D1562566

Getting Tough

Politics and Society in Modern America

William Chafe, Gary Gerstle, Linda Gordon, and Julian Zelizer, editors

Getting Tough: Welfare and Imprisonment in 1970s America by Julilly Kohler-Hausmann

The Rise of a Prairie Statesman: The Life and Times of George McGovern by Thomas Knock

The Great Exception: The New Deal and the Limits of American Politics by Jefferson Cowie

The Good Immigrants: How the Yellow Peril Became the Model Minority by Madeline Y. Hsu

A Class by Herself: Protective Laws for Women Workers, 1890s–1990s by Nancy Woloch

The Loneliness of the Black Republican: Pragmatic Politics and the Pursuit of Power by Leah Wright Rigueur

Don't Blame Us: Suburban Liberals and the Transformation of the Democratic Party by Lily Geismer

Relentless Reformer: Josephine Roche and Progressivism in Twentieth-Century America by Robyn Muncy

Power Lines: Phoenix and the Making of the Modern Southwest by Andrew Needham

Lobbying America: The Politics of Business from Nixon to NAFTA by Benjamin C. Waterhouse

For a full list of books in this series see: http://press.princeton.edu /catalogs/series/pstcaa.html

Getting Tough

WELFARE AND IMPRISONMENT
IN 1970s AMERICA

Julilly Kohler-Hausmann

Princeton University Press

Princeton and Oxford

Published by Princeton University Press, 41 William Street, Princeton, New Jersey 08540

In the United Kingdom: Princeton University Press, 6 Oxford Street, Woodstock, Oxfordshire OX20 1TR

press.princeton.edu

Jacket photograph: Ronald Reagan and Nelson Rockefeller, 1968 / Getty Images

ISBN 978-0-691-17452-5

Library of Congress Control Number 2017931926

British Library Cataloging-in-Publication Data is available

This book has been composed in Sabon LT Std and Helvetica Neue family

Printed on acid-free paper ∞

Printed in the United States of America

10 9 8 7 6 5 4 3 2 1

For Mark Leff

Contents

Contents

Figures

Acknowledgments

It is ironic that a book about the dangers of sorting people between good and bad is dedicated to man who was all good. For over a decade Mark Leff was the first person and last person who read anything I wrote. I would send him the first inchoate draft to see if it was headed in the right direction. And it was only after consultation with him that I would declare a piece finished. It would be too embarrassing to admit how many versions he read in between. He had a remarkable analytical ability to evaluate intellectual structures on their own terms. No matter the topic, he could easily discern the central pillars, the gratuitous clutter, and the fundamentally unsound elements in any historical argument. Whenever Mark started self-deprecatingly insisting he had no productive feedback, I braced myself. He usually then proceeded to make a single comment that destabilized or reoriented the entire conceptualization. His rigor and acuity were matched only by his kindness, humor, and infinite generosity. He expected the best of people and demanded even more from himself. It is the custom for authors to take responsibility for all the errors in their books, but in this case I'd like to share responsibility for any problems with cancer. For if Mark were still alive, he would have commented on everything ranging from the analytical to the grammatical. It is daunting to send this book off without the benefit of his final questions. It is even harder to know that he did not live to see it finished and dedicated to him.

A broad web of family, friends, colleagues, and institutions supported me during the years I spent working on this project. At the University of Illinois, Urbana-Champaign, Jim Barrett, Clarence Lang, Elizabeth Pleck, and David Roediger each offered critical readings and extensive comments that steered the project in profound ways. Dana Rabin, Leslie Reagan, and Stephen Hartnett also offered kind and wise mentorship. Even though my research has far too many elites for his taste, Jim Barrett adopted me into the fold of labor and working-class history students and he greatly enriched my years in Champaign. I was lucky to have had the intellectual and social community provided through the Working Class History Reading Group that he organized. These faculty were models of intellectual generosity and engagement.

At the University of Illinois, I also cherished the friendship and advice of Will Cooley, Sarah Forhardt-Lane, Amy Hasinoff, Erica Hill, Karlos Hill, Maurice Hobson, Brian Hoffman, Abdulai Iddrisu, Jason Kozlowski, Anna Kurhajec, Marie Leger, Shoshana Magnet, Sascha Meinrath, Brian

Nicholson, Edward Onaci, Kerry Pimblott, Craig Robinson, Melissa Rohde, Mike Rosenow, Martin Smith, and Roswell Quinn. In particular, I would like to thank the small group that became my core conspirators: Brandon Mills, Anthony Sigismondi, Kwame Holmes, and Brian Yates.

I could not have asked for a more supportive environment to finish this book than the History Department at Cornell University. For their kindness and counsel, I am particularly grateful to Ed Baptist, Judy Byfield, Ray Craib, Holly Case, Barb Donnell, Maria Christina Garcia, Sandra Greene, T. J. Hinrichs, Katie Kristof, Tamara Loos, Jon Parmanter, Barry Straus, Kay Stickane, Eric Tagliacozza, Robert Travers, and Judy Yonkin. I'd also like to thank colleagues who provided feedback on my research at critical junctures: Oren Falk, Itsie Hull, Durba Gosh, Mary Beth Norton, Camille Robcis, Claudia Verhoven, Aaron Sachs, Penny Von Eschen, Margaret Washington, and Rachel Weil. A cohort of magnificent junior scholars arrived at Cornell around the same time as I did. Ernesto Bassi, Louis Hyman, Mostafa Minawi, Russell Rickford, and Victor Seow have made these years less stressful and considerably more fun. Derek Chang and Larry Glickman have both gone far beyond what should ever be expected and dedicated their time and wisdom to assist me on too many occasions to enumerate. Two gifted Cornell students, Janelle Bourgeois and John Hall, provided expert research assistance during the final stages of the book. I have also benefited from the comments of and discussions with the growing concentration of scholars researching inequality and incarceration in other units at Cornell, particularly Peter Enns, Maria Fitzpatrick, Chris Garces, Anna Haskins, Jamila Michener, Aziz Rana, Rob Scott, and Chris Wildeman. I feel especially privileged to have the support of and an ongoing dialogue with Joe Margulies and Mary Katzenstein. Our friendship with the family of Jenny Mann and Guy Ortolano has greatly enriched our time in Ithaca.

A wide range of other scholars have also offered invaluable comments at different stages. I thank Seth Ackerman, Dan Berger, Nancy Campbell, Merlin Chowkwanyun, Will Cooley, Thomas Dorrance, Kelly Lytle Hernandez, David Herzberg, Max Felkor-Kantor, Volker Janssen, Felicia Kornbluh, Naomi Murakawa, Khalil Gibran Muhammad, Donna Murch, Julie Netherland, Jessica Neptune, Anne Parsons, Kimberly Phillips-Fein, Peter Pihos, Eric Schneider, Christopher Seeds, Stuart Schrader, Karen Tani, and Mason Williams. Audra Wolfe, Sanford Schram, and Katherine Beckett provided astute feedback on the structure and content of the entire manuscript that was essential in guiding my final revisions. My conversations with Elizabeth Hinton both enrich my scholarship and sustain me personally. My frequent text storms and phone calls with Kwame Holmes have been a critical source of wisdom and solace. During my year at the Institute for Advanced Study, I benefited immensely from discussions about my project with Danielle Allen, Manduhai Buyandel-ger, Brian Connolly, Didier Fassin, Hugh Gusterson, Michael Hanchard, Nann Koehane, Jill Locke, Jennifer Morgan, Charles Payne, Sophie Rosenfeld, and Joan Scott. It would be impossible to overstate Heather Thompson's influence on my intellectual and professional trajectory. She has believed in and pushed this project since the first time we met when we spent over three hours brainstorming about my research. Ever since then, I have been in awe of the intellectual sophistication and endless energy she has dedicated to illuminating the history of the carceral state.

I am grateful for the assistance of archivists at the California State Archives, the Illinois State Archives, the New York City Municipal Archives, the New York State Archives, the Rockefeller Archive Center, and the Ronald Reagan Presidential Library. Generous grants and fellowships from the following organizations made the research and writing possible: American Association of University Women, Institute for Social Sciences at Cornell University, Heyman Center for the Humanities at Columbia University, American Council of Learned Societies, the Illinois Program for Research in the Humanities, Illinois State Historical Society, School of Social Science at the Institute for Advanced Study in Princeton, New York State Archives, and the University of Illinois, Urbana-Champaign History Department and Graduate College. Early iterations of this research were published in the *Journal of American History*, the *Journal of Social History*, and the *Journal of Urban History*, and I am grateful to the reviewers and editors who assisted with those articles.

For incredible work shepherding the book through production, I would like to thank Julian Zelizer and the staff working with Princeton University Press, particularly Jenn Backer and Eric Crahan. The press enlisted three ideal readers for the manuscript. Matt Lassiter, Robert Self, and Vesla Weaver each provided painstakingly detailed and incisive reviews that strengthened the book immeasurably.

My family and friends have been an anchor throughout the often hectic, tumultuous years that I worked on this book. It is impossible to articulate my gratitude for the love and ceaseless support of my parents, Julilly Kohler and Charles and Jean Hausmann. They are my most trusted advisors and role models for how to live with compassion and integrity during both adversity and good fortune. I am so grateful to have married a man whose family I adore, especially Kay Pickard and Lara Bury and her family. My mother-in-law, Kay, has an endless reservoir of energy and creativity and strength that is an ongoing inspiration. My three stepsisters, Bridget Madigan-Sharp, Kate Madigan, and Kelly Reese, and their families sustained me with humor, perspective, and love through what often seemed like a never-ending endeavor. Issa Kohler-Hausmann, my little sister and closest friend, has been intimately involved in every aspect of this book, from its conceptualization to designing the graphs to final footnote queries. She and Marty LaFalce have deeply informed my own understanding of penal system. Just when I think I cannot get more cynical, they share another horror story from their daily encounters with the courts and the prisons. I am so proud of the amazing scholar and advocate my sister has become. I could not imagine doing this work without her company at every step. While I cannot list my entire network of social support, I want to express my deep gratitude to Caroline Burghardt, Dana Carter, Marie-Christine Fox, Marie Leger, Marie Kohler, Anne MacDougald, Betsy Nordlander, Jessica Owley, Gretchen Wilson, and the Kohler and Capellero families. I also want to acknowledge that this project grew out of my years working with anti-poverty, union, and welfare-rights activists in Washington State. I hope this research can in some small way honor and buttress the work they and others like them do every day.

As someone who researches the tensions between paid work and the work of parenting, I was still unprepared for the difficulty of caring for young children while starting my own career. Thankfully, I was blessed with trusted teachers and child-care providers. I will be forever grateful to Alicia Aubin, Vickie Fernandez, Shena Griffith, Melanie Allen Guidi, Stacy Huchison, Stephany Item, Wynter Latorre-Ovasaka, Sompit and Walter Oerlemans, Blythe Sanford, Kala Savage, and the teachers at Ithaca Community Childcare Center, Friends Child Care Center, Aspen Grove Preschool, and Fall Creek Elementary School. I am also indebted to my mother and mother-in-law, who stepped in over and over again to provide arduous and desperately needed assistance, often on only hours' notice, during conference travel, sickness, and the inevitable complications that arise when parents hold jobs in two separate cities.

My husband, Victor Pickard, is the love of my life, and his dedication, curiosity, tenacity, and brilliance are a constant inspiration. I could not have finished this book without his ceaseless encouragement and assistance. Every facet of my life is richer and more filled with joy because I do it with him. Our two young children, Zaden and Lilia, made it much harder to finish this book. They are such magical, hilarious, fascinating people that it was often simply too difficult to take my eyes away from them and turn back to the computer. But at the same time, my children have bound me even more tightly to the nation they will inherit and made me more determined to help make sense of the persistent inequality that mars it. More than anything, they have inspired me to try to do work that will make them proud someday.

Getting Tough

Introduction

"Why don't we just remove [welfare recipients'] citizenship?" a New York State senator asked during a 1973 interview. "Then they're not our problem."[1] The senator's question was meant sarcastically; he was condemning yet another restriction in the supports available to low-income parents. Nonetheless, the question captures a critical feature of policymakers' response to the social and economic upheaval throughout the final decades of the twentieth century. During that period, American lawmakers "got tough" on drugs, welfare, and crime. In the process, they restructured the state and citizenship. Beginning in the 1970s, politicians and law enforcement professionals steadily increased the number of people sent to prison, the amount of time they spent there, and the frequency with which they were returned to prison after release. These political choices drove one of the most dramatic expansions of a penal system in world history.[2] But policymakers did not simply increase the number and severity of penal sanctions. They also continued degrading the civic standing of those convicted of crimes, imposing limitations on their access to state benefits, employment opportunities, and civil and political rights.

As lawmakers and state officials funneled more resources into the penal system, they also retrenched many social welfare programs, particularly those imagined to be serving poor, "nonworking" people of color. In 1980, the United States spent three times more money on food stamps and welfare grants than on corrections. By 1996, the balance had reversed, with the nation devoting billions more to corrections than the two principal programs for the poor.[3] Policymakers paired diminishing levels

[1] Senator Sidney Von Luther was opposing a proposal that reduced recipients' protection from service interruptions when they were unable to pay their utility bills. Amy Plummer, "Albany Notes," *New York Amsterdam News*, April 14, 1973, 20.

[2] The penal system had been steadily accruing capacity for decades, but its growth spiked dramatically in the last decades of the twentieth century. On the long history of institutional development and legitimization of state and federal law enforcement, see Kathleen J. Frydl, *The Drug Wars in America, 1940–1973* (Cambridge: Cambridge University Press, 2013); Marie Gottschalk, *The Prison and the Gallows: The Politics of Mass Incarceration in America* (Cambridge: Cambridge University Press, 2006); and Naomi Murakawa, *The First Civil Right: How Liberals Built Prison America* (New York: Oxford University Press, 2014).

[3] Loïc Wacquant, "Class, Race, and Hyper-incarceration in Revanchist America," *Daedalus* 139, no. 3 (Summer 2010): 76–77. The program popularly called "welfare" provides cash support to poor parents. Congress replaced the original program, Aid to Families with Dependent Children (AFDC), with Temporary Assistance for Needy Families (TANF) in 1996.

of support with policies constraining beneficiaries' privacy and freedom. They subjected welfare recipients to marriage-promotion programs, drug testing, home searches, fingerprinting, sanctions, and prohibitions on where they could spend their money.[4] Many marginalized populations that had been regulated through social welfare institutions moved under the purview of the criminal justice system. Undocumented immigrants, low-income drug users, and people with psychological disorders or charged with sex offenses have become increasingly managed through penal institutions.

This book attempts to make sense of the link between these transformations in the penal and welfare systems. By integrating institutions, policy issues, and political actors that are usually studied separately, it sheds a different light on these concurrent trends and reveals mass incarceration, the War on Drugs, and welfare state retrenchment to be intertwined phenomena. These institutional transformations were symptoms of a profound shift in *governing strategies and logics* for the most subordinated groups and spaces in society. When confronted with a series of political challenges and economic upheavals that crested in the 1970s, broad coalitions of policymakers repudiated the declared commitment to rehabilitating marginalized populations, particularly those living in racially segregated, deindustrializing urban cores. In its place, an increasingly dominant group of policymakers championed "getting tough": an emphasis on strategies of punishment, surveillance, coercion, sanctions, quarantine, or containment linked with limitations on rights, freedom, and access to economic opportunity and state benefits. These policies actively degraded the social, economic, and political status of already stigmatized categories of Americans.

Getting Tough offers a window into the historical processes that displaced rehabilitation as a dominant approach to the social problems imagined to be emanating from black and Latino "ghettos." It chronicles three key state-level political struggles over drug use, poverty, and crime during the 1970s. Proponents offered tough strategies as solutions to a host of governance problems arising from the era's significant economic

---

[4]Shoshana Magnet, "Bio-Benefits: Technologies of Criminalization, Biometrics, and the Welfare System," in *Surveillance: Power, Problems, and Politics*, ed. Sean Hier and Joshua Greenberg (Vancouver: University of British Columbia Press, 2009), 169–84; Amy Sherman, "Judge Temporarily Halts Drug-Testing for Welfare Applicants," October 26, 2011, http://www.politifact.com/florida/promises/scott-o-meter /promise/600/require-drug-screening-for-welfare-recipients/; Matt Taibbi, *The Divide: American Injustice in the Age of the Wealth Gap* (New York: Spiegel and Grau, 2014), 316–25; "New Kansas Law Limits Spending of Welfare Benefits on Concerts, Pools, Lingerie," NBC News, April 16, 2015, http://www.nbcnews.com/news/us-news/new-kansas -law-limit-spending-welfare-benefits-concerts-pools-lingerie-n343176.

transformations and social movement challenges.[5] In response to the upheaval, moderate politicians in both major parties promised to secure social order by rehabilitating and integrating marginal individuals and spaces. However, these efforts encountered political criticism from both the Left and the Right, vexing programmatic complications, and strident challenges from the subjects of rehabilitative projects. Conservatives mobilized with growing sophistication and energy against liberalism and the New Deal order. Many activists and thinkers on the Left publicly challenged the assumption that disorder and inequality were evidence of individual or group deficiencies and instead interpreted them as symptoms of economic exploitation and racial domination. People targeted for rehabilitation put forth alternative explanations for their conditions. They resisted coercive policies that constricted their rights or made civic standing and social services contingent upon proper performance. By the early 1970s, these factors converged to undermine the rationale for and commitment to rehabilitation.

In this context, various groups advanced interpretations of the turmoil and visions for a path forward. Politicians and their constituents used social and criminal policy as a forum to hash out these issues. These debates became key sites in the ongoing renegotiation of the social contract raging in the post–civil rights era. This book excavates the clashing interpretations of drug use, concentrated poverty, racial inequality, political insurgency, and crime, and it explores why some narratives were more resonant and enduring than others. Policy elites, grassroots supporters of tough policy, and those subject to welfare and penal institutions never spoke with one voice, nor did they break into neat categories that mapped directly onto the usual categories of political actors or ideologies (such as liberal and conservative or Republican and Democrat). They are best distinguished by the ways they interpreted social dynamics and the strategies they proposed to secure social peace. The solutions that different groups advanced depended on their assessment of state capacity and the subjectivity of "problem people": whether they interpreted crime and inequality as primarily functions of individual pathology, cultural or environmental dysfunction, "root causes," the legacy of racial injustice, "blocked opportunities," or economic and social structures.

In the midst of this upheaval, it was not at all clear which narrative would prevail. The events recounted in this book happened at a moment

[5]This frame helps reveal that tough crime and welfare policies proliferated and have been politically intractable precisely because they did so much for so many different people. Focusing on the political economy, Ruth Wilson Gilmore illustrates how penal expansion resolved multiple crises and served multiple ends, absorbing surplus land, capital, and populations. Ruth Wilson Gilmore, *Golden Gulag: Prisons, Surplus, Crisis, and Opposition in Globalizing California* (Berkeley: University of California Press, 2007).

when the political and programmatic efficacy of "getting tough" was neither assured nor assumed. In fact, many believed the country was heading in the opposite direction. Instead of constricting the number of people eligible for state aid, Congress seriously considered enacting President Nixon's guaranteed minimum income proposal that would have added roughly ten million people to the public assistance rolls.[6] Before politicians enacted a frenzy of harsh sentencing laws in the 1970s and 1980s, there was broad agreement, especially among policy elites, that long prison terms were programmatically ineffective at controlling crime. In 1970, the United States Congress passed and President Nixon signed comprehensive drug policy reforms that abandoned federal mandatory minimum sentences for drug selling and possession.[7] Many commentators deduced from the rapid progress toward deinstitutionalization of psychiatric hospitals that massive custodial institutions were destined for irrelevance. Some criminologists and other specialists even predicted that the prison would eventually vanish from the landscape.[8]

Yet tough politics won out in the three episodes chronicled in this book. Their proponents insisted this was because of the unambiguous failure of liberal programs and the inherent ungovernability of the poor in African American and Latino communities.[9] Yet close scrutiny of the history suggests we should question this logic. These policies did not reflect the inevitable failure of the state or the congenital degeneracy of poor communities of color. Instead, they actually helped entrench these assertions in the political vernacular. To understand why civic degradation triumphed over the range of other liberal, social democratic, libertarian, or more radical approaches, it is critical to situate these strategies within the era's political landscape, particularly the structure of state institutions, contractual notions of citizenship, and popular conceptions of class, gender, and racial difference.[10]

[6]Felicia Kornbluh, "Who Shot FAP? The Nixon Welfare Plan and the Transformation of American Politics," *The Sixties: A Journal of History, Politics, and Culture* 1/2 (December 2008): 126.

[7]David Courtwright, "The Controlled Substances Act: How a 'Big Tent' Reform Became a Punitive Drug Law," *Drug and Alcohol Dependence* 76, no. 1 (October 5, 2004): 9–15, especially 12.

[8]David Garland, *Culture of Control: Crime and Social Order in Contemporary Society* (Chicago: University of Chicago Press, 2001), 1–2.

[9]For scholarship challenging the narrative that the War on Poverty "failed," see Annelise Orleck, "Introduction: The War on Poverty from the Grass Roots Up," in *The War on Poverty: A New Grassroots History, 1964–1980*, ed. Annelise Orleck and Lisa Gayle Hazirjian (Athens: University of Georgia Press, 2011), 1–31.

[10]In this sense, this is a state-centered history that explores how discourse and political culture, particularly racial and gender ideology, influenced policymakers' efforts to manage urban space. For examples of a state-centered interpretation, see Frydl, *Drug Wars in*

Tough policy won out because its proponents offered solutions to vexing governing problems that were culturally resonant, politically salable, and feasible within the configuration of state institutions and civic culture. "Getting tough" was often the path with less political resistance from powerful interests in society. These policies subordinated groups that rehabilitative welfare programs had already marked as suspect by virtue of their need for individual-level transformation or reform. While expanding the penal system was fervently contested and fiscally and bureaucratically cumbersome, alternative proposals— such as the complete renunciation of state responsibility or full employment and guaranteed income programs—confronted even more profound political and institutional stumbling blocks. It was certainly more broadly palatable than the fundamental redistribution of power and resources called for by many organized drug users, welfare recipients, and prisoners. "Getting tough" aggrandized the views of people with cultural, political, and economic capital at the expense of those who had very little.

While ostensibly color-blind, these narratives mobilized deeply rooted assumptions about gender and racial difference and the powerful stigmatizing force of criminalization to produce the vision of distinct subjects: drug pushers, welfare queens, and criminals. This political project built upon longstanding tropes of black criminality and gender hierarchy. Calls for tough drug and crime policies rested upon claims that social problems sprang from "permissive," maternalist social welfare programs and pathologizing parenting by African American and Latina mothers. Proponents exalted punitive strategies of containment and civic degradation by linking them to masculinist visions of "tough" state power and disparaging alternative strategies as effeminate and "soft."[11]

America and Gottschalk, *The Prison and the Gallows*. For studies of shifting understandings of poverty and its causes, see Alice O'Connor, *Poverty Knowledge: Social Science, Social Policy, and the Poor in Twentieth-Century U.S. History* (Princeton: Princeton University Press, 2002) and Michael Katz, "What Kind of Problem Is Poverty? The Archeology of an Idea," in *Territories of Poverty: Rethinking North and South*, ed. Ananya Roy and Emma Shaw Crane (Athens: University of Georgia Press, 2015), 39–78. On the powerful role of racism in federal crime policy, particularly the ideology of racial liberalism and its naturalization of links between criminality and blackness, see Elizabeth Hinton, *From the War on Poverty to the War on Crime: The Making of Mass Incarceration in America* (Cambridge, Mass.: Harvard University Press, 2016) and Murakawa, *The First Civil Right*.

[11] While the role of tropes about masculinity and toughness have been less scrutinized in histories of penal expansion, the critical importance of notions of black criminality is well established in the extant literature. For example, see Hinton, *From the War on Poverty to the War on Crime*; Khalil Gibran Muhammad, *The Condemnation of Blackness: Race, Crime, and the Making of Modern Urban America* (Cambridge, Mass.: Harvard University Press, 2010); and Murakawa, *The First Civil Right*.

The political process of enacting tough policy had profound implications beyond the obvious effects of increasing incarceration and constricting state aid. It helped produce popular knowledge about the terms
of citizenship, the state's capacity to affect society, and who and what
were responsible for social marginality and inequality. Political discourse,
especially when codified in public policy, helped constrict the terms of the
debate, limiting the range of what could be considered feasible and desir-
able state action. Passing tough policies in legislatures and implementing
them on the ground fortified individualist and cultural explanations of
social problems at a time when responsibility was fiercely contested. They
transformed the disorder arising from economic dislocations and ardent
social movements into problems of incorrigible, racialized groups—
especially African Americans' criminogenic "culture of poverty."

Advancing tough policies helped absolve government of responsibility
for marginalized people's well-being and accountability to their voices.
Through "getting tough," policymakers altered the purported mission
of government that had ascended in the postwar era: it shifted from an
emphasis on transforming marginalized individuals to protecting good,
deserving citizens from these groups. Although politicians' rhetoric often
positioned rehabilitation and punishment as opposing strategies, programs aiming to normalize and assimilate deviant groups were not the
antithesis of those aiming to punish or warehouse. While never func-
tionally interchangeable, they both tended to approach inequality, crime,
and drug use as rooted in individual behavioral or cultural problems.
And they both operated within a contractual understanding of citizenship where the state was empowered to degrade the rights and benefits
of people deemed unwilling or incapable of performing their civic obligations. Proponents presented these populations as uncontrollable without coercion and ultimately undeserving of full civic standing. According
to the supporters of tough policy, drug pushers, welfare recipients, and
criminals forfeited their rights and claims on the state by breaking the
law or drawing state aid. As civil rights and other movements pried open
notions of citizenship, the civic subordination entailed in "getting tough"
entrenched stark racialized gradations within the polity. These punitive
policies helped produce the trope of a nation divided between rights-
bearing, taxpaying Americans and a racialized, denigrated "underclass."

Legislative debates over drug, welfare, and crime policy became a platform to salvage and remake political authority for politicians confronted
with the perception of a governance crisis. Through the spectacle of passing and implementing these policies, lawmakers elevated this muscular
vision of state power during a period when government's efficacy and
legitimacy were under assault from critics on the Left and the Right. The
perceived need to "get tough" undermined social welfare institutions and

their expertise while bolstering the prestige and resources of other state actors and institutions, particularly law enforcement. Punitive policy rested on (and reified) the assumption that the state was incapable of distributing social and material security to all citizens. But it was not anti-government.[12] The state remained very much responsible for protecting those defined as upstanding and worthy citizens.[13]

Mutating States: Joining the Welfare State and Carceral State in Modern U.S. History

Joining the history of the welfare and penal institutions sheds new light on each. Popular narratives about the U.S. welfare state identify a rightward shift in U.S. politics whereby conservatives set out to shrink government down to the size "where you can drown it in a bathtub," as conservative strategist Grover Norquist famously described his aim.[14] However, incorporating penal expansion reveals that the late twentieth century was a period of state mutation, not withdrawal or shrinkage. In

[12] Ruth Wilson Gilmore (*Golden Gulag*) has termed this general phenomenon an "anti-state state." See also David Garland's discussion of debates over whether the massive penal system should undermine characterizations of the United States as a "weak state." David Garland, "Penality and the Penal State," *Criminology* 51, no. 3 (2013): 475–517.

[13] Other scholarship suggests that these reorientations happened on multiple registers. Robert Self argues that the state reoriented from serving families materially to protecting them morally during this period. See Robert O. Self, *All in the Family: The Realignment of American Democracy since the 1960s* (New York: Hill and Wang, 2013).

[14] Jeremy Peters, "Grover Norquist, Author of Antitax Pledge, Faces Big Test," *New York Times*, November 19, 2012, http://www.nytimes.com/2012/11/20/us/politics/grover -norquist-author-of-antitax-pledge-faces-big-test.html. Theorists of neoliberalism refine popular characterizations of conservatives as anti-statist and pursuing small government. They identify the ascendance of a new neoliberal governing order—typically dated to the 1970s—marked by economic policies favoring laissez-faire (or "unregulated") markets, privatization, and the abandonment of the state's social welfare functions. According to these accounts, neoliberalism displaced and supplanted the Keynesian and redistributive welfare state but did not abandon an active role for the state. Instead, under neoliberalism, theorists argue, the state remains a productive force—dedicated to actively promoting favorable conditions for market expansion and extending market logics into all aspects of social relations. The literature on neoliberalism is vast. For two influential but different takes on neoliberalism, see David Harvey, *A Brief History of Neoliberalism* (New York: Oxford University Press, 2007) and Wendy Brown, *Undoing the Demos: Neoliberalism's Stealth Revolution* (Cambridge, Mass.: MIT Press, 2015). Some scholars who theorize the relationship between neoliberalism and the penal system are Bernard Harcourt, *The Illusion of Free Markets: Punishment and the Myth of Natural Order* (Cambridge, Mass.: Harvard University Press, 2012); Loïc Wacquant, *Punishing the Poor: The Neoliberal Government of Social Insecurity* (Durham, N.C.: Duke University Press, 2009); and Joe Soss, Richard C. Fording, and Sanford F. Schram, *Disciplining the Poor: Neoliberal Paternalism and the Persistent Power of Race* (Chicago: University of Chicago Press, 2011).

the political struggles chronicled in this book, the central debate was not over the size of government but whom the state should serve. The most contested question was over *whom* the state should hire to do the job and *what tactics* it should deploy to manage inequality and deviance. When it came to crime or regulating the poor, the Republican Party (along with frequent support from Democrats) pursued policies that enlarged the scale and scope of government, regularly overruling concerns about size, cost, or the sanctity of individual rights. These impulses were not limited to functions that secured domestic security (a frequent caveat in calls for limited government), as conservatives pursued state intervention to regulate many different arenas, such as poor women's employment, marriage, and reproduction—all areas that represented few threats to public safety. Instead of marking the end of big government, massive state-building projects accompanied this reorientation.

Of course, discrepancies between rhetoric and action are a hallmark of democratic governance. Party ideologies are rarely internally coherent and reflect uneasy alliances and other practical necessities of electoral politics. Nonetheless, the tension between calls for limited government and policies of state expansion points to a more fundamental feature of politics during the final decades of the twentieth century: freedom from intensive state regulation and surveillance was a privilege reserved for those defined as full, rights-bearing citizens. Those defined as criminal or dependent were relegated to a subordinated status that allowed—even demanded—coercive state supervision and coercion. And aggressive state intervention within many impoverished communities of color in turn helped mark them as inherently suspect spaces.[15]

Social welfare programs transformed unevenly through the late twentieth century, but the state neither withdrew from social provision nor ceased to redistribute resources. Many social services and social insurance programs serving those popularly understood to be deserving citizens—such as middle-class, aged, or white populations receiving benefits through Social Security and Medicare—withstood most efforts at privatization and benefit reduction.[16] The state continued to distribute significant resources with the tax code through, for example, the Earned Income Tax Credit or income tax deductions for child care, home mort-

[15]Increased policing, stop and frisks, and surveillance in urban communities of color increased arrests, reports of which were in turn used as evidence of black and Latino criminality. For a cogent analysis of this dynamic, see Hinton, *From the War on Poverty to the War on Crime*.

[16]See, for example, Julian E. Zelizer, "Reflections: Rethinking the History of American Conservatism," *Reviews in American History* 38, no. 2 (2010): 367–92 and Paul Pierson, *Dismantling the Welfare State?: Reagan, Thatcher and the Politics of Retrenchment* (New York: Cambridge University Press, 1995).

gages, and employer- provided health care.[17] It was welfare programs imagined to be serving undeserving populations—predominantly African Americans, Latinas, and the "nonworking" poor—that have been drastically curtailed since the 1970s. The highest-profile example is the fate of Aid to Families with Dependent Children (AFDC), the program that provided cash support to poor parents. While Social Security benefits maintained their value between the 1970s and 1990s, AFDC benefits shrank by over half in real dollars. Analysis that focuses principally on state withdrawal and privatization can inadvertently reproduce obfuscations in politicians' rhetoric by eliding the profound ways the state continued to enhance the material and social position of many Americans. Furthermore, it can misconstrue the transformations in poor communities. During the final decades of the twentieth century, many people residing in racially segregated urban areas faced not only economic abandonment and diminished state aid but also intensified entanglement with the state, particularly police and the burgeoning penal system.[18]

Despite the incessant coupling of welfare and crime in popular rhetoric, there has been limited historical scholarship scrutinizing the relationship between them. Historians of recent developments in welfare programs tend not to engage the concurrent, dramatic growth in carceral institutions, just as scholars of crime and punishment tend not to integrate developments in the welfare state.[19] This book builds upon the literature in the social sciences that has examined welfare and penal systems together. Much of that work conceives of the two as integrated systems implicated in the regulation of social marginality and conceptualizes an inverse relationship where penal systems expand as social welfare supports contract. Researchers, for example, discovered a degree of negative correlation between welfare spending and imprisonment rates across various U.S. states.[20] But since there is no formal mechanism

[17] Christopher Howard, *The Hidden Welfare State: Tax Expenditures and Social Policy in the United States* (Princeton: Princeton University Press, 1999); Suzanne Mettler, *The Submerged State: How Invisible Government Policies Undermine American Democracy* (Chicago: University of Chicago Press, 2011).

[18] On the ways new police and prosecutorial practices regulate urban space, see Issa Kohler-Hausmann, "Misdemeanor Justice: Control without Conviction," *American Journal of Sociology* 119, no. 2 (September 2013): 351–93. On the ways intensive policing has led residents to alter their public movements and comportment, see Forrest Stuart, *Down, Out, and Under Arrest: Policing and Everyday Life in Skid Row* (Chicago: University of Chicago Press, 2016).

[19] An important exception is Elizabeth Hinton's new research on the War on Poverty and federal crime policy, *From the War on Poverty to the War on Crime.*

[20] Katherine Beckett and Bruce Western, "Governing Social Marginality: Welfare, Incarceration, and the Transformation of State Policy," in *Mass Imprisonment: Social Causes and Consequences*, ed. David Garland (London: Sage, 2001), 35–50. Two other researchers who

beyond budgetary trade-offs that inversely link welfare and penal systems, this book contributes to our understandings of this relationship by mapping the contingent historical processes that produced these shifts in three historical cases. Because penal (or law enforcement) and welfare agencies often operated simultaneously and symbiotically on the ground, I approach them as alternative—but not necessarily antithetical—tools for social regulation.[21] The fractured nature of the U.S. state prevented monolithic operation or centrally dictated coordination between various government-run and state-funded programs. For example, the various institutions encompassing the penal system—courts, prisons, jails, and probation, parole, and police departments—all faced distinct constraints and imperatives, leading them to sometimes coordinate haphazardly or work at cross-purposes. There were even more institutional and political impediments to any systematic synchronization between the penal and welfare systems.

Research about the origins of mass incarceration has largely focused on what inspired elites to embrace "law and order" and crime politics in the 1960s. Scholars emphasizing the role of grassroots pressure debate the extent to which "law-and-order" politics were animated by alarm with rising crime (either from whites or communities of color) or a white "backlash" against civil rights organizing and urban uprisings.[22] The

conducted an international comparison concluded that although the relationship between welfare and carceral spending was not simple or direct, "it is difficult to believe that the consistent finding of an inverse relationship between the commitment to welfare and the scale of imprisonment, both cross-nationally and across the United States, is simply accidental or coincidental." David Downes and Kirstine Hansen, "Welfare and Punishment in Comparative Perspective," in *Perspectives on Punishment: The Contours of Control*, ed. Sarah Armstrong and Lesley McAra (Oxford: Oxford University Press, 2006), 154. Some contemporary studies—particularly ethnographies—powerfully reveal how social welfare and penal systems intersect constantly in people's daily lives. See Lynne Haney, *Offending Women: Power, Punishment, and the Regulation of Desire* (Berkeley: University of California Press, 2010); Megan Comfort, *Doing Time Together: Love and Family in the Shadow of the Prison* (Chicago: University of Chicago Press, 2008); Dorothy E. Roberts, *Shattered Bonds: The Color of Child Welfare* (New York: Basic Books, 2001); Stuart, *Down, Out, and Under Arrest*; and Jill McCorkel, *Breaking Women: Gender, Race, and the New Politics of Imprisonment* (New York: New York University Press, 2013).

[21] For influential works on these regulatory functions, see Frances Fox Piven and Richard Cloward, *Regulating the Poor: The Functions of Public Welfare*, updated ed. (New York: Vintage, 1993); Wacquant, *Punishing the Poor*; and Soss, Fording, and Schram, *Disciplining the Poor*; and Beckett and Western, "Governing Social Marginality," 35–50.

[22] For two different arguments linking crime policy to a backlash to civil rights, see Thomas Byrne Edsall and Mary Edsall, *Chain Reaction: The Impact of Race, Rights, and Taxes on American Politics* (New York: Norton, 1991) and Michelle Alexander, *The New Jim Crow: Mass Incarceration in the Age of Colorblindness* (New York: New Press, 2012). For scholarship on popular pressure arising from consternation about crime, see Michael Javen Fortner, *Black Silent Majority: The Rockefeller Drug Laws and the Politics*

scholars who emphasize elite's proactive role in elevating law-and-order politics debate which groups were the chief architects and their motivations. Some argue Republicans used racially coded language about crime to mobilize frustration about the civil rights movement and urban disorder to gain electoral advantage and fracture Democratic coalitions.[23] Subsequent research has emphasized the role of liberals, particularly their racial ideology, in facilitating the War on Crime and penal expansion.[24] Another group of scholars locate the deeper roots of penal expansion in U.S. political culture and institutions.[25] Some argue that mass incarceration should be interpreted as a function of the rise of late modernity or an effort to manage whole spaces and populations rendered superfluous by the rising "neoliberal" order of the late twentieth century.[26] This book devotes less time trying to disentangle the relative significance of these important factors than highlighting the particular ways rhetoric bundled them together. I focus on the critical role political discourse played in ascribing meaning to the economic dislocations and political insurgency that collided in the period.[27] I also endeavor to move beyond top-down versus bottom-up debates by rendering the dynamic interplay in the policy arena between political elites, "backlash voters," social movements, drug sellers, welfare recipients, and prisoners. Incorporating the participation and perspective of those who sponsored, supported, opposed, and were targeted by tough policies reveals how their tangled interactions propelled these changes.

of Punishment (Cambridge, Mass.: Harvard University Press, 2015); Peter K. Enns, *Incarceration Nation: How the United States Became the Most Punitive Democracy in the World* (New York: Cambridge University Press, 2016); and Michael Flamm, *Law and Order: Street Crime, Civil Unrest, and the Crisis of Liberalism in the 1960s* (New York: Columbia University Press, 2005).

[23] See, for example, Vesla Weaver, "Frontlash: Race and the Development of Punitive Crime Policy," *Studies in American Political Development* 21 (Fall 2007): 230–65 and Kathleen Beckett, *Making Crime Pay: Law and Order in Contemporary American Politics* (New York: Oxford University Press, 1997).

[24] Murakawa, *The First Civil Right*; Hinton, *From the War on Poverty to the War on Crime*.

[25] For examples, see James Q. Whitman, *Harsh Justice: Criminal Punishment and the Widening Divide between America and Europe* (New York: Oxford University Press, 2005); Lisa L. Miller, *The Perils of Federalism: Race, Poverty, and the Politics of Crime Control* (New York: Oxford University Press, 2010); Robert Perkinson, *Texas Tough: The Rise of America's Prison Empire* (New York: Metropolitan Books, 2010); and Gottschalk, *The Prison and the Gallows*.

[26] For examples, see Garland, *Culture of Control*; Wacquant, *Punishing the Poor*; and Gilmore, *Golden Gulag*.

[27] Vesla Weaver also calls for scholars to denaturalize the assumption that rising violence or crime rates invariably results in punitive policy. See Weaver, "Frontlash," 235.

By connecting welfare and penal history, *Getting Tough* illustrates that many of the policies that expanded the penal system were answers to political problems arising when the U.S. welfare state confronted the upheaval of the 1960s and 1970s. Cracking down on pushers, welfare queens, and criminals was a response to contestation within the welfare state, and it also produced narratives about the welfare state. An increasingly dominant segment of politicians and the public interpreted disruptive social movements, rising crime rates, and economic downturns as evidence of the failure of welfarist programs and the ungovernability of marginalized groups. Codifying these logics in public policy helped suppress alternative interpretations in the public dialogue. It rationalized welfare-state retrenchment and remade state legitimacy and the terms of citizenship.[28] The penal system's expansion must therefore be at the center of our narratives about political change, the transformations of the state, and the rationalization of persistent racial, class, and gender hierarchies in the wake of the movement challenges of the 1960s and 1970s. Tough crime and welfare policy were not only a symptom of broader electoral and ideological shifts; they were instrumental in catalyzing them.

Degrading Citizenship: Producing Civic Stratification and "Common Sense"

This book argues that tough politics helped shape common sense about American citizenship and the state. It is a political history that scrutinizes the dialogic relationship between public policy, civic hierarchies, and popular understandings of the social world. Drug, welfare, and crime policies were implicated in both the day-to-day regulation of poor communities and the production of knowledge about inequality, deviance, and different categories of Americans.[29] Political rhetoric and public pol-

---

[28] In this sense, this book is one answer to Heather Thompson's call for historians of mass incarceration to not just do the important work of chronicling developments within the penal system but also show how the carceral expansion intervened in other transformations. Heather Thompson, "Why Mass Incarceration Matters: Rethinking Crisis, Decline, and Transformation in Postwar American History," *Journal of American History* 97, no. 3 (December 2010): 729–31.

[29] There are a number of approaches to analyzing the broader political effects of state punishment and social policy. The following works differ in orientation and emphasis but have all informed my analysis. Punishment's role in solidifying social solidarities is most famously associated with the writings of Émile Durkheim. David Garland makes the case for integrating Durkheim's work with other theoretical traditions, illustrating the ways the expressive functions of punishing that produce and enforce social norms and collective identities can coexist with other functions, such as class domination and social control. See David Garland, *Punishment and Modern Society: A Study in Social Theory* (Chicago:

icy initiatives helped isolate which social dynamics became "problems" in the first place. Anti–welfare fraud campaigns pushed welfare cheating into newspaper headlines and political speeches for decades while increasing economic inequality and stagnating real wages, arguably much more broadly registered trends, did not emerge as dominant political issues. Furthermore, struggles over the policy response to particular acts were necessarily also contests over the popular understandings of the definition, meaning, and cause of the problem behavior. The appropriate state response to burglary, for example, shifted depending on whether policymakers assumed thieves were desperate drug addicts, the victims of the poor parenting by welfare mothers, political revolutionaries, or economically desolate. Defining a phenomenon as part of a "drug epidemic," a "welfare crisis," or a "culture of poverty" went a long way toward dictating the appropriate response.

Because it is more broadly and immediately understood, I refer to "common sense" to reference the constellation of popular assumptions, logics, values, and affects surrounding particular social issues. It could also be called the social imaginary or the moral economies of crime, drugs, and welfare.[30] Elites could not simply inject these formulations

---

University of Chicago Press, 1993). The most famous exploration of punishment's role in normalization and social control is Michel Foucault, *Discipline and Punish: The Birth of the Prison* (New York: Vintage, 1995). On the ways crime discourse in the media and politics helps transform elites' definitions and logics about social conditions into popular "common sense," see Stuart Hall, Chas Critcher, Tony Jefferson, John Clarke, and Brian Roberts, *Policing the Crisis: Mugging, the State and Law and Order* (New York: Palgrave Macmillan, 2013). On the promise and pitfalls of employing a Gramscian analysis, see T. J. Jackson Lears, "The Concept of Cultural Hegemony: Problems and Possibilities," *American Historical Review* 90, no. 3 (1985): 567–93. Research in the social sciences has examined how welfare policy shapes notions of citizenship, institutional trajectories, and people's connections to the state. See, for example, Suzanne Mettler and Joe Soss, "The Consequences of Public Policy for Democratic Citizenship: Bridging Policy Studies and Mass Politics," *Perspectives on Politics* 2, no. 1 (March 2004): 55–73; Andrea Louise Campbell, *How Policies Make Citizens: Senior Political Activism and the American Welfare State* (Princeton: Princeton University Press, 2003); and Joe Soss and Joe Brian, *Unwanted Claims: The Politics of Participation in the U.S. Welfare System* (Ann Arbor: University of Michigan Press, 2002). On the broader political effects of the penal system, see Amy E. Lerman and Vesla M. Weaver, *Arresting Citizenship: The Democratic Consequences of American Crime Control* (Chicago: University of Chicago Press, 2014). On how state agents articulate and embody the state's morality, see Fassin, *At the Heart of the State*, 1–14. For a general discussion of the role of policy in "social construction," see Ann Schneider and Helen Ingram, "Social Construction of Target Populations: Implications for Politics and Policy," *American Political Science Review* 87, no. 2 (June 1, 1993): 334–47.

[30] For examples of other discussions of the social imaginary, see Samuel Moyn, "Imaginary Intellectual History," in *Rethinking Modern European Intellectual History*, ed. Darrin M. McMahon and Samuel Moyn (Oxford: Oxford University Press, 2014), 112–30 and Alice Kessler-Harris, *In Pursuit of Equity: Women, Men, and the Quest for Economic*

into a pliant populace. They were embedded in and constrained by political culture, which they in turn helped shape. The dominant narratives coexisted with alternative and discordant ones, although the rhetoric of political elites exerted powerful force—especially once concretized in law and ritually performed through state administration. For example, many people disagreed vehemently with racist representations of lazy, sexually deviant "welfare queens" but nonetheless had to navigate this feature of the political landscape when discussing AFDC.

"Getting tough" reverberated powerfully because its proponents often had large platforms and loud megaphones amplified through the media. Their narratives rested upon resonant racial and gender scripts. But it was not only their force, historical resonance, and volume that made these narratives so powerful. Once codified as state policy, "getting tough" created legally sanctioned gradations within the polity that were subsequently enacted in daily encounters with government agents.[31] Incessantly stopping and frisking young African American men, denying the vote to people with felonies, or searching welfare recipients' homes signaled—on a repeated and ongoing basis—these groups' degraded status. Stigmatizing routines and the denial of key rights and benefits denoting political belonging worked to discredit their targets' interpretations of the social order and their claims on the state. These formal, subordinated civic categories persevered and even hardened in the post–civil rights era—the period popularly celebrated as the realization of an equal, universal citizenship. Conceptions of full citizenship continued to be constructed through and defined against these racialized and subordinated civic categories.[32]

Citizenship in 20th-Century America (Oxford: Oxford University Press, 2001). Ethnographer and sociologist Didier Fassin explains that "moral economies represent the production, circulation, and appropriation of values and affects regarding a given social issue. Consequently, they characterize for a particular historical moment and a specific social world the manner in which this issue is constituted through judgments and sentiments that gradually come to define a sort of common sense and collective understanding of the problem." See Didier Fassin, ed., *At the Heart of the State: The Moral World of Institutions* (London: Pluto Press, 2015), 9.

[31] Different scholars have emphasized how welfare state programs became key sites for citizenship negotiations. See, for example, Kessler-Harris, *In Pursuit of Equity*; Linda Kerber, *No Constitutional Right to Be Ladies: Women and the Obligations of Citizenship* (New York: Hill and Wang, 1998); Nancy Fraser and Linda Gordon, "Civil Citizenship against Social Citizenship? On the Ideology of Contract-versus-Charity," in *The Condition of Citizenship*, ed. Bart van Steenbergen (London: Sage, 1994), 90–108; and Michael Katz, *The Price of Citizenship: Redefining the American Welfare State* (New York: Metropolitan Books, 2001). Others have argued that crime policy became a forum to oppose civil rights gains and claims for full citizenship by African Americans, even a vehicle through which to create a "new Jim Crow." See Alexander, *The New Jim Crow* and Weaver, "Frontlash."

[32] I conceive of the boundaries of the polity to be contiguous with the nation-state and any individuals therein to be members of the political community with civic agency,

Although there are many dimensions and conceptualizations of citizenship, I am concerned with the mechanisms that affect *standing within the polity*, particularly how penal and welfare policy constrained or enhanced people's ability to make claims on the state and gain leverage in public debates.[33] My focus here is not on the boundary between citizens and noncitizens but on the range of civil statuses within formal citizenship.[34] While it was not always the case, the policies in this book typically assumed that drug sellers, welfare recipients, and prisoners were citizens and subordinated these groups' civic status on the basis of their position vis-à-vis welfare or penal bureaucracies.

Hierarchy and differentiation within the polity have been constant features of U.S. society, perpetually remade in different alignments throughout the nation's history. Instead of breaking into easily delineated categories of "first-class" and "second-class" citizens, the country developed a complex gradation of different statuses, with different packages of rights, civil disabilities, and benefits attached. For much of U.S. history, policymakers categorically delimited the rights and benefits of entire groups on the basis of factors such as race, ethnicity, citizenship status, disability, or

---

regardless of they are undocumented immigrants or felons without basic political and civil rights. I am drawing here on conversations with political theorist Danielle Allen and her conceptualizations of the polity, civic agency, and citizenship more broadly. See also Danielle Allen, *Talking to Strangers: Anxieties of Citizenship since Brown v. Board of Education* (Chicago: University of Chicago Press, 2006). For a general discussion of alterity as a condition of citizenship, see Engin F. Isin, *Being Political: Genealogies of Citizenship* (Minneapolis: University of Minnesota Press, 2002), 1–5. See also Lisa Marie Cacho, *Social Death: Racialized Rightlessness and the Criminalization of the Unprotected* (New York: New York University Press, 2012).

[33] On standing, see Judith N. Shklar, *American Citizenship: The Quest for Inclusion* (Cambridge, Mass.: Harvard University Press, 1998). On the law's role in the civic subjection of racialized others, disabled persons, and women throughout the nineteenth century, see Barbara Young Welke, *Law and the Borders of Belonging in the Long Nineteenth Century United States* (New York: Cambridge University Press, 2010).

[34] Although notions of citizenship and the development of immigration control and the criminal justice systems were deeply intertwined, I do not take up that critical history in this book. For examples of research that investigate these dynamics, see Kelly Hernandez, "Amnesty or Abolition: Felons, Illegals, and the Case for a New Abolition Movement," *Boom: A Journal of California* 1, no. 4 (2011): 54–68 and Torrie Hester, "Deportability and the Carceral State," *Journal of American History* 102, no. 1 (June 1, 2015): 141–51. For examples of the rich literature on immigration and the shifting legal and social position of Indigenous people and various groups of noncitizens, see Mae M. Ngai, *Impossible Subjects: Illegal Aliens and the Making of Modern America* (Princeton: Princeton University Press, 2004); Aziz Rana, *The Two Faces of American Freedom* (Cambridge, Mass.: Harvard University Press, 2010); and Cybelle Fox, *Three Worlds of Relief: Race, Immigration, and the American Welfare State from the Progressive Era to the New Deal* (Princeton: Princeton University Press, 2012).

gender.[35] As these rationalizations for civic subordination faced escalating challenges in the civil rights era, policymakers advancing tough policies rationalized gradations within the polity through contractual understandings of citizenship that were already deeply anchored in U.S. history. Criminal and welfare policy did not restrict rights or withhold benefits on the basis of increasingly discredited theories of biologically grounded gender or racial inferiority. Instead, architects of tough public policy mobilized a longstanding and venerated logic in U.S. political culture that reserved full civic standing for those deemed "productive" and "independent." They insisted, with much popular support, that many of the rights and benefits of citizenship must essentially be *earned*—that they were contingent upon fulfilling civic obligations.[36] They argued that pushers, welfare recipients, and prisoners had failed to follow the law or to contribute to the polity by paying taxes or working and thereby forfeited their claims to material security, voice in public deliberations, and full civil and political rights. This discourse veiled the profound ways that gender, race, class, sexuality, and policy concerning immigration and Indigenous people structured which groups could position themselves as "law-abiding," "taxpayers," "independent," "workers," and "citizens" in the first place.

Welfare and crime policies helped produce a spectrum of civic statuses ranging from full, rights-bearing citizens to degraded groups positioned as distinct from the "public." Policies designed for deserving citizens aimed to enhance the rights, resources, and standing of beneficiaries. They produced programs, like the GI Bill and Social Security, that were rarely means or morals tested, entailed minimal surveillance, and in many cases obscured any notion of dependence on the state by framing benefits as earned or obscuring the state assistance altogether. Despite the ostensibly universal character of many such programs, access has been highly racialized and gendered and limited to those with certain kinds of work histories.[37]

[35] See, for example, Welke, *Law and the Borders of Belonging*; Rana, *The Two Faces of American Freedom*; Nancy F. Cott, *Public Vows: A History of Marriage and the Nation* (Cambridge, Mass.: Harvard University Press, 2000); and Linda K. Kerber, "The Meanings of Citizenship," *Journal of American History* 84, no. 3 (December 1, 1997): 833–54.

[36] On how contractual understandings of citizenship can be at odds with efforts to secure broader social rights, see Fraser and Gordon, "Civil Citizenship against Social Citizenship?" 90–108. For one argument about different visions of citizenship throughout U.S. history, see Rogers M. Smith, *Civic Ideals: Conflicting Visions of Citizenship in U.S. History* (New Haven: Yale University Press, 1999). For how exclusion can be rationalized from within (as opposed to in tension with) liberalism, see Mary Katzenstein, Leila Ibrahim, and Katharine D. Rubin, "Felony Disenfranchisement and the Dark Side of American Liberalism," *Perspectives on Politics* 8, no. 4 (September 2010): 1035–54.

[37] Even some means-tested cash transfers are issued through unstigmatizing procedures. For example, the Earned Income Tax Credit has ameliorated the poverty of millions of families by subsidizing low wages through a refundable tax credit triggered through tax

On the other end of the spectrum were policies that explicitly denigrated their targets' political standing through limitations on their rights, freedoms, or access to economic opportunity and state benefits. The penal system mobilized many of the most powerful techniques of civic subordination, but did not monopolize them. For example, the institutionalization, sterilization, and disenfranchisement of people with intellectual disabilities happened through the welfare state.[38] In contrast to Europe, the United States developed uniquely degrading habits of punishment.[39] People marked as criminal in the United States have been sentenced to different degrees of "civil death"—the loss of particular civil, social, and political rights—that vary widely and wildly depending on criminal offense, jurisdiction, and historical period.[40] Even after the completion of their sentence, convicts have been barred from voting, participating on juries, holding elected office, drawing certain welfare benefits, and becoming licensed in a host of professions.

---

filing. New Deal policymakers built a fragmented welfare state, making domestic and agricultural workers ineligible for social insurance and relegating many of the most vulnerable workers, people of color, and single mothers to paltrier and stigmatized programs that were typically means and morals tested. They effectively barred many immigrants, Asians, Native Americans, Latinos, and African Americans. On how policy design can enhance the political standing of program beneficiaries, see Campbell, *How Policies Make Citizens* and Mettler and Soss, "The Consequences of Public Policy for Democratic Citizenship," 55–73. On how state benefits and services are obfuscated from the public, see Mettler, *The Submerged State*. On the development and effects of the bifurcated welfare state, see Ira Katznelson, *When Affirmative Action Was White: An Untold History of Racial Inequality in Twentieth-Century America* (New York: Norton, 2006); Linda Gordon, *Pitied But Not Entitled: Single Mothers and the History of Welfare, 1890–1935* (New York: Free Press, 1994); and Kessler-Harris, *In Pursuit of Equity*.

[38]Allison Carey, *On the Margins of Citizenship: Intellectual Disability and Civil Rights in Twentieth-Century America* (Philadelphia: Temple University Press, 2010).

[39]While criminal punishment typically entails a degree of status degradation, there is actually significant variation across time and place. In some other countries, those convicted of crimes or drawing state aid are not targeted as aggressively by policies intended to degrade their status and do not forfeit as many rights. For example, many penal systems in Europe endeavor to limit the civil degradation of prisoners and convicts and have explicitly rejected the public shaming that has often characterized punishment in the United States. Prisoners in France and Germany, for example, are almost never disenfranchised, continue to wear their own clothes while incarcerated, and are addressed as "sir" by their captors. Although status degradation has not been central to analyses of public policy in the modern period, James Q. Whitman has argued for its centrality. He explores how the habit of status degradation and "leveling down" of punishment explains the United States' markedly distinct penal development as compared to European systems. Whitman, *Harsh Justice*. For a classic article on the sociology of degradation, see Harold Garfinkel, "Conditions of Successful Degradation Ceremonies," *American Journal of Sociology* 61, no. 5 (1956): 420–24.

[40]Rebecca McLennan, "The Convict's Two Lives: Civil and Natural Death in the American Prison," in *America's Death Penalty: Between Past and Present*, ed. David Garland, Michael Meranze, and Randall McGowen (New York: New York University Press, 2011), 191–219.

In between these poles are a range of policies that position subjects in a probationary or suspect status. Historically, "paupers" and others drawing poor relief have been forced to surrender certain political and civil rights while receiving aid.[41] While many programs offered services unconditionally, there were others—such as public housing and AFDC—that have made benefits contingent upon performance, such as sobriety, wage work, and proper comportment or sexual conduct. Programs committed to rehabilitation typically offered social assimilation on elites' terms and often interpreted economic and social marginality as a symptom of personal failure. They had mechanisms for sorting between corrigible and incorrigible subjects, and there were always certain individuals, often people of color, who were not deemed candidates for social integration. For example, in the northern penal system, assumptions about African Americans' innate criminality that solidified in the Progressive Era made them less viable candidates for rehabilitative programming.[42] The promise of rehabilitation and full civic standing was often delimited by race, contingent upon proper performance, and coerced through the threat of punishment or sanction.

These different civic statuses were largely produced through law, popular discourse, and administrative practices. There were no corresponding fixed, objective divisions between different types of people on the ground, and state endeavors to sort individuals were messy, contested, and historically contingent. Nor was there necessarily any correspondence between a person's civic status as a convict or welfare recipient and his or her individual subjectivity. Despite the much-publicized demands that offensive groups be quarantined, banished, or stripped of their rights, "getting tough" failed to expel these populations from the political community. Nonetheless, moving from a policy rhetorically committed to reintegration to a policy of social expulsion constricted the ability of collectives, once defined by their status as convicts or welfare recipients, to leverage space in political debates. Describing people as excluded from "the public" or "civilly dead" elided the ways they remained enmeshed in society as family members, friends, laborers, objects of exploitation, or referents against which "good citizens" were defined. But the capacity to effect political change has never been limited to those with full standing. People subjected to civic degradation remained ac-

---

[41] Chad Alan Goldberg, *Citizens and Paupers: Relief, Rights, and Race, from the Freedmen's Bureau to Workfare* (Chicago: University of Chicago Press, 2007); Michael B. Katz, *The Undeserving Poor: America's Enduring Confrontation with Poverty* (New York: Oxford University Press, 2013).

[42] Muhammad, *The Condemnation of Blackness*; Khalil Gibran Muhammad, "Where Did All the White Criminals Go?: Reconfiguring Race and Crime on the Road to Mass Incarceration," *Souls* 13, no. 1 (2011): 72–90.

tive agents in society and continued to fiercely assert their humanity and make demands on the state.

Rehabilitation and the Crucible of the "Urban Crisis"

For a period in the twentieth century that reached its zenith in the 1960s, rehabilitation became a dominant strategy in the state's response to social marginality and economic inequality. The political and economic upheavals that escalated in the 1960s destabilized this governing logic and the existing patterns of civic stratification. This opened new space to debate who and what were responsible for urban disorder and how best to respond. Some social movement participants called for revolution, others for radical democracy or locally controlled social services. Others called for more robust social welfare programming. Their political opponents insisted instead that the time had arrived to get tougher on seemingly hostile and unruly residents of racially segregated urban communities. Those defending the status quo felt increasingly besieged.

The focus on catalyzing transformation within individuals ascended in the decades after the Great Depression amid skepticism of direct assistance and the ongoing repression of movements advocating structural interventions in the economy. Renewed business mobilization and the anti-communist crusades accompanied the rapid economic growth after World War II, leaving fewer and fewer voices advocating for redistribution and state control or management of the market. Politicians embraced a pro-growth and Keynesian orientation in economic policy and a focus on developing human capital in social policy.[43] The emphasis on individually targeted rehabilitation spanned diverse institutions. As courts and medical authorities began approaching drug addiction as a disease, states mounted new treatment programs aiming to transform addicts into responsible, taxpaying citizens.[44] AFDC, for example, ceased to focus on subsidizing parenting labor and increasingly committed to remaking the habits and character of welfare recipients to facilitate their entrance into

[43] On the retreat of plans for more aggressive intervention and regulation of capitalism during and after the New Deal era, see Alan Brinkley, "New Deal and the Idea of the State," in *The Rise and Fall of the New Deal Order, 1930–1980*, ed. Steve Fraser and Gary Gerstle (Princeton: Princeton University Press, 1990), 85–121. See also Landon R. Y. Storrs, *The Second Red Scare and the Unmaking of the New Deal Left* (Princeton: Princeton University Press, 2013).

[44] William L. White, *Slaying the Dragon: The History of Addiction Treatment and Recovery in America* (Bloomington, Ill.: Chestnut Health Systems, 1998).

the paid labor force.[45] Rehabilitative objectives also anchored the penal system: prisons were dedicated to corrections and offered a combination of psychological, vocational, and educational services. While these programs often delivered important services and benefits, their coercive features also left them as vulnerable to criticism from their ostensible beneficiaries as their ideological opponents. As we will see in the coming pages, subjects of rehabilitative projects often found their treatment stigmatizing, unresponsive, coercive, and sometimes outright punitive.

In the 1960s, social movement pressure and the increasing popular attention to poverty in the midst of unprecedented economic abundance helped inspire Presidents John F. Kennedy and Lyndon Johnson to call upon the federal government to ameliorate, even eradicate, poverty.[46] They were particularly concerned about the "social dynamite" of American "ghettos": the risk of disorder arising from the concentrated poverty in segregated, crowded, urban African American communities.[47] In 1964, President Johnson declared a War on Poverty that reflected confidence that social welfare initiatives and continuing economic prosperity would enable the country "to open for all Americans the opportunity that is now enjoyed by most Americans."[48] Under his leadership, Congress created Medicare and Medicaid in 1964 and 1965, respectively, dramatically expanding access to health care for the poor and elderly. They initiated Head Start, which provided early childhood education for low-income children, and launched the food stamp and indigent legal services programs. The rhetoric advancing War on Poverty programs often acknowledged the structural factors producing urban conditions, but the policies mostly focused on reforming individuals and communities, eschewing direct intervention in the economic system. Many of the architects of the programs also interpreted racial inequality as the result of the allegedly matriarchal black family, blocked opportunities, and lack of training and skills. Although many programs, such as Head Start, became significant sources of employment for low-income parents, politicians emphasized job training over job creation.[49]

The War on Poverty and the state's rehabilitative programs soon confronted a series of escalating challenges. Slowing economic growth and increased spending on the Vietnam War undermined plans to subsidize

---

[45] Jennifer Mittelstadt, *From Welfare to Workfare: The Unintended Consequences of Liberal Reform, 1945–1965* (Chapel Hill: University of North Carolina Press, 2005), 11.

[46] Julian E. Zelizer, *The Fierce Urgency of Now: Lyndon Johnson, Congress, and the Battle for the Great Society* (New York: Penguin, 2015).

[47] Hinton, *From the War on Poverty to the War on Crime.*

[48] Lyndon Johnson, "Annual Message to Congress on the State of the Union," January 4, 1965, http://www.lbjlib.utexas.edu/johnson/archives.hom/speeches.hom/650104.asp.

[49] On the War on Poverty, see Katz, *The Undeserving Poor*, particularly 102–55.

the War on Poverty through the dividends of continuing economic expansion. Capital migration, "urban renewal," and discriminatory housing and hiring practices joined to facilitate suburban expansion and drain jobs and capital from urban communities. These dynamics exacerbated material hardship, particularly in urban communities of color that had never reaped as many benefits from the earlier growth. They also increased demands on the state for social and economic assistance.[50]

Marginalized groups intensified their demands, which had always been present, for a voice in negotiating the terms of their "inclusion." After black freedom movements assailed the varied pillars supporting white supremacy in the North and South, other social movements followed suit, prying open and destabilizing categories of citizenship and challenging the gendered and racial exclusions of the New Deal welfare state. People on the ground in poor communities seized on the political opportunity of the War on Poverty, particularly the emphasis on encouraging the "maximum feasible participation" of the poor in Community Action Programs, to claim new resources and political power.[51] This organizing challenged the power of local political elites, which eroded establishment support for these federal initiatives.

The urban uprisings of the 1960s escalated the stakes of these debates and thrust conditions in urban "ghettos" into the national spotlight. In city after city throughout the mid-1960s, authorities sent tanks and the National Guard into burning streets. After Martin Luther King's assassination in 1968, urban residents rebelled in over one hundred cities. The national media closely covered the violence, property destruction, and disorder. For many present or watching on television, the scenes looked eerily like a war zone. Indeed the uprisings at home and political insurgencies in Africa, Asia, and Latin America collapsed into each other. Politicians, law enforcement, and activists with different agendas identified an interconnected global rebellion underway challenging colonialism, racism, and capitalism.

[50] On the history of urban segregation, municipal politics, and suburban expansion in the postwar era, see, for example, Kevin Kruse, *White Flight: Atlanta and the Making of Modern Conservatism* (Princeton: Princeton University Press, 2007); Matthew D. Lassiter, *The Silent Majority: Suburban Politics in the Sunbelt South* (Princeton: Princeton University Press, 2007); Robert Self, *American Babylon: Race and the Struggle for Postwar Oakland* (Princeton: Princeton University Press, 2003); and Thomas J. Sugrue, *The Origins of the Urban Crisis: Race and Inequality in Postwar Detroit*, 2nd ed. (Princeton: Princeton University Press, 2014).

[51] On the ways poor communities struggled to reshape the War on Poverty on the ground, see Orleck and Hazirjian, *The War on Poverty* and Alyosha Goldstein, *Poverty in Common: The Politics of Community Action during the American Century* (Durham, N.C.: Duke University Press, 2012). On "maximum feasible participation," see Orleck, introduction to *The War on Poverty*, 2.

Political rhetoric blurred riots together with foreign threats, concentrated urban poverty, rising crime rates, and civil rights activism into an acute "urban crisis."[52] Throughout the ensuing years, Americans debated the appropriate response to this tangle of issues that were now constructed as interlocking and indigenous to poor communities of color. Disputes raged over the appropriate balance of social welfare spending and law enforcement needed to manage this racialized vision of urban disorder and political insurgency. Johnson again advanced rehabilitative strategies, arguing that crime was rooted in social deprivation and could be mitigated by expanding opportunities through the Great Society programs. He redeployed his War on Poverty programs as tactics in another newly declared war, explaining that "the War on Poverty is . . . a war against crime and a war against disorder."[53]

As Johnson continued to press for more robust social programs, he also pursued martial approaches to securing "law and order." In 1965, he signed the Law Enforcement Assistance Act that began an unprecedented transfer of federal resources to local law enforcement, which had traditionally been primarily the responsibility of state and local governments. Echoing the counterinsurgency expertise that circulated transnationally, he argued that economic development, the penal system, and social welfare programs were complementary and necessary partners in the efforts to secure order: "Effective law enforcement and social justice must be pursued together, as the foundation of our efforts against crime."[54] Critics of Johnson, however, positioned the strategies as starkly oppositional. They challenged the assumption that social welfare programs were the government's most effective tools for maintaining social order and diffusing political uprisings. Law-and-order proponents argued that new civil rights laws and enlarged social welfare programs not only failed to reduce disorder but actually created it.

By the mid-1960s, domestic law enforcement agencies often interpreted the conditions in inner cities as wars and had begun to turn to the military for training, technology, and even terminology to handle the situations.[55] When Congress passed the Omnibus Crime Control and Safe

---

[52] For how civil rights activism, crime, and rioting came to blur together, see Naomi Murakawa, "The Origins of the Carceral Crisis: Racial Order as 'Law and Order' in Postwar American Politics," in *Race and American Political Development*, ed. Joseph Lowndes, Julie Novkov, and Dorian Warren (New York: Routledge, 2008), 234–55.

[53] On "The War on Poverty is," see Flamm, *Law and Order*, 47.

[54] Lyndon Johnson, "Special Message to the Congress on Crime and Law Enforcement," March 9, 1966, American Presidency Project, http://www.presidency.ucsb.edu/ws/?pid=27478.

[55] I explore the ways knowledge and strategies circulated between foreign and domestic space in Julilly Kohler-Hausmann, "Militarizing the Police: Officer Jon Burge's Torture and Repression in the 'Urban Jungle,'" in *Challenging the Prison-Industrial Complex: Activism,*

Streets Act in 1968, it facilitated the transfer of expertise and technology from the military to local law enforcement agencies. Aiming to rationalize and strengthen the crime-fighting powers of the state, the bill weakened the federal legal protections of criminal defendants that the Supreme Court had just articulated. The Safe Streets Act also created the Law Enforcement Assistance Administration (LEAA), which strengthened ties between local police and the federal government and enabled a further influx of federal dollars into local police departments. While LEAA funded some programs intended to tackle "root causes" of crime, such as drug addiction, the vast majority of resources subsidized the expansion of local police forces and their acquisition of military riot control gear.[56] Therefore, throughout this period, social programs proliferated alongside this deployment of increasingly militarized and strident law enforcement. While these different endeavors to secure social order coexisted on the ground in poor communities, debates raged over what should become the dominant rationale guiding state action. By the early 1970s, there was no inevitable path forward. Struggles over public policy, like the ones chronicled in this book, became key sites where people continued the fights over governance and authority that were left open by the era's upheaval. The outcome—which can appear overdetermined decades later—seemed up for grabs in the early 1970s.

Three Studies in Tough Politics

This book unfolds in three parts, each chronicling the enactment of influential state-level drug-, welfare-, and criminal-sentencing policies during the 1970s. Each part examines pivot points within the histories of these policies where old rationales for state intervention had been destabilized and what would replace them was unclear. It illuminates the profoundly different "problems" that elites tried to solve using civic degradation and tough politics. At these critical junctures, I examine how

---

Arts, and Educational Alternatives, ed. Stephen Hartnett (Urbana: University of Illinois Press, 2010), 43–71. For examples of the new work that theorizes and historicizes the transnational circulation of counterinsurgency knowledge, see Ananya Roy, Stuart Schrader, and Emma Shaw Crane, "Gray Areas: The War on Poverty at Home and Abroad," in *Territories of Poverty* (Athens: University of Georgia Press, 2015), 289–315 and Micol Seigel, "Objects of Police History," *Journal of American History* 102, no. 1 (June 1, 2015): 152–61.

[56] On the Safe Streets Act and LEAA, see Hinton, *From the War on Poverty to the War on Crime*; Thompson, "Why Mass Incarceration Matters," 729–31; Christian Parenti, *Lockdown America: Police and Prisons in the Age of Crisis* (New York: Verso, 2000), 6–23; and Jonathan Simon, *Governing through Crime: How the War on Crime Transformed American Democracy and Created a Culture of Fear* (Oxford: Oxford University Press, 2007), 89–102.

competing interpretations of social dynamics were hashed out through policy struggles, resulting eventually in an altered dominant rationale for government action.

Part 1 of the book, "Pushers," illustrates how politicians endeavored to resolve broad problems of urban governance through intensifying the criminalization of drug sellers. It explores how New York governor Nelson Rockefeller repudiated the state's varied drug-treatment programs and enacted the nation's most severe drug penalties. The 1973 "Rockefeller drug laws" targeted (and thereby helped reify) the figure of the "drug pusher," whom the governor held responsible for increasing crime, drug use, and general social disorder. These debates helped entrench the idea that low-level drug sellers were irredeemable and state efforts to transform deviant, racialized groups into full citizens were futile.

In the second part, "Welfare Queens," I explore the ways increasingly stringent and punitive welfare policy arose from efforts to accommodate the profound renegotiation of women's roles and responsibilities in the postwar era. It follows the efforts of Illinois and California state lawmakers to reform AFDC in the 1970s. Instead of relying on rehabilitation and economic incentives to induce poor mothers into the labor force, legislators, led by California governor Ronald Reagan, endeavored to limit AFDC program size through criminalization, anti-fraud campaigns, and work mandates. These policy struggles gave birth to the racialized caricature of the "welfare queen" and intensified the public stereotype of AFDC beneficiaries as lazy, financially secure, and criminally suspect. Anti–welfare fraud campaigns recast the caseload increases resulting from embryonic articulations of an economic citizenship—expanded AFDC eligibility and access and new "welfare rights"—as the work of these deviant cheaters.

The final part, "Criminals," reveals how fixed criminal sentencing responded to problems of institutional governance and social movements within prisons. It chronicles California's passage in 1976 of a trendsetting determinate sentencing law that abandoned rehabilitation as an aim of incarceration. This transformation ultimately facilitated the dramatic increase in mandatory minimum sentences. Lawmakers paired longer prison terms with new civic liabilities, thereby deepening the moat between full citizenship and the status of "convict" that had just been narrowed by a host of challenges to convicts' "civic death." In advancing tough criminal policies, their proponents asserted that those convicted of street crime were either hopelessly irredeemable or only responsive to draconian punishment.

Although federal politics and policy played an increasingly central role in the state transformations of the late twentieth century, it was state and local governments that administered AFDC and the majority of the penal and drug-treatment institutions. Therefore, many of the most important developments in crime and welfare policy happened at the state level.[57] Yet benefit levels and incarceration rates varied significantly by state and region, and no single state can stand in for the national story. The social upheaval in New York, Illinois, and California was particularly dramatic, and the policy struggles in those states were historically significant on their own terms. They made news across the country and helped sculpt national discourse about poverty, crime, and drug addiction.[58]

These state-level struggles responded to developments in federal politics while also transforming them. California governor Ronald Reagan and New York governor Nelson Rockefeller used "getting tough" to jockey for leadership of the Republican Party and the presidency. Reagan's welfare reforms in California were instrumental in derailing President Richard Nixon's guaranteed minimum-income proposal, the Family Assistance Plan. They set a course in state and federal legislative trends that culminated in the 1996 welfare reforms that abolished AFDC. Rockefeller's drug laws helped extinguish President Nixon's enthusiasm for his ambitious drug-treatment initiatives of the early 1970s. They starkly illustrated the political dividends of draconian drug and crime policy for the politicians who would embrace similar postures as the War on Drugs crescendoed in the ensuing years. California's 1976 determinate sentencing law was the first major experiment in a sentencing trend that swept the nation. It transferred sentencing authority to prosecutors and lawmakers, who in turn became two of the most significant drivers of penal expansion.

Each of the three studies is divided between two chapters. The first chapter in each section investigates the construction of the "problem": the political and governance issues that drugs, welfare, or criminal sentencing

[57] On the pivotal role of federal policy in the development of mass incarceration, see Hinton, *From the War on Poverty to the War on Crime* and Weaver, "Frontlash." On the importance of state-level studies and regional variation, see Mona Lynch, *Sunbelt Justice: Arizona and the Transformation of American Punishment* (Stanford: Stanford Law Books, 2009) and Vanessa Barker, *The Politics of Imprisonment: How the Democratic Process Shapes the Way America Punishes* (New York: Oxford University Press, 2009).

[58] More local- and state-level histories are needed to unearth how punitive policy spread and how dynamics differed between regions and changed after penal capacity and authority expanded in the 1980s and 1990s. While social scientists have attempted to identify factors influencing state-level variation, less work has explored the historical process by which these logics and policies migrated between various states, the federal level, and foreign territories. Examples of state-level studies are Perkinson, *Texas Tough* and Lynch, *Sunbelt Justice*. For research on the differences between states, see Barker, *The Politics of Imprisonment*; Soss, Fording, and Schram, *Disciplining the Poor*; Michael C. Campbell and Heather Schoenfeld, "The Transformation of America's Penal Order: A Historicized Political Sociology of Punishment," *American Journal of Sociology* 118, no. 5 (March 1, 2013): 1375–1423; and Beckett and Western, "Governing Social Marginality."

procedures endeavored to manage and the divergent ways people interpreted them. The second chapter then traces the ways "getting tough" provided partial and contested political resolutions to these problems and to broader social conflicts. Throughout the book, I focus on the interactions between street-level policy implementation, social movements, constituent pressure, electoral politics, and public policy formation. While principally tracking statutory changes at the state level, the book also incorporates the interplay between federal and municipal politics.

I also highlight the dialogue between political elites and their constituents. I recognize elites' disproportionate power but also examine how ordinary people pressured leaders and shaped public debates within asymmetrical power relations. With varying levels of influence, people steered politicians toward certain issues and interpretations and away from others. Through face-to-face interactions, letters to newspapers and politicians, voting (or not voting), cultural productions, activism, and public opinion polls, the public registered its concerns and signaled which framings of issues resonated most powerfully. Within even more highly constrained parameters, people convicted of drug crimes, welfare recipients, and prisoners intervened in these historical developments, and I have incorporated some of the ways those targeted by these policies dialogued with the state. Although the proponents of tough policies insisted that targeted groups' voices were illegitimate, they were nevertheless forced to confront them. Indeed, this book reveals that subordinated groups played a critical role in this history. They advocated for themselves through activism, protests, political participation, and their incessant demands that state programs better serve their interests.[59] Just as frequently, they created political pressure through their survival strategies, informal acts of resistance, and failure to act in the ways elites stipulated. They precipitated political change, although not always the type of change they would have hoped for.

---

[59] To illustrate the ways non-elites registered in these deliberations, I draw heavily upon constituent mail and public hearing testimony. With few archival windows into these perspectives, these sources offer welcome insight into non-elites' participation. They are, however, like any source, a product of the context in which they are produced and reflect gross power differentials. The writings of drug users, prisoners, and welfare recipients about statutory change are particularly fraught sources for many reasons. For example, in many cases, state agents may even have had power to retaliate against letter writers or otherwise affect their circumstances. For this reason, I do not consider letters undistorted or even honest reflections of the writers' views. Nor do I assume the letters or statements are indicative of the opinions of others who did not write to legislators or testify. Instead, the letters and testimony reveal some of the ways that those people, operating within severely constrained parameters (including official censorship), discussed the state's role in their lives when in dialogue with its representatives.

These three political struggles reveal how fights over drug, welfare, and crime policy became central staging grounds in the long historical struggle over the social contract: who deserved voice in the polity, what were citizens' rights and obligations, and what, in turn, were the state's responsibilities to its citizens. While the studies are presented separately for narrative purposes, the politics of drugs, welfare, and crime were intertwined ideologically and overlapped chronologically. The logics they shared developed strength, consistency, and legitimacy as they spread, although they did not operate the same way in every setting. The drug pusher, welfare queen, and criminal all collapsed into the racialized and unassimilable "urban underclass": a powerful political construction that would hover menacingly over the politics of the 1980s and beyond.

Tough politics did not simply index popular opinion or reflect a conservative drift in the American electorate; they were instrumental in producing it. Rather than an inevitable consequence of the "failures of liberalism," they reified that narrative in public discourse. These policies paid political dividends, naturalized social hierarchies, and deflected social movements' demands. In the process, they helped criminalize entire populations and spaces by reinscribing the idea that suspect groups were entirely ungovernable without force or coercion. Unearthing this fraught history denaturalizes the assumptions that tough politics advanced—assumptions that hardened into common sense over the ensuing decades.

PART I

Pushers

The addict, no matter what his psychological perceptions about himself, no matter what theorizing psychiatrists do, is a social type generated in response to changes in the social economy in a time of world crisis. A mistake frequently made is to view drug consumption merely as an indulgence, a gratification, an escape rather than a market response to economic and social dislocation.

—Sol Yurick, author of *The Warriors*, in "The Political Economy of Junk"

Drugs make people feel good, not bad. They give people pleasures available in no other way. And they provide a near perfect escape from reality. The truth is that we are a drug taking society, with nine million alcoholics, hundreds of thousands of respectable pill takers who can afford prescriptions, thousands who drink to excess on occasion, including before driving, untold millions who continue to shorten their lives with tobacco, and five hundred seventy thousand heroin addicts. The truth is we are all in the same boat.

—Harvard Hollenberd, chief counsel of Narcotic Addiction Control Commission, to Harriet Michel, director of Mayor's Narcotic Control Counsel, 1972[1]

Alarm about illicit drugs crescendoed in the 1960s and 1970s. Drugs seemed to threaten the nation at every turn. "Junkies," "pushers," and "addicts" loomed large in public consciousness. Newspapers warned that

[1] The epigraphs to the part introduction come from Sol Yurick, "The Political Economy of Junk," *Monthly Review* 22, no. 7 (December 1970): 23 and Harvard Hollenberd to Harriet Michel, director of Mayor's Narcotic Control Counsel, October 11, 1972, 4th Administration, Reel 61, Central Subject and Correspondence Files of Governor Nelson A. Rockefeller, New York State Archives, Albany, N.Y. (hereafter Rockefeller Gubernatorial Papers, NYSA).

hunger for drugs drove people to steal, mug, and even kill to sustain their habits. Commentators attributed the era's crime rates to surging heroin use and claimed that addicts transformed once welcoming neighborhoods into dangerous, forbidding spaces. Simultaneously, many were alarmed that heroin no longer seemed confined to poor communities of color. Media broadcasts reported that soldiers were using the high-quality, affordable heroin in Southeast Asia to manage the boredom and terror of the Vietnam War.[2] Reports of white middle-class substance abuse and experimentation led parents to worry that drugs—like so many problems at the time—had breached the carefully guarded borders of suburban America.[3] These specific crises were all the more ominous because of the general upheaval throughout society. Drugs joined with the mass movements, the rebellions of youth, and the war in Vietnam to threaten traditional authority structures. And the more attention and resources state and federal governments devoted to drug treatment and law enforcement, the worse the situation seemed to get. For many, drugs appeared to be the final straw, pushing the country into mayhem and chaos.

Nowhere was the issue more salient than New York. New York City, a main entry point for heroin into the country, was supposedly home to half of the nation's heroin addicts.[4] The perception of a drug epidemic was both crisis and opportunity for lawmakers in New York State, and few politicians more persistently leveraged the issue than Nelson Rockefeller, who governed the state during the crisis. Drugs, he explained in 1970, imperiled the nation's fundamental stability: "The fiber of the American character has traditionally been strong. That is why the nation grew great. Drugs threaten to destroy that very fiber and to destroy the American future along with it."[5]

As the son of the powerful philanthropist and financier John D. Rockefeller Jr., Nelson Rockefeller was born into the spotlight as an heir to one of the country's great fortunes. Before entering electoral politics, he worked for Presidents Roosevelt and Truman to advance U.S.

[2]Michael Massing, *The Fix* (New York: Simon and Schuster, 1998), 100–131; Baum, *Smoke and Mirrors: The War on Drugs and the Politics of Failure* (Boston: Little, Brown, 1996), 39–62. See also "As Common as Chewing Gum," *TIME*, March 1, 1971, and "New Withdrawal Costs," *TIME*, June 7, 1971.

[3]Baum, *Smoke and Mirrors*, 34–35; Eric Schneider, *Smack: Heroin and the American City* (Philadelphia: University of Pennsylvania Press, 2008), 142–59. For contemporary news reports, see Martin Tolchin, "Involvement of Middle Class in the Narcotics Problem Arouses Demands for Action," *New York Times*, March 9, 1970, 29 and Tom Buckley, "The Fight against Drugs Is in a Mess," *New York Times*, March 22, 1970, 184.

[4]Schneider, *Smack*, x, 1–16.

[5]"Draft of Crime Speech," [1970], Folder 320, Box 32, Series 10.4, Nelson A. Rockefeller Gubernatorial Records, Rockefeller Archive Center, Sleepy Hollow, N.Y. (hereafter RAC).

interests abroad, particularly in Latin America.[6] He served as New York's governor from 1959 to 1973, but his ambition was always to hold the nation's highest office. Rockefeller ran for the Republican presidential nomination in 1960, 1964, and 1968. He was the quintessential moderate Republican during a period when a revived conservative movement mobilized within the party, pulling it to the right and frustrating his presidential ambitions.

In the last decade of Rockefeller's tenure as governor, he dedicated unprecedented physical, institutional, and monetary resources to a series of rehabilitative programs that approached drug addiction as a medical disease. Then, in January 1973, Rockefeller shocked the political establishment by declaring that these drug-treatment efforts—programs he had championed for over a decade—were abject failures. He proposed instead that the state make the penalty for selling hard drugs, regardless of quantity, a lifetime in prison without any option of plea bargaining, probation, or parole. A few months later, the New York legislature answered Rockefeller's call and passed a mildly diluted version of his proposal, enacting the harshest narcotics laws in the nation.

This book's first part traces the genesis and enactment of these punitive proposals, which came in time to be known as the Rockefeller Drug Laws. Chapter 1 explores the governing problems that set the stage for the 1973 drug laws and the ways different groups struggled to interpret and respond to them. It chronicles New York's efforts to manage heroin through drug rehabilitation and explores how the varied therapeutic approaches coexisted with criminalization. Chapter 2 explores the ways Rockefeller's 1973 tough proposal attempted to resolve the governing problems that arose from the therapeutic regime. It analyzes the ideological and political work accomplished by the tough proposal and the response by policymakers, opponents, drug users, and the diverse members of the general public.

Political and media narratives tethered the "drug problem" to political upheaval, economic change, and rising crime rates, which inflamed public anxiety. There was no consensus about how to respond: politicians and their constituents rushed into the fray offering a host of diverse interpretations of the problem and appropriate reactions. Far from purely elite, rarified policy debates, people from all quarters shaped and engaged these questions. From prisons to the state capital to neighborhood meetings to newspapers' editorial pages to new drug-treatment groups, people

---

[6] On the formative role of Rockefeller's experience in Latin America for the evolution of his anti-communism and domestic political postures, see Micol Seigel, "Nelson Rockefeller in Latin America: Global Currents of U.S. Prison Growth," *Comparative American Studies* 13, no. 3 (July 3, 2015): 161–76.

wrestled over what caused drug use and what authority and strategies were best employed to manage it. Did drug abuse result from individual pathology, either criminality or illness? Did it originate in certain suspect spaces or cultures? Were drug abuse and drug markets a function of larger social and economic structures or perhaps a permanent feature of American culture? How should society respond to widespread drug use and illicit drug markets: punitive sanction, coerced medical treatment, rehabilitation directed and controlled by ex–drug users, legalization, or, perhaps, revolution? Hashing out these questions through drug-policy debates not only helped produce popular knowledge about the state's capacity to manage drug users and sellers. It ultimately also amplified some narratives about the causes of addiction, crime, urban disorder, and social inequality and drowned out others.

CHAPTER ONE

Addicts into Citizens

THE TRIBULATIONS OF NEW YORK'S TREATMENT REGIME

When Nelson Rockefeller proposed his draconian drug penalties in 1973, he presented them as a rupture with the recent past—a sharp repudiation of the drug-treatment programs he had championed for almost a decade. Many scholars and commentators have largely echoed this assessment, positioning the Rockefeller Drug Laws as the origins of the modern, punitive War on Drugs. There is no doubt that the political theater of enacting these policies reverberated nationally and dramatically escalated the prescribed penalties for selling illicit drugs. But emphasizing only the radical departure the laws entailed risks obscuring the continuities with the earlier period and impeding our ability to understand the transformation. Carefully locating Rockefeller's dramatic proposal in the longer history of the state's efforts to manage drug use and street crime reveals that the 1973 policy both repudiated and built upon the treatment regime that came before them.

Contemporary political rhetoric also obscured the complexities and continuities. A newspaper at the time captured the tidy narrative in the simple title: "Drug Addiction in NY: Once an Illness, Now a Crime."[1] Though Rockefeller emphasized drug rehabilitation before 1973 and penal sanction afterward, it is imperative analytically to recognize that criminalization and medicalization are concurrent, intertwined, and at times mutually dependent strategies. Rockefeller—and most other participants in these debates—never categorically rejected a role for treatment or law enforcement. They more typically debated the appropriate balance between them. Policymakers endeavored to establish which strategy was appropriate for which groups: what enticements, services, and deterrents were needed to manage different consumers and sellers of illicit drugs. In other words, the architects of New York's drug policy were engaged in a (largely futile) effort to sort the various participants in the drug economy into distinct categories: between victims and perpetrators, addicts

---

[1] "Drug Addiction in NY: Once an Illness, Now a Crime," *Daily News Tribune* (Fullerton, Calif.), September 8, 1973, Reel 61, Rockefeller Gubernatorial Papers, 4th Administration, NYSA.

and pushers, or the redeemable and incorrigible. As has often been the case throughout the state's frustrated efforts to regulate intoxicating substances, a person's social location—race, ethnicity, neighborhood, gender, and class—had a profound influence over where in the state's taxonomy he or she landed.

While rhetoric in the 1970s presented "addicts" and "pushers" as stable, essential identities, these terms are best understood as artifacts of the ongoing historical struggles over narcotics. Instead of objective divisions within the social body, the distinct categories of drug users were actually constituted through debates over policy. The term "addict" suggested that habitual drug users suffered from a uniform affliction rooted in individual pathology and that there was some consistency in the perils generated by physical or psychological dependence on substances.[2] Although the rhetoric of addiction typically worked to affix an indelible label to a person, the relationship of drug users themselves to the concept of addiction often changed depending on context, policy regime, and time period. The same person might desperately struggle to be certified by the state as an addict in one setting while shunning the label and its stigma in another.

"Pusher" referred to someone who sold drugs at the street level and was typically imagined to be an African American or Latino man. There was considerable slippage between this term and "addict," since many habitual users, particularly with little income, sold and traded drugs to sustain their habit. The term "pushers" implied that drug sellers were involved in aggressively recruiting new customers and creating more addicts, as opposed to responding to consumer demand. The distinctions between "victims," "addicts," "pushers," and "addict-pushers" grew increasingly important as addiction was medicalized and consternation about crime and drugs grew. While these categories were highly fluid, mutable, and contested on the ground, the state's prescribed classification would have profound consequences for the fates of those labeled.

When New York faced escalating drug use after World War II, politicians and their constituents offered a range of interpretations of it and policy responses to it. Doctors, activists, law enforcement, and an emerging cadre of addiction treatment experts—some of whom were themselves

---

[2] On the history of medicalization and addiction research, see Caroline Jean Acker, *Creating the American Junkie: Addiction Research in the Classic Era of Narcotic Control* (Baltimore: Johns Hopkins University Press, 2002); David T. Courtwright, *Dark Paradise: A History of Opiate Addiction in America* (Cambridge, Mass.: Harvard University Press, 2001); and Nancy D. Campbell, *Discovering Addiction: The Science and Politics of Substance Abuse Research* (Ann Arbor: University of Michigan Press, 2007). On conceptions of addiction and shifting efforts to regulate drugs in New York, see Maureen Mahoney, "Fighting 'Addiction': African-American and Hispanic Activism and New York City's Illegal Drug Policies, 1946–1999" (PhD diss., University of Wisconsin–Madison, 1999).

"ex-addicts"—also entered the fray to assert their own authority and policy proposals. The result of these deliberations was an evolving set of therapeutic programs and criminal sanctions aimed to manage drug users and mitigate crime and drug use. The state's varied anti-drug programs rested on distinct conceptualizations of addiction, empowered different groups, and produced divergent outcomes. Each presented political problems stretching beyond the considerable difficulties entailed in controlling drug markets and users. Building a substantial network of treatment programs proved to be controversial and expensive. It was dependent on fraught political coalitions, opposed by powerful interests, besieged by critics of all political persuasions, and ostensibly designed to serve some of the most reviled groups in society. Drug users and their allies began using the state's purported commitment to rehabilitation to make demands for very different programs and more profound reforms. And in the midst of these ordeals, other local, national, and international developments intervened in the early 1970s to make the drug use in New York an even more explosive issue. It was this thorny landscape that Rockefeller would endeavor to navigate with his infamous 1973 proposal.

The Menace of Heroin

World War II interrupted heroin supply routes, but the drug reappeared as trade reopened after 1945 and it soon presented a host of new challenges for the state. The estimated number of heroin users increased tenfold during the 1960s, from fifty thousand nationally in 1960 to approximately a half million in 1970.[3] A number of forces contributed to this rising use. Between 1960 and 1970, the gross national product doubled, increasing consumer demand for all types of commodities, legal and illegal, at the same time that a large cohort of baby boomers reached the ages most prone to initiate drug use.[4]

New York City's heroin markets were primarily concentrated in the densely populated African American and Latino communities created by mass internal migration and discriminatory housing practices.[5] Just as international conflicts and the escalating Cold War shaped the global supply and circulation of heroin, the profound political economic transformations and dislocations in the decades after World War II shaped

[3] David Musto, *The American Disease: Origins of Narcotic Control* (New York: Oxford University Press, 1999), 247–48. On some of the dynamics that expanded heroin supply in the postwar era, see Alfred McCoy, *The Politics of Heroin: CIA Complicity in the Global Drug Trade* (Brooklyn, N.Y.: Lawrence Hill Books, 1991).

[4] Courtwright, *Dark Paradise*, 145–85; Musto, *American Disease*, 247–48.

[5] On heroin markets, see Schneider, *Smack*.

the domestic heroin markets. Decline in the industrial and manufacturing sectors started early in New York City, driven in part by relatively high production costs, corporate migrations, and changes in technology and infrastructure. At the same time, substantial groups of Puerto Ricans and African Americans migrated to the city, searching for jobs that were increasingly unavailable or simply nonexistent. Many of them encountered instead extreme residential segregation that concentrated the poor and people of color into ghettos systematically underserved by state programs. This spatially structured economic and racial inequality was the product of market forces and state action (and inaction). "Urban renewal" and highway and bridge developments displaced and disrupted many working-class neighborhoods. These infrastructure projects, coupled with discriminatory lending and real estate practices, facilitated rapid suburban development and the mass migration (of the predominantly white middle class) to hitherto less accessible areas, such as Long Island and Staten Island.[6] The unemployment rate for teenage African American men was consistently higher than that of other groups and doubled between 1960 and 1970 to 35 percent.[7]

Declining licit economic opportunities propelled more and more young men into drug markets, which in turn increased access to and use of heroin. Police neglect and corruption also served to corral drug markets into urban communities of color, further multiplying the number of people exposed to drugs and the drug trade. Accurate or consistent measurements of drug users and addicts were notoriously elusive. At one point, government officials estimated that the number of addicts increased from 25,000 in 1966 to 200,000 in 1973. The New York State Narcotic Control Commission, however, claimed that there were 60,000 heroin users living in New York City in 1967, three-quarters of whom were African American or Puerto Rican.[8]

This mounting drug use became an increasingly politically urgent issue through its connection to the era's rising crime rates. Although many researchers rejected a direct link between addicts and violent crime, politicians and popular media alleged that heroin users who needed money to purchase drugs were responsible for street crime, particularly mugging

---

[6] François Weil, *A History of New York* (New York: Columbia University Press, 2004), 259–85; Kim Moody, *From Welfare State to Real Estate: Regime Change in New York City, 1974 to the Present* (New York: New Press, 2007), 1–62.

[7] Schneider, *Smack*, 102.

[8] Schneider, *Smack*, 10, 17–51, 121; Edward Jay Epstein, *Agency of Fear: Opiates and Political Power in America* (London: Verso, 1990), 41. Estimates varied significantly and it was remarkably difficult to establish the number of addicts with certainty.

and robbery.[9] The vexed political rhetoric of the period often inflated the amount of theft committed by heroin users. For example, in assessing the extent of crime heroin addicts committed, the Rockefeller administration would multiply the estimated number of addicts by the amount of money it cost to maintain a daily heroin habit; thus addicts were said to have stolen $1,095,000,000 worth of goods in 1970. Since there was never more than $100 million of property reported stolen in all of New York during this period, the billion-dollar figure was clearly inaccurate.[10]

This association between crime and drugs was especially salient in an era when dramatic rises in crime rates were widely reported and highly politicized. Since crime statistics are imprecise and malleable, debates raged at the time (and continue today) over the actual extent of the "crime wave" during this period. They are affected by factors such as changes in police departments' reporting practices or police discretion in arrests and crime classification. They were inflated to some degree in this period by demographic factors. Since the large cohort of babies born after World War II began reaching early adulthood—the age bracket most prone to commit crime—in the late 1950s, some increases in crime were predictable. Between 1960 and 1968, burglary in New York City increased 480 percent and the number of reported robberies grew by 825 percent. Some of this growth reflected the more diligent crime reporting initiated by New York City mayor John Lindsay.[11] Despite these factors, crime rates were not wholly statistical artifacts. The murder rate—one of the more reliable crime measurements—also increased significantly when compared to that of preceding decades. There were 390 murders in the city in 1960 and 1,117 in 1970.[12] While it was still lower than it was at many points in the first half of the twentieth century, the national murder rate escalated from 5.5 per 100,000 in 1965 to 7.3 per 100,000 in 1968.[13]

---

[9] For an article quoting multiple experts debunking a direct link between addiction and violent crime, see James M. Markham, "Heroin Hunger May Not a Mugger Make," *New York Times*, March 18, 1973, SM281.

[10] Epstein, *Agency of Fear*, 42.

[11] For discussions at the time, see Sidney Zion, "The Police Play a Crime Numbers Game," *New York Times*, June 12, 1966, 122; Fred J. Cook, "Law and Order Is the Battle Cry of the Campaign But There's Always a Crime Wave—How Bad Is This One?" *New York Times*, October 6, 1968, SM38; and Murray Schumach, "A Numbers Game: Police Here Find 14% Rise in Major Violations, But Figures Are Deceptive; Crime Statistics Often Numbers Game," *New York Times*, February 4, 1968, 1. For the academic treatments that engage the relationship between crime rates and growing incarceration, see, for example, Garland, *The Culture of Control*; Weaver, "Frontlash"; Flamm, *Law and Order*; Thompson, "Why Mass Incarceration Matters"; Enns, *Incarceration Nation*; and Hinton, *From the War on Poverty to the War on Crime*.

[12] Schneider, *Smack*, 117, 123.

[13] Thompson, "Why Mass Incarceration Matters," 727.

Regardless of their imprecision, crime and drug figures had very real consequences for policy and public perception. A 1968 *New York Times* article explained that "the public does not weigh the unseen forces behind statistics. Their ears and eyes are exposed daily to television and radio accounts of the most sensational aspects of crime. Newspapers tend to group isolated crimes into 'waves.' Dinner conversations and office chatter are filled with personal knowledge of crime."[14] New Yorkers' daily experience and individual fears were contextualized and given meaning by the persistent media reports about broader crime patterns.

But crime alone cannot account for the timing and fervency of the popular sentiment that "law and order" had eroded during the 1960s. The high-profile unrest and movements of the time exacerbated anxieties about social stability. These upheavals were not a news story from far away; New Yorkers directly participated in or witnessed the high-profile resistance. In 1963, housing activist Jesse Gray helped organize widespread rent strikes of 4,500 tenants in Harlem to redress degraded living conditions. The next year, the shooting of a fifteen-year-old African American boy by a white police officer triggered the "Harlem Riots." Many white citizens resisted the fundamental renegotiation of rights and privileges that such movements demanded. In political rhetoric and media portrayals, activism, especially African American civil rights organizing, was increasingly portrayed as crime.[15] Street crime, urban rebellions, and protests blurred together, and the "drug epidemic" offered one explanation for the ills that seemed to threaten the nation. In many instances, it also became a racially sanitized way to blame urban problems on pathological individual criminals and drug users instead of on the factors identified by movement participants, such as moneyed elites, racial subordination, and gross economic disparities.

The anxiety about drug use in the 1960s was not historically unprecedented. The United States has experienced cycles of intense public consternation about intoxicating substances, usually influenced as much by who was publicly associated with the drug as the dangers posed by the substance itself. Efforts to control drug use have typically been connected to state-building projects and efforts to manage suspect populations and enforce societal norms.[16] These long struggles over the appropriate societal, governmental, and personal responses to drug use resulted in the uneven yet steady development of two seemingly contradictory phenomena: the increasing medicalization of drug abuse and criminalization of drugs and their users. On one hand, the twentieth century witnessed an escalating pro-

[14] Schumach, "A Numbers Game," 1, 58.
[15] See Murakawa, "The Origins of the Carceral Crisis."
[16] See Courtwright, *Dark Paradise* and Musto, *American Disease*.

hibition of drugs (along with the prohibition and subsequent legalization of alcohol), coupled with the development of various state institutions and programs, such as the Federal Bureau of Narcotics, designed to prosecute their use and trade. On the other hand, the growing number of adherents to the "disease concept of addiction" enabled the development of new specialists, bodies of knowledge, and institutions dedicated to curing individuals of the compulsion to consume alcohol or drugs.[17] Despite political rhetoric that consistently positioned medicalization and criminalization as oppositional strategies, the disease concept of addiction was not the antithesis of criminalization. Both law enforcement and addiction scientists approached illicit drug use as an aberrant behavior that was a threat to public order. Both saw addiction as an individual pathology, located in a person's biology or personality. Both assumed that public institutions beyond the family or social network should be enlisted in encouraging sobriety and abstinence.[18]

As the notion that compulsive drug or alcohol use was a medical problem gained currency in many circles, the federal government established two narcotic farms in Lexington, Kentucky, and Fort Worth, Texas, in the mid-1930s. Addicts could be committed to these hybrid prison-hospitals by court order or "voluntarily" (although they were also often under duress from family or threat of prosecution).[19] When drug use increased in the postwar period, policymakers intensified both treatment efforts and criminal penalties. Panic about juvenile delinquency, particularly the fear that white middle-class teens were becoming addicted to drugs through contact with urban pushers, helped inspire Congress to enact the 1951 Boggs Act. The law dramatically increased penalties and introduced harsh mandatory minimum sentences for drug distribution and possession. Five years later, Congress doubled the penalties for selling heroin and marijuana and limited the availability of parole and probation. For the first time in U.S. history, the law allowed juries to sentence those convicted of distributing drugs to life in prison and those selling drugs to minors to death.[20] These harsh penalties failed to curtail drug use and, for many, the dramatic spread of heroin in the late 1950s and early 1960s strengthened the case for treating addiction as a disease. It emboldened groups such as the American Medical Association and the American Bar Association to advocate for reevaluation of punitive law enforcement strategies.[21]

[17] White, *Slaying the Dragon*, 122–26.

[18] Nancy Campbell, "Toward a Critical Neuroscience of 'Addiction,'" *BioSocieties* 5, no. 1 (2010): 89–104.

[19] Campbell, *Discovering Addiction*; Acker, *Creating the American Junkie*.

[20] White, *Slaying the Dragon*, 234; Musto, *American Disease*, 230–31; Matthew D. Lassiter, "Impossible Criminals: The Suburban Imperatives of America's War on Drugs," *Journal of American History* 102, no. 1 (2015): 128–30.

[21] Musto, *American Disease*, 232–33.

The courts also registered the broadening acceptance of the disease concept of addiction. In the 1962 case *Robinson v. California*, the Supreme Court ruled unconstitutional a California law that sentenced people to ninety days in prison for being an addict. Writing for the majority, Justice Potter Stewart explained, "It is unlikely that any State at this moment in history would attempt to make it a criminal offense for a person to be mentally ill, or a leper, or to be afflicted with a venereal disease. . . . We cannot but consider the statute before us as of the same category." The Court declared imprisonment for being an addict cruel and unusual punishment and a violation of the Eighth and Fourteenth amendments: "To be sure, imprisonment for ninety days is not, in the abstract, a punishment which is either cruel or unusual. But the question cannot be considered in the abstract. Even one day in prison would be a cruel and unusual punishment for the 'crime' of having a common cold."[22] This ruling opened the possibility that illness relieved addicts of legal responsibility. It was another decade before courts settled the legal questions raised in *Robinson* by narrowly interpreting the decision to simply prohibit criminalizing the status of addiction if accompanied by no other illegal act.[23] The exact same ruling that decriminalized addiction also enabled the civic subordination of addicts by affirming the states' power to confine them indefinitely. *Robinson v. California* explicitly allowed for coerced, involuntary institutionalization, as long as it was to treat and not penalize: "A State might determine that the general health and welfare require that the victims of these and other human afflictions be dealt with by compulsory treatment, involving quarantine, confinement, or sequestration."[24] Therefore, this foundational case forbid civic diminishment and containment for punitive ends but sanctioned restricting the liberty and rights of drug users for therapeutic purposes or when deemed necessary to protect the general welfare.

It was state-level lawmakers who endeavored to translate these principles into practice.[25] New York and California led the way by giving courts discretion to transfer drug users out of the criminal justice system

[22] Robinson v. California, 370 U.S. 660 (1962).

[23] In the interim, however, defendants and their lawyers challenged the criminal sanctions for drug possession and purchase, as well as other crimes against property they claimed were the inevitable consequence of their disease. Herbert Fingarette, "Addiction and Criminal Responsibility," *Yale Law Journal* 84 (1974–75): 413; Edward Henry Benton, Andrew Bor, William H. Leech, and Joyce Adler Levy, "Drugs and Criminal Responsibility Special Project," *Vanderbilt Law Review* 33 (1980): 1145–1218. For another discussion, see Frydl, *Drug Wars in America*, 326–28. For an example case, see People of New York v. Nelson Borrero, 19 N.Y.2d 332, 227 N.E.2d 18, 280 N.Y.S.2d 109 (1967).

[24] *Robinson*, 370 U.S. 660.

[25] David F. Weiman and Christopher Weiss, "The Origins of Mass Incarceration in New York State: The Rockefeller Drug Laws and the Local War on Drugs," in *Do Prisons Make*

for custody and treatment. New York's embrace of the disease concept of addiction was reflected in the passage of the Metcalf-Volker Law in 1962. It allowed those charged with drug offenses to choose between a prison term and rehabilitative treatment in a state hospital.[26] Recognizing that the habitual use of illicit drugs constituted a crime and often led to other legal transgressions, the law hoped to divert addicts from prison to psychiatric hospitals. In practice, the policies instituted by Metcalf-Volker did little to curb drug use. The law was underfunded and the Department of Mental Hygiene lacked the expertise and enthusiasm for handling drug users. The minimum ninety-day stay did not seem long enough to isolate addicts from society or catalyze personal transformation.[27] Although the legislation had intended for patients to have access to community-based aftercare programs, the state funded and developed few of these.[28] Those charged with drug offenses frequently opted for the prison term because it was usually considerably shorter than the treatment stays in the typically dour state hospitals.[29] Studies reported that a huge percentage of patients absconded from supervision, and a majority of those who did receive treatment were subsequently rearrested.[30]

In the midst of ongoing reports of drug use and crime, the issue of narcotics stalked the gubernatorial race. Worries of a tight election loomed for Rockefeller in 1966, and his past promises of decisive, effective action on crime and drugs promised to haunt his campaign. His opponents were united in their criticism of the Metcalf-Volker Law. The policy had satisfied few constituencies.[31] Democratic challengers critiqued the status quo and favored either compulsory custody or drug maintenance. Rockefeller also encountered legislative pressure from his right within the Republican Party to counter what they saw as excessive judicial discretion and lenience in the sentencing of drug sellers. They criticized his veto of a

---

Us Safer?: The Benefits and Costs of the Prison Boom, ed. Steven Raphael and Michael A. Stoll (New York: Russell Sage Foundation, 2009), 73–116.

[26] Schneider, Smack, 131; Samuel Roberts, "Rehabilitation as 'Boundary Object': Medicalization, Local Activism, and Narcotics Addiction Policy in New York City, 1951–62," Social History of Drugs and Alcohol 26, no. 2 (2012): 147–69.

[27] John Martin, Stephen David, and Barbara Lavin, A Political History of the New York State Narcotic Addiction Control Commission, 1976–September, 1972 (Bronx: Institute for Social Research, Fordham University, 1972), 9.

[28] Schneider, Smack, 131.

[29] Arthur Pawlowski, "New York State Drug Control Policy during the Rockefeller Administration, 1959–1973" (PhD diss., State University of New York at Albany, 1984), 86–88.

[30] Robert Howe Connery, Rockefeller of New York: Executive Power in the Statehouse (Ithaca: Cornell University Press, 1979), 267.

[31] Martin, David, and Lavin, A Political History of the New York State Narcotic Addiction Control Commission, 10–12.

1965 law that would have imposed minimum prison terms on anyone convicted of selling drugs to people under the age of twenty-one.

The governor confronted this criticism from political opponents alongside constant demands for action from urban communities and vexing reports of growing heroin use in the predominantly white suburbs. Aware of the issue's growing significance, Rockefeller announced a new initiative in a speech to the legislature in February 1966. To make the case for his proposal, he explicitly invoked the threat of crime and middle-class drug use by warning that "narcotic addicts are said to be responsible for one-half the crimes committed in New York City alone—and their evil contagion is spreading to the suburbs."[32] Rockefeller now advocated for wide-ranging civil commitment programs that would seek rehabilitative ends through coercion, quarantine, and stark limitations on the civil liberties of drug users.

The civil commitment of addicts was a strategy being employed in California without significant success, though it had just weathered challenges to its constitutionality. California had passed a groundbreaking civil commitment law in 1961. It allowed the state to assign people certified as addicts who had been convicted of felonies or misdemeanors to a seven-year program that combined inpatient and outpatient treatment.[33] Those who failed to comply with the rules and maintain their sobriety could be incarcerated. Despite the mixed reports from California, the United States Congress soon followed suit and passed the Narcotic Addict Rehabilitation Act (NARA) in 1966. The bill designated new funding for addiction treatment and research and strengthened the government's power to civilly commit certified addicts. People convicted of a federal offense who were deemed eligible could choose between criminal sanction and treatment (usually at the federal narcotic farms).

Rockefeller's civil commitment program, administered by the Narcotic Addiction Control Commission (NACC), a newly created state agency, authorized the removal of any person certified as an addict to a state-run treatment facility. Under the plan, addicts convicted of felonies faced a maximum of five years and other users faced treatment for a maximum of three years. Unlike the provisions in Metcalf-Volker, civil commitment was compulsory and long term: addicts would not be given the freedom to decide whether they needed treatment. Anyone could initiate civil commitment under the new program. Those not arrested for a crime could be committed to the program by friends, family members, or any person who swore before authorities that the individual was an addict unwilling to

[32]Bernard Weinraub, "Confinement of Addicts Proposed by Rockefeller: Rockefeller Asks New Addicts," *New York Times*, February 24, 1966, 1, 24.

[33]White, *Slaying the Dragon*, 250–51.

undergo treatment. The new strategy appealed to various constituencies by promising to deliver on two missions: first, to reduce crime by sweeping addicts from the streets, and second, to rehabilitate addicts. With this dual agenda, Rockefeller mobilized support among those who demanded long-term institutionalization of addicts and those who wanted to see the state develop a more extensive treatment infrastructure. To neutralize opposition and garner backing from New York mayor John Lindsay, the governor amended his original plan to also direct significant funds to the burgeoning network of private and public treatment programs.[34]

Although the NACC rhetorically prioritized its custodial and treatment missions, the agency's creation was paired from the outset with an escalation in punishment. Rockefeller proposed a measure amending the penal code to increase the mandatory minimum sentence for selling narcotics to someone over the age of twenty-one from five to seven years. The minimum penalty for sale to someone under twenty-one went from seven to ten years.[35] The proposal disaggregated the forces animating drug abuse into two social categories: addicts and sellers. The first was marked as a candidate for coerced rehabilitation and the other for criminal sanction; both faced intensified state pressure and increasingly degraded civic status. Structuring this proposal was the assumption that drug users and sellers spread addiction. Where addiction specialists argued that it was people with disordered personalities and disordered lives who were predisposed to addiction, Rockefeller presented addiction as communicable and therefore a risk to the entire civic body.[36] He called for an unprecedented mobilization of state resources and promised dramatic results: "The war [on crime and narcotics] can be waged only as an offensive—an all-out push to achieve human renewal on a scale never before attempted by any state or nation." His emphasis on "human renewal" not only was a nod to his therapeutic ambitions for the program; it also reflected the governor's vision for funding this massive state expansion. He hoped to receive two-thirds of the money from the federal government. "Human renewal should command as much support as urban renewal," he argued.[37]

Critics of the governor noted immediately that the program entailed more human removal than renewal. Senator Manfred Ohrenstein, a

[34] Martin, David, and Lavin, *A Political History of the New York State Narcotic Addiction Control Commission*, 17.

[35] Sydney Schanberg, "Rockefeller Signs Bill on Narcotics: Names Head of Controversial Program for Addicts California Law Cited Present Law Differs," *New York Times*, April 7, 1966, 35.

[36] White, *Slaying the Dragon*, 250. For an example of how specialists discussed addiction in the media, see Markham, "Heroin Hunger May Not a Mugger Make."

[37] Weinraub, "Confinement of Addicts Proposed by Rockefeller," 24.

liberal Democrat from New York City's west side, opposed the legislation, highlighting how medicalization was used to rationalize internal social exile: "What we're doing here is establishing a leprosy colony—just to isolate these people from society."[38] He predicted that "it will prove to be a failure and is a colossal waste of money and is a hoax."[39] Only three senators and seven members of the State Assembly voted against the law, although lawmakers—including some representing urban and African American districts—claimed they supported the measure reluctantly and voiced opposition during the floor debates to its coercive features.[40]

The new civil commitment law paid immediate political dividends in Rockefeller's third gubernatorial campaign. He championed the new policy, which was about to go into effect, throughout the 1966 race, running newspaper ads that stoked the racialized fear of addict crime. In one, an image of a dark arm with a hypodermic needle ran next to the words: "The stealing. The mugging. The Killing. All for this." It concluded, "Get the addicts off the streets, put the pushers behind bars, and this crime will stop."[41] By suggesting that violent crime would end by removing addicts from public space, Rockefeller presented an apparently tidy solution to urban disorder.[42] Rockefeller's Democratic challenger, Frank O'Connor, campaigned against civil commitment as a violation of addicts' civil rights and advocated its repeal.[43] Rockefeller capitalized on his rival's opposition to compulsory treatment, warning voters that "O'Connor's election would mean that addicts were free to continue to roam the streets: to mug, to purse-snatch, to steal, and even to murder."[44] When Rockefeller won the race, both camps believed that his opponent's stand against compulsory treatment cost him the election.[45]

[38]Ibid. The complex politics of using medicalization to combat social stigma can be seen in other contexts. For example, people with leprosy faced this dilemma after organizing for a more medical approach to their condition. See Michelle Therese Moran, *Colonizing Leprosy: Imperialism and the Politics of Public Health in the United States* (Chapel Hill: University of North Carolina Press, 2007).

[39]Weinraub, "Confinement of Addicts Proposed by Rockefeller," 24.

[40]John Silbey, "State Senate Votes Rockefeller Plan for Compulsory Treatment of Addicts," *New York Times*, March 29, 1966, 19; Schanberg, "Rockefeller Signs Bill on Narcotics," 35.

[41]Pawlowski, "New York State Drug Control Policy during the Rockefeller Administration," 122.

[42]On the reports that claims of heroin addicts' violence were dramatically exaggerated by Rockefeller, see Epstein, *Agency of Fear*, 35–46.

[43]Pawlowski, "New York State Drug Control Policy during the Rockefeller Administration," 122.

[44]Homer Bigart, "Rockefeller Links Rival and Crime," *New York Times*, October 29, 1966, 23.

[45]Sydney Schanberg, "A 'Major Error' Laid to O'Connor," *New York Times*, November 14, 1966, 30.

The "Candy Coated Penitentiary"

While politically profitable in the short term, the new civil commitment programs faced a number of serious challenges that eventually doomed their ability to deliver on the ambitious promises of Rockefeller and his allies.[46] They would ultimately prove incapable of accomplishing either the custodial or therapeutic goals or satisfying any of the multiple constituencies they endeavored to accommodate. The new program's twin commitments caused tension immediately. In early meetings of the NACC, members, who hailed from distinct institutional backgrounds, clashed over the most basic attributes of the program: Should employees carry batons and badges and be able to give half rations as punishment as was the case in prison? Do patients who run away from the program "escape," as they do from prison, or "abscond," as they would from a mental hospital?[47] In 1974, a state audit would find that a tension between curative and custodial mission hamstrung its entire performance.[48]

The state's efforts to establish these facilities, colloquially called the "Rockefeller Programs," were plagued from the outset by other logistical, bureaucratic, and political complications. And that was before the drug users arrived. Although the state was determined to get the program running immediately, finding facilities and appropriately trained staff proved difficult. Public support for removing addicts from the streets did not easily translate into welcoming treatment facilities into neighborhoods.[49] Local communities fought fervently to prevent placement of new treatment centers in their neighborhoods, considerably slowing the acquisition of facilities and resulting in many centers locating within commercial and industrial areas, some in repurposed old prisons. In 1967, Rockefeller admitted that "we have not found a single community that did not protest." He continued to explain the need for new centers in terms that were probably not particularly comforting to his audience: "The investment in this program by the state is nothing compared to the losses in crime and in terms of murder and fear. What are we going to do with these people?

[46] "Candy coated penitentiary" is a resident's description of a NACC facility quoted in Richard Severo, "Addicts and the State: Aim Unfulfilled," *New York Times*, April 21, 1969, 42.

[47] Pawlowski, "New York State Drug Control Policy during the Rockefeller Administration," 130–33.

[48] "The Acquisition and Construction of Drug Abuse Treatment Facilities," Program Audit, Legislative Commission on Expenditure Review, January 18, 1974, Reel 60, Rockefeller Gubernatorial Papers, 4th Administration, NYSA, S-9, S-15.

[49] Ibid.

Sacrifices must be made, even if it means a facility comes into your own neighborhood."[50]

In the initial five months, one-third of the first 1,200 who entered the program had not been arrested for a crime. Half of those presented themselves voluntarily for treatment and the other half were confined against their will, usually after being turned in by a spouse or other family member. The remaining 800 were committed after arrest for a crime and faced up to five years of compulsory treatment.[51] The conditions residents encountered at NACC facilities solidified their subordinated civic status. Residents were called "patients," but staff controlled visitation policy and surveilled their mail; there were three head counts a day.[52] With no coherent therapeutic philosophy and insufficient staff training, the caliber of care was widely condemned. An in-depth study by the *New York Times* two years into the program found almost nothing positive to report about the institutions' therapeutic capacities.[53] After a 1968 riot at the Woodward Center (housed in a refurbished prison), the guards won the right to carry clubs on the job.[54] The director insisted, nonetheless, that the guards, who were mostly trained at reformatories and prisons, did lots of "informal counseling."[55] Even people who voluntarily submitted themselves for treatment were led away in handcuffs. One man explained, "I am being treated like an animal in a locked cage."[56] As word of the conditions spread, many of those arrested or committed fought desperately against being certified as an addict through procedural challenges or hearings, especially if the "treatment" length exceeded the criminal sentence for their crimes.

When legal avenues were exhausted, residents of the Rockefeller Programs often took drastic measures to escape. According to government reports, more than 7,000 of the 24,000 committed to NACC programs absconded, either from residential programs or aftercare.[57] Of the departing residents placed in aftercare between March 1969 and March 1970,

[50]Murray Schumach, "Day of Compulsory Care Is Near for Uneasy Addicts in State; Up to Five Years Due; Program, Starting Saturday, Aiming at Breakthrough in Rehabilitating Victims," *New York Times*, March 27, 1967, 1, 26.

[51]Murray Schumach, "Narcotics Board to Act on Ruling," *New York Times*, August 19, 1967, 27.

[52]Pawlowski, "New York State Drug Control Policy during the Rockefeller Administration," 112.

[53]Severo, "Addicts and the State," 1, 42.

[54]"Guards Get Clubs after Addicts Riot," *New York Times*, June 24, 1968, 32.

[55]Severo, "Addicts and the State," 1, 42.

[56]Ibid.

[57]Emeel Betros, "*Anomalies in Drug Abuse Treatment:* Interim Report of the Temporary State Commission to Evaluate the Drug Laws," Legislative Document #11 (Albany: State of New York, 1975), 151.

only 19 percent were still enrolled nine months later; the remaining 81 percent relapsed, dropped out, or were rearrested.[58] Such reports reflected the Rockefeller Programs' highly permeable boundaries and emboldened program critics who charged that the state failed to isolate drug users from the community.

While many drug users endeavored to escape the new treatment programs, others used the state's commitment to rehabilitation to maneuver within the criminal justice system to affect their fates. Some arrested for drug offenses often wrote to the governor, pleading for him to intervene in their case and asserting their status as addicts to gain entry into treatment programs or evade prison. One woman wrote to Rockefeller when her son was diverted to prison after being certified as an addict. After fighting with various officials to have her son committed to an NACC facility, the mother was finally able to reach someone in the governor's office who intervened on her behalf. Although her son was transferred from prison to a treatment facility that was itself housed in an old prison, she wrote to the governor about her relief at the change of venue and her gratitude to the man who had helped her. She also challenged the state's individualized response to drug use and questioned the criminalization of drug users:

> Governor Rockefeller, do you think the time will ever come when legislators, society, and government will accept part of the blame, and realize that drug addiction is a great social disease, not a crime? . . . Surely, the hundreds of thousands of our young people involved in today's "drug culture" cannot possibly all be criminals. . . . By expressing my views, Governor Rockefeller, I do not wish to imply that my son is an innocent in the woods. I am not, unfortunately, naïve enough to believe that anyone, other than himself injected that heroin filled needle into his arm—or that anyone forced him to [do] things he may have done to obtain drugs. I am inclined to believe that he can be saved; and that rather than a criminal, he is merely a victim of his times.[59]

In arguing that her son, although responsible for his own actions, suffered from a "social disease," this mother attributed drug use to the broader contemporary milieu, rejecting narratives of individual pathology or contamination by other addicts. Her letter rhetorically embedded

---

[58] Pawlowski, "New York State Drug Control Policy during the Rockefeller Administration," 211.

[59] Ida C. M. to Governor Rockefeller, n.d., 4th Administration, Reel 9, Rockefeller Gubernatorial Papers, NYSA. Throughout this book, I have removed the last names of people who might have been unaware that their correspondence would become part of the public record. I have retained the last names of those who spoke in public forums, such as to the media or at legislative hearings.

the addict back into society, held out the possibility of redemption, and, most emphatically, rejected the brand of criminality.

NACC policy also inspired people who were not narcotic users to seek therapeutic custody themselves. One man wrote to the governor to protest the failure of the state to commit any resources or legal allowances for alcoholics. The author began his letter by associating himself with the more socially marginalized category of drug addict to plead for access to treatment:

I, sir, am an "addict" of a sort, also a criminal, substantiated by numerous convictions and most of my adult life spent in prison, but also and most important sir, I am a alcoholic, for over 20 of my 36 years. I have never committed a crime while sober, I have never hurt, injured or assaulted anyone in anyway in my entire life . . . I need professional help, rather than punishment and prison, the psychiatrist of this institution is in agreement—but there is no place for the judge to send me, no alcohol program for the criminal alcoholic, no hospitals . . . I sir humbly pray for some help, some understanding, some understanding and intervention, from someone who cares, for someone to step forward and prevent a bigger crime from being committed against me than I ever committed against society.[60]

By juxtaposing his crimes to the state's crimes against him, the author flipped the conventional narrative about societal victimization. Instead of the alcoholic offending society, society and the state failed alcoholics by neglecting to build institutions that addressed their circumstances.

Contrary to the state's emphasis on the personality, drug users often depicted job training and education as integral to their vision of rehabilitation. A veteran who became addicted to heroin after his nervous breakdown in battle explained, "A state prison term would be of no help to me. I want to help myself." Reflecting the growing consensus that prisons served little rehabilitative function, he asserted a claim, as a certified addict, to treatment: "There are stipulations [that allow treatment instead of prison]. A program where I will be able to finish school and learn a trade. A program where I can receive the therapy that I need so bad."[61] While letter writers mostly approached Rockefeller as supplicants and rarely claimed a "right to drug treatment," some endeavored, like this man, to harness the state's rehabilitative ambitions. Many probably just hoped to minimize the negative consequences of engagement with the state, but others may have genuinely hoped that government could

[60]Daniel M. to Governor Rockefeller, n.d. [1972?], 4th Administration, Reel 60, Rockefeller Gubernatorial Papers, NYSA.

[61]James E. to Senator Jacob Javits, June 9, 1973, 4th Administration, Reel 61, Rockefeller Gubernatorial Papers, NYSA.

help catalyze a positive personal transformation. These individual letters reveal drug users' active engagement with the struggles over defining the causes of and appropriate responses to addiction. Though many found little of value in the Rockefeller Programs, the state's therapeutic commitment provided drug users more discursive space than criminalization. And many seized on that space to build and gain access to programs that more effectively addressed their circumstances.

Among political elites, the enthusiasm for the NACC programs barely outlasted the initial huge outlays to secure staff and facilities.[62] The Rockefeller Programs did not fully satisfy a single constituency. With the limitations in funding and state capacity, they were incapable of delivering on their therapeutic and custodial ambitions. It proved incredibly challenging to commit any substantial proportion of New York's drug users. Officials had originally hoped to have almost one-third of the "known addicts"—19,000 people—in custody by 1969. However, as of November 1968, the Rockefeller Programs interned only 4,244 of the 64,240 "known addicts."[63] Institutional factors also hindered the program. Police proved hesitant to arrest every drug user they encountered. Prosecutors often avoided the time- and energy-intensive civil commitment process and instead used the threat of institutionalization in a Rockefeller Program to coerce defendants to plead guilty to a criminal charge with a shorter prison term. To remedy this, policymakers committed to quarantine advocated making civil commitment easier by further diluting drug users' protections and weakening procedural guarantees within the certification process.[64]

The lackluster progress reports and the inability to house any significant percentage of New York's heroin users conspired to undermine political support for the program after only a few years, and the legislature was increasingly unwilling to fund it. State Senator Samuel Greenberg captured the general mood when he offered his verdict on the program: "The program is a failure. It is failing to get the addicts off the street. It is failing to rehabilitate those few addicts under its care. It is failing to halt crime."[65] In mid-1971, the legislature allocated only $91.7 million of the NACC's $117 million requested operating budget. They recommended deemphasizing residential care and reorienting existing programs toward non-residential treatment. That year, the NACC phased out seven of

[62] "The Acquisition and Construction of Drug Abuse Treatment Facilities."

[63] Bill Kovach, "Democratic Senators Assail State over Narcotics Control," *New York Times*, November 20, 1969, 32; Martin, David, and Lavin, *A Political History of the New York State Narcotic Addiction Control Commission*, 24–26.

[64] Martin, David, and Lavin, *A Political History of the New York State Narcotic Addiction Control Commission*, 25–41.

[65] Kovach, "Democratic Senators Assail State over Narcotics Control," 32.

the twenty-three facilities, returning four of them to the Department of Correctional Services. They increased overall treatment slots by cutting residential treatment capacity by half and introduced aftercare and outpatient services in the remaining facilities.[66] And the NACC increasingly served as a conduit for funds to municipal and private drug-treatment agencies. They invested state resources in two other treatment modalities, methadone maintenance and therapeutic communities, that had been developing steadily since the 1950s. Both now received new funding, attention, and controversy as the determination to mitigate drug use and crime intensified.[67]

The Addict as Expert: New York's Therapeutic Communities

People who sincerely sought to end dependence on drugs rarely found institutionalization in the Rockefeller Programs helpful. Instead, many turned to therapeutic communities, a new and innovative trend in drug treatment where ex-users designed and directed recovery. Evolving from the same general treatment philosophy as Alcoholics Anonymous (AA), therapeutic communities relied upon a fellowship of substance users to catalyze personal transformation and sobriety. Unlike the outpatient meeting format of AA, therapeutic communities were drug-free residential treatment programs. They aimed to fundamentally rebuild the addict's personality and lifestyle before facilitating reintegration into society. Understanding drug abuse to be a symptom of a deeper character dysfunction, therapeutic communities facilitated emotional development through cultivating self-awareness and self-discipline. To achieve these ends, centers employed confrontational group therapy, which encouraged high levels of personal and collective responsibility and an elaborate system of demotions and rewards that moved patients within a strict hierarchy of residents. As residents progressed through their multiyear stay, they took on increasing leadership and control in the community. Therefore, while strictly autocratic, therapeutic communities were typically controlled and staffed by ex-addicts, many of whom had completed the same programs.[68]

Charles Dederich founded Synanon, the first therapeutic community, in Ocean Park, California, in 1958. A recovering alcoholic and originally

[66]"The Acquisition and Construction of Drug Abuse Treatment Facilities," 15–17.

[67]Martin, David, and Lavin, *A Political History of the New York State Narcotic Addiction Control Commission*, 30–48.

[68]White, *Slaying the Dragon*, 245–50.

a fervent Alcoholics Anonymous adherent, Dederich developed an enthusiastic following for his unique program of communal living and group confrontation sessions. These raucous group encounters, or "games" as they were called, were based on the rejection of the traditional, restrained treatment environments. The leaders of the Probation Department of New York's Kings County Supreme Court turned to Synanon as a model when they wanted to start an experimental program for the male drug felons under their department's supervision in 1963. They founded Daytop Village and recruited David Deitch, a former Synanon resident, to oversee the program in 1964. Like Synanon, Daytop emphasized the addict's role and responsibility in ending dependence on drugs. There was constant support but also mutual surveillance of every aspect of daily life. For seemingly minor transgressions, colleagues and staff publicly berated residents. For example, a resident might be forced to wear a sign and a diaper to admit that he had acted "like a baby" or carry a lightbulb all day after forgetting to turn out the lights. The regimented, intense environment was designed to create stressful conditions that residents learned to manage with new, healthy strategies.

By positioning the ex-addict as the expert on rehabilitation, therapeutic communities saw ex–drug users as role models and agents of positive change in society, as opposed to corrosive, permanent outsiders. Within the program, people derived authority about recovery not from academic or clinical training but from the direct, personal confrontation with addiction. In an inversion of modern notions of therapeutic expertise, patients were the catalysts of their own cures. Although some therapeutic communities, such as Odyssey House in New York, employed professional counselors, a significant percentage of most centers' staff were prior residents or other ex–drug users. The programs appeared harsh to some, but proponents felt that professional social workers' techniques of gentle questioning and observation could not meaningfully pierce an addict's elaborate shield of defenses, withdrawal, and self-delusion.[69]

Searching for a meaningful state response to growing drug use, politicians experimented with funding therapeutic communities. Mayor Lindsay's decision to back these programs reflected his administration's experimentation with more locally controlled, community-based programs and an appeal to the Puerto Ricans and African Americans who had been instrumental in his electoral victory. In 1966, the city hired Efren Ramirez to lead New York City's treatment efforts. Dr. Ramirez,

[69] On the functions, philosophy, and organization of Daytop Village, see Barry Sugarman, *Daytop Village: A Therapeutic Community* (New York: Holt, Rinehart and Winston, 1974).

a proponent of therapeutic communities who had directed programs in Puerto Rico, felt that the addict, once "reformed," was the best authority on recovery. He explained, "The rehabilitated addict, in our opinion, is an expert in drug addiction."[70] He helped establish the Phoenix House and develop a burgeoning network of therapeutic communities. This treatment modality—for a number of years—became the centerpiece of the city's drug-treatment efforts, subsidized increasingly with state funds channeled through the NACC.[71]

Although funding for these programs was motivated by the political desire to control drug use and crime, adherents felt their mission to be fundamentally distinct. A cofounder of Daytop Village explained the difference:

> But we must be careful not to confuse steps taken to protect society from the addict (jails, the "Rockefeller program," the federal facilities in Fort Worth, Texas, and Lexington, Kentucky, and in my opinion, methadone maintenance) with those now being taken to rehabilitate the addict himself.[72]

Casting addicts themselves as agents of their own rehabilitation inverted the dominant characterizations of the period, which depicted addicts as either unredeemable or requiring the intervention of specialists. These programs positioned addicts as not only redeemable but—once sober— integral to the treatment of other drug users and, therefore, to the general social welfare.

As a state strategy to control drug use and crime, therapeutic communities posed their own set of problems for politicians determined to pacify communities and reduce crime rates before the next electoral contest. They were residential programs with average stays of two years and were thus expensive to establish and operate. Although they proliferated rapidly, the houses were necessarily small and intimate, and there were not enough funds, time, or trained ex-addict staff to treat even a small percentage of the addict population in New York. Additionally, membership in a therapeutic community was considered a privilege and the strictly regimented environment led many residents to be expelled or simply leave before completing the program. Statistically, the program was successful for those who finished, but a significant majority dropped

[70] Poppy Cannon White, "New Hope for Drug Addicts," *New York Amsterdam News*, August 6, 1966, 13.

[71] Barbara Rawlings and Rowdy Yates, *Therapeutic Communities for the Treatment of Drug Users* (London: Jessica Kingsley Publishers, 2001), 62–65; Martin, David, and Lavin, *A Political History of the New York State Narcotic Addiction Control Commission*.

[72] Daniel Casriel, *Daytop; Three Addicts and Their Cure* (New York: Hill and Wang, 1971).

out.[73] Moreover, local communities engaged in extensive grassroots organizing to oppose the placement of treatment houses in their neighborhoods. In one of many examples, hundreds of community members picketed the Daytop program on Staten Island to oppose its placement and successfully delayed funding for many months.[74] These confrontations forced politicians to choose between supporting addicts, an unpopular if not completely demonized constituency, and the significantly more politically powerful and resourceful neighborhood groups, churches, and business owners.

Some African Americans and Puerto Ricans charged that white program leaders and funders preyed on their communities, just like drug peddlers, and built institutions that were not sufficiently accountable to or controlled by local communities. Influenced by struggles for community control in schools and buoyed by a federal commitment to encourage "maximum feasible participation" of local people in their own social services, proponents demanded culturally relevant programs. They called for programs led by and responsible to their communities that built up the self-esteem of drug users (as opposed to breaking them down) and instilled cultural pride. Many would come to see political education and activism as integral parts of their programs.[75]

Critics also challenged the basic philosophical tenets of therapeutic communities that located the source of addiction in individual personality defects. An article in *Health/Pac Bulletin*, a publication produced by health activists affiliated with the New Left, explained, "The therapeutic community tends to reduce drug addiction to the level of an individual problem. This position derives from the concept of the addict as a sociopathic personality. If on the other hand, addiction is attributed at least partially to a sick society, then its cure is to involve the ex-addict in changing society."[76] These critics questioned the emphasis on reintegrating addicts into society, since they claimed society produced the very problems that generated drug addiction in the first place.

[73] These statistics vary considerably depending on time period and research methods. See, for example, Sugarman, *Daytop Village*, 5–7.

[74] See Clayton Knowles, "Narcotics Center Faces Opposition," *New York Times*, April 12, 1965, 36 and "Daytop Lodge, House of Hope for Addicts," *New York Amsterdam News*, February 15, 1964, 43. There was community opposition at almost every step to establishing treatment centers.

[75] Mahoney, "Fighting 'Addiction,'" 54–96.

[76] "Editorial: Who Benefits from the American Drug Culture?" *Health/Pac Bulletin*, June 1970, Reel MR 72, Departmental Files, Folder: Drugs, John Lindsay Mayoral Papers, New York City Municipal Archives, New York City (hereafter NYCMA), 20. See also Merlin Chowkwanyun, "The New Left and Public Health: The Health Policy Advisory Center, Community Organizing, and the Big Business of Health, 1967–1975," *American Journal of Public Health* 101, no. 2 (February 2011): 238–49.

But therapeutic communities captured the imagination of many New Yorkers in the late 1960s. Famous musicians, such as Pete Seeger, Duke Ellington, and the Grateful Dead, played in a four-day musical festival and fund-raiser for Daytop in Manhattan.[77] There were television documentaries about Daytop and the members staged a long-running, critically acclaimed off-Broadway show about their experiences in recovery. While the desire to mitigate the crime and disorder associated with drug users motivated much of the support for these programs, many people also were attracted to the struggle for human redemption that recovering addicts represented.[78] The prominence of Daytop, the Phoenix House, and other therapeutic communities illustrates the extent to which societal responses to drug abuse were up in the air in the late 1960s. While many people only approved of programs that approached drug users as criminal pariahs, concern about a "heroin epidemic" also provided openings for groups to advance alternative sources of authority and knowledge about addiction. However, the costs, limitations, and political liabilities of these therapeutic communities, coupled with the intractable nature of much chronic drug use, pushed lawmakers to search for other strategies to control it.

A Many-Headed Hydra: The Diverse and Escalating Threat of Heroin

The political stakes of the issue escalated further as heroin use in three different social spaces received increased attention. Politicians, who had long confronted pressure from within urban communities to address crime and the concentration of drug markets, now also faced popular anxiety about suburban drug use and a short-lived but profound panic about addiction among the troops in Vietnam. In each setting, the social position of heroin users influenced debates over the best way to respond.

For people living in New York's urban African American and Latino communities, the effects of crime and concentrated illicit drug markets were viscerally evident and less mediated through the popular press. For decades, residents had been agitating for state action. African Americans admonished police for their unresponsiveness, neglect, and indifference to the drug use and markets. Some activists—such as revered labor organizer and civil rights leader A. Philip Randolph—argued that it was

---

[77]"4-Day Music Fete Aids Ex-Addicts," *New York Times*, June 16, 1968, 58.

[78]Walter Kerr, "They Grow Their Own Play," *New York Times*, June 2, 1968, D1; Dan Sullivan, "The Theater: 'The Concept' Pictures Narcotics Victims' Ordeal," *New York Times*, May 7, 1968, 51; Casriel, *Daytop*.

police negligence and corrupt complicity with organized crime that had transformed Harlem into a vice district in the first place.[79] For many, concentrated drug use was one of numerous manifestations of the long historical failures of the state and political machines to serve and be accountable to African American citizens. Criticism of police neglect and police brutality may seem contradictory, but many saw police unresponsiveness, corruption, and abuse as diverse symptoms of the state's general abdication of its responsibility to the safety and welfare of black citizens.

While many African American commentators agreed that the police were ineffective at mitigating the harm of drug use, they did not speak with one voice as to the appropriate response to the problem. Local middle-class leaders organized marches and campaigns calling for more strident enforcement and policing, as well as state narcotic hospitals. For example, Reverend Oberia Dempsey, an avid organizer around issues of crime and drugs in Harlem, advocated for intensive drug treatment but also (and increasingly as time went on) better policing and longer prison sentences for pushers.[80] Other African Americans and Latinos were skeptical about turning to police and longer prisons terms as a vehicle to improve conditions in their communities. This was exacerbated by widespread recognition of police brutality, corruption, and complicity in the drug trade.[81] Activists worked for decades to create mechanisms—such as the Civilian Review Board—to make police more accountable to the local community.

By 1968, some African Americans were calling for increasingly punitive action, especially against pushers, explaining that crime had grown to devastating levels.[82] The National Association for the Advancement of Colored People (NAACP) issued reports and initiated campaigns calling for more and better police officers, more convictions, and longer punishments for drug pushers. At a joint legislative hearing on crime in Harlem in 1969, Assemblyman Hulan Jack and others testified that they and their families avoided leaving their homes at night because muggings and other assaults were so rampant. Witnesses attributed the crime to desperate drug addicts but faulted police neglect and corruption for the lawlessness.

[79] Mahoney, "Fighting 'Addiction,'" 29–31, 45–47.

[80] For a longer treatment of Dempsey's career, see Fortner, *Black Silent Majority*.

[81] Schneider, *Smack*, 106–13.

[82] See, for example, Homer Bigart, "Middle-Class Leaders in Harlem Ask Crackdown on Crime," *New York Times*, December 24, 1968, 25; "Addicts' Victims Turn Vigilante," *New York Times*, September 23, 1969, 1; and Gerald Fraser, "Harlem: A Matter of Life and Death," *New York Times*, December 15, 1968, E14. For an interpretation that positions anti-crime frustration and punitive sentiments within African American communities as an engine behind the Rockefeller Drug Laws, see Fortner, *Black Silent Majority*.

Vincent Baker, chairman of the NAACP's crime commission, demanded more strident state action, warning of the risk of vigilante patrols if police failed to mitigate the situation. In his comments, he deployed Nixon's metaphor of the "silent majority" to present opponents of increasing police and punishment as a loud but unrepresentative minority: "The silent majority in Harlem would welcome a police order to get tough. . . . The climate in Harlem favors law enforcement."[83] Some community groups took matters into their own hands, organizing campaigns to protect citizens from robbery, mugging, and other crimes. Reverend Dempsey, infuriated by state inaction and police neglect, argued African Americans had no choice but to organize for their own protection and, by 1969, had formed vigilante and self-defense groups to push drug sellers out of their neighborhoods.[84]

These calls from within the black middle and working classes for more intensive policing and harsh punishment diverged in important ways from rhetoric associated with the white "silent majority." These voices less frequently positioned enhanced punishment and policing as the antithesis to social welfare expenditures or enhanced local community control. Even among those advocating a hard line, calls for harsh punishment for drug sellers were often paired with demands for more systemic reforms and greater social supports. Demands for more strenuous policing were often connected to wider structural critiques that implicated other factors, such as police neglect and corruption, in concentrating crime and vice markets in Harlem. Baker explained that "organized crime cannot exist without the partnership of politicians and police."[85] Reverend Dempsey also critiqued the ways that organized crime, the economic exploitation of inner-city consumers, and police conduct intersected to undermine public security. Organized crime depended on addicts to buy drugs, and addicts depended on people desperate for affordable consumer goods to buy stolen merchandise at a fraction of the retail cost. Dempsey explained that "in many cases, those who buy stolen goods are those who have long been and are still being exploited by Harlem merchants who cheat them, beat them, charge them the highest prices for the poorest quality products and drag them into court when they get behind." Consumers of stolen goods were "thus helping the addict to continue on drugs and the organized criminal to continue to drain Harlem and other ghettos dry."[86] These comments suggest that it was not the dearth of resources in the

[83]M. S. Handler, "Harlem Officials Testify on Crime: They Warn State Hearing of Possible Vigilante Action," New York Times, February 21, 1969, 50.

[84]See, for example, "Harlem Vigilantes Move on 'Pushers,'" Chicago Daily Defender, June 23, 1965, 2 and "Addicts' Victims Turn Vigilante," 1.

[85]Handler, "Harlem Officials Testify on Crime," 50.

[86]"Crime Fight Moving," New York Amsterdam News, March 8, 1969, 1, 45.

"ghetto" but lucrative opportunities for exploitation that exacerbated residents' problems.[87]

These calls for "getting tough" also generated debate and bitter exchanges between different groups claiming to represent African Americans. Some critics insisted that "law and order" operated as a euphemism for anti-black and anti–civil rights sentiments. Leonard De Champs, chairman of the Harlem Chapter of the Congress of Racial Equality (CORE), excoriated the NAACP, calling it "oppressive and Nazi-like for its Fascist proposals regarding law and order in the streets of Harlem and New York City's other Black communities." He charged that "Vincent Baker's love for mandated jail sentences and tightened-up parole procedures conclusively proves that the NAACP is an effective enemy of the 1.2 million Black people in this city."[88] Floyd McKissick, a longtime civil rights activist and another leader of CORE, claimed that the NAACP's punitive recommendations reflected the interests of the black middle class. He wrote that "the arguments used in the report of the NAACP smack suspiciously of the Ronald Reagan-George Wallace school of repressive 'law and order,' at any cost. They appeal to the fears and prejudices of citizens who have even a little bit worth protecting."[89] He pointed to "a gap of understanding between middle class and poor Blacks along economic lines" and explained that "we should know by now the addition of more white cops in the ghetto solves nothing. The ones who suffer more from such measures are the poor blacks; not necessarily the guilty ones." Instead of harsher punishment, McKissick called for community control: "The ghetto must be safe for its citizens, but it cannot be made so by police state tactics. All efforts must be directed toward the ending of conditions which breed crime and chaos; all efforts much be directed toward the development of a Black-orientated, Black controlled law enforcement agency—an agency dedicated to the aid and protection of Black people, not to their suppression."[90]

During this period, a host of community groups and organizations set up treatment programs, many of which received New York City and state funds, intended to be more directly accountable to the communities

[87]Beryl Satter explores how federally enabled residential segregation made African American communities vulnerable and lucrative targets for exploitative real estate practices in Chicago, particularly contract sales. Beryl Satter, *Family Properties: How the Struggle over Race and Real Estate Transformed Chicago and Urban America* (New York: Picador, 2010).

[88]"Hits NAACP on Crime," *New York Amsterdam News*, April 24, 1971, 31.

[89]Floyd McKissick, "NAACP—In Crime in the Streets," *New York Amsterdam News*, January 11, 1969, 15.

[90]Ibid.

in which they were embedded.[91] Some grew out of churches and established community groups, while others were connected to more radical political organizing. For example, in March 1969, eighty volunteers and twenty-two drug addicts took over a three-story building in Harlem and set up a drug-treatment program. They hoped to bring attention to "the inadequacy of the state's narcotic program and the entire health program for the black people." The addicts involved told the *New York Times* that they had faced a maze of waiting lists and applications in their efforts to secure treatment. One had never heard back from a program he had applied to three years earlier in 1966. The journalist reported that all of the patients interviewed complained that the state's drug addiction programs were "more punishment than rehabilitation." One addict asked if "I should turn myself in to the state and be locked up for rehabilitation." They contrasted the civic degradation of the state treatment programs with guerrilla programs, claiming that in the latter, they "talk to you like a man, not a statistic—the people really want to help you and it makes you want to help yourself." After a police eviction order, the center was closed and the patients transferred to an "underground hospital."[92] In subsequent years, other groups also established treatment programs. The Young Lords, a radical group dedicated to Puerto Ricans' self-determination, were integral to establishing a detox program at Lincoln Hospital.[93]

Drastic fluctuations in policing further intensified frustration within urban communities. In 1969, the city initiated a major intensification in street-level enforcement of drug markets. At a press conference in September, Mayor Lindsay announced that the police department intended to shift the narcotics division's 500-person force to the pursuit of upper-level drug arrests and direct the entire remaining patrols to prioritize narcotic arrests at the street level.[94] This sweep produced a considerable uptick in narcotics arrests in New York City: they jumped from 7,199 in 1967 to 26,378 in 1970.[95] Then, in 1971, at a high point in the surge of heroin use, the NYPD abandoned their campaign of intensive street-

[91] On struggles for community-controlled drug treatment, see Mahoney, "Fighting 'Addiction,'" 125–31. On funding for "indigenous" programs, see Martin, David, and Lavin, *A Political History of the New York State Narcotic Addiction Control Commission*.

[92] "Protesters Give Up Harlem Building: Protesters in Harlem Give Up Building Seized to Treat Addicts," *New York Times*, March 11, 1969, 1.

[93] Mahoney, "Fighting 'Addiction,'" 125–31.

[94] "Police to Step Up Narcotics Fight: Lindsay Vows Funds Needed for Decoys' Purchases—All Patrolmen Alerted," *New York Times*, September 10, 1969, 1.

[95] Joint Committee on New York Drug Law Evaluation, *The Nation's Toughest Drug Law: Evaluating the New York Experience: Final Report of the Joint Committee on New York Drug Law Evaluation* (New York: Association of the Bar of the City of New York, 1977), 90.

level drug policing.[96] Police officials claimed that the policy was ineffective and expensive and resulted in low conviction rates because the court system did not have the capacity to process the arrests.[97] The result was a dramatic fall-off in arrests. New York City police conducted over 24,025 felony drug arrests in 1970, 18,694 in 1971, 10,370 in 1972, and 7,041 in 1973.[98]

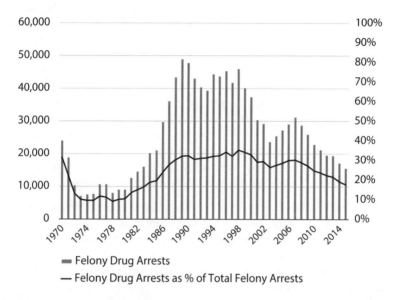

Figure 1.1. Felony drug arrests, total and as a percent of all felony arrests, in New York City, 1970–2014. (*Source*: New York State Department of Criminal Justice Services)

An explosive scandal that erupted in 1970 also motivated this retreat from aggressive narcotics policing. After unsuccessful attempts to handle corruption through channels within the police department, police officers Frank Serpico and David Durk worked with the *New York Times* on a series of articles revealing the extent of graft and extortion in the

[96]Ibid., 14, 89–91.
[97]Ibid., 88–91.
[98]These data are from the New York State Department of Criminal Justice Services. Although they both show the same patterns, there are discrepancies between data reported by the Joint Committee on New York Drug Law Evaluation (from NYPD statistical reports) and the data provided to the author by New York State Department of Criminal Justice Services (represented in the graph). Joint Committee on New York Drug Law Evaluation, *The Nation's Toughest Drug Law*, 88–91.

NYPD.[99] Their public reports forced Mayor Lindsay to finally address the longstanding problem and he appointed a commission to investigate the charges. The Knapp Commission's 1972 report concluded that well over half of the police force was involved in some form of corruption. It singled out corruption within narcotics enforcement, claiming that "high-ranking officials acknowledge it to be the most serious problem facing the department." The commission exposed that there were NYPD officers profiting from every aspect of the narcotics trade: police financed drug sales, provided protections for drug trades, seized drugs and cash during busts, and blackmailed sellers.[100] The Knapp Commission's report generated national controversy, but it was hardly news for Harlem residents. In a *New York Amsterdam News* article, Floyd McKissick wrote that the *"New York Times* has finally acknowledged what every Black man in New York already knew—that the New York City Police Department is corrupt from top to bottom."[101] For some, the Knapp Commission highlighted the hypocrisy of championing "law and order" and policing as the antidote to social problems. Michael Keating expressed his disgust with corruption in an article for the *New York Amsterdam News*:

> We have learned that while many policemen and their many politician followers were loudly proclaiming their virtue and their mission to save society, they at the same time were spending most of their time on a Sunday, not chasing thieves, rapists and muggers, but shaking down some poor guy for trying to make ends meet by keeping his bodega open on Sunday. . . . They were at the same time dealing dope.[102]

The Knapp Commission's revelations confirmed longstanding complaints of Harlem residents, but they did not translate into a more responsive police force. The official reaction to the revelations of systemic corruption and extortion by both state and federal law enforcement was to deemphasize the policing of open-air drug markets. Police officials, convinced that interactions with retail drug sales provided a dangerous invitation for graft, discouraged patrol officers from direct confrontation with drug sellers. Specialized units and federal agents assumed primary responsibility for drug policing and concentrated on higher levels of the distribution system.[103]

[99] Vincent Cannato, *The Ungovernable City* (New York: Basic Books, 2002), 466–79.

[100] "Report Says Police Corruption in 1971 Involved Well over Half on the Force," *New York Times*, December 28, 1972, 22.

[101] Floyd McKissick, "Police Corruption," *New York Amsterdam News*, May 23, 1970, 15.

[102] Michael Keating, "Knapp Panel Revealed Nothing New on Cops," *New York Amsterdam News*, February 26, 1972, A5.

[103] Richard Curtis, "The War on Drugs in Brooklyn, New York: Street Level Markets and the Tactical Narcotics Team" (PhD diss., Columbia University, 1996), 13–17. On the Knapp Commission, see Cannato, *The Ungovernable City*, 532–34, 466–78.

Although some residents undoubtedly welcomed the retreat from more aggressive drug market policing, the African Americans who were calling for more concerted action probably felt abandoned by the state in the midst of a crisis.

As those within New York's urban communities amplified their longstanding calls for an effective state response to the growing heroin use, concerns about drug use in other spaces made the issue even more explosive. The fervor over drug use cannot be teased apart from the anxiety produced by the mass social movements of the time. A vocal counterculture rejected the mainstream values of their parents, embracing drugs and new notions of sexuality. Movements demanded the rise of a society dramatically reformed and reborn. Politicians' claims that drugs unraveled the country's social fabric were politically resonant in part because they helped give meaning to the turmoil throughout society. Drugs, therefore, were inextricably tangled up with anxiety about young people's political rebellion.

Although the predominantly white counterculture was originally associated with marijuana and hallucinogenic use, they increasingly experimented with a wider array of drugs in the late 1960s. Heroin use grew more popular, in part as a way to manage coming down from amphetamines. The throngs of young people moving through San Francisco's Haight-Ashbury and the East Village and Greenwich Village in New York City brought their drug knowledge and habits back to their communities, driving a marked expansion of heroin use in white suburban areas between 1967 and 1973.[104] A 1968 anti-drug advertisement designed by the Ad Council featured large type simply and ominously stating: "Heroin is moving to the suburbs."[105]

As the new decade began, more reports of heroin use in the high schools of affluent areas of Brooklyn, Long Island, and Westchester heightened concern that drugs were "spreading" from inner cities. The popular references to an "epidemic" depicted drug use as a contagion transmitted with minimal human volition. An article from the *Washington Post* noted: "One thing is certain—the drug culture is spreading rapidly. It is spreading from the ghettos, where it has long been deeply embedded, to the white suburbs."[106] In articles such as these, drugs were presented as indigenous to inner cities; if they did appear in other communities, they were imagined as a weed or disease that had escaped from its traditional

[104] Schneider, *Smack*, 142–58.

[105] "Drug Abuse Is Moving to the Suburbs" advertisement, Advertising Council Historical File, RS 13/2/207, Box 45, Folder: "Drug Abuse Information, July 1971," American Advertising Council Archives, University of Illinois Archives.

[106] Marquis Childs, "Drugs Spreading from the Ghettos," *Washington Post*, November 23, 1970, A17.

ecosystem to infect new territory. This language naturalized the high rates of drug addiction in poor areas and elided the abuse of substances— including alcohol and prescription pills—in affluent communities. It located the genesis of social problems in urban communities of color and deflected attention from other social, economic, and cultural factors that could inspire young white people to use drugs.[107]

The changing demographics of heroin use intensified the political urgency of the problem.[108] At a Senate hearing in 1971, Mayor Lindsay warned that drug addiction could now strike any family:

> For too long, people thought of the problem of narcotics in the same way they thought of slums, unemployment, and welfare checks—all problems confined to the poor and to minorities, and to central cities. But the explosion of the drug culture has proven that wrong. Today, no family in America is immune from the possible discovery that their son or daughter suffers from drug abuse.[109]

Some officials would occasionally publicly acknowledge that reports about more affluent users changed the entire political calculus. An unnamed official in the Lindsay administration told a reporter, "As long as drugs were primarily a problem of the lower classes, there was a minimum amount of pressure to do any more than research the problem."[110] In 1970, an official from the White House Office of Management and Budget generated controversy when he admitted before a House committee on drug abuse that as long as heroin was a problem isolated to the "ghetto," "it was a problem we could live with."[111]

Commentators frequently noted the urgency inspired by the new concerns about white middle-class drug use. A columnist for the African American newspaper *New York Amsterdam News* wrote in 1970:

> Drug addiction is nothing new. Black kids have been destroyed for years by the heroin plague. Ghetto youth were easy prey for pushers whose little bags of dope brought the promise of escape from the dismal trap of poverty and racism. But now there is general alarm about the inroads dope is

[107] David Herzberg, *Happy Pills in America: From Miltown to Prozac* (Baltimore: Johns Hopkins University Press, 2010).

[108] Tolchin, "Involvement of Middle Class in the Narcotics Problem Arouses Demands for Action," 29; Buckley, "The Fight against Drugs Is in a Mess," 184. See also Connery, *Rockefeller of New York*, 266.

[109] "Testimony of Mayor John V. Lindsay before the U.S. Senate Subcommittee on Alcoholism and Narcotics," Washington, D.C., May 5, 1971, Reel 16, Subject Files, Folder: Drugs, John Lindsay Mayoral Papers, NYCMA.

[110] Tolchin, "Involvement of Middle Class in the Narcotics Problem Arouses Demands for Action," 29.

[111] Baum, *Smoke and Mirrors*, 35.

making. The reason isn't hard to find. More and more victims are coming from white middle-class families. When black kids were hooked, society was silent. But now everyone is up in arms about it.[112]

Some linked the growing reliance on therapeutic expertise to the seeming inappropriateness of the civic degradation of criminalization for this new population of drug users. An editorial in the *Health/Pac Bulletin* explained:

> Heroin, they say, is no longer an affliction of the "amoral or ignorant" lower classes and black and brown ghetto dwellers alone; its use is spreading like wildfire among the children of the respectable, white, middle class. As the daily rep fans the flames, and as frightened (and voting) middle class parents begin to demand action which will deal with "the problem," treatment "experts" and politicians are moving to the fore with the "solutions."[113]

Therefore, growing white involvement served to heighten panic about drugs as well as interest in therapeutic or medical remedies. Although concern about middle-class drug use probably inspired some more lenient, treatment-based responses to drug users, it had the inverse effect on attitudes toward drug sellers, the "pushers" who were held responsible for foisting the habit on new groups. The editorial continued:

> And now, the move afoot to reduce drug penalties for the mere possession of a drug (heroin and marijuana) and to increase the penalties for pushers, once again is in response to the needs of a frightened middle class segment of our society. In effect, the "liberalized" laws only represent a liberalization for the drug user who can afford to purchase his drugs. The poor, ghetto addict (who must sell to support his habit) will continue to be prosecuted to the full extent of an even harsher law.[114]

Since many street dealers were low-income users themselves, the trend of increasingly harsh punishment for "pushing" perpetuated a race- and class-based penalty structure for drug crimes. Those with resources had a greater chance of being diverted to less stigmatized punishments or treatment programs while the working class and poor, especially people of color, were more regularly channeled into the penal system. These dynamics fueled visions of a criminalized, racialized threat emanating from American central cities, while asserting that drug use throughout society could be mitigated through escalating punishment of street-level sellers.

[112] Whitney M. Young Jr., "The Drug Danger," *New York Amsterdam News*, March 14, 1970, 14.
[113] "Editorial: Who Benefits from the American Drug Culture?" 1.
[114] Ibid., 1.

As the discourse endeavored to divide addicts and pushers on the domestic scene, politicians encountered a new, vexing category of drug user abroad. The panic about heroin use thousands of miles away would reshape New York's treatment infrastructure by channeling federal resources into a new, controversial treatment: methadone maintenance. Heroin use exploded into a political crisis when two congressmen who had returned from a trip to Vietnam reported staggering levels of heroin use among U.S. armed forces: 10 to 15 percent of troops, between 26,000 and 39,000 people, used the drug on a regular basis.[115] Republican Robert H. Steele warned that "the soldier going to South Viet Nam today runs a far greater risk of becoming a heroin addict than a combat casualty."[116] Press coverage of soldiers' drug use reached a frenzied pitch in the summer of 1971. Politicians warned of the dangers posed by weapons-trained veterans joining the domestic drug culture. Iowa senator Harold Hughes predicted that "within a matter of months in our large cities, the Capone era of the '20s may look like a Sunday school picnic by comparison."[117]

The Nixon administration was intent on preventing the chaos and public relations nightmare of a wave of displaced, heroin-addicted veterans returning to the United States. With heroin use among the white middle class registering as a political priority, and now threatening military operations, President Nixon took the stage at a press conference in June 1971 to declare that "America's Public Enemy Number One is drug abuse."[118] In contrast to earlier explanations of domestic drug consumption, which posited that drug use was the result of individual pathology or disease, rhetoric about the situation in Vietnam often acknowledged that circumstantial factors, such as stress or availability, could contribute to drug use. President Nixon explained in a speech outlining his administration's efforts to tackle the problem that "peer pressures combine with easy availability to foster drug use."[119] Soldiers also ascribed their drug use to their context; some claimed that marijuana and heroin even helped manage the terror of combat. "All our guys used it [pot] in my outfit," one explained. "I was point man for our squad . . . and I smoked and

[115] For an in-depth investigation of the political uses of the panic over heroin use in Vietnam, see Jeremy Kuzmarov, *The Myth of the Addicted Army: Vietnam and the Modern War on Drugs* (Amherst: University of Massachusetts Press, 2009). David E. Smith, *"It's So Good, Don't Even Try It Once": Heroin in Perspective* (Englewood Cliffs, N.J.: Prentice-Hall, 1972), 60; "The New Public Enemy No. 1," *TIME*, June 28, 1971.

[116] "New Withdrawal Costs."

[117] Quoted in Baum, *Smoke and Mirrors*, 49.

[118] "The New Public Enemy No. 1."

[119] President Richard Nixon, "Special Message to the Congress on Drug Abuse Prevention and Control," June 17, 1971, American Presidency Project, http://www.presidency.ucsb.edu/ws/index.php?pid=3048&st=nixon&st1=drugs.

shot up a little scag [heroin] you know, just to save my own ass! When you get high, in a way it calms you down so you don't shit your pants."[120]

While U.S. forces used all manner of intoxicating substances while in Vietnam, much of the public attention centered around heroin. The troops who used heroin were rarely characterized as "junkies." This had much to do with the low-cost, high-quality heroin readily available in Southeast Asia. With such pure narcotics, troops had little need to inject heroin and, instead, were able to use less-stigmatized delivery mechanisms such as smoking or snorting. Most important, a heroin habit in Vietnam cost between two and seven dollars daily, well within the budget of an average GI, as compared to the $50 to $100 a day that officials estimated users needed to purchase the weaker heroin in the United States.[121] Nixon explained that "a habit which costs $5 a day to maintain in Vietnam can cost $100 a day to maintain in the United States, and those who continue to use heroin slip into the twilight world of crime, bad drugs, and all too often a premature death."[122]

The federal response to drug use in the military sought to affirm soldiers' political standing and largely repudiated strategies of civic degradation. Years later, Dr. Beny Primm, a drug-treatment specialist from New York, explained that the situation demanded a different strategy than had been previously employed:

> What we did in Vietnam, we said these were soldiers, these were good American boys over there fighting a war, red-blooded Americans, who happened to be in a stressful situation and used drugs. We began to find other ways to describe addiction rather than to say, "They're second-class citizens. They're the worst in the world. They're the dregs of the earth."[123]

In June 1971, Nixon publicly announced the United States' "new, all-out offensive" against the domestic and foreign threat of drug abuse. He then announced the formation of the most extensive federal drug-treatment initiative in U.S. history. He established the Special Action Office for Drug Abuse Prevention (SAODAP), which was directly accountable to the president. The new program would be headed by Jerome Jaffe, a leading methadone researcher who had developed innovative treatment programs in Illinois.[124] SAODAP diverged from

[120] Smith, *"It's So Good, Don't Even Try It Once,"* 67.

[121] Ibid., 7; "As Common as Chewing Gum."

[122] Nixon, "Special Message to the Congress on Drug Abuse Prevention and Control."

[123] Program Transcript: Night 1, "Drug War," *Frontline*, http://www.pbs.org/wgbh/pages /frontline/shows/drugs/etc/script.html.

[124] Richard Nixon, "Remarks about an Intensified Program for Drug Abuse Prevention and Control," June 17, 1971, American Presidency Project, http://www.presidency.ucsb.edu /ws/?pid=3047.

past initiatives because it invested a majority of funds into treatment and education, as opposed to law enforcement. With a Republican administration spearheading an unprecedented and massive treatment investment favoring methadone maintenance, the disease concept of addiction appeared ascendant. National drug policy was securely under the direction of specialized treatment experts. The architects of Nixon's program spoke hopefully of a growing consensus that the state was responsible for reintegrating drug users into society: "As the notion of the right to rehabilitation evolves into the consciousness of America, it will get us away from the archaic thinking that the drug addict is an evil character."[125]

Since drug use in the military was the administration's priority, Jerome Jaffe was on a plane to Vietnam the day after Nixon announced his new initiative. There Jaffe implemented a drug-screening program where two huge newly minted machines tested the urine of every service member about to be discharged. Those testing positive spent an extra week in detoxification—without the assistance of methadone—before returning to the United States for three more weeks of treatment. To enable this plan, Nixon reversed the longstanding policy of dishonorably discharging or court-marshaling those caught using drugs in the military. In a single memo, he ordered the secretary of defense to stop considering drug use a crime in the Uniform Code of Military Justice. This decriminalization reflected the pragmatism of the Nixon administration, which was desperate to get a handle on the problem, but it also revealed the range of state responses available beyond intensifying punishment.[126] When the results of the urine screenings began to trickle back, White House officials were relieved to find far fewer heroin users than they had feared. In the first seven weeks, only 5.4 percent tested positive for drugs.[127] Though the initial estimates that had provoked the panic might have been inflated, Jaffe had anticipated that many soldiers would probably stop using once word got out about the drug tests and that positive results could delay soldiers' much-anticipated discharge. While many users probably brought their heroin addiction home with them, many others left their habit in Vietnam along with the stressful war that had helped inspire it.[128]

[125] Program Transcript: Night 1, "Drug War."

[126] Baum, *Smoke and Mirrors*, 52.

[127] "Shrinking the Drug Specter," *TIME*, August 9, 1971.

[128] Schnieder, *Smack*, 160; Kuzmarov, *The Myth of the Addicted Army*; Nancy D. Campbell, "The Spirit of St. Louis: The Contributions of Lee N. Robins to North American Psychiatric Epidemiology," *International Journal of Epidemiology* 43, no. suppl. 1 (August 1, 2014): i23–25.

Methadone Maintenance and the Limits of Reintegration

With ceaseless reports of rising crime rates and expanding drug use within these different populations, heroin use became an increasingly volatile and charged political issue. A vicious cycle accelerated: the more attention to drugs and crime, the more fervent the calls for state action became. The more ambitious the political promises of action, the more inept the state appeared when the next election cycle produced new terrifying statistics and troubling anecdotes of state impotence. Few felt that the Rockefeller Programs and therapeutic communities were managing the situation sufficiently. New York City officials reported that 50 percent of the inmates in jail were addicts.[129] The problem seemed impervious to state action.

These discouraging trends were of particular concern to Rockefeller as he eyed his 1970 reelection campaign. While commentators often attribute Rockefeller's rightward drift to his presidential ambition, the governor faced volatile political dynamics within his home state. The governor confronted pressure rightward from the New York State Conservative Party, which had formed in 1962 and fielded a challenger— Paul Adams—in both the 1966 and 1970 races. He faced an increasingly un-unified Republican electorate that had 600,000 fewer registered members than the Democrats. The *New York Times* reported that some observers wondered whether Rockefeller's victory was not assured.[130] As early as 1969, the *New York Times* reported that a series of political maneuvers signaled the governor's intention to tack rightward to navigate these perilous waters. Endorsements of party conservatives and new austerity budgets "confirmed for many politicians a growing conviction that the Governor is approaching 1970 as a more conservative Republican than he has been since he assumed office 10 years ago."[131] To top it off, commentators and campaign insiders predicted that the governor stood little chance of retaining the 35 percent of the African American and Jewish vote that he had won in the 1966 race. To respond to these shifts within his own coalition, the Rockefeller campaign attempted to capitalize on divisions within traditional

---

[129] "Testimony of Mayor John V. Lindsay before the U.S. Senate Subcommittee on Alcoholism and Narcotics."

[130] See Richard Reeves, "Rockefeller's Strength and Weakness Are Analyzed," *New York Times*, March 30, 1970, 47 and Bill Kovach, "Rockefeller Campaigning Year before Election Day: Rockefeller Opens Campaign for Fourth Term a Year before Election Day to Bind Up Party Wounds," *New York Times*, October 27, 1969, 1, 39.

[131] Kovach, "Rockefeller Campaigning Year before Election Day," 39.

Democratic coalitions by appealing to "white ethnic" voters in areas such as Bay Ridge, Brooklyn, and Buffalo.[132]

Faced with this political landscape, Rockefeller increasingly emphasized a new approach to heroin addiction that was attracting national attention. Abetted by the Nixon administration's enhanced investment in this treatment, New York directed funding to a controversial experiment in methadone maintenance that had been gaining adherents for years and offered some promise in arresting escalating drug use and crime. In the mid-1960s, a small research study conducted at New York City's Rockefeller Hospital had begun dispensing methadone, a heroin substitute, to addicts.[133] Methadone, a long-acting, synthetic opiate that sated the craving for heroin, was particularly appealing because it supposedly mitigated the need to commit crimes to support the habit. Patients required only one dose daily and, its advocates claimed, experienced little if any euphoria. Proponents saw the drug as treating the chemical imbalance that caused compulsive heroin cravings and acknowledged that some people would need to continue treatment indefinitely. They often compared methadone maintenance to diabetics' long-term reliance on insulin. Although methadone users technically remained addicted, treatment experts emphasized their transformation into law-abiding, productive citizens who could work and raise families. The treatment, they hoped, could slash crime statistics while reintegrating heroin users into mainstream society. They would function normally and perform all social, work, and family obligations. Vincent Dole, one of the study's two principal researchers, described the profound transformation methadone would catalyze in drug users' status: "Our objective, after all, is to make citizens out of addicts."[134]

National interest in the new treatment was piqued when the psychiatrist Robert DuPont conducted a highly publicized study that purportedly established a direct link between crime rates and burgeoning heroin use. DuPont's researchers interviewed or tested the urine of approximately 200 people booked into Washington, D.C., jails during August and September 1969 and discovered 45 percent tested positive for or admitted to heroin use.[135] In the following months, the Department of Corrections instituted a methadone program that claimed to markedly reduce crime. Nixon staffers, searching for ways to contain drug use, funneled federal money toward the program and started crafting a national program. By

[132] Richard Reeves, "Rockefeller's Strategy: Drive for 'White Ethnic' Vote Appears to Be Succeeding against Goldberg," *New York Times*, September 21, 1970, 37.

[133] Courtwright, *Dark Paradise*, 163–65.

[134] William Claiborne, "Rules Urged in Dispensing Methadone," *Washington Post*, November 15, 1970, D1.

[135] Baum, *Smoke and Mirrors*, 19.

the 1972 presidential election, crime rates in Washington defied national trends and fell by half from their high in 1969.[136] The White House declared the federally supported citywide experiment a success.

For politicians, promoting methadone risked seeming dangerously permissive and endorsing government drug handouts. However, the chance to quickly and dramatically reduce crime rates at a relatively low cost was attractive for politicians—such as Nixon and Rockefeller—who had made high-profile pledges to manage crime during their election campaigns.[137] Methadone was probably particularly attractive to Rockefeller because his compulsory treatment program faced all manner of public criticism: for its punitive emphasis, its inability to "sweep addicts from the streets," the alleged slow pace of getting programs on line, its high cost, and its failure to dramatically reduce crime. Rockefeller's Democratic opponent in the gubernatorial race, Arthur Goldberg, made the governor's failure to stem drug use one of his two main issues in the campaign. Rockefeller's own polling confirmed the centrality of the issue, showing drug abuse to be one of voters' primary concerns.[138] The Conservative Party's candidate for governor also attacked Rockefeller's record on combating drug use, calling for the death penalty for people convicted of distributing, importing, or wholesaling narcotics.[139] Acknowledging the limitations in his compulsory treatment programs, the governor began deemphasizing the Rockefeller Programs. The funding and new admissions for civil commitment centers declined and their resources were redirected toward local drug-free treatment centers and short-term detoxification programs. And increasingly, the NACC funds also subsidized the new and expanding methadone infrastructure.[140]

As had been the case with previous expansions of drug treatment, the state's expansion of methadone treatment did not preclude a role for the penal system in managing drug use. Rockefeller's 1970 campaign rhetoric ratcheted up tough talk about drug pushers and emphasized the role of long prison sanctions. One advertisement featured the image of an aging drug dealer sitting in a prison cell while a stern, booming narra-

[136] Transcript of interview with Robert DuPont for "Drug Wars," *Frontline*, http://www .pbs.org/wgbh/pages/frontline/shows/drugs/interviews/dupont.html.

[137] White, *Slaying the Dragon*, 251–56.

[138] Frank Lynn, "Rivals for Governor Cite Drug Issue," *New York Times*, September 19, 1970, 13; Frank Lynn, "Goldberg Opens Radio-TV Campaign," *New York Times*, September 18, 1970, 46. Not surprisingly, the issue was particularly relevant in and around New York City.

[139] "Conservative Candidate Labels Rockefeller Drug Policy Failure," *New York Times*, September 23, 1970, 41; "Narcotics Action Sought by Adams: Drug Abuse Also Is Cited by Walinsky and Rockefeller," *New York Times*, September 9, 1970, 39.

[140] Martin, David, and Lavin, *A Political History of the New York State Narcotic Addiction Control Commission*, 40–44.

tor cautioned his colleagues: "A warning to dope pushers in New York State, Rockefeller has increased the maximum punishment for selling hard drugs to life imprisonment. And now, pusher, when you're caught it can be for keeps . . . Rockefeller. He's done a lot. He'll do more."[141] Speaking directly to pushers in the ad provided the public spectacle of an empowered Rockefeller disciplining the recalcitrant drug pusher. While this rhetoric did not match the penal practices of the time, Rockefeller's tactics paid off. Facilitated no doubt by the infusion into his campaign of millions from his personal fortune, he handily won a fourth term in office. He made up for significant losses in the Jewish and African American vote by attracting support from traditionally Democratic "white ethnic" voters.[142]

The NACC, with financial help from the federal government, expanded methadone treatment dramatically by establishing clinics throughout New York. Funding for the Rockefeller Programs decreased as methadone became the more dominant treatment modality. In its execution, methadone treatment was a particularly complicated program with diverse and seemingly contradictory implications. It was simultaneously politically promising and risky. The program proved more successful than other strategies at mitigating the drug trade's social costs and property crime, and in many cases allowed politicians the rare opportunity to declare some measure of progress in their anti-drug campaigns. It also appealed to lawmakers because it cost far less than custodial care. While some methadone treatment centers offered basic services, such as health or employment counseling, many of the new clinics simply dispensed methadone to patients once a day.[143]

Methadone was embraced first and foremost as a crime control strategy, as both critics and supporters acknowledged. By approaching addiction as an individual, biologically rooted pathology that could be managed by a simple daily medication, the modality absolved lawmakers of addressing the larger social forces many blamed for widespread drug use. Individualized treatment diverted attention from the profound economic crises and police practices that concentrated vice markets (and therefore drug access and use) in central cities. William Raspberry, a *Washington Post* columnist, alluded to this dimension of methadone's appeal when he wrote in 1971 that "methadone is not so much a means for treating addicts as a way of fighting crime. . . . [M]ethadone not only blocks the

[141]Richard Reeves, "This Is the Battle of the Titans?" *New York Times*, November 1, 1970, 70.

[142]Richard Reeves, "4-Term Governor: Victory Helps Party Retain Control of the Legislature," *New York Times*, November 4, 1970, 1.

[143]Walter Goodman, "The Choice for Thousands: Heroin or Methadone?" *New York Times*, June 13, 1971, SM14; Richard Severo, "Addiction: Chemistry Is the New Hope," *New York Times*, March 19, 1971, 1, 23.

effects of heroin in the addict; it blocks the effects of drug addiction on society, rendering addiction a merely personal problem."[144] Many who promoted methadone treatment did so out of a willingness to accept any opportunity to control crime, regardless of its impact on drug users. One Lower East Side resident explained he had lost all interest in protecting the rights or well-being of addicts: "I wouldn't care if someone came along with a machine gun and killed all of them . . . I've been robbed, my wife has been robbed—I'm sorry, but I don't care any more."[145] A social worker's comment to the *New York Times* reflected the popular belief that methadone was needed to protect the city, even if it did not address the root causes of addiction. "If your goal is to get people off the streets, you can give them methadone," she explained. "If you are considering why they became addicted and you want to help them make their lives more productive, then you have to do something else. But you look around and you wonder if you shouldn't get people off the streets before the city is destroyed."[146]

Despite these politically alluring features, methadone treatment presented a series of political problems. It immediately generated political controversy. For many critics, especially those in the drug-free treatment community, administering methadone was akin to drug maintenance and denied more substantive healing to an addict. That these new, less expensive treatment programs threatened to divert funding from more established ones only intensified the already pronounced philosophical tensions between the proponents of therapeutic communities, methadone, and other neighborhood-based treatment efforts.[147] Other critics worried that methadone symbolized tolerance of the "drug culture" and accelerated social decay. Some radical black and Latino activists saw methadone treatment as a strategy to forestall organized political resistance by sedating their communities.[148]

Much public concern about methadone centered on how it was "misused." Though methadone, prescribed at a sufficient dose, inhibited the effects of other opiates, it could also be used to get high, either on its own or when combined with other substances. Initially methadone was attractive primarily to heroin users seeking to regulate their own habit, but it

[144] Quoted in Helena Hansen and Samuel Roberts, "Two Tiers of Medicalization," in *Critical Perspectives on Addiction*, ed. Julie Netherland (Bingley: Emerald, 2012), 89–90.

[145] Severo, "Addiction: Chemistry Is the New Hope."

[146] Ibid.

[147] See, for example, Martin, David, and Lavin, *A Political History of the New York State Narcotic Addiction Control Commission* and "ASA: There Are Enough Junkies for Us All," *Health/Pac Bulletin*, June 1970, Reel MR 72, pp. 9–13, Departmental Files, Folder: Drugs, John Lindsay Mayoral Papers, NYCMA.

[148] Courtwright, *Dark Paradise*, 170–74.

eventually became attractive to new, recreational users as well. Employees of clinics and pharmacies siphoned methadone into illicit markets, as did clients selling individual doses. This problem became particularly acute during a heroin draught in the early 1970s that was produced in part by the Nixon administration's efforts to interrupt international drug supply chains between Turkish opium and the U.S. retail markets. The resulting shortages caused heroin costs to spike and the street-level drug purity to plummet.[149] For a short period in the mid-1970s, heroin-related deaths decreased, as did hepatitis B infections, an indicator of intravenous drug use levels. However, reducing supply drove up demand for heroin substitutes, leading new and seasoned heroin users alike to embrace methadone. Between 1973 and 1976, there were more deaths from methadone overdose than from heroin overdose. Most of the fatalities resulted from "unsupervised" and illicit methadone use, not from methadone administered in treatment programs.[150] By 1974, Mexican heroin had stepped in to fill the void left by Turkish opium; prices declined and drug purity again increased. Turkey resumed opium cultivation in the same year.[151] Therefore, while the heroin supply bounced back quickly, methadone became more controversial. The diversion of methadone into illicit markets undermined program advocates' claims that the treatment heightened social stability and public safety.[152]

Methadone treatment also lost community support, and therefore political support, because drug users remained enmeshed and marked in public space. Methadone's failure to "get people off the streets" and ultimately undermined much of its support. The emphasis on producing normative, socially conforming citizens was at odds with the methadone dispersal system, which marked clients as requiring surveillance and careful regulation. While methadone treatment was ostensibly devoted to social reintegration and disentangling people from criminal networks, the state designed a delivery system that both stigmatized patients and criminalized the space around the clinics. In order to curtail the diversion of methadone into illicit markets, methadone could only be dispensed in specially regulated and licensed clinics. While some clinics might even-

[149] Schneider, *Smack*, 175–83. The Nixon administration's ongoing initiatives resulted in a 1972 treaty with Turkey where the United States provided $32 million for crop substitution in exchange for a ban on opium production. Around the same period, French authorities, working closely with U.S. law enforcement, targeted many of the heroin-processing centers in Marseilles that had been the infamous "French Connection" between Turkish opium and the U.S. retail markets.

[150] Joint Committee on New York Drug Law Evaluation, *The Nation's Toughest Drug Law*, 57–58.

[151] Ibid., 39–41; Schneider, *Smack*, 182–85.

[152] Joint Committee on New York Drug Law Evaluation, *The Nation's Toughest Drug Law*, 41, 50–58.

tually allow patients to take home individual extra doses to continue treatment over a weekend, most were required to visit a clinic daily and consume the methadone, typically mixed with some orange-flavored beverage, in front of the staff.[153]

Although methadone treatment showed some promise of reducing crime rates, the visible, salient presence of addicts in neighborhoods all over New York exacerbated hostility toward heroin users and government treatment efforts. Residents of neighborhoods with methadone programs often recoiled at the groups of addicts congregating for their daily doses of the drug. All over the country, methadone clinics faced active and organized opposition from neighborhood groups opposed to the placement of clinics in their community. Locals fiercely resisted the clinics through lobbying, pickets, letter-writing campaigns, and even vigilante attacks and sabotage.[154] Methadone centers attracted even more attention than drug-free programs because they served higher numbers of people who had to pass through neighborhoods to visit a clinic daily. Residents claimed that the clients lingered, accosted locals, and were a magnet for drug sellers and people looking to buy methadone (and other illicit drugs) on the street. Race factored in many of these conflicts, as illustrated by a report to Mayor Lindsay concerning a public nuisance lawsuit again a private methadone clinic treatment facility. It explained simply, "In the case of Ithaca, there have been thinly veiled racial overtones. The patients are predominantly Black and Puerto Rican and this is basically a white middle class neighborhood."[155] Opposition to methadone centers was not isolated to white communities; many African Americans resisted what they viewed as an unfair concentration of drug-treatment centers in their neighborhoods.

Since the political acceptance of methadone arose from a desire to protect "the public" from the addict, in many senses it further strengthened the perceived distinction between the two. In letters opposing drug centers, people often voiced a zero-sum understanding of rights, where services or programs understood to help one group directly disadvantaged another. One letter to Mayor Lindsay that opposed a rehabilitation center reasoned that "bringing hardcore disadvantaged people and taking whites out of our area who represent middle income status is racially discriminating." The author continued by asserting that her aversion to the neighborhood becoming a "ghetto" was not racist: "We don't want to

[153] For more on the racialization of methadone, see Hansen and Roberts, "Two Tiers of Medicalization," 89–90.

[154] Courtwright, *Dark Paradise*, 170–74; "The Methadone Jones," *Newsweek*, February 7, 1977, 29; White, *Slaying the Dragon*, 251–56.

[155] Memo from Laura Blackburne to Jay Kriegel re: Ithaca Methadone Program, July 25, 1973, Reel 37, Subject Files, Folder: Narcotics, John Lindsay Mayoral Papers, NYCMA.

increase the density of population in this vicinity and especially the extension of another possible ghetto made of Hispanics and Blacks. This does not mean any feeling of discrimination either."[156] Writers repeatedly asserted their status as homeowners and taxpayers to legitimize their claims on the state, while also rhetorically positioning the racialized population of addicts outside the political community. For example, U.S. representative (and future mayor) Ed Koch wrote to Mayor Lindsay about his constituents' complaints regarding methadone centers. He argued that "we must strike a balance between the addict's needs and the public's right for protection."[157] This seemingly mundane language saturated these debates and reflected the assumption that addicts and the public were separate and their interests were inversely related—what helped the addict hurt the public and vice versa.

Methadone clinic patients struggled to counter this image. *Breakthrough*, a newsletter written by the patients and staff of a clinic at Jamaica Hospital, attempted to counter presentations of methadone patients as an alien element. "We are part of the local community," one author asserted, despite the fact that local residents felt differently:

> Most residents of this area still consider us junkies and a menace to their children, their businesses, and their peace of mind. . . . The fact that we are on "methadone" does nothing to alleviate their fears for too many of them it is just another form of drug abuse . . . we are no longer addicts but human beings with the same ambitions, desires and feeling that they have. We have learned from our mistakes, which is one of the reasons we are on methadone, and this alone should show them our desire to become a productive part of society again.[158]

The author did not challenge the idea that active users were "nonproductive" members of society; instead he struggled against the permanency of the degraded status by transforming methadone treatment into a mark of civic responsibility and belonging.

The determination to subordinate the civic status of drug users in treatment centers undermined their programmatic efficacy. The limits of methadone's inclusionary promise were starkly revealed in the debates over employing ex-users. In a society where full citizenship was dependent on the ability to earn and consume, few issues were more signifi-

[156]Eugenie W. to Mayor Lindsay, June 12, 1973, Reel 34, Subject Files, Folder: Methadone Maintenance, John Lindsay Mayoral Papers, NYCMA.

[157]Congressman Ed Koch to Mayor Lindsay, December 5, 1972, Reel 34, Subject Files, Folder: Methadone Maintenance, John Lindsay Mayoral Papers, NYCMA.

[158]Jimmy H., "Community Outlook," *Breakthrough Newsletter* of Jamaica Hospital Clinic, #1, Reel 34, p. 4, Subject Files, Folder: Methadone Maintenance, John Lindsay Mayoral Papers, NYCMA.

cant to rehabilitation and social integration than access to jobs. However, cultural and political rhetoric that positioned heroin users as nonworking, dangerous outsiders poisoned the efforts of former illicit drug users to secure even the most basic work.

Recognizing that no promise of rehabilitation was viable if employers refused to hire people undergoing treatment in the state's programs, some state actors attempted to mitigate discrimination against former addicts in the job market. For example, the chief council of the NACC complained to city officials that their anti-drug advertisements directly sabotaged his efforts to convince employers to hire rehabilitated addicts. He argued that the campaign, which painted a frightening, sordid image of addicts as the "living dead," was irrelevant to potential users since it failed to acknowledge the real reasons people started using drugs. He wrote to city officials:

> The phrase, "living dead" suggests, as do all of the ads, no return for the rehabilitated addict. This is scary, all right, but it is scaring all the wrong people for all the wrong reasons, such as employers who recoil from hiring rehabilitated addicts. Your campaign has reinforced a stereotype in the most persistent and unenlightened way.[159]

A state commission in 1975 also found that these representations made employers reluctant to hire addicts. Members of the commission discovered from interviews that major employers "receive their information about addiction from the media; they constantly refer to such information, which they deem highly reliable; and they view the addict, as does the media, as a source of all of society's problems." The representations of addicts intended to discourage drug use undermined the assimilative mission of treatment: "[The] exaggeration of addict-related crime through the media and certain otherwise responsible agencies of government is a significant factor in leading the major employers to believe that since addiction means crime, and most crime at that, rehabilitation is impossible."[160] State agents worked at odds with each other, some attempting to build support for reintegrating a population that other state agents constructed as the "living dead."

Individuals in treatment programs were, of course, the most acutely aware of the contradictions between policies claiming to produce self-supporting citizens but effectively inhibiting it. One man's experience illustrated how these policies intersected in individuals' lives. "I have tried

[159]Harvard Hollenberd to Harriet Michel, director of Mayor's Narcotic Control Counsel, October 11, 1972, 4th Administration, Reel 61, Rockefeller Gubernatorial Papers, NYSA.
[160]Temporary State Commission to Evaluate the Drug Laws, Chester Hardt Chairman, "Employing the Rehabilitated Addict, Interim Report" (Albany, N.Y., 1973), vi.

every existing program at that time and failed at all the programs," John Browski explained in his testimony before the Temporary Commission to Evaluate Drug Laws. "I was at Kentucky [federal drug-treatment center] five times; I detoxed at hospitals five times. . . . As soon as I would find work, I would spend the money on drugs and if it wasn't enough, I would steal from the company." This all changed when he enrolled in a methadone program: "From the first day of the program until this day, I have not touched a drop of junk which surprises me more than anybody." Once stabilized on methadone and looking for employment, Browski lied in his interview with Western Electric about his drug use. He worked at the company for a year and a half without incident until he was hospitalized after a workplace accident and informed his doctor he needed methadone. When the doctor reported this to Western Electric, Browski was fired:

> I had a good work record and I thought that I had proven myself after working for them for two years. But I was informed that it is company policy not to hire meth patients and if I had told them at the time, they would not have hired me. So my services were terminated . . . I have been collecting compensation from the company for 1 1/2 years.[161]

His union did not take up his cause because they also viewed methadone treatment as continued drug dependence. These interactions between state policies, employer practices, and cultural stigma effectively stymied recovering addicts' job opportunities, often forcing them to either forgo sustainable employment or risk repercussions by misrepresenting their histories. Therefore the government program purportedly dedicated to transforming addicts into productive, contributing citizens actually marked them as dangerous and risky propositions for employers. In the process, the state helped reproduce the permanent social and economic segregation that it was ostensibly dedicated to undermining.

These issues were particularly acute in urban communities of color, where profound structural and economic barriers made integration of low-income African American and Latino drug users into the mainstream U.S. economy even more challenging. Beny Primm, the director of a methadone program in Brooklyn, described the unique challenges of dealing with heroin use in African American communities. He reported that the most outstanding benefit of methadone "has been the conceptual transformation of the 'junkie' from criminal to patient."[162] This shift in

---

[161]Ibid., 63–65.
[162]Beny J. Primm, MD, "Methadone Is Not the Answer," n.d., Reel 2, p. 1, Subject Files, John Lindsay Mayoral Papers, NYCMA.

civic status was limited, however, especially for poor drug users from poor, racially segregated areas. He explained:

> Even if we are able to overcome the psychic inertia among our patients— the lack of self-confidence, the lack of basic skills, and the lack of accept- able patterns for dealing with society's demands—we have not altered the environment in which they developed and in which they must survive. Thus we are placed in a position of attempting to prepare individuals in- tellectually and emotionally to enter a society which really doesn't want them. . . . Society, and I'm talking about the white establishment, has made the black ghetto resident a deviant to begin with. Thus it is of little con- sequence in the eyes of society and in the individual's own mind that he becomes an addict, a criminal, or dependent on welfare. What option does he really have?[163]

According to Primm, transforming the psyches of individual addicts from urban communities of color would accomplish little when their commu- nities remained marginalized. The job migrations and general economic abandonment of urban communities of color joined with the slowing economic growth to make Lyndon Johnson's dream of fully incorporat- ing poor spaces into American prosperity an increasingly hollow and improbable proposition. In this sense, dreams of assimilating deviant in- dividuals and dreams of incorporating entire marginalized spaces floun- dered on the same obstacles. They both interpreted social problems as the product of exclusion: blocked opportunities and personal or group- level barriers to integration. For rehabilitation to have real purchase in the communities he served, Primm explained that the community "must begin to accept treatment programs in their midst . . . community resi- dents must accept ex-addicts as fellow citizens and workers."[164] And yet it was precisely the alternative vision of rehabilitation that decoupled treatment or other social support from technologies of civic subordina- tion that aroused such fierce political resistance.

At the onset of the 1970s, the narcotics problem presented New York politicians, and Nelson Rockefeller especially, with a serious political challenge. A perceived crisis in state legitimacy helped make the drug use of the 1960s and 1970s a particularly volatile political issue. It became entangled with struggles over the causes and remedies for gross social, economic, and racial inequality that black and Puerto Rican activists

[163] Ibid., 4–6.
[164] Ibid., 10.

forced into the public arena. The governor also confronted the shifting terrain of electoral politics, not just within the national Republican Party but also within the politics of New York State and New York City. Rockefeller's political moves operated within and responded to these public debates, while also exerting a powerful impression.

The state's constrained funds and institutional capacity also structured Rockefeller's political options, as did evolving medical and legal norms surrounding drug addiction. Methadone maintenance, along with therapeutic communities and civil commitment, failed to pacify urban space or the popular anxiety arising from incessant reports of drug use and crime. They failed to deliver favorable crime statistics at electorally expedient intervals. Whether because of dependence or a simple disinclination to forgo their attendant pleasures, many people simply kept using drugs. Treatment programs never received the resources or infrastructure they would have required to intern or treat all of New York's drug users. While policymakers enlisted police, courts, prisons, and social welfare programs to manage drug users, they could not completely control the various state agencies' enthusiasm or efficacy for the assignment.

Efforts to build therapeutic state capacity faltered on tensions within the project. The programs, chiefly dedicated to securing social order, endeavored to reintegrate drug users through programs that marked addicts as a distinct, suspect category. This feature of the rehabilitative programs rendered them vulnerable to criticism from multiple angles. Those subject to treatment often resisted the punitive, custodial features and chafed under the constraints on their freedom and rights. Others used the state's purported commitment to their well-being and social reintegration to challenge the programs they encountered and make space for alternative visions of rehabilitation. At the same time, dispensing state benefits and offering social assimilation to some of society's more reviled groups, particularly low-income black and Latino drug sellers, antagonized those who felt criminals must surrender rights and claims on the state. In other words, the treatment programs floundered against limitations of political will, state capacity, and internal tensions as much as the stubborn persistence of drug use and crime. There was no obvious or easy next move as Rockefeller faced this fraught and complicated landscape. While the governor had been championing different policies and programs for decades, it was the tough law he sponsored in 1973 that became the central pillar of his political legacy.

CHAPTER TWO

The Public versus the Pushers

ENACTING NEW YORK'S ROCKEFELLER DRUG LAWS

Drug policy had no preordained course in the early 1970s. By 1973, the state had spent $124.9 million to acquired or build twenty-five facilities for its NACC residential and outpatient programs.[1] There were 56,522 people enrolled in different types of drug treatment in New York City: 34,149 in methadone programs and 22,373 in drug-free treatment. Meanwhile, a host of different indicators—such as overdose deaths, serum hepatitis cases, and reports of "addict-related crime"—suggested a leveling off and decline in addiction.[2] All of this did little to appease public anxiety about street crime and new drug cultures. For politicians promising safer streets and the cessation of narcotic use, the treatment programs originally intended to bolster their anti-drug credentials often became liabilities. There were serious political, fiscal, and institutional problems with every strategy championed by Governor Rockefeller. Opponents used the programs as evidence of their rivals' missteps and the state's failure to manage the threats posed by drugs and their ominous pushers. In some communities, the proliferation of programs and the controversies about their placement actually made the problem more salient and vexing.

Reports of the problem doggedly appeared in the press. Abandoning efforts at precision, newspapers offered wide ranges in their estimates of the extent of drug use; one article, for example, put the number of addicts in New York City between 150,000 and 300,000 in 1973.[3] Yet despite the public fear about addicts and addict crime and the popularity of "law-and-order" political appeals, a vast majority of the population reported to pollsters that they viewed drug abuse as a medical problem. Specialists and significant swathes of the public saw harsh punishment as an outmoded, discredited approach. In 1971, Governor Rockefeller released a poll showing that 87.6 percent of respondents reported that drug

[1] "The Acquisition and Construction of Drug Abuse Treatment Facilities," 1.
[2] Memo from Gordon Chase, Health Services Administration, to Mayor John Lindsay, "Six-Month Status Report on Addiction," July 9, 1973, Reel 2, Subject Files, Folder: Addiction Services, John Lindsay Mayoral Papers, NYCMA.
[3] James Markham, "Is It True Nothing Works?" *New York Times*, January 14, 1973, 5.

addicts should be treated as sick people, not criminals.[4] Mayor Lindsay, a man with national political ambitions, publicly floated the idea of imitating Britain's network of heroin maintenance clinics and actually dispensing heroin to addicts.[5]

It was in this context that Nelson Rockefeller proposed a dramatic escalation in punishment that opponents and supporters alike would herald as the "toughest drug laws in the nation." This chapter illuminates the genesis, passage, and implementation of his proposal. The drug laws were the result of the interaction between Rockefeller's personal political ambitions, diverse popular frustration with the period's social movements and political insurgency, and the persistence of heroin use and street crime in New York during the late 1960s and early 1970s. All of these dynamics refracted through the architecture of the limited U.S. welfare state, particularly the burgeoning drug-treatment infrastructure. In short, Rockefeller's "tough" proposal was an attempt to resolve the problems that had arisen from the caustic interaction between the state's ambitious political promises to control drugs and crime and the political, programmatic, and institutional complications of doing so through individualized treatment programs. Rockefeller's dramatic and harsh proposal was built upon the premise that therapeutic programs failed to curtail drug use and street crime. He attributed the "failure" of the rehabilitative project to incorrigible addicts and pushers, only rarely acknowledging the other factors that hindered treatment programs. Having thus defined the problem, the new laws promised to manage urban disorder and violence by quarantining these irredeemable pushers and intensifying the coercive pressure on drug users to stop taking narcotics.

Citizens Demand Their Rights Back: The Problem of Misplaced Rights

Rockefeller's decision to embrace draconian penalties for drug selling is best understood in the context of the period's raging struggles over the social contract—the fierce disagreements over who deserved rights, benefits, and standing and on what terms. The governor himself framed his decisions in these terms. His political choice was not random personal whim or simply an unavoidable response to local conditions. He was em-

---

[4] Press release from Executive Chamber of Governor Nelson Rockefeller, June 24, 1971, Reel 37, Subject Files, Folder: Narcotics, John Lindsay Mayoral Papers, NYCMA.

[5] James Markham, "What's All This Talk of Heroin Maintenance?" *New York Times*, July 2, 1972, SM6; Press release re: Investigating Heroin Maintenance Program, Mayor's Office, June 3, 1971, Reel 72, Departmental Files, Folder: Drugs, John Lindsay Mayoral Papers, NYCMA.

bedded in the popular zeitgeist—which he in turn helped sculpt through his rhetoric and legislative agenda—marked by particular beliefs about the causes of crime and the appropriate responses to it. The origin story of his infamous drug laws that he relayed to the press illuminates how his proposal intersected with wider negotiations over rights and citizenship underway at this time.

Rockefeller's narrative begins at a party in early 1972 when he was talking with William Fine, the president of Bonwit Teller department stores. Fine became concerned about narcotics after his own son's struggle with addiction and he had subsequently become board chairman of the Phoenix House, a therapeutic community in New York City.[6] That night Rockefeller asked Fine if he'd be willing to go to Japan to find out why it had the lowest addiction rate of any industrialized nation. Fine agreed, financed the trip himself, and spent a weekend meeting with health officials in Japan. He submitted his findings to the governor in March 1972. He reported that drug addiction in Japan was negligible, affecting less than 1 percent of the population, and the relapse rate after treatment was a paltry 0.13 percent.[7] Fine's memo outlined Japan's aggressive responses to drug use: seventy-two-hour detentions in all suspected cases of drug use (with an additional ten- to twenty-day hold if ordered), detoxification without any medical treatment to soften withdrawal symptoms, mandatory hospitalization for up to six months for confirmed addicts, community mentors to facilitate the transition from treatment programs, and the possibility of a life sentence for drug sellers. Although Fine detailed all the various features in Japan's aggressive anti-drug program, Rockefeller fixed on a single component: life sentences for drug sellers. He also took to heart the lesson Fine said he took away from the trip:

> The thing that impressed me most of all is the single minded conviction they have that *public interest is above human rights when it comes to an evil.* In other words, it becomes a detriment to the public interest when there is drug abuse; therefore, the human rights of those who get involved in narcotics, or push narcotics, are brushed aside—quickly, aggressively, and with little or no recourse. . . . It is incredible to me that they have had such success, but then, it really all comes down to what people are willing to give up to get, and the Japanese, obviously, were willing to give up the soap box movement on human rights in order to rid the public of the evil abuses of drugs.[8]

[6] William Kennedy, "Rocky Is 64, Going on 35," *New York Times*, April 29, 1973, 17.
[7] Joseph E. Persico, *The Imperial Rockefeller: A Biography of Nelson A. Rockefeller* (New York: Simon and Schuster, 1982), 144; William Fine to Rockefeller, March 15, 1972, 4th Administration, Reel 61, Rockefeller Gubernatorial Papers, NYSA.
[8] Fine to Rockefeller; emphasis in original.

Fine's analysis barely touched upon the complex set of cultural, economic, and political factors that made drug use and treatment profoundly distinct phenomena in Japan versus the United States.[9] For him, the takeaway message from the Japanese was not the specifics of their policy but what he considered their strategic disregard for the rights of the addict.

Of course, Rockefeller hardly had to cross the globe to hear calls for draconian punishment of drug sellers. Fine's letter was probably more of an echo than a shocking wake-up call. Tough mandatory minimum sentences had been the dominant approach when he took office, and hardliners in the state had been pushing such proposals, even including the death penalty, for years. Fine's letter resonated with the demands for a new balance between individual rights and the "public's" social welfare that saturated Rockefeller's constituent mail and other politicians' rhetoric at the time. The governor would eventually make these themes the ideological underpinning of his new drug laws.

Particularly because of his longstanding presidential ambitions, Rockefeller was embedded in politics that were simultaneously local and national. At the national level, calls for law and order grew increasingly popular through the 1960s and were a hallmark in the presidential campaigns of both Barry Goldwater in 1964 and Richard Nixon in 1968. The demands for social stability and the restoration of order were deeply enmeshed in the ongoing struggles over whom the state served. Calls for law and order were never isolated to white populations, but hostility and resistance to African American demands for full citizenship and economic security were often articulated through this language. "Law and order" was often a euphemism for racial animus or opposition to civil rights and black power movements. According to the political logic, African American and Latino activists undermined the rule of law through disruptive protests, particularly civil disobedience, and thereby promoted lawlessness and crime. Nixon claimed he would counter these forces by championing the interests of the "silent majority": that mass of public who did not agitate to end the Vietnam War or endeavor to reshuffle the distribution of rights and resources in the polity.

Letters to Rockefeller offer a window into the public attitudes he confronted at a more local level, and they help reveal the particular ways Rockefeller's constituents framed their concern about drugs and crime. During his years in office, the governor received hundreds of letters on the need to "reestablish order" and control crime. One rhetorical theme

---

[9] In other places, reporters acknowledged the particular cultural and social context of drug treatment in Japan that made it a singularly unhelpful model for American social policy. See, for example, Edwin McDowell, "Tokyo, Where Law Means Order," *Wall Street Journal*, November 28, 1973, 4th Administration, Reel A16, Rockefeller Gubernatorial Papers, NYSA.

that manifested consistently in this correspondence was the tendency to attribute rising crime and drug use to liberalism's failures and civil rights organizing. Rockefeller's constituent mail persistently blamed crime on the permissiveness of courts and social programs, asserting a causal connection between newly won legal and social rights for marginalized populations and "worsening" conditions in society. Some constituents interpreted their experiences as victims of horrible crime through this frame. One woman, whose brother was murdered, wrote to the governor about what she saw as the problematic balance of rights and responsibility in society:

> There is too much emphasis on rights and the various minority groups and not enough on responsibilities and the majority. . . . The convict or guy with a record has more rights than anyone. Money that is presently being handed out for welfare, Medicaid, youth services, senior citizens and the various minorities or gravy trains might better be used to create a responsible society. There is too much appealing, protests, etc. for more funds and not enough common sense to administer sensible programs that are for the majority and create a more responsible society.[10]

Letters such as these pointed to the substantive renegotiations underway over the terms of citizenship for a variety of marginalized groups. While the race of letter writers was rarely explicitly stated and people of all races expressed deep exasperation with crime, many clearly linked rising crime and disorder to the high-profile demands by "minorities" for new rights and protections.

The civil rights victories in Congress in 1964 and 1965 were accompanied by the Supreme Court's revision of criminal procedures during the 1960s. It granted defendants a whole series of new protections. For example, people charged with crimes won the right to a public defender if unable to pay for counsel, the right to have a lawyer present during interrogations, and the right to be informed of their rights upon arrest.[11] Critics of these changes often attributed incidents of crime to these new legal protections. In a letter advocating the reinstatement of the death penalty, one person wrote:

> Over the past several years I have been increasingly deprived of certain rights and guarantees, granted to me under the Bill of Rights. I refer to the right to walk the streets in peace and security and to feel safe within my home. We have, in fact, arrived at a reversal of the normal: the criminal walks the streets and the law-abiding, tax-paying citizen is locked

[10] Janet R. to Rockefeller, March 5, 1973, 4th Administration, Reel A16, Rockefeller Gubernatorial Papers, NYSA.

[11] Parenti, *Lockdown America*, 5.

up—voluntarily at his home, with several locks at the door and a lock at each window.[12]

In this and other similar correspondence, constituents declared that their status and protection had been eroded as criminal defendants gained rights.

These arguments flipped a dominant tenet of the era—advanced by both mainstream liberals and some social movements—that stressed the role of social inequality and racial injustice in producing criminal behavior. For example, President Lyndon Johnson argued that crime was rooted in social conditions and could be mitigated by expanding opportunities, which he proposed accomplishing through his Great Society programs.[13] Contesting this narrative, letter writers insisted that liberal programs and civil rights laws encouraged crime instead of lessening it and—in a zero-sum formulation of rights where one group's gain is another's loss—subordinated the rights of "taxpayers" or "the majority." Another woman wrote to express these frustrations after her home was robbed:

> This letter is written to you by a law abiding citizen who feels she is discriminated against in favor of dope addicts and welfare cheats. I am a widow who lives alone, works every day, pays taxes and lives by the rules. I get very little from my taxes when I can no longer walk on the streets and when I am afraid in my own home. . . . Sorry this letter is not typed. My typewriter was stolen.[14]

This woman employed the language of activists challenging discrimination to articulate her belief that the state had betrayed the reciprocal arrangement between itself and the citizenry. The government failed in its responsibility to maintain her safety, even as she upheld her responsibilities of working, following the law, and paying taxes. She linked her growing insecurity directly to the state's increasing accountability to marginalized groups, specifically the "dope addicts" and "welfare cheats."

Many also believed that the liberals who advocated for attention to "root causes" lived in segregated, suburban communities apart from the problems facing urban spaces. One man wrote to Rockefeller about his father's murder. He explained that "on January 20, 1973, two black men attempted a robbery at my father's place of business in New York City. My father died because of gunshot wounds to the heart, lungs, and face." He then expressed his frustration that working-class people had been abandoned to deal with problems in the cities from which elites fled:

---

[12] Otto S. G. to Rockefeller, August 28, 1973, Reel A16, Rockefeller Gubernatorial Papers, 4th Administration, NYSA.

[13] Flamm, *Law and Order*, 47.

[14] Ann S. to Rockefeller, February 6, 1971, 4th Administration, Reel A16, Rockefeller Gubernatorial Papers, NYSA.

"Why? The impunity with which murder can be committed and excused for by guilt ridden liberals who, because of the privilege of their affluence in the socio-economic spectrum make concessions to the criminal element. . . . The social experiments they espouse for the majority rarely, if ever, affect their own family prerogatives of freedom of choice guaranteed by their socio-economic sanctuary." The author ascribed rising crime to efforts to understand its root causes: "Conversely, once murder has been committed, they bend backwards to find root causes thereby condoning the very act of violence itself. The cycle of excuse and permissiveness feeds on itself until there is no safe society for anyone and the vast majority walk with fear." He went on to posit a dichotomy where granting rights to a murderer restricts and devalues the victim:

> It must be reaffirmed that we value the life of the victim of violent crime more dearly than the imagined civil rights of the murderer, that the full extent of punishment that fits the crime is not cruel and inhuman but merciful to the memory of the victims and his family and is a proper deterrent to the commission of violence. . . .
>
> The legal structure unjustly sets aside the rights of that life and stupidly seeks redemption and social value in the salvation of the murderer, instead of bringing all power to bear to the prevention of such crimes.[15]

For this writer, recognizing the "imagined rights" or seeking the social reintegration of violent criminals denigrated the standing of their victims and endangered law-abiding people generally.

Constituents repeatedly insisted that they lived in a world turned upside down, where the wrong people had rights and the right people were punished. One police officer wrote, "It seems like the law abiding citizens have no rights whatsoever, except the responsibility and obligation 'to work in order to support and care for the parasites of society, the common and habitual criminal.'"[16] Another police officer articulated a similar point when he wrote Rockefeller that "it's really ironic that prisoners have a union and policemen don't. It seems that as a policeman you lose some of your privileges and as a prisoner you gain. . . . Let's treat a prisoner like a prisoner and not like a poor unfortunate who because of his social environment acted in a criminal manner."[17] According to this logic, being treated "like a prisoner" necessarily precluded rights or procedural protections and, most important, determining the "root causes" of criminal behavior.

---

[15] Joseph B. to Rockefeller, April 30, 1973, 4th Administration, Reel A16, Rockefeller Gubernatorial Papers, NYSA.

[16] Wayne R. to Rockefeller, January 18, 1973, 4th Administration, Reel A16, Rockefeller Gubernatorial Papers, NYSA.

[17] William A. to Rockefeller, February 18, 1972, 4th Administration, Reel A16, Rockefeller Gubernatorial Papers, NYSA.

Among the myriad factors to hold accountable for rising crime, these letters often faulted government permissiveness, systemic explanations of deviance, and the expansion of rights for marginalized populations, especially racial minorities. Instead of repudiating government intervention in society, this logic called for a new kind of state action, characterized by tough, retributive strategies that constricted targeted groups' rights. A state legislator captured this logic in a letter to Rockefeller explaining his support for a new death penalty law: "In the name of decent people who obey the laws of our country and contribute to our society, let's stop playing nurse-maid to these cut-throats and murderers and give them what they deserve."[18] In this sense, sanctifying and honoring law-abiding citizens required that criminal deviance be dramatically avenged.

The rhetoric in these letters often belittled and discredited welfare-state and therapeutic programs by linking them with attributes typically associated with bad mothering. Letter writers implied that paying attention to structural inequalities and policies of rehabilitation were "permissive" and "over-indulgent" and, therefore, had the pernicious effect of excusing and ultimately encouraging antisocial behavior. Again and again, citizens called for "tough" responses to these problems, such as the death penalty or a military presence in the streets. One man wrote Rockefeller, "We need the national guard in NYC. This educated moron [Mayor John] Lindsay is all but destroying us. I would rather see martial law or civil war than present conditions."[19]

While many would adopt "law-and-order" political rhetoric, some politicians did not see it as the only viable path to power. Some directly challenged it, as well as the more general conservative shift in the Republican Party. In a speech on crime, Mayor Lindsay questioned the practical value of these tactics:

> The rise of crime in the 1960s makes many Americans long for the comparative tranquility of the 1950s. . . . Now that feeling of security—if it really existed—is gone. . . . The security all of us have lost will not be restored by hard words. The rhetoric of a George Wallace or a Ronald Reagan or a Richard Nixon can exploit this nation's fear but it will not stop the rise of crime on your streets and mine.[20]

[18] Gerald Soloman, Assembly Member, to Governor Rockefeller, July 26, 1973, 4th Administration, Reel 60, Rockefeller Gubernatorial Papers, NYSA.

[19] Ron H. to Rockefeller, n.d., 4th Administration, Reel A16, Rockefeller Gubernatorial Papers, NYSA.

[20] John Lindsay, "Address by Mayor John Lindsay to Young Lawyers of Dade County Bar Association, Breakfast Meeting," February 15, 1972, Reel 14, Subject Files, Folder: Crime, John Lindsay Mayoral Papers, NYCMA.

As the Republican Party grew more accountable to a cadre of conservative activists, Lindsay switched his affiliation in 1971, registering as a Democrat before pursuing that party's presidential nomination in the 1972 race. Rockefeller took the opposite tack. At the 1964 Republican National Convention, Rockefeller had critiqued the party's growing conservative "extremism" and met with a hostile reception from Goldwater's supporters (the crowds booed him). Instead of moving away from the party as Lindsay did, Rockefeller appeared to be courting his party's more conservative factions by the early 1970s.

The governor's response to the events that transpired at Attica Correctional Facility, an upstate New York prison, aligned him with the law-and-order stalwarts in his party. On September 9, 1971, prisoners rebelled and took control of a section of the institution, holding forty-two guards hostage. In the standoff that ensued, the prisoners released a list of demands, including amnesty for the revolt and remedies for the poor conditions, racism, and abuse at the prison. Russell Oswald, a reputably liberal prison warden, attempted to negotiate with the prisoners through a group of intermediaries chosen by the inmates. Rockefeller, in one of the most controversial decisions of his administration, refused to visit the scene to take part in the negotiations and, on September 13, ordered state police to suppress the uprising. In the brutal attack that retook Attica, state agents killed ten hostages and twenty-nine inmates.[21]

Much of the country considered the violent repression at Attica a travesty and a state massacre. The governor's actions inspired fierce criticism from prisoners' allies, civil liberties advocates, and even much of the mainstream press. However, Rockefeller's actions simultaneously built his credibility among other groups, particularly the more conservative Republicans who were increasingly essential for his professional ambitions. Newspapers cited the handling of Attica as evidence of his growing viability with the Right as a 1976 presidential candidate.[22] For many, the state response at Attica represented the rejection of negotiations with and accommodations for marginalized groups demanding rights and representation. One constituent wrote:

> Frankly, many times your actions have been too liberal for my taste, but this time I was delighted and fully supported your actions, as did almost everyone I know in business here in NYC and elsewhere. It seems to most

[21]Tom Wicker, *A Time to Die* (New York: Quadrangle/New York Times Book Company, 1975); Persico, *The Imperial Rockefeller*, 140. See also Heather Thompson, *Blood in the Water: The Attica Uprising of 1971 and Its Legacy* (New York: Pantheon, 2016).

[22]Helen Dewar, "Southern GOP Chiefs Soften on Rockefeller," *Washington Post*, August 29, 1974, A4.

of us middle class Republicans that all the rights nowadays belong to the drug addicts, burglars, rapists and murderers, with little thought given to the rights of their victims. I know that you know this is the true viewpoint of the majority and the majority gratefully supported you in your actions on Attica. Hooray![23]

As another person explained in a letter celebrating Rockefeller's decision, "The liberal over compensation has proven that bowing to unreasonable demands does not appease the complainants, but increases the clamor for more outlandish demands."[24] This author joined with many others at the time who championed strong, decisive, and—if need be—violent action to establish the limits of acceptable political action and starkly demarcate who were viable civic participants. While Rockefeller received much criticism for the state's violent retaking of Attica, many among his key constituencies (as well as his political rivals on the national stage) either tacitly or explicitly endorsed resolute, muscular action against unruly and restive populations.

The Tough Solution

As Rockefeller confronted the diverse fallout from his tough posture at Attica, he faced the continuing political challenges arising from New York's drug-treatment infrastructure and ongoing popular concern about drug use and crime. And he seems to have concluded that he had less to gain and increasingly more to lose through further political investment in the therapeutic regime. At the very least, Rockefeller recognized the potential political utility of more aggressive measures as he circled back to the "Japanese model." Two months after sending his report, William Fine again found himself at a party with New York's governor. This time, California's governor, Ronald Reagan, was also in attendance. Reagan was intrigued by Fine's description of his trip to Japan and requested a copy of his recommendations. However, when Fine walked across the room and asked Rockefeller if he would mind sharing the report with Reagan, the governor refused. Joe Persico, the Rockefeller aide who recounted the story in a book, explained Rockefeller's thinking: "This thunderbolt was to be hurled by him."[25] Rockefeller's refusal makes even more sense in light of the fact that

[23] Patricia B. to Rockefeller, May 1, 1972, 4th Administration, Reel 18, Rockefeller Gubernatorial Papers, NYSA.
[24] Anglo C. to Rockefeller, September 14, 1972, 4th Administration, Reel 18, Rockefeller Gubernatorial Papers, NYSA.
[25] Persico, *The Imperial Rockefeller*, 144.

Reagan was widely perceived as one of Rockefeller's chief opponents for the 1976 Republican presidential nomination.[26]

The governor's aides did not hear about his new idea until they met at the end of 1972 to discuss the following year's legislative program and begin drafting the "State of the State" address. According to Persico, the staff was uneasy as Rockefeller announced his plan to sentence all drug sellers to life in prison without parole or any other way to reduce their sentence. Their reservations about the plan infuriated the governor and he demanded that they advance it despite their misgivings. Michael Whitman, Rockefeller's chief counsel, risked his relationship with the governor to express his distaste for the idea.[27] Howard Jones, head of the NACC and therefore technically a key figure in state narcotics policy, was never consulted about the plan. He spoke with Rockefeller about the proposal only after he got wind of it from other sources and requested a meeting. When they met, Jones outlined the many problems with the proposal: juries would hesitate to convict addicts for such long sentences; jails could not hold them all; the budget could not afford the mandate; judges would lose sentencing discretion; and, finally, the law offered no hope for rehabilitation or second chances. Rockefeller listened coldly and silently throughout the meeting. After Jones left, he dismissed the logistical and philosophical arguments against the plan. He simply said, "He's just worried about his people," referring to the fact that the NACC head was African American.[28] Rockefeller's staff advanced the law despite the concerns many shared. In retrospect, Persico claimed, "I never understood the psychological milieu in which the chain of errors in Vietnam was forged until I became involved in the Rockefeller drug proposal."[29]

The fact that Rockefeller rejected the counsel of drug-treatment experts was not merely incidental to the plan. The flagrant renunciation of modern, social scientific knowledge was a key part of its appeal. By advancing his own "commonsense" solution and brazenly rejecting established expertise, Rockefeller tapped into and helped solidify a deep frustration with modern bureaucracy and liberal state policy. He later told reporters that it was not law-enforcement experts who proposed a central feature of his plan—the $1,000 reward for information leading to the arrest of a drug pusher. The bounties were

[26] Marquis Childs, "Reagan vs. Rockefeller: The Race for '76 Is On," *Washington Post*, December 25, 1973, A23; William White, "Campaign Begins for '76 Nomination," *Chicago Tribune*, January 21, 1973, A6.
[27] Persico, *The Imperial Rockefeller*, 140–42.
[28] Ibid., 142.
[29] Ibid., 145.

the idea of his college- and high-school-aged stepsons.[30] He explained to another reporter that his conversations with Fine inspired him *to be his own drug expert*. He continued, "So out of this I got to feel maybe we've got to focus on who is being mugged, mobbed, robbed, murdered, raped, and so forth—so how to restore civil liberties to our citizens."[31] Here Rockefeller underscored policy's role in affirming or effacing different groups' standings within the polity and signaled that he had changed the professed aim of legislation from curing and reintegrating addicts to protecting society and the victims of crime. He advanced a zero-sum understanding of rights, where the restoration of "civil liberties to our citizens" was predicated upon renouncing state accountability for the care and well-being of people convicted of crime. While rehabilitation had always been a conflicted and partially hollow mission, the new proposal made it clear that the social and mental condition of addict-pushers would not be a barometer of policy success.

Rockefeller publicly unveiled his plan in the State of the State speech on January 3, 1973. Beginning his discussion of drugs by establishing the depth of public concern about the issue, he said, "Virtually every poll of public opinion concerns documents that the number one, growing concern of the American people is crime and drugs—coupled with an all-pervasive fear for the safety of their person and their property." He continued by declaring that citizens were right to demand firm action from the state to protect their interests: "The law abiding people of this State have the right to expect tougher and more effective action from their elected leaders to protect them from lawlessness and crime." He predicated this call for new, resolute action upon the failure of all previous state efforts to curb addiction, declaring:

> It is a time for brutal honesty regarding narcotics addiction. . . . In this state, we have allotted over $1 billion to every form of education against drugs and treatment of the addict through commitment, therapy, and rehabilitation. But let's be frank—let's tell it like it is: We have achieved very little permanent rehabilitation—and have found no cure.[32]

He explained that in spite of these massive state efforts, "addiction has kept growing." The dangers were escalating since "a rising percentage of our high school and college students, from every background and

[30] Kennedy, "Rocky Is 64, Going on 35," 17.

[31] M. A. Farber, "How Governor Decided on 'Tougher' Approach," *New York Times*, August 31, 1973, 16.

[32] "Annual Message 1973," January 3, 1973, Box 76, Folder 810, Series 10.4, p. 16, Nelson A. Rockefeller Gubernatorial Records, RAC.

economic level, have become involved, whether as victims or pushers."[33] By endeavoring to cleave participants in the drug economy into separate groups of victims and pushers, Rockefeller forwarded a particular narrative where drug sellers engendered the drug use of others. The governor positioned addicts as outsiders, without claims to citizenship protections, and as a military enemy solely responsible for the destruction of entire communities: "Whole neighborhoods have been effectively destroyed by addicts as by an invading army."[34] According to Rockefeller, the fate of the nation hung in the balance: "We face the risk of undermining our will as a people—and the ultimate destruction of our society as a whole."[35]

"This has to stop," he declared, pounding the lectern. "This is going to stop." He then outlined his intention to sentence dealers to life in prison without the option of probation, parole, or plea bargaining. Additionally, $1,000 bounties for information leading to a dealer's arrest would ensure that "for the first time ever, there would be a cash incentive to work for society instead of against it."[36] By proposing life sentences for all pushers, big and small, Rockefeller moved "pushers," the street-level vendors who were often poor, habitual users, from possible candidates for therapeutic intervention to candidates best managed through harsh punishment and social quarantine. He collapsed the distinction he had made in his early drug proposals between addict-pushers and non-addict-pushers and between the high-volume wholesalers and traffickers and lower-level retailers. Elevating any drug selling to the most severe sanction accommodated medicalized rhetoric about addiction by preserving a path for reintegrating addicts or "victims" who were not as directly implicated in the drug trade. It maintained the heaviest stigma on the most marginalized users who did not have alternative sources of money and had to sell drugs (or engage in other illegal "hustles") to subsidize their habit. In other words, targeting pushers further criminalized addiction for the poor while also holding them responsible for drug use more broadly.

Rockefeller narrated the state's therapeutic efforts in a way that positioned punitive measures as inevitable. "These are drastic measures," he acknowledged. "But I am thoroughly convinced, after trying everything else, that nothing less will do."[37] Despite this rhetorical emphasis on a dramatic repudiation of earlier strategies, the new proposal built on Rockefeller's earlier commitment to quarantine addicts

[33] Ibid.
[34] Ibid.
[35] Ibid.
[36] Ibid.
[37] Quoted in Massing, The Fix, 127.

through civil commitment centers. The governor rationalized his proposal by redeploying medical metaphors that had traditionally framed addict-pushers as victims of illness. He now persistently cast them as infectious agents spreading heroin addiction. "It is time to start protecting ourselves," he explained. "There is no question that young people who are sharing and selling relatively small amounts of heroin must be removed from society and isolated like carriers of a dangerous contagion."[38]

At a press conference, Rockefeller was explicit that tough punishment and rehabilitation were complementary—not conflicting—strategies. "This is not a substitute for the rehabilitation programs," he told the assembled reporters. "I would just like to remind you that I have put $31 million additional into the budget this year for rehabilitation programs. This brings the total of the state to $136 million for this coming fiscal year for rehabilitation." He insisted that the new law would amplify the state's efforts to manage drug use, explaining that "we're not talking about this as a means of abandoning rehabilitation, substituting for rehabilitation." He went on to explain that the new punishment would increase drug users' motivation to seek treatment: "We're just saying that rehabilitation, which a great many addicts have not been willing to take . . . , that this is not stopping the problem."[39] Therefore, the logic of the proposal was simultaneously predicated upon the failure of treatment to handle drug abuse and dependent upon the continued availability of treatment.

Although Rockefeller insisted that addict-pushers' reluctance to embrace treatment dictated his embrace of penal quarantine, his answers to some of the reporters' questions at the press conference revealed that there were other factors that complicated his treatment programs. He acknowledged that the limits of state capacity and resources constrained the ability to offer treatment on the scale he had promised in his campaigns. He explained that the state had not utilized its power to institutionalize addicts on a wide scale "simply because of the horrendous undertaking that would be involved."[40] He suggested that this calculation could shift if the federal government covered the cost of

[38]Neil Mehler, "Rockefeller Here, Urges War on Drugs," *Chicago Tribune*, February 10, 1973, 2.

[39]Statement by Nelson Rockefeller, transcript of news conference with Governor Nelson Rockefeller, Reverend Oberia Dempsey, Reverend Earl Moore, Mr. Glester Hinds, Dr. George McMurray, and Dr. William Baird, Albany, N.Y., January 22, 1973, Folder 1837, Box 89, Series 25 Press Office, p. 11, Nelson A. Rockefeller Gubernatorial Records, RAC.

[40]"Questions and Answers: Governor Nelson Rockefeller, Testimony at Joint Hearing Senate and Assembly Codes Committee," January 30, 1973, Folder 1837, Box 89, Series 25 Press Office, p. 38, Nelson A. Rockefeller Gubernatorial Records, RAC.

compulsory treatment, explaining that "this could be a very interesting, different and additional phase, but that is beyond our capacity as a state alone." The governor also admitted how profoundly political resistance limited efforts to build out the physical infrastructure for treatment. He reminded the audience of "the tremendous bitterness in one community after another to opening treatment centers anyplace in this state. Every community had rallies and meetings to oppose it, to fight it, to stop it."[41] He continued by identifying a public desire for a geographical fix to the drug problem, not necessarily a social solution: "This has been our reaction as a society. We don't want this [heroin] problem but don't bring these people anywhere near us for treatment."[42] In this sense, Rockefeller acknowledged that public reluctance to shoulder the costs of rehabilitation had impeded the project.

Rockefeller's rhetoric persistently positioned citizens and pushers as opposing categories. He explained to a gathering of the Empire State Chamber of Commerce that "we, the citizens, are imprisoned by the pushers. I want to put the pushers in prison so we can come out, ladies and gentlemen."[43] His new plan promised to erect the impermeable boundaries between addicts and the rest of society that so many desired. The proposal politically insulated Rockefeller on multiple fronts. First, legislators and pundits who remembered how O'Connor's opposition to Rockefeller's harsh drug proposal had undermined his 1966 gubernatorial campaign probably recognized the peril. Rockefeller's plan left opponents open to being branded as soft on crime and soft on drugs, both politically hazardous in the contemporary climate. Second, since the logic of the new, punitive proposal rested upon the notion that New York's treatment efforts were total failures, Rockefeller turned his earlier programs into evidence to support his new direction, thereby neutralizing them as political liabilities in upcoming campaigns.[44] Lastly, by presenting the range of debate as between (usually coerced) treatment and punishment, Rockefeller forced outside of this binary other proposals circulating at the time, such as heroin maintenance clinics (which New York mayor John Lindsay considered) or community-controlled policing and treatment.[45]

[41] Ibid., 41.

[42] Ibid., 42.

[43] Quoted in John Hamilton, "Hooked on Histrionics," *New York Times*, February 12, 1973, 27.

[44] Kennedy, "Rocky Is 64, Going on 35."

[45] Markham, "What's All This Talk of Heroin Maintenance?" SM6; McKissick, "NAACP—Crime in the Streets," 15.

Engaging Rockefeller's Plan

The response to the governor's proposal ranged from scorn to incredulity to fervent support, revealing deep divisions in the understandings of the causes of and appropriate responses to drug use. And it was these public understandings that the law also ultimately helped sculpt. Some legislators jokingly called it the "Attila the Hun Law," apparently referencing the law's invocation of a ruthless, barbaric masculinity.[46] Organizations such as the American Civil Liberties Union and Legal Aid immediately opposed the policy, but they were soon joined by less likely opponents, such as the Conservative Party. The *New York Times* editorialized against the program, calling the governor's speech "vengeful." They also challenged Rockefeller's claim that "society had no alternative," charging that he was abandoning treatment programs that showed results although they had never been fully implemented or funded.[47] The editorial pointed to an "irony in Governor Rockefeller's defeatism," particularly since the "state's pioneering program in methadone maintenance . . . has recently appeared to be making significant impact on the addiction problem."[48]

John Lindsay, who as New York City's mayor would face much of the logistical fallout from the policy, was another powerful opponent. He called it "impractical, unworkable and vindictive" and questioned the motivation for the proposal:[49]

> We all know the urge to lash out, to take some drastic step, which will yield a final answer to this corrosive evil. . . . We all know how empty it is to promise victory over crime by an emotional call to lock the criminals up and throw away the key. That is not a battle plan. It is merely a deceptive gesture, offering nothing beyond momentary satisfaction and inevitable disillusionment.[50]

Other commentators charged Rockefeller with irresponsible politicking and throwing a tantrum.[51] Pointing to the governor's presidential ambitions, many dismissed the entire announcement as a ploy to rework his liberal image and appeal to the increasingly powerful right wing

[46] Epstein, *Agency of Fear*, 43.

[47] "Hard Line in Albany," *New York Times*, January 4, 1973, 36.

[48] Ibid.

[49] Max Seigel, "Lindsay Assails Governor's Plan to Combat Drugs," *New York Times*, January 10, 1973, 1.

[50] "Statement by Mayor John V. Lindsay," January 9, 1973, Box 79, Folder 845, Series 10.4, Nelson A. Rockefeller Gubernatorial Records, RAC.

[51] "Rockefeller & Kleindienst: Life and/or Death," *Washington Post*, January 9, 1973, A16.

of the Republican Party that had thwarted his previous efforts at the nomination.[52]

Drug users and sellers were almost entirely absent from the public deliberations about the bill, although some people spoke on their behalf or challenged the wisdom of permanently segregating them in prison. In one rare instance where users were interviewed, an "ex-junkie" quoted by the *New York Times* challenged the governor's assertion that the threat of life in prison would deter drug use: "The trouble with the deterrent theory is that politicians think that there was a logical process to my behavior . . . that I was thinking rationally about sentences, prisons, and deterrence while I was pursuing a white powder to inject into my body and which would strip me of any decency of purpose."[53] In a few limited forums, family members spoke against abandoning the hope of their loved ones' rehabilitation.[54] The father of one heroin user insisted that there were some former addicts who were "probably doing more to help their fellow man than the average citizen."[55]

Paul Good, a prominent television and print journalist, admitted in an op-ed that his son was a recovering heroin addict. He explained that he understood the governor's desire for retribution against pushers since he had often fantasized about murdering his son's dealer. But he realized the futility of holding drug sellers responsible for his son's actions:

> I put the idea aside because I knew that virtually all of my son's suppliers were addicts like he, hustling money in any way to insure their fix. . . . My son did the same thing at times, buying bags cheap in Harlem and the South Bronx, and selling them at a profit in our Connecticut suburb, the profits going back into his arm.

Acknowledging his own son's culpability, Good also challenged the stark dichotomy between sympathetic addicts and malicious suppliers. He went on to suggest that Rockefeller had intended to punish and internally exile sellers as an answer to growing fears about drug use among young whites. "Where was Rockefeller when addiction began gaining a foothold as a basically black problem?" he asked. "He was nowhere to be heard."[56] (In testimony before a joint legislative committee, Rockefeller responded directly to Paul Good's column, assuring him that he considered Good's son a dangerous pusher who should also face the new harsh punishments.)

[52]See, for example, White, "Campaign Begins for '76 Nomination."

[53]David Rothenberg, "The Governor's Deterrent Theory," *New York Times*, March 2, 1973.

[54]Lawrence Vangelder, "Drug Users' Relatives Call Governor's Plan Too Hard on Youths," *New York Times*, January 14, 1973.

[55]Ibid.

[56]Paul Good, "My Son—Perhaps Yours," *New York Times*, January 29, 1973, 29.

Debate over the drug proposal became a site of contestation over who genuinely represented the "African American community." The reality was complicated as African American opinion was obviously not uniform and varied by gender, age, and class position, among others factors. In its efforts to gauge support for the drug legislation among African Americans, the press found mixed reactions. Some African Americans claimed that the policies, while ostensibly racially neutral, were part of ongoing sabotage and oppression of their communities. One man in a high administrative state post said that Rockefeller "is out of his mind—we see him now for what he is. He's not dealing with social dynamics. When he starts talking about narcotics, he's talking about the minority population." An African culture educator told a reporter that the governor was looking to "round up young black kids, young black boys, and put them in concentration camps."[57]

While many believed the law explicitly targeted black people, others welcomed aggressive action on a problem they felt had been too long ignored by law enforcement in their communities.[58] Some hoped that a crackdown would mitigate the harms caused by the drug trade. One Harlem social worker told the *New York Times* that "such a measure is long overdue and I support it 100 percent."[59] Some of the African American leaders who had been demanding harsher sentencing for years now supported the governor's effort to secure the legislation's passage. The Rockefeller administration organized a news conference where the governor presented five community leaders from Harlem who supported his bill.[60] Among them was Reverend Oberia Dempsey, the pastor who had called for organized vigilante resistance to drug peddlers in the mid-1960s and would now travel with the governor to promote the bill. Dempsey grounded his support for the governor's proposal in a causal narrative about how "the nation's number one state, New York, became a state of fear for more than 18 million law abiding citizens." He explained that "dope pushers made this so. . . . [They] have made jungles out of our schools, they have made jungles out of our low-income and middle-income housing projects. The hard drug pushers have made jungles out

[57] Gerald Fraser, "Harlem Response Mixed," *New York Times*, January 5, 1973, 1.

[58] See, for example, Bigart, "Middle-Class Leaders in Harlem Ask Crackdown on Crime," 25; "Harlem Vigilantes Move on 'Pushers,'"; and "Addicts' Victims Turn Vigilante," 1.

[59] Fraser, "Harlem Response Mixed."

[60] Francis Clines, "Harlem Leaders Back Life Terms for Drug Sale," *New York Times*, January 23, 1973, 43. For discussions of African American support for Rockefeller's proposal with different emphases and interpretations, see Jessica Neptune, "Harshest in the Nation: The Rockefeller Drug Laws and the Widening Embrace of Punitive Politics," *Social History of Alcohol and Drugs* 26, no. 2 (Summer 2012): 170–91 and Michael Fortner, "The Carceral State and the Crucible of Black Politics: An Urban History of the Rockefeller Drug Laws," *Studies in American Political Development* 27 (2013): 14–35.

of our world-famous Times Square and Greenwich Village."[61] When reporters asked Dempsey if he disagreed with the governor's decision to punish addict-pushers and non-addict-pushers in the same way, Dempsey responded that "years ago I would have," but explained that his exasperation with social conditions had grown to the point that he ceased drawing a distinction.[62]

While Rockefeller claimed he consulted African American community leaders and they supported him, some African Americans challenged this claim. One state senator dismissed the endorsements from Harlem leaders: "They were just palace pets, the usual ones who endorse him. The community can't be fooled by that."[63] In early February, two African American state legislators presided over a community meeting where most participants opposed the proposed reforms. Participants disputed Rockefeller's claims to having consulted community leaders. "He didn't confer with me," declared Senator Von Luther. He added: "When he rounded up some ministers and other leaders to support him, he created a stacked deck; many of those people have gotten money from the Governor to run the very programs that have failed to solve the problem."[64] During the debate on the Assembly floor in May, Representative Woodrow Lewis criticized the governor's use of Harlem ministers, including Reverend Dempsey, "as puppets and instruments to engender and be partners in the creation of hysteria."[65] Although many black and Puerto Rican legislators agreed about the need to get drug sellers off the streets, there was not consensus on the best approach. Members acknowledged considerable frustration on the issue from their constituents, but only a minority openly endorsed the plan. The *New York Times* reported that of the eighteen black and Puerto Rican legislators, "the positions range from endorsement by two legislators, at least partial acceptance by many, guarded neutrality by a few and flat denunciation by six members."[66] Senator Vander Beatty

[61] Statement by Reverend Dempsey, transcript of news conference with Governor Nelson Rockefeller, Reverend Oberia Dempsey, Reverend Earl Moore, Mr. Glester Hinds, Dr. George McMurray, and Dr. William Baird, Albany, N.Y., January 22, 1973, Folder 1837, Box 89, Series 25 Press Office, p. 1, Nelson A. Rockefeller Gubernatorial Records, RAC.

[62] Ibid., 12.

[63] Francis Clines, "Governor's Drug Bill Splits Black and Puerto Rican Legislators," *New York Times*, March 4, 1973, 38.

[64] Robert Thomas, "New Drug Laws Scored in Harlem; Residents Voice Opposition to Governor's Proposals," *New York Times*, February 3, 1973, 30.

[65] Statement by Assemblyman Woodrow Lewis, "Drug Law Transcripts: Transcript of Debate on Drug Bills," May 3, 1973, New York State Assembly Public Information Office (Albany, N.Y.), 152.

[66] Clines, "Governor's Drug Bill Splits Black and Puerto Rican Legislators," 38.

supported Rockefeller's proposal and endorsed the death penalty for big-time pushers.[67]

There were voices outside legislative circles that urged African Americans to be wary of supporting (and thus facilitating) the state's constriction of drug sellers' rights. In a column published in *New York Amsterdam News*, Leroy D. Clark wrote, "I would like to give some warnings—which shouldn't even be necessary—warnings against us—you and I—making the addict and even the addict pusher the 'new nigger' and the 'new spick'—for it can't be done without your help." He cautioned that fear and demonization of the drug seller enabled a more general expansion of state power and that "the addict has been used as the tool and the cover" for a series of "recent incremental moves to constrict civil liberties and to enhance the general potential for governmental control and repressive surveillance." Indeed, Clark saw "the problem of addiction being used by cynical, covert nigger baiting politicians to create a plethora of repressive police techniques which will quickly be used first against any militant efforts in our communities, and, secondly, against us, all of us, whenever it suits the 'man's' purpose." Clark suggested that opponents of Rockefeller's proposal recognized the support for punitive responses among other African Americans. "I know that I ask for a restraint," Clark explained, "which our communities now do not feel—because they feel the community is being immobilized by the addict." He prophetically warned that new police powers—such as "no knock" entries and "stop and frisk" powers—which were justified as crucial weapons in the anti-narcotic campaigns might ultimately be deployed wantonly throughout entire African American and Latino communities, not just against addicts: "I only hope that we don't get invited into a hall for the lynching of the addict—and look up to find the doors locked when the ceremony is over."[68]

Although there was a range of opinions about Rockefeller's plan, it quickly became clear that, similar to his decision to authorize the brutal retaking of Attica, the governor had mobilized a frustrated segment of society and directed its antagonism toward the most marginalized groups. His drug proposal became a national story, garnering valuable publicity for his anticipated presidential run. By early February, Gallup public opinion polls showed that 67 percent of the country supported his plan. Support was lowest among "nonwhites" but still substantial: 59 percent supported putting pushers away for life.[69] The governor's

---

[67] Plummer, "Albany Notes," 20.

[68] Leroy D. Clark, "What Does Civil Liberties Mean in Drug Context?" *New York Amsterdam News*, January 13, 1973, A5.

[69] "Public Supports Drug-Pusher Law," *New York Times*, February 11, 1973, 46.

mail was even more enthusiastically behind the plan; according to early reports, it ran 20–1 in his favor.[70] By the end of 1973, Rockefeller had received 3,042 letters about his proposal; 2,353 of them, or 77 percent, supported it.[71]

Support came from all over the country. A woman from Florida wrote to express her enthusiasm for the drug plan: "Bravo! For the first time since 1964, I have the feeling that society is on my side in the struggle to raise my children to be decent, honorable, responsible citizens."[72] To this woman, the harsh punishment of pushers symbolized the recapture of the state and society from other antagonistic interests. A number of letters commented on the "courage" and "guts" it took for Rockefeller to get tough and stand up to the established medical and legal authorities.[73] Many people were moved to contact Rockefeller after watching him and Reverend Dempsey debate the proposal with a doctor on Barbara Walters's television show. One woman wrote, "I wanted to stand up and applaud after you spoke. I am sick to death of hearing these doctors and liberal lawyers be 'so holier than thou.'"[74] This proposal therefore both validated people's perception of pushers as irredeemable and galvanized hostility toward liberals and specialists' authority.

Some politicians also used the new drug plan to evidence the folly of pursuing idealistic ends through social policy. The deputy Republican majority leader in the Senate connected his support of Rockefeller's proposal to the larger project of restoring faith in the justice system:

> Seldom in my lifetime have so many citizens expressed such failing confidence in our system of justice than they do today. . . . Ironically, too often, we are thwarted by the very instruments created by our own hand. We are captives of both our compassion and our idealism.[75]

Characterizing therapeutic programs as the product of misplaced compassion helped undermine drug-treatment and social welfare programs

[70] Kennedy, "Rocky Is 64, Going on 35," 16.

[71] Weekly Mail Reports, 4th Administration, Reel 1, Rockefeller Gubernatorial Papers, NYSA.

[72] Beatrice B. to Rockefeller, September 7, 1973, 4th Administration, Reel 61, Rockefeller Gubernatorial Papers, NYSA. It is impossible to know why this author cited 1964 as a turning point, but 1964 was the year the Civil Rights Act passed and President Johnson defeated Barry Goldwater in the presidential election.

[73] See, for example, Mrs. E. to Rockefeller, September 21, 1973, 4th Administration, Reel 61, Rockefeller Gubernatorial Papers, NYSA.

[74] Genevieve W. to Rockefeller, March 20, 1973, 4th Administration, Reel 16, Rockefeller Gubernatorial Papers, NYSA.

[75] William Conklin to Rockefeller, February 20, 1973, Box 79, Folder 846, Series 10.4, Nelson A. Rockefeller Gubernatorial Records, RAC.

more broadly. By asserting that the programs faced inevitable failure because they were hopelessly idealistic, this and similar charges directed attention away from a host of other political vulnerabilities and institutional and fiscal limitations that circumscribed the programs' operations. Proponents of the drug laws promised governance shorn of naïve sentimentality; they presented civic degradation as the only resolute, firm, and realistic alternative strategy.

A letter to the editor in the *New York Times* from a doctor at SUNY's Community Medicine Department illustrated the ways that the medicalized rhetoric about a drug epidemic was mobilized for this expansion of penal sanctions.

> Governor Rockefeller's new proposals for dealing with the drug problem by attacking sellers are strongly supported by epidemiological theory. . . . Thus heroin addiction is similar in many ways to diseases such as malaria with its identifiable vector, the mosquito. Malaria has been controlled in many parts of the world, not by treating sick individuals and not by warning people against swamps, but by eliminating swamps and mosquitoes. Governor Rockefeller, having previously tried treatment (including methadone maintenance) and education programs for heroin addiction and seen them fail to control its spread, has opted for a public health approach which . . . has some real chance of success.[76]

By equating pushers with mosquitoes, the letter writer positioned the wholesale *elimination* of drug sellers as a sound—even scientific—solution. He characterized this criminalization strategy as being fundamentally grounded in a public health approach to drug use.

While many lined up in support of the plan, the governor also encountered serious opposition from within the very institution he was designating to grapple with the drug pushers. In their series of meetings across the state soliciting feedback, legislators repeatedly confronted law enforcement officials critical of the proposal, particularly its logistical implications and its limitations on their discretion. Commentators predicted catastrophic consequences for the state's budget and prison and court systems.[77] Judges expressed reservations about the proposed limitations to their discretion and the elimination of plea bargaining, which they claimed prevented trial backlogs and induced low-level dealers to

---

[76] Steven Jonas, letter to the editor, *New York Times*, January 12, 1973, 32.

[77] See William Raspberry, "Rockefeller's Stand on Drugs: Would It Do Any Good?" *Washington Post*, January 10, 1973, A23; Francis Clines, "Legislators See Problems in Stiff Drug-Crime Laws," *New York Times*, January 10, 1973, 49; Lesley Oelsner, "2 Top Judges See Court Paralysis under Drug Plan," *New York Times*, January 6, 1973, 1; Tom Wicker, "The Fallacy of 'Getting Tough,'" *New York Times*, February 20, 1973, 33; and Michael Kaufman, "Reaction Mixed on Drug Penalty," *New York Times*, January 8, 1973, 19.

turn against the larger operators in the business.[78] The District Attorney's Association, the Judicial Conference, and the New York City police commissioner all opposed the proposal. The police commissioner flew to Albany to personally lobby against the bill during the final debates.[79]

Aware that the law did not have the votes to pass the State Assembly, Rockefeller had to decide between pursuing a coalition with conservative opponents worried about the limits to prosecutorial discretion or reaching across the aisle to negotiate with Democrats. The governor chose to allow Republicans to maintain ownership of the legislation and compromise with the conservatives and criminal justice officials worried about jail overcrowding and court backlogs.[80] He agreed to remove hashish from the drugs covered by the law and to allow for limited plea bargaining and parole.

Under the new version, drug offenders would receive a sentence range dictated by the type and quantity of drug they sold. All drug sale offenses were considered class A felonies and carried a maximum sentence of life in prison. There were three subcategories within the A category, each with different mandatory minimum terms. For example, an A-1 felony constituted the sale of at least one ounce of any narcotic or the possession of two or more ounces. This conviction carried a mandatory minimum sentence of fifteen years to life in prison, meaning that the person would not be eligible for parole until he or she served at least fifteen years. After serving their minimum sentence, prisoners still faced parole boards that could set release dates at any time between the completion of the minimum sentence and the maximum, life in prison. Once released, people convicted of class A felonies could never be removed from parole; they were to be monitored by state agents until their death.[81] The only way to avoid the prison time and be placed directly on parole was to become an informant for the authorities.[82] In practice, this provision rarely applied to street-level sellers since they seldom had significant intelligence on higher-level drug operations. Since the law prohibited plea bargaining out of class A, people arrested with small amounts of drugs and charged with the A-3 felony could not plead down to a lower class to evade lifetime

[78]Oelsner, "2 Top Judges See Court Paralysis under Drug Plan."

[79]Plummer, "Albany Notes," B10.

[80]Francis X. Clines, "G.O.P. in Assembly Delays Drug Bill," *New York Times*, May 1, 1973, 86; Francis X. Clines, "Vote on Drug Bill Is Again Delayed," *New York Times*, May 2, 1973, 23; Francis X. Clines, "Drug Bill Pressed by G.O.P. Leaders," *New York Times*, May 3, 1973, 39.

[81]M. A. Farber, "Opinion Remains Divided over Effect of State's New Drug Law," *New York Times*, August 31, 1973, 16.

[82]William E. Farrell, "Governor's Bill on Drug Traffic Voted by Senate," *New York Times*, April 28, 1973, 69; William E. Farrell, "Revised Narcotics Measure Is Voted 80–65 in Assembly," *New York Times*, May 4, 1973, 77.

parole or the possibility of life in prison. They had to be sentenced with at least one year to life.

As an effort to secure support from the Republicans and members of the Conservative Party, the governor agreed to simultaneously advance the Second Felony Offender Act. The act dramatically constrained judicial discretion by subjecting all second felony offenders to new mandatory minimum prison sentences. This statute received less attention than the drug laws but ultimately had an equally, if not more, significant effect on expanding New York's prison population.[83] With these compromises and heavy lobbying by the governor, the legislation came before the state lawmakers five months after Rockefeller proposed the idea.[84]

The Republican-controlled Senate passed Rockefeller's bill on April 27, 1973, with 41 votes in favor and 14 opposed.[85] Nine Democrats crossed the aisle to endorse the bill, among them Senator Vander Beatty—the only black legislator to vote for the bill in either house.[86] The bill then moved to the State Assembly, where the floor debate on May 3 lasted seven hours.[87] Critics of the law attempted to challenge both the inherent virtue of tough strategies and the governor's rationale for abandoning an emphasis on treatment. Many insisted that tough action was not the only possible response to exasperation with the drug problem and challenged the governor's narratives about the failure of treatment programs. Others pointed out that Rockefeller's rhetoric obscured how past experiments with harsh sentencing, such as the federal mandatory minimums enacted in the 1950s, had failed to stem the rising tide of drug use only a decade earlier. Assemblyman Richard Gottfried challenged the premise of treatment's failure upon which the drug laws were built, telling the chamber that "in announcing his new proposal in January, the Governor stated, and other members here have stated, that we have tried everything in the drug field, and it has all failed." He explained that "it would be much more accurate to say that in the drug field we have tried almost nothing."[88] Reminding the assembled lawmakers that the state

[83] Pamala Griset, *Determinate Sentencing: The Promise and the Reality of Retributive Justice* (Albany: State University of New York Press, 1991), 66–67. See also William E. Farrell, "Mandatory Sentence Proposed for 2d-Felony Drug Offenses: Rockefeller Plan Cited Example Given One-Third Provided," *New York Times*, April 5, 1973, 49.

[84] Alan Chartock, "Narcotics Addiction: The Politics of Frustration," in *Governing New York: The Rockefeller Years*, ed. Robert Connery and Gerald Benjamin (New York: Academy of Political Science, 1974), 247.

[85] Farrell, "Governor's Bill on Drug Traffic Voted by Senate," 1.

[86] Plummer, "Albany Notes," B10.

[87] Farrell, "Revised Narcotics Measure Is Voted 80–65 in Assembly," 77.

[88] Statement of Assemblyman [Richard] Gottfried, "Transcript of Debate on Drug Bills," May 3, 1973, obtained from the New York State Assembly Public Information Office (Albany, N.Y.), 131.

and federal governments had long used lengthy mandatory penalties for drug users and sellers, Gottfried continued:

> There is not any evidence anywhere to suggest that concept of deterrent has the slightest effect in the drug field, and I think our experiences [have] proven that time and time again. Yet, now in New York State, because we say we have got to do something, we are trying the same thing that we have tried time and time again across this county with no success.[89]

The legislator therefore flipped the governor's narrative, insisting that criminalization was actually the tried and failed drug policy. Six of the eleven black legislators in the Assembly spoke against the law during the debates. Representative Woodrow Lewis was on the verge of tears at times, insisting during his statement that "efforts in matters of treatment had not been exhausted."[90]

Other legislators also charged that the new policy was more political theater than a genuine effort to deter drug sellers. In his speech, Assemblyman John LaFalce sarcastically suggested that legislators were simply pursuing politically rewarding postures: "Let's not solve the drug problem. Let's make the people think they are solving the drug problem."[91] He warned that the vote would be used as a weapon in upcoming contests: "Now, I know, I know that in the fall of 1974 a great campaign issue is going to be made of the votes that we take on this bill . . . and I know a great attempt will be made to cast every single legislator who votes against the Governor's bill as soft on drugs."[92] During the floor debates, other legislators asked lawmakers to acknowledge the political capital Rockefeller stood to amass upon enacting these policies. Assemblyman Brian Sharoff explained:

> Well, Gentlemen, it just seems to me that none of us are leveling with anybody here. This drug bill, if it is anything, is the opening wedge in Governor Rockefeller's 1974 gubernatorial race, nothing more and nothing less. Today we are making Governor Rockefeller's television commercials for him. We are helping the ad agency that he gets put the language at the bottom of the screen to create the impression in the minds of millions of New Yorkers that somehow the streets will be safer, and homes will be safer, and the drug problem will be solved.[93]

The critiques, however, did not halt the legislation's passage. Despite these charges and questions about the bill's feasibility from both sides

[89] Ibid, 133.
[90] Plummer, "Albany Notes," B10.
[91] Statement of Assemblyman John LaFalce, "Transcript of Debate on Drug Bills," 84.
[92] Ibid., 86.
[93] Statement by Assemblyman [Brian] Sharoff, "Transcript of Debate on Drug Bills," 145.

of the aisle, the State Assembly passed the bill on May 3. The final count was 80 to 65, with only one Republican voting against the measure.[94] At the bill signing, Rockefeller explained that the state finally had the "tools to protect law abiding citizens from the drug pushers" and commended lawmakers for their courage in passing the bill:

> This is the toughest anti-drug program in the nation. It ignited a heated debate and generated enormous pressures on our lawmakers. I applaud the courage of the majority leaders and members of the state legislature who stood firm against this strange alliance of established interests, political opportunists and misguided soft-liners who joined forces and tried unsuccessfully to stop this program.[95]

Rockefeller felt that that the law had provided an opportunity for leaders to show their manly resolve in confronting the drug problem.

The Logic and Practice of Quarantine

To deal with implementation of the law, the governor signed legislation that dedicated new funds to prepare the treatment facilities for a surge of addicts seeking help. It also authorized the creation of new judgeships and courts to handle the increased volume of drug crime trials.[96] The state sponsored a $500,000 public information campaign warning of the harsh new rules and established hotlines to access treatment and report drug dealers (and possibly qualify for the $1,000 bounty).[97] In the weeks during which the hotline was aggressively promoted, 100 callers a day reported mostly low-level drug dealing in their areas.[98] New York City's Addiction Services Agency sponsored a "3 Day Drug Treatment Recruitment Marathon," sending six vans around to high

[94]Farrell, "Revised Narcotics Measure Is Voted 80–65 in Assembly," 77.

[95]"Bill Signing Ceremony, Narcotics Bills," May 8, 1973, Folder 265, Box 14, Series 12.3, Nelson A. Rockefeller, Vice Presidential, RAC.

[96]At the same time, lawmakers changed the name of NACC to the Drug Abuse Control Commission (DACC) and expanded the agency's authority to drugs beyond narcotics. The DACC was empowered to certify people for dependence on drugs such as barbiturates, amphetamines, and hallucinogens. "The Acquisition and Construction of Drug Abuse Treatment Facilities," 19–23. On the thirty-one new Supreme Court judges in New York City, see Association of the Bar of the City of New York and the Drug Abuse Council, "The Nation's Toughest Drug Law: Evaluating the New York Experience, Final Report of the Joint Committee on New York Drug Law Evaluation" (Washington, D.C.: Drug Abuse Council, 1977), 103–8, 73–79.

[97]Chartock, "Narcotics Addiction," 246.

[98]M. A. Farber, "Officials Say Narcotics 'Hot Line Is Working,'" *New York Times*, October 14, 1973, 34.

drug use areas to round up addicts for rehabilitation before the law went into effect.[99] These campaigns reveal yet again the complicated relationship between treatment and punishment. The call to draconian sentencing was premised on rehabilitation's failure while at the same time rationalized through the ongoing availability of drug treatment and its purported ability to motivate drug users into welfare programs. Those who failed to avail themselves of treatment were marked as defiant and incorrigible and therefore deserving of more profound limitations on their rights and freedoms.

The publicity campaign's tagline was "Don't get caught holding the bag." Its half-page advertisement in the *New York Times* targeted not just drug users but all citizens, running under big black letters that read: "How the New Drug Laws Affect You." Under the heading "Why did the State make this law in the first place?" officials listed the legislature's motivations:

> To make it tough for the addicts, the junkies, the pushers to infect others. And to give them a chance to end their addiction. To stop the mugging and the crime which is a tragic by-product of drug abuse. To make the streets safe for you and your family.

These announcements declared that treatment was available for anyone finally convinced that the state was serious about cracking down on drugs. But the ads also announced the dedicated funds for new judges and prison space and warned that, like a stern parent, "the State Means Business."[100] While these advertisements may have informed some drug users of the increasing risks of their habit, they were also declarations to wider audiences of the state's new stance toward drugs and invigorated commitment to acting as guarantor of public safety.

When the new drug laws went into effect on September 1, 1973, they were probably a bigger spectacle in the media and the political realm than at the street level. If people living in high-crime areas assumed the new policy implied stepped-up enforcement or more aggressive arrests, they were disappointed. Police did not undertake high-profile raids and generally kept arrest levels steady. Addicts did not seek treatment in dramatically higher numbers, nor did they flee to other states as many had predicted. A few reporters heard that dealers stayed inside or stuck to regular customers for a period of weeks. Later reports by law enforcement

[99] Press release from Health Services Administration, "Addiction Service Agency Sponsors Pre–September 1 Three-Day Drug Treatment-Recruitment Marathon," August 29, 1973, Reel 2, Subject Files, Folder: Addiction Services, John Lindsay Mayoral Papers, NYCMA.

[100] New York State Drug Abuse Program, "How the New Drug Laws Affect You," advertisement in *New York Times*, August 24, 1973, 15.

and treatment officials estimated that the law restrained the heroin trade for two to four months.[101] Many reported higher drug prices. One profound effect on the ground was that sellers began to rely increasingly on minors as drug runners because they were not sentenced as harshly as adults. Overall, users continued to buy and sell drugs to maintain their habit without dramatic interruption.[102]

Barely three months after the statute became law, Nelson Rockefeller resigned as governor, claiming he wanted to devote more time to his National Commission on the Critical Choices for America.[103] Most assumed that the real reason he resigned was to get a jump start on his presidential campaign in 1976 and avoid a potentially bruising gubernatorial election. Though many hoped that Rockefeller's early departure would give his lieutenant, Malcolm Wilson, a leg up in the gubernatorial election of 1974, Democrat Hugh Carey defeated Governor Wilson in a post-Watergate election that went badly for Republicans nationwide.

After failing to stop Rockefeller's policy in the legislature, opponents turned to state and federal courts in their efforts to derail the law. Legal Aid groups challenged some of the early sentences on the grounds that the law was "disproportionately severe" and therefore unconstitutional. The ensuing legal battles revealed in stark terms that the policy's logic and legality rested on holding sellers responsible for the entire "drug epidemic." In 1973, Imogene Broadie, a twenty-four-year-old woman, received the mandatory indeterminate life sentence for selling $1,300 worth of cocaine. She challenged the sentence and the entire drug law in state court, claiming they were unduly harsh. Both appeals courts rejected her plea, acknowledging that the laws were severe but privileging the state's need to address the urgent drug situation. The highest state court, the Court of Appeals, based its decision on the perceived failure of other strategies to manage the problem: "Facing a high recidivism rate in drug related crimes and an inadequate response to less severe punishment, the Legislature could reasonably shift the emphasis from rehabilitation to isolation and deterrence."[104] The court explicitly echoed Rockefeller's assumptions about drug use: pushers were the

[101] Association of the Bar of the City of New York and the Drug Abuse Council, "The Nation's Toughest Drug Law," 46.

[102] M. A. Farber, "Users, Pushers Haven't Noticed It So Far," *New York Times*, December 2, 1973, 4; M. A. Farber, "Wilson Is 'Disappointed' Addicts Don't Seek Help," *New York Times*, January 11, 1974, 35; M. A. Farber, "Drug Flow Noted Despite New Laws," *New York Times*, June 25, 1974, 1; Lena Williams, "Thousands of Harlem Drug Runners, 9 to 16, Find the Rewards Are High, the Risks Low," *New York Times*, April 21, 1977, 53.

[103] Stephen Isaacs, "Rocky Is Due to Quit Today; 1976 Bid Seen," *Washington Post*, December 11, 1973, A2.

[104] People v. Broadie, 37 N.Y.2d 100 (1976), 113.

force driving the drug epidemic and were therefore responsible for all of its consequences:

> The drug seller, at every level of distribution, is at the root of the pervasive cycle of destructive drug abuse. . . . The legislature could reasonably have found that drug trafficking is a generator of collateral crime, even violent crime. And violent crime is not, of course, the only destroyer of men and the social fabric. Drug addiction degrades and impoverishes those whom it enslaves. The debilitation of men, as well as the disruption of their families, the *Legislature could also lay at the door of the drug traffickers* [emphasis added].[105]

The court claimed that the lengthy sentences, which might at first seem grossly disproportionate, appeared rational once drug sellers were defined as the malignant force behind the social problems associated with drugs.

In the case of *Carmona v. Ward*, a U.S. District Court ruled the new drug laws unconstitutional because they were out of proportion to the severity of the crime. Martha Carmona, a forty-one-year-old Puerto Rican woman, sold drugs on consignment and pled guilty to one count of possessing more than an ounce of cocaine in her apartment.[106] After a plea reduction, she was sentenced to six years to life. Her codefendant, Roberta Fowler, a twenty-three-year-old mother of two, was sentenced to four years to life for selling $20 of cocaine to an undercover agent. Since anyone convicted of a drug felony faced the possibility of life in prison regardless of the degree of involvement in the drug trade, the lower court saw little proportionality in the law and ruled it unconstitutional. The U.S. Court of Appeals disagreed and reversed the decision in 1978, claiming that the legislature, not the courts, should determine what punishment was appropriate for a crime. Thwarted at the appellate level, Carmona and Fowler asked the Supreme Court to consider their case.

Although the highest court denied their petition, Justices Thurgood Marshall and Lewis Powell took the unusual step of issuing a dissenting opinion that argued why the Court should have heard the case. Justice Marshall wrote that the punishments were disproportionate and unfairly held Carmona and Fowler responsible for the entire consequences of the drug trade: "In sum, by focusing on the corrosive social impact of drug trafficking in general, rather than on petitioners' actual—and clearly marginal—involvement in that enterprise, the Court of Appeals substantially overstated the gravity of the instant charges."[107] The justice

---

[105] Ibid.

[106] Carmona pled to a lesser charge. She was actually arrested for selling almost eight ounces and three ounces of cocaine to an undercover agent on separate occasions in 1974.

[107] Carmona v. Ward, 439 U.S. 1091 (1979), 61.

also attacked the notion that the particular severity of New York's drug problem shielded extreme, draconian policy from constitutional challenge: "However serious its narcotics problem, New York cannot constitutionally [punish] those with peripheral involvement in drug trafficking as if they were responsible for the problem in its entirety."[108] Despite these dissents, the courts generally affirmed the logic animating the Rockefeller Drug Laws, holding sellers accountable for the social harms of drug use and the drug trade.

Not surprisingly, people charged with drug crimes had a very different perspective on the laws. Many prisoners wrote to Governor Carey after he signaled his intent to moderate the laws upon entering office in 1975. While some letter writers clearly hoped to inspire direct intervention in their individual cases, others simply wanted to share their view. Many felt the drug laws were profoundly unfair, both in conception and application, and often blended their criticisms of the policies with descriptions of how prison had failed to address their struggles. One man explained:

> I am married and have 3 children and I miss them very much. I write this letter to ask you to please amend this drug law, this is the first time I have ever been in trouble and I feel I was sentenced very harshly just because I was a sick man and didn't realize it until it was too late. . . . This law is ridiculous. I agree that a man who is trying to get rich by selling drugs should be put in prison for a long time, but that should be left up to the judge, not Mr. Rockefeller . . . I lost my home because my wife couldn't keep up the cost without going on welfare which I feel very strongly should be avoided, she is working and living at her mother's house till I get home. The last year that I worked (1974) I paid $2,000 dollars in taxes and this year because of a mistake any man could make I am costing the state thousands of dollars to keep me in a place like this.[109]

He persistently asserted his connection to society as a father, a husband, a taxpayer, and a worker—all identities explicitly erased in popular rhetoric about addicts. He points to the consequences of extracting him from his community, costs rarely acknowledged because addicts were consistently presented as isolated and apart from "the public."

Other writers struggled to communicate how the policy interfaced with their lives, the drug trade, and drug addiction in ways that politicians could not have intended. One man wrote:

[108] Ibid., 63.
[109] Raul S. to Carey, n.d., 1st Administration, Reel 135, Carey Gubernatorial Papers, NYSA.

Are such laws effective in achieving the desired end? I say no! Not when, in an effort to circumvent them, the drugs are put into the hands of our youth for sale and distribution, thus spreading the disease to the most vulnerable of our population. Not when the increased sanctions only serve to raise the price of drugs thus enhancing the profits of those willing to take the chance. Not when we realize that the addict is a sick person who cannot be frightened away from his drug dependence by harsher penalties. Not when the flow of drugs into this country continues unmitigated. Not when addicts are sent to a prison, only to return to society with the same problem they went in with.[110]

The author concluded that some balance must be struck between his well-being and that of "society": "In such laws, some equipoise must be arrived at between the rights and interests of society and those of the addict criminal victim."[111] In this formulation, the writer gestured toward the zero-sum formulation of rights that structured so much of these debates. He upended the discourse that positioned victims, criminals, and addicts as separate and mutually exclusive entities by collapsing them all into a single category.

Self-identified addicts repeatedly insisted that the threat of punishment would not dissuade drug users from pursuing intoxicants. They challenged the popular notion that long prison sentences, even without access to narcotics, would break the compulsion to do drugs. One letter outlined the futility of a punishment that did not address addiction:

Holding a man in prison for a long span of time does not liquidate the disease of drug addiction. You and I both know this. . . . My sentence of six to twelve years will not serve any purpose unless I can receive the proper treatment and return to the mainstream of society as a meaningful and productive citizen.[112]

Others prisoners explicitly challenged the prison's claim to reintegrate those charged with crimes. Despite the semantic emphasis on "corrections," one author insisted that prison instead reinforced the fundamental divide between full citizens and those who were incarcerated: "Reformation and rehabilitation is the rhetoric and systematic dehumanization is the reality. . . . The penitentiary today amounts to a banishment from civilized society to a dark and evil world completely alien to the free world, a world that is administered by criminals

---

[110] Gerard P. to Carey, January 31, 1975, 1st Administration, Reel 135, Carey Gubernatorial Papers, NYSA.

[111] Ibid.

[112] Cornell A. to Carey, February 26, 1976, 1st Administration, Reel 136, Carey Gubernatorial Papers, NYSA.

under unwritten rules and customs completely foreign to free-world culture."[113] The author positioned the prison as an instrument of civic degradation and social elimination.

Other letter writers spoke about the ways poverty and racism dictated one's fate within the criminal justice system. One man explained that "like me most of the inmates here at Attica Correctional Facility are poor black and addicted." He claimed that both race and poverty made people criminally suspect and that long prison sentences rarely produced positive outcomes for those incarcerated:

> This world don't make any sense to me any more. I am serving a six year to
> life sentence for selling a drug I don't remember doing. . . . On the behalf
> of the inmate serving time all over the state can we look forward to the
> day when someone will stop and take a good look at those that have long
> histories of drug addiction and help us. Most of us are not violent criminals
> but people with heavy mental problems; drugs ease that problem when we
> are high. . . . Being black is enough to get you convicted always.[114]

The author went on to highlight the vast gulf between his subjectivity as an addict who does not recall being arrested, much less committing a crime, and the subjectivity of the white juries and district attorney who pride themselves on jailing him.

> Even the all white middle class juries think they have did their thing for
> justice with the young assistant district attorney walking out of the court
> room proud as a father of a newly born baby. A meaningless conviction.
> But it look good to those who don't know any better including the member
> of the juries. Just another junkie off for a life bid in prison. Not just a black
> junkie, but any member of a poor family in New York state. There is no
> justice for the poor. Those who are caught in the web of dope world justice
> are out of the picture.[115]

The author recognized that the jury and district attorney seemed to sincerely feel justice was served by his conviction, that the whole process looked valid "to those who don't know any better." Yet he failed to acknowledge that his critique of penal operation was actually quite consistent with Rockefeller's rationale for advancing his bill. Its proponents never intended it to be judged primarily on its ability to "help" drug sellers, nor did its success depend upon prison playing a meaningful role for those arrested. For the purposes of the bill, long prison terms were

[113]Gilbert J. to Wilson, n.d., 1st Administration, Reel 11, Wilson Gubernatorial Papers, NYSA.

[114]Lawrence D. to Carey, n.d., 1st Administration, Reel 135, Carey Gubernatorial Papers, NYSA.

[115]Ibid.

a technology of social quarantine and a deterrent. With regard to those charged and sentenced, these punishments simply positioned addict-pushers "out of the picture."

A Lasting Legacy

Over the course of the 1970s, the laws had little measurable success in curtailing drug use. A comprehensive study published in 1978 found that while the laws may have temporarily deterred drug sales, they had no significant long-term impact on heroin use or crime rates. In fact, according to the report, "serious property crime of the sort often associated with heroin users increased sharply between 1973 and 1975. The rise in New York was similar to increases in nearby states."[116] The report also noted that "heroin use was as widespread in mid-1976 as it had been when the 1973 revision took effect, and ample supplies of the drug were available."[117] While the laws failed to significantly reduce drug use and related crime, they did set in motion a range of political and institutional transformations. They created gross discrepancies between New York State punishments and those of other jurisdictions. In fact, New York's sentences were so out of step with those in the federal system that some federal agents would coerce full cooperation by threatening to transfer drug offenders' cases to New York courts. A lawyer illuminated the sharp contrast in a 1975 letter to Governor Carey: "My office is half way between the Federal Courthouse at Foley Square and Special Narcotics Courts at 11 Center St. The difference between these two courts is the difference between life imprisonment and probation."[118]

Even though the police did not scale up drug arrests in 1973, the policy soon began presenting logistical problems within the penal system. It created backlogs that clogged the court system, especially in New York City.[119] Because the law prohibited small-time drug sellers from plea bargaining, a growing percentage of defendants demanded a trial. Before the laws' implementation, only 6 percent of drug indictments went to trial; afterward, that number rose to 16 percent.[120] This forced the state to

[116] Association of the Bar of the City of New York and the Drug Abuse Council, "The Nation's Toughest Drug Law," 9.

[117] Ibid., 7.

[118] Alvin G. to Governor Carey, January 29, 1975, 1st Administration, Reel 135, Carey Gubernatorial Papers, NYSA.

[119] Weiman and Weiss, "The Origins of Mass Incarceration in New York State," 73–116.

[120] Association of the Bar of the City of New York and the Drug Abuse Council, "The Nation's Toughest Drug Law," 17.

spend a disproportionate amount of time handling A-3 felons, the lowest-level charge. Between 1974 and June 1976, they represented 41 percent of all class A drug indictments in New York City and 61 percent of the class A trial workload.[121]

These trends inhibited the work of prosecutors, defense attorneys, and judges, and their critiques helped convince lawmakers to reexamine the drug laws. In July 1975, the legislature amended the statute to liberalize the restrictions on plea bargaining and parole. While some lawmakers may have been motivated by compassion for small-time drug sellers facing long sentences, these amendments were predominantly an accommodation to prosecutors. It allowed A-3 felons to plead guilty to as low as a class C felony with the consent of a judge and prosecutor. Legislators balanced these reforms by toughening other sections of the law and restricting plea bargaining for other felony classes. Reforms gave more discretion to prosecutors to entice people charged with drug crimes to accept plea bargains or cooperate with law enforcement. They did not fundamentally alter the mandatory prison terms and life sentences.[122] Even after the amendments were enacted, New York's drug penalties were still the most severe in the nation. There were few other attempts to significantly reduce penalties during the rest of the decade, though Governor Carey did pardon some groups of people with sympathetic cases.[123]

Treatment programs, on the other hand, suffered a much more dramatic fate in the 1970s. The Rockefeller Drug Laws had helped displace treatment as a dominant strategy for regulating drug use and its harms, making the state funds allocated for drug-treatment programs particularly vulnerable during the unrelenting budgetary pressures of the mid-1970s. Although police and fire departments also faced layoffs, programs for the most marginalized populations were decimated in the wake of New York City's fiscal crisis. The city's municipally funded treatment programs fared poorly and did not recover. In 1974, New York City provided $15 million for Addiction Services Agency activities. Four years later, by the fiscal year 1978, the city invested only $3.3 million, a 77 percent decrease. In 1977, there were still 53,310 people in New York State treatment, costing about $135 million a year. At the same time, the

---

[121] Ibid., 9.

[122] "The Tough Drug Law Is Changed," *New York Times*, July 13, 1975, 5; Tom Goldstein and Peter Bramley, "Even as Amended, It's the Toughest in the United States," *New York Times*, July 20, 1975, E16.

[123] For example, see Goldstein and Bramley, "Even as Amended, It's the Toughest in the United States" and "Carey Acts to Free 4 Jailed for Drugs," *New York Times*, January 28, 1979, 21.

state spent $190 million to house 13,900 "addicts" in prison.[124] Treatment advocates persistently couched their opposition to program cuts in comparative terms, defending treatment on the grounds of cost savings. A letter from the Phoenix House protested a proposed 25 percent cut to youth drug treatment:

> Although austerity is needed in our present financial crisis, the above cutbacks are both cruel and senseless. Cruel in terms of human suffering, and senseless in terms of economic illogic. It costs $13,634 a year to imprison an addict, and for juveniles the cost is even higher. In residential, drug-free treatment facilities such as the Phoenix House, the cost is only $2,677 a year. In other words, one of your tax dollars goes to jailing an addict and 25 cents to treat him. "Either way, you must pay."[125]

These economic tradeoffs, no matter how often and forcefully they were pointed out, failed to significantly undermine support for criminalizing poor drug users, particularly from urban communities of color.

New York State, after leading the nation in drug-treatment programs, largely retreated from the field, leaving private and nonprofit programs to offer addiction services with more limited government support. Decreases in funding and the repudiation of therapeutic objectives did not imply the complete disappearance of drug treatment on the ground. Courts continued to intertwine mandated treatment with penal sanctions in their regulation of those convicted of drug crimes. Furthermore, the emphasis on the "failures" of treatment did little to inhibit the dramatic expansion of private drug-treatment programs serving middle-class populations with insurance or cash. During the periods when politicians abandoned treatment as the principal response to the low-income addict-pusher, residential drug treatment became a dominant social response to middle-class and affluent drug abuse. Therapeutic communities became increasingly privatized and professionalized. Both Daytop Village and the Phoenix House grew into large, independent, drug rehabilitation programs.[126]

Over the next few years, national studies and frequent press investigations would confirm that the Rockefeller Drug Laws had few posi-

---

[124] Memo from Jerome Hornblass, Commissioner ASA, to Mayor Abraham Beam, January 12, 1977, Mayor Beam Department Correspondence, 74-77, Reel 10, Subject Files, Folder: Addiction Services Agency, Abraham Beam Mayoral Papers, NYCMA.

[125] Irvin Simmons to Justice Pleary, March 3, 1977, 1st Administration, Reel 136, Carey Gubernatorial Papers, NYSA. The letter, from Phoenix House staff, implores the judge to contact lawmakers and oppose drug-treatment cuts.

[126] On Daytop Village, see www.daytop.org/; for the Phoenix House, see http://www.phoenixhouse.org/about/.

tive programmatic effects.[127] Although the drug laws were in part a response to street-level frustration with the drug trade, the NYPD did not immediately translate the legislation into more aggressive attention to street-level drug markets or wide-scale street sweeps.[128] The number of felony drug arrests for heroin in the city actually declined dramatically from 22,301 in 1970 to fewer than 4,000 between 1973 and 1975.[129] Police reluctance to enthusiastically enforce the new laws was due in part to their experience with intensive policing in the late 1960s. They feared flooding courts and prisons with arrests that the system was ill-equipped to handle.[130] Their hesitation was also probably connected to the NYPD's response to the Knapp Commission's revelations of police corruption and concerns that police interaction with narcotics markets risked further scandal. Drug felony arrests declined 71.9 percent between 1970 and 1973, and New York City's fiscal crisis during the following years further diminished police staffing and morale.[131] Between 1976 and 1984, the city saw a 29 percent decline in uniformed officers, from around 24,000 to 17,000.[132] In this context, police prioritized violent and more serious drug crimes, and the proportion of state prisoners serving time for drug violations held steady, growing only from 11 percent in 1972 to 12 percent in 1977.[133]

The mid-1970s saw open-air drug markets flourish in New York City, particularly in Harlem and the Lower East Side. Supplies stabilized after the heroin draught of the early 1970s with drugs from Mexico and Asia.[134] Descriptions of the drug markets on the Lower East Side in the early 1980s evoke a carnival atmosphere. Streets were crowded with lines of customers, double-parked cars, and drug sellers

---

[127]"U.S. Study Backs Critics of New York's Drug Law," *New York Times*, September 5, 1976, 1; "Drug Abuse and Drug Laws," *Washington Post*, September 11, 1976, A14; Selwyn Raab, "Impact of Stiff Drug Law Is in Dispute after 2 Years," *New York Times*, March 29, 1976, 1.

[128]For a comprehensive account of the delayed implementation of the Rockefeller Drug Laws and the role of local actors, see Mason B. Williams, "Street-Level Drug Police and the Rise of Mass Incarceration in New York City, 1973–1989" (paper delivered at the Violence & the City Conference, City University of New York, 2015) and Weiman and Weiss, "The Origins of Mass Incarceration in New York State," 73–116.

[129]Association of the Bar of the City of New York and the Drug Abuse Council, "The Nation's Toughest Drug Law," 91.

[130]Ibid., 89–91.

[131]Weiman and Weiss, "The Origins of Mass Incarceration in New York State," 89.

[132]L. Zimmer, "Operation Pressure Point: The Disruption of Street-Level Drug Trade on New York's Lower East Side," Center for Research in Crime and Justice (New York: New York University Law School, 1987), 2.

[133]Weiman and Weiss, "The Origins of Mass Incarceration in New York State," 88.

[134]Paul Goldstein et al., "Marketing of Street Heroin in New York," *Journal of Drug Issues*, no. 3 (1984): 565.

shouting the names of their particular products. In some instances, street vendors offered hotdogs and soda.[135] One police officer explained to a researcher that "there were some blocks in the precinct that I avoided as much as possible because it was embarrassing to be a police officer and see the law broken in front of your eyes and know there was nothing you could do." A drug user articulated a similar sense that police had largely withdrawn from managing the retail drug markets: "There was nothing the police could do. There were more of us than there were of them and for every seller they arrested, there were ten people waiting to take his place on the street. The police were more of a nuisance than anything. I'd think 'like, why do they bother coming out here at all?'"[136]

It was not until the 1980s that the New York penal system began to have the capacity or enthusiasm to produce the arrests and incarceration rates that would eventually become the law's legacy.[137] Police capacity recovered as the city rebounded slowly from the austerity measures during the fiscal crisis. Between 1980 and 1988, the administration of New York City mayor Ed Koch increased the police force by 19 percent.[138] Distance from the corruption scandals surrounding the Knapp Commission diminished officials' defensiveness and hesitation to intervene more directly in the drug trade.[139] In 1981, the NYPD initiated a new campaign of street-level drug enforcement, deployed a new one-hundred-officer undercover force to engage in buy-and-bust operations. Ostensibly responding to incessant citizen complaints, the campaign's original focus on Times Square, the financial district, and Bryant and Washington Square parks also suggests a connection to efforts to attract investment and tourism and remake New York City's image in the wake of the high-profile fiscal and social crises of the 1970s.[140] In 1984, the NYPD expanded street-level enforcement and implemented Operation Pressure Point, which entailed more aggressive "quality of life" policing that focused on low-level felony and

[135]Curtis, "The War on Drugs in Brooklyn," 13–17; Zimmer, "Operation Pressure Point," 1–3.

[136]Zimmer, "Operation Pressure Point," 3.

[137]On the importance of street-level implementation and recognizing that punitive legislation in itself does not trigger penal expansion, see Williams, "Street-Level Drug Police and the Rise of Mass Incarceration in New York City."

[138]Weiman and Weiss, "The Origins of Mass Incarceration in New York State," 73–116.

[139]Curtis, "The War on Drugs in Brooklyn," 16–21.

[140]Leonard Buder, "New Police Unit to Battle Drugs in Public Places," *New York Times*, July 31, 1981, 1, B4; Williams, "Street-Level Drug Police and the Rise of Mass Incarceration in New York City"; Miriam Greenberg, *Branding New York: How a City in Crisis Was Sold to the World* (New York: Routledge, 2008). See also Figure 1.1 for drug arrests in New York City between 1970 and 2014.

misdemeanor drug sales to areas including Harlem and the Lower East Side. Between 1979 and 1984, felony drug arrests grew from 11,300 to 23,500 in New York State. The growing number of arrests compounded with higher rates of indictments, convictions, and imprisonment throughout the penal system.[141] In this way, aggressive policing and more ardent prosecution mobilized the punitive machinery established by Rockefeller years earlier to produce steadily increasing levels of incarceration. The policy helped flood the prison system with low-level drug offenders, disproportionately from the communities of color targeted by the newly intensified policing. By 1988, 25.4 percent of New York prisoners were drug offenders, 37 percent of all new admissions; in 1980, only 9 percent of the state's prisoners had been convicted of drug offenses.[142]

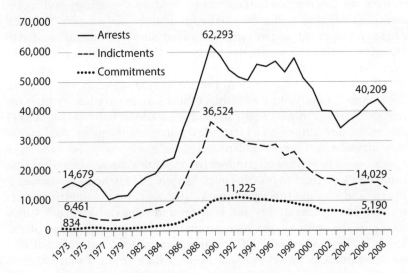

Figure 2.1. "Trends in Felony Drug Arrests, Indictments, and Commitments in New York State, 1973–2008." (*Source*: Reproduced from Office of Justice Research and Performance, "New York State Felony Drug Arrest, Indictment, and Commitment Trends, 1973–2014," Division of Criminal Justice Services, Criminal Justice Research Report, February 2010, http://www.criminaljustice.ny.gov/pio/annualreport/baseline_trends_report.pd)

[141] Weiman and Weiss, "The Origins of Mass Incarceration in New York State," 97.
[142] Ibid., 89.

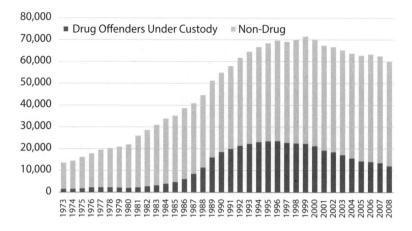

Figure 2.2. "Drug Offenders and Total Offenders under Custody in New York State Department of Corrections, 1973–2008." (*Source*: Reproduced from Office of Justice Research and Performance, "New York State Felony Drug Arrest, Indictment, and Commitment Trends, 1973–2014," Division of Criminal Justice Services, Criminal Justice Research Report, February 2010, http://www .criminaljustice.ny.gov/pio/annualreport/baseline_trends_report.pdf)

Although heroin use slowed in the 1980s because of supply interruptions, demographic changes, and the petering out that typically characterizes cycles of drug use, the Rockefeller Drug Laws failed to halt the next drug spate on the horizon—crack-cocaine—which would inspire a new level of hysteria, misery, and repression in the following decade.[143] Yet the laws endured, despite delivering much of the disaster opponents predicted: they did little to lessen drug use, addiction, or trafficking while dramatically increasing pressure on courts and the penal system.[144] Of all the people incarcerated for drug offenses in 1999, almost 80 percent had never been convicted of a violent felony. At the turn of the twenty-first century, approximately 90 percent of drug offenders in New York State prisons were African American or Latino, despite the fact that a majority of

[143] Courtwright, *Dark Paradise*, 170–85.
[144] See, for example, J. P. Caulkins et al., "Mandatory Minimum Drug Sentences: Throwing Away the Key or the Taxpayers' Money?" (Santa Monica, Calif.: Rand Corporation, Drug Policy Research Center, 1997), 1–193. The Drug Policy Alliance also offers analysis of the laws and their ineffectiveness at curtailing drug use, as well as a bibliography of studies on mandatory minimum drug sentencing. See http://www .drugpolicy.org/.

drug users and sellers were white.[145] In his January 2009 State of the State speech, New York governor David Paterson, a longtime critic of the policies, again reiterated the near total failure of the drug laws to mitigate the harms associated with illicit drugs: "Few public safety initiatives have failed as badly and for as long as the Rockefeller Drug Laws."[146] Yet despite some reforms, the Rockefeller Drug Laws were remarkably resilient, resisting decades of activists' efforts to repeal or seriously amend them. It was not until 2009 that the combination of a Democratically controlled legislature, serious state deficits, and relentless grassroots pressure created the opening for more substantial reform of the state's narcotics policy. Finally, in that spring, legislators dramatically revised New York drug sentencing. They restored a degree of judicial discretion and allowed judges to divert low-level drug offenders from prison to treatment programs.[147]

While focusing only on their high costs and decades-long record of failure, it is difficult to understand the political longevity of these and other punitive drug laws. However, when viewed from another perspective, their perseverance is less confounding. Punishing policies may not have dramatically mitigated drug abuse or crime rates, but they did critical work for important constituencies. "Law-and-order" legislation paid handsome political dividends, and Rockefeller's case was no exception. Rockefeller's tough drug laws proved to be an invaluable asset to his political fortunes in the following years. All over the country, people explained that his viability as a Republican presidential candidate in an increasingly conservative party rested on his tough posture at Attica, his crackdown on "welfare cheaters," and his passage of the harshest drug laws in the nation.[148] Although Rockefeller did not capture the presidency, Gerald Ford appointed him vice president after President Nixon's resignation in 1974.[149]

[145]The Campaign to Repeal the Rockefeller Drug Laws, "General Fact Sheet," Drop the Rock, http://www.droptherock.org/?page_id=2; New York City Legal Aid Society, "Rockefeller Drug Laws," Drug Policy Alliance, http://www.drugpolicy.org/library/factsheets/rockefeller_fact2.cfm, 2002.

[146]Governor David A. Paterson, "State of the State Address 2009," http://www.ny.gov/governor/keydocs/speech_0107091.htm.

[147]The legislature also enacted some reforms to the Rockefeller Drug Laws in 2004 and 2005. See, for example, Jeremy Peters, "Albany Reaches Deal to Repeal '70s Drug Laws," *New York Times*, March 25, 2009 and Jeremy Peters, "Deal on State's Drug Laws Means Resentencing Pleas," *New York Times*, March 28, 2009.

[148]Dewar, "Southern GOP Chiefs Soften on Rockefeller," A4; Albert Hunt, "Will Rocky Finally Make It in '76?" *Wall Street Journal*, December 4, 1973, 26.

[149]President Ford replaced Rockefeller with Kansas senator Bob Dole on the Republican ticket before facing Jimmy Carter in the 1976 election. Despite Rockefeller's rightward tack

Beyond their influence on Rockefeller's personal political fortunes, the drug laws helped resolve problems that arose from the interactions between therapeutic social programs and the dynamics of drug use, the illicit trade, and the shifting political economy. They forged for their supporters a path out of the fraught terrain created by high-profile political promises to establish social order and social reintegration and the difficulties of delivering on that promise. When confronted with this host of political and programmatic challenges, Rockefeller built his new policy upon the premise that therapeutic programs failed because its targets were ungovernable through welfarist strategies. And the political spectacle of enacting these policies was instrumental in reifying these assumptions as common sense. They explicitly denigrated the civic and legal status of the racialized addict-pusher at a time when society wrestled over activists' demands for full, equal citizenship for all Americans. Holding pushers responsible for widening drug use addressed consternation about heroin use in and outside of the "ghetto," while holding open the possibility of reintegration and rehabilitation for drug users from more affluent space. The laws facilitated the ongoing bifurcation of society's response to drug use. Drug users that authorities understood as redeemable (often white and middle class) encountered mild penalties and increasingly privatized treatment while drug sellers understood as incorrigible (often the poor and black and Latinos drug sellers) encountered unforgiving entanglement with prisons, parole, and probation.[150] These were not simply divergent strategies for different populations; they actually depended on each other. In many incantations, the narratives of innocent victims and helpless addicts depended upon the malevolence of the irredeemable pusher.

Even though therapeutic programs were never devoid of stigmatizing practices, Rockefeller's move in 1973 from a policy rhetorically committed to reintegrating drug addicts (even addict-pushers) to a project of social and physical quarantine was significant. However coercive in practice, rehabilitative intent in policy was theoretically democratizing, committed to reabsorbing marginalized citizens into the polity (on elites' terms). The shifting emphasis in governing strategies empowered some groups, institutions, and experts while disempowering others. Treating drug users as patients, instead of criminals, logically prescribed a different economy from what would arise with the punitive War on Drugs. Drug-treatment programs hired more social workers than guards, and more women, people of color, and ex–drug users than did penal institutions.

---

on some social policies, party officials viewed Rockefeller's lingering reputation as an East Coast moderate as a liability.

[150] For further discussion of the processes of decriminalizing drug use in white and suburban spaces, see Lassiter, "Impossible Criminals," 126–40.

The earlier emphasis on rehabilitation, however compromised, had provided drug users and their families with some discursive leverage in negotiations with the state over their fates. As drug users and other community groups began forcefully using the therapeutic commitments to advance their own visions of rehabilitation, Rockefeller's drug policy symbolically severed state responsibility to many of its most vulnerable citizens.

By abandoning rehabilitation as the dominant rationale, policymakers changed the definition of success. What program administrators and politicians had presented as efforts to cure addicts of their disease they now framed as efforts to protect "the public" from the addict and pusher. By positioning addict-pushers as outside of the "public" in a highly degraded civic status, they constricted this already narrow path through which to make claims in the polity. As the stigma associated with drug selling reached a crescendo, those ensnared by law enforcement and the drug economy found they were entitled to fewer and fewer rights and services from the state.

While Rockefeller's drug laws ultimately did little programmatically to mitigate crime rates or drug use, they offered clear answers to fiercely contested political questions. Enacting this punitive policy helped produce knowledge about "problem people" and the limits of the state's capacity to integrate or transform them into "good citizens." This may help explain why, instead of avoiding New York's example, forty-eight states instituted anti-drug laws with mandatory minimum sentencing in the decade after the Rockefeller Drug Laws passed.[151] The laws helped resolve a host of governance problems by renarrating the limits of political will as the problems of incorrigible, racialized deviants. They transformed the aversion to "reintegrating" poor drug users, funding diverse treatment programs, and tackling racial and economic subordination into evidence of irredeemable drug sellers. In terms of the dominant medical metaphor of addiction, they had moved pushers from being considered *diseased* to being cast *as the disease*.

[151] Musto, *American Disease*, 273–74. The Rockefeller Drug Laws are often credited in popular and scholarly accounts with instigating the deluge of punitive legislations that followed. While the laws were undoubtedly highly publicized political theater that garnered national attention and evidenced the political utility of "getting tough," detailed historical research into the political struggles in others states would be needed to establish precisely what role the New York laws played in other lawmakers' decisions to enact tougher drug laws.

PART II

Welfare Queens

Linda Taylor received Illinois welfare checks and food stamps, even though she was driving three 1974 autos—a Cadillac, a Lincoln, and a Chevrolet station wagon—claimed to own four South Side buildings, and was about to leave for a vacation in Hawaii.

—George Bliss, "Cops Find Deceit—But No One Cares," *Chicago Tribune*, September 29, 1974

There are some [that commit welfare fraud] who are determined to get a piece of the Great American Pie. Mothers who have tried to make it honestly, by working hard or trying to manage on the pittance allowed them each month by Public Aid; mothers who have probably seen their children scorned or put down because of the way they dress; mothers who are determined that their children will live in decent housing without plaster falling and rate running; mothers who are determined that their children will eat until they are full; nourishing meals, and attend schools where they will be able to get more than a mediocre education; mothers who are determined that their children will get good medical care and not be treated like lepers because the state is paying.

—Elaine Fitzpatrick, letter to the editor regarding "Busted Queen," *Chicago Defender,* November 26, 1974

By the 1960s, AFDC, the program that provided cash support to poor parents, had few enthusiastic defenders. President Johnson acknowledged in 1968 that "the welfare system pleases no one." He explained, "It is criticized by liberals and by conservatives, by the poor and the wealthy, by social workers and politicians, by whites and Negroes in every part of the nation."[1] Of course, everyone was not engaged with (and enraged by) welfare for the same reasons. Politicians, bureaucrats, and recipients had different concerns than did people not directly involved with the program. Nonetheless, their hostilities informed and amplified each other and left few voices defending the status quo.

During the 1960s, an unprecedented interracial movement of welfare recipients critiqued the program's paltry benefits and demeaning bureaucratic regulations, claiming it withheld the resources needed to raise their families with dignity. Many program beneficiaries organized into a national federation of welfare-rights groups demanding an expansion in the level of support and societal recognition and remuneration for the work of caregiving. Through pressure from recipients, the federal government, and new court rulings, state welfare programs expanded the amount of aid they offered and the number of people they served. While elites faced an exploding demand for welfare benefits with few politically attractive revenue sources to offset the budgetary pressures, many working- and middle-class voters were more disturbed by the moral and symbolic implications of welfare than any budgetary concerns. Welfare became a terrain to articulate a host of frustrations, particularly about hard economic times and changing racial, gender, and sexual relations.

Part 2 begins by chronicling how politicians bundled this host of issues together into what they called a "welfare crisis." Chapter 3 explores the ways lawmakers and administrators, at the state and federal levels, attempted to narrate and respond to the conditions. The landmark welfare reforms Ronald Reagan spearheaded as governor of California in the early 1970s constricted eligibility standards, heightened bureaucratic scrutiny, instituted work requirements, and enlisted the penal system to handle fraud and child-support collections. Reagan's California campaign was embedded in both national and state politics and was intended in part to counter President Nixon's Family Assistance Plan. The California welfare reform campaign also ultimately helped solidify a powerful narrative about the causes of the "welfare mess."

Restrictive welfare reforms and anti-AFDC rhetoric mobilized a host of racially charged frustrations to halt the tentative steps toward a broader economic citizenship. The tangled, dialogical (or perhaps caustic) interaction between elites and the grassroots gave these issues force and propelled their course. Animosity toward recipients intensified during the highly publicized efforts to shrink welfare rolls through work requirements, surveillance, and fraud prosecutions. But

---

[1] Quoted in Molly Michelmore, *Tax and Spend: The Welfare State, Tax Politics, and the Limits of American Liberalism* (Philadelphia: University of Pennsylvania Press, 2012), 76.

the intensity of public vitriol against welfare recipients not only emboldened proponents of tough welfare reforms in the legislature (and chilled their critics) but also steered the campaign in subtle ways, for example toward concern about recipients' access to consumer goods and services.

Chapter 4 explores the central role of criminalization and welfare fraud in degrading the civic status of welfare recipients and the declining support for the program. Politicians, such as Reagan, blamed soaring caseloads not on the economic conditions or the recent legal reforms that prohibited states from denying aid on the basis of race or morality but on personal failings of recipients, particularly the alleged preponderance of sexually deviant welfare "cheaters." To manage this problem, they often enlisted law enforcement and penal rituals. The press amplified politicians' narrative through sensationalized, often anomalous, tales of recipients' shiftlessness, devious scams, and extravagant consumption. Like Rockefeller's drug laws, restrictive welfare policies further suppressed the civic standing of already suspect groups by subjecting AFDC recipients to state discipline, work mandates, and new criminal scrutiny.

The chapter then turns to how Illinois transplanted the strategies initiated in California to address its own political conditions. Focusing closer to the street level reveals how the anti-fraud campaign created suspect citizenship statuses that others could exploit. Ordinary people leveraged this vulnerability and reported their acquaintances for welfare fraud for a host of distinct motivations. Their participation, in turn, helped reshape the state's anti-fraud campaign. Recipients found that anti-fraud initiatives further constrained their ability to make ends meet on low monthly cash grants. Some charged that the campaign essentially criminalized poverty and abrogated recipients' citizenship.

Legislators' punitive policy responses to welfare abuse—especially their recruitment of the criminal justice system—solidified welfare recipients' cultural position as the antithesis of "workers" and therefore the opposite of taxpaying, respectable, productive citizens. Anti-fraud campaigns crystallized these conceptions and enshrined them in popular mythology while also clashing with—and stifling—the perspectives of welfare recipients. At a time when recipients were organizing a vocal welfare-rights movement, these state initiatives directly challenged activists' claims to state support by virtue of their roles as mothers, citizens, and consumers. In fact, tough welfare policies positioned welfare recipients as without legitimate claims on the state. In the process, these campaigns helped derail efforts to erect a national income floor for families and discredited other visions of social citizenship that included a right to basic material security. Instead of building a more expansive citizenship, policymakers degraded the civic position of the nation's poorest citizens. Similar to the Rockefeller Drug Laws, the anti-fraud campaigns reoriented the purported mission of state programs from reforming or serving a marginalized group to protecting the "public" from that population.

CHAPTER THREE

The Welfare Mess

REIMAGINING THE SOCIAL CONTRACT

The political scientist Lawrence Mead was one of the cohort of conservative intellectuals who articulated a theoretical rationale for "workfare" and other restrictive welfare reforms. A self-professed big-government conservative, Mead favored deploying state power to enforce social norms and compel recipients into wage work. In his 1986 book he wrote that "low-wage work apparently must be mandated. . . . Government need not make the desired behavior worthwhile to people. It simply threatens punishment (in this case loss of benefits) if they do not comply."[1] Mead's call for coercive, "paternalistic" social policy was predicated upon a contractual understanding of citizenship that had deep historical roots and popular resonance. This vein of popular and academic thought essentially insisted that work was a prerequisite to full citizenship. A constituent's 1970 letter in support of disenfranchising welfare recipients put the argument in extreme terms. He explained to California governor Ronald Reagan that "these people add nothing to our economy but, because they are citizens of the United States, they exercise their right to vote. Actually, they are, in my opinion, no more than second rate citizens and because they continually draw welfare, I do not believe they should have the right to have a say in our government or how our tax money is spent."[2]

While disenfranchising welfare recipients was a marginal (and constitutionally dubious) proposal in the early 1970s, full citizenship has long been constructed as contingent upon performing civic obligations like working, paying taxes, and serving in the military.[3] Yet popular references to the social contract typically obfuscate the ways access to full citizenship have been delimited by race, sexuality, class, and gender. Under the tradition of coverture, women owed their civic obligations

[1] Lawrence M. Mead, *Beyond Entitlement: The Social Obligations of Citizenship* (New York: Free Press, 1986), 84.

[2] Harold J. to Governor Reagan, September 15, 1970, Correspondence Unit Administrative, Box 1970/79, 1/2, Ronald Reagan Governor's Papers, Ronald Reagan Presidential Library, Simi Valley, Calif. (hereafter RRGP).

[3] Kerber, *No Constitutional Right to Be Ladies*, 304; Kessler-Harris, *In Pursuit of Equity*; Fraser and Gordon, "Civil Citizenship against Social Citizenship?" 90–108.

to their husband and family, not to the political community. This excused women from many critical responsibilities such as serving on a jury, serving in the military, and performing "productive" labor and diminished their claims on full citizenship.[4] Furthermore, the ostensibly universal social contract has historically explicitly and implicitly excluded nonwhite populations.[5] Policymakers often did not consider nonwhite women to be governed by the domestic ideology of separate spheres and instead used various mechanisms to coerce them into low-wage labor.

In the decades after World War II, a number of factors converged to upset the gendered and racial arrangements that undergirded dominant conceptions of citizenship.[6] Federal oversight during the 1940s and 1950s helped secure new access to state benefits for growing numbers of black citizens.[7] When black freedom movements disrupted the legal and institutional machinery of white supremacy, they challenged the subordinate civic status of African Americans in the North and the South. AFDC became a lightning rod for frustration with this broader renegotiation of rights and services. As more and more women entered the formal workforce, popular understandings of women's appropriate roles and obligations also transformed. Welfare became a flashpoint for those reckoning with the disappearance of "family wage jobs" and accompanying pressure on women to enter the labor market while still balancing their domestic responsibilities. Many women who felt compelled (by economic pressure and personal ambition) to perform remunerated labor were enraged by reports that welfare allowed other women to stay home—particularly the nonwhite women understood as unsuited for domesticity. Of course, few groups of mothers were more acquainted with the pressures of managing wage work and unpaid domestic labor than women of color. But the alleged failure of poor and nonwhite mothers in society to "work" became evidence of their profound dereliction of civic duties and grounds to discredit their voices and oppose their claims on the state.

[4]Kerber, *No Constitutional Right to Be Ladies*, 305.

[5]Although I focus here on popular invocations of rights and obligations, political philosophers have critiqued social contract theories along these lines. On the function and maintenance of a "racial contract" that excludes nonwhites from the social contract, see Charles W. Mills, *The Racial Contract* (Ithaca: Cornell University Press, 1997). On gender, see Carole Pateman, *The Sexual Contract* (Stanford: Stanford University Press, 1988).

[6]For further discussion of these themes, see Marisa Chappell, *The War on Welfare: Family, Poverty, and Politics in Modern America* (Philadelphia: University of Pennsylvania Press, 2011) and Kessler-Harris, *In Pursuit of Equity*.

[7]Karen M. Tani, *States of Dependency: Welfare, Rights, and American Governance, 1935–1972* (New York: Cambridge University Press, 2016).

These broad historical transformations converged with other economic and political dynamics to make AFDC one of the era's most volatile political issues. This chapter maps the ways political rhetoric explained a host of diverse dynamics by sweeping them together into a "welfare mess." In the postwar period, economic dislocations, increases in single-parent families, federal oversight, and the mass migration of African Americans expanded ADC caseloads. States attempted to mitigate these increases with the tools they had used for decades: eligibility restrictions, anti-fraud campaigns, and intensified scrutiny of the caseloads. However, by the late 1960s, they confronted new and powerful impediments. Federal administrators, poverty lawyers, many funded through the War on Poverty, and welfare-rights activists pushed states to recognize new "rights" to public assistance. New rulings and policies constrained administrators' ability to deny aid on the basis of morality—which had often served as a proxy for race. This ballooned the welfare rolls even further.[8]

With the convergence of these dynamics, ADFC became the front line in ongoing battles over the terms of citizenship and the role of the state. As Lawrence Mead explained, "The repeated national debate over welfare since the mid-1960s can be seen as a struggle to define a new social contract."[9] Elites and non-elites engaged in debates over how to clean up the welfare mess by negotiating this new contract. Many activist welfare recipients and others on the Left advocated for more robust social rights—the right to an adequate standard of living as a function of citizenship or parenting. Opponents of expanding social rights and welfare rights blamed AFDC for a host of frustrations, such as rising taxes and unwieldy state budgets. But the copious constituent letters to Reagan reveal that many at the grassroots level had slightly divergent motivations than those of conservative anti-welfare politicians. Many letter writers did not oppose state assistance categorically and instead complained bitterly about a patchwork and paltry welfare state that offered them few services. Much like letter writers who expressed frustration about crime in New York, grassroots welfare opponents were most often enraged that benefits and rights went to the "wrong people." They typically did not call for smaller government but instead for a renegotiation of the social contract—a restructuring of who gets a voice and benefits and on what terms. Both Richard Nixon and Ronald Reagan attempted to mobilize this popular frustration for their own political projects.

---

[8]Tani, *States of Dependency*; Premilla Nadasen, Jennifer Mittelstadt, and Marisa Chappell, *Welfare in the United States: A History with Documents, 1935–1996* (New York: Routledge, 2009).

[9]Mead, *Beyond Entitlement*, 85.

Making the Welfare Mess

The reform initiatives in the 1960s and 1970s were embedded in the long history of welfare bureaucracies' struggles to limit costs while policing intersecting racial, gender, and class hierarchies. Contrary to popular rhetoric, women have always labored in and outside the home. The idea of separate spheres of responsibility for men and women solidified in the nineteenth century with the growing importance of wage labor. Throughout the early twentieth century, male workers organized for a "family wage" that would enable them to support their entire family. These campaigns positioned women's proper role as performing the unremunerated, "reproductive" work of the domestic sphere.[10] Although the labor movement and economic growth helped deliver this domestic arrangement to some families, many jobs—especially those available to African Americans, Latinos, and other immigrants—never paid enough to support entire families. Working-class women of all races frequently performed wage labor, particularly before marriage and childbirth.

In the Progressive Era, middle-class reformers established mothers' pensions, which provided support to single mothers so that they would be able to raise their children in the home. Proponents insisted that these benefits were not charity and their beneficiaries were not "paupers" who traded civic standing for economic support. Reformers argued that mothers' pensions were recognition of a valued social contribution, akin to veterans' pensions. After the onslaught of the Great Depression, Congress incorporated many features of mothers' pensions into the federal welfare program, Aid to Dependent Children (ADC), later renamed Aid to Families with Dependent Children (AFDC). Inaugurated in the landmark 1935 Social Security Act, ADC was originally intended to enable single mothers, usually imagined as widows, to stay at home and raise their children. To prevent undermining the male breadwinner ideal, the sculptors kept grant levels low to ensure that remarriage remained more lucrative than receiving welfare.[11] ADC, while not particularly controversial at its inception, was nonetheless relegated to a secondary position vis-à-vis the more robust social insurance programs designed to affirm the economic security and social belonging of male, typically white, breadwinners.[12]

[10]Chappell, The War on Welfare, 6–9; Lawrence Glickman, A Living Wage: American Workers and the Making of Consumer Society (Ithaca: Cornell University Press, 1999).

[11]Gordon, Pitied But Not Entitled.

[12]There is a rich literature on maternalism, mothers' pensions, and the founding of ADC. See, for example, Molly Ladd-Taylor, Mother-Work: Women, Child Welfare, and the State, 1890–1930 (Urbana: University of Illinois Press, 1994); Gordon, Pitied But Not Entitled; Joanne Goodwin, Gender and the Politics of Welfare Reform: Mothers' Pensions in Chicago, 1911–1929 (Chicago: University of Chicago Press, 1997); Theda Skocpol, Protecting

Racism and racial politics fundamentally shaped the development of social welfare programs instituted during the New Deal.[13] Lawmakers deemed domestic and agricultural workers, commonly understood to be African Americans (but, in application, also many other workers), ineligible for the federally controlled Unemployment Insurance and Old Age Insurance. When they were able to access state support, African American families were forced to rely on the paltrier programs, such as ADC. States had considerable discretion in the implementation of ADC. They received federal matching funds to help cover the costs of the program and operated with some federal regulation and oversight, but state officials set grant levels and eligibility conditions.[14] This allowed for dramatic variation in benefit levels and conditions between different regions. In the South, many states effectively barred African American women from state aid, especially when their labor was in high demand during harvest times.

In the second half of the twentieth century, women began entering the workforce at unprecedented rates.[15] This trend would accelerate in the 1970s, when the average female worker was no longer single and unmarried but a married mother.[16] Where only 30 percent of women with children under six years old worked outside the home in 1970, 43 percent were employed in 1976. By 1985, half of all mothers with preschool-age children held paying jobs.[17] During the same period that women entered the workforce in record numbers, poor women—especially Latina and African American women—gained increased access to welfare, allowing a modest reprieve from wage labor.

Soldiers and Mothers: The Political Origins of Social Policy in the United States (Cambridge, Mass.: Belknap Press of Harvard University Press, 1992); Katz, *The Undeserving Poor;* Winifred Bell, *Aid to Dependent Children* (New York: Columbia University Press, 1965); and Gwendolyn Mink, *The Wages of Motherhood: Inequality in the Welfare State, 1917–1942* (Ithaca: Cornell University Press, 1995).

[13]See Mary Poole, *The Segregated Origins of Social Security: African Americans and the Welfare State* (Chapel Hill: University of North Carolina Press, 2006) and Linda Faye Williams, *The Constraint of Race: Legacies of White Skin Privilege in America* (University Park: Pennsylvania State University Press, 2003).

[14]On the intertwined development of ADC and federal, state, and local authority, see Tani, *States of Dependency.*

[15]The state and economy enlisted droves of women into industry during World War II to support themselves and the war effort. After the war, state and popular pressure encouraged women to relinquish their jobs to returning veterans, and many white middle-class women embraced domestic roles in the quickly expanding suburban landscape. Yet the dramatic movement of women into the paid labor force had irrefutably begun. Stephanie Coontz, *The Way We Never Were: American Families and the Nostalgia Trap* (New York: Basic Books, 1993).

[16]Chappell, *The War on Welfare*, 135.

[17]Beth Bailey, "She Can Bring Home the Bacon," in *America in the Seventies*, ed. Beth Bailey and David Farber (Lawrence: University Press of Kansas, 2004), 109.

Many of the same forces that led to the expansion of drug use and the drug trade in New York contributed to a growing demand for social welfare programs. For much of the nation, increased prosperity accompanied the rapid economic expansion and suburban growth of the postwar period. But capital migration, monetary policy, and racially discriminatory lending and hiring practices increasingly encumbered the economy in urban communities of color, particularly in the North and West. The mass migration of African Americans out of the South, where highly restrictive welfare regimes limited access to AFDC, to comparatively more generous states increased caseloads and shifted their racial composition. Although the majority of welfare recipients had always been white, almost half were people of color after 1958.[18] Rising divorce rates and the increase in the number of single mothers also drove up ADC enrollments. The number of families receiving ADC doubled between 1945 and 1950, and by 1960 the program served more than three million clients.[19]

Throughout the 1950s, social workers and policymakers placed less emphasis on offering material support to poor families. They increasingly emphasized individually targeted rehabilitation services designed to strengthen families and encourage "independence." More and more, this meant enacting policies that not only tolerated but explicitly encouraged women to perform wage work outside the home. In 1962, Congress enacted a series of amendments that reoriented welfare away from providing cash assistance to support women's socially valued domestic labor toward a new emphasis on encouraging mothers' movement into the paid labor force.[20]

The increased emphasis on "rehabilitating" welfare recipients coexisted with efforts to purge ineligible and "unworthy" families from the rolls. Consternation about undeserving people receiving benefits had always been part of welfare administration, but officials deployed fraud investigations more consistently as states faced the growing demand for services in the postwar era. Cities like New York, Detroit, Indianapolis, and Baltimore undertook campaigns to investigate recipient "chiseling" and fraud during the 1940s and 1950s.[21] In 1961, the city of Newburgh, New York, instituted a collection of draconian welfare policies that concentrated unprecedented national attention on welfare

---

[18] Gwendolyn Mink, *Welfare's End* (Ithaca: Cornell University Press, 1998), 52.

[19] Nadasen, Mittelstadt, and Chappell, *Welfare in the United States*, 23–24.

[20] Ibid. For the history of rehabilitative emphasis in ADC, see Mittelstadt, *From Welfare to Workfare*. To signal the program's concern with the parents as well as the children in poor families, legislators changed the name of the program from Aid to Dependent Children (ADC) to Aid to Families with Dependent Children (AFDC).

[21] See Tani, *States of Dependency* and Bell, *Aid to Dependent Children*.

politics.[22] The city manager's plan eliminated benefits to women with "illegitimate" children or those who refused to take any job offered. It forced all recipients, who were commonly pictured as Puerto Ricans and African American migrants from the South, to pick up their checks at the police station for eligibility audits to "weed out the chiselers."[23] In 1962, a U.S. Senate hearing vilified the allegedly lax social workers in Washington, D.C., who tolerated welfare fraud. These nationally publicized, anti-fraud initiatives targeted African American communities and inflamed hostility toward welfare recipients.[24] States also policed morality by enforcing "suitable homes" regulations and "man-in-the-house" rules, which made women ineligible for welfare if they were found to be living with a male companion.[25] In practice, these policies typically targeted African Americans, allowing program administrators to protect ADC from public criticism while keeping costs low and enforcing racial hierarchy.[26]

Welfare officials conducted unannounced "midnight raids" of clients' homes in search of male companions. If a man was discovered, administrators could cancel benefits by either defining the home as "unsuitable" (because of the moral transgression) or ineligible (because officials claimed the man was "assuming the role of the spouse" and should support the family). The 1962 "Operation Weekend" inaugurated in Kern County, California, is an example of these strategies. The program entailed a series of early morning raids on welfare recipients' homes to detect men or other violations of program regulations. Officials replicated the strategy with "Operation Bedcheck" in Alameda County in 1963. They dispatched pairs of social workers or welfare investigators to recipients' homes at 6:30 in the morning in search of "unauthorized males." While one member of the team requested admittance at the front door, the other

[22]Lisa Levenstein, "From Innocent Children to Unwanted Migrants and Unwed Moms: Two Chapters in the Public Discourse on Welfare in the United States, 1960–1961," *Journal of Women's History* 11, no. 4 (2000): 10–33; Tani, *States of Dependency*, 1–7, 224–36.

[23]Rick Perlstein, *Before the Storm: Barry Goldwater and the Unmaking of the American Dream* (New York: Hill and Wang, 2001), 130.

[24]Kenneth J. Neubeck and Noel A. Cazenave, *Welfare Racism: Playing the Race Card against America's Poor* (New York: Routledge, 2001), 92–114.

[25]See, for example, Gordon, *Pitied But Not Entitled*; Bell, *Aid to Dependent Children*; Ladd-Taylor, *Mother-Work*; Goodwin, *Gender and the Politics of Welfare Reform*; and Nadasen, Mittelstadt, and Chappell, *Welfare in the United States*, 11–22.

[26]Bell, *Aid to Dependent Children*. The perception of the program's caseload suffered after 1939 when reforms granted widows access to the Old Age Insurance benefits of their deceased husbands. Transferring widows out of ADC made the program more politically vulnerable by removing the least stigmatized women and increasing the percentage of women of color and divorced, separated, or unmarried women on the caseload. By having critical benefits of citizenship flow through the male breadwinner, it also further concretized in the welfare state the normative vision of heterosexual, nuclear families.

staked out the back door to make sure no one fled the premises. The two then proceeded to search the dwelling, paying special attention, according to the court decision about the constitutionality of these campaigns, "to beds, closets, bathrooms, and other places of concealment."[27] After searching hundreds of homes, officials prosecuted four women for fraud and opened thirty-three other investigations.[28]

In the 1960s, states faced mounting pressure from inside and outside government to expand accountability and access to AFDC. Since ADC's inception, state officials had struggled with federal administrators who used the notion of a right to welfare to make ADC administration more rule bound and uniform. Federal administrators were able to coerce compliance and more substantial public assistance through the threat of withholding critical matching funds from recalcitrant states.[29] Local welfare-rights groups were active throughout the 1960s, particularly in New York and California. In 1966, groups met to form a national consortium for welfare rights that became the National Welfare Rights Organization (NWRO). A significant percentage of the leadership and membership of this vocal interracial welfare-rights movement was black women receiving AFDC. They demanded and in many cases received larger grants, a more responsive grievance procedure, and greater accountability from the welfare program. In the case of California, the nascent welfare-rights movement also drew energy, strategies, and expertise from organizing by the civil rights movement, the blind, and farm workers.[30] The War on Poverty and its Community Action agencies provided funds and infrastructure that activists used to challenge local welfare administrators.[31] The new commitment to provide legal services for the poor facilitated an energetic litigation strategy committed to expanding welfare rights. At first, much of the focus was on simply securing the benefits and resources, such as winter coats, that the program itself allowed but were frequently withheld through the discretion of caseworkers. As time went on, activists also weighed in on policy struggles at the state and federal levels.

They articulated a unique feminist ideology that challenged stigmatizing practices and claimed the right to state support by virtue of their

---

[27] Benny Max Parrish, Plaintiff and Appellant, v. The Civil Service Commission of the Country of Alameda, etc., et al., Defendants and Respondents. Docket No. S.F. 22429, Supreme Court of California, 66 Cal.2d 260 (1967), March 27, 1967.

[28] Felicia Ann Kornbluh, *The Battle for Welfare Rights: Politics and Poverty in Modern America* (Philadelphia: University of Pennsylvania Press, 2007), 29.

[29] Tani, *States of Dependency.*

[30] Kornbluh, *The Battle for Welfare Rights*, 27–33.

[31] Annelise Orleck, *Storming Caesars Palace: How Black Mothers Fought Their Own War on Poverty* (Boston: Beacon Press, 2005).

status as mothers, citizens, and consumers.[32] Welfare-rights activists resisted the deeply rooted practice of civically subordinating people who received economic assistance. They asserted a right to economic security that did not depend on participation in the formal workforce and encompassed access to the consumer goods that were becoming the hallmarks of full citizenship in an affluent society.[33] Unlike white feminists' demands for greater access to the workplace and various professions, many in the welfare-rights movement fought for state support sufficient enough to allow parents the choice to forgo wage labor and focus on their domestic and caregiving labor. In this sense, they advocated opening to poor women and women of color the domestic arrangements historically limited to white upper- and middle-class women.

As welfare-rights organizing committees coalesced around the country, two sociologists—Frances Piven and Richard Cloward—published an influential article in a 1966 issue of the *Nation* magazine outlining a new strategy to end poverty in the United States.[34] They argued that organizers should focus on enrolling in AFDC the huge numbers of families that were eligible but did not receive state support. This campaign would not only improve families' material conditions but create a crisis for state budgets that would ultimately force politicians to establish a national minimum income. In the years that followed, it appeared that this might actually come to pass. During the mid-1960s and early 1970s, the combined pressure from War on Poverty programs, "poverty lawyers," and civil and welfare-rights activists helped increase the numbers of people applying for and receiving aid.[35] Welfare grants increased in real economic terms, and courts ruled states' "substitute parent" or "man-in-the-house" laws unconstitutional by the early 1970s.[36] These and other landmark cases greatly expanded access to welfare programs by constricting the state's ability to arbitrarily cancel grants or use morality or race to deny aid. In the pivotal 1970 case, *Goldberg v. Kelly*, the Supreme Court ruled that welfare could not be summarily suspended

[32] For detailed histories of this activism, see Kornbluh, *The Battle for Welfare Rights* and Premilla Nadasen, *Welfare Warriors: The Welfare Rights Movement in the United States* (New York: Routledge, 2005).

[33] Lizabeth Cohen, *A Consumers' Republic: The Politics of Mass Consumption in Postwar America* (New York: Vintage, 2003).

[34] Richard Cloward and Frances Piven, "The Weight of the Poor: A Strategy to End Poverty," *The Nation*, May 2, 1966.

[35] Rickie Solinger, *Beggars and Choosers: How the Politics of Choice Shapes Adoption, Abortion, and Welfare in the United States* (New York: Hill and Wang, 2001), 139–48. See also Piven and Cloward, *Regulating the Poor*.

[36] Mink, *Welfare's End*, 55.

without an evidentiary hearing, which amounted to a robust procedural protection.[37]

As more and more eligible families applied for benefits and welfare administrators accepted growing percentages of these applicants, AFDC size and costs ballooned. The rolls expanded from 3.1 million in 1960 to 10.8 million in 1974.[38] The program's size doubled just between 1965 and 1970, growing from 3.3 to 7 million people.[39] While critics often interpreted this growth as a "welfare crisis" symptomatic of an incompetent state or the pathology and laziness of the parents it served, it was—in many ways—the result of the state finally beginning to pay a great percentage of its citizens the benefits to which they were entitled. In the early 1960s, about one-third of eligible families were enrolled in AFDC. By 1971, about 90 percent were receiving benefits.[40] With these expansions, AFDC faced intensifying attacks and increasingly became a centerpiece in arguments that positioned poor mothers as the source of social disorder.

Nixon's Family Assistance Plan

As welfare budgets grew and people saw the program as disproportionately serving Latinas and African Americans, the public's already limited approval of AFDC waned. Welfare administrators who had long managed costs and allayed public hostility by denying aid to the most stigmatized women now found many of their tools ruled illegal or unviable by legal challenges and activist pressure. In this climate, program administrators and politicians endeavored to find new ways to limit expenditures while simultaneously managing the socially marginalized populations now contained within the welfare program instead of excluded from it.

In 1967, the U.S. Congress responded to mounting criticism of AFDC by passing a series of amendments to the Social Security Act designed to both incentivize and coerce recipients into the paid workforce. They instituted the Work Incentive Program (WIN), requiring any AFDC recipient deemed ready for employment to get a job or enter a training program. States technically received the authority to designate what constituted "employable" and could refer any mother, no matter the age of her chil-

---

[37]Ibid., 49–52; Solinger, *Beggars and Choosers*, 145–52. On key court decisions regarding welfare in the late 1960s and early 1970s, see Tani, *States of Dependency*, 260–69.

[38]Nadasen, Mittelstadt, and Chappell, *Welfare in the United States*, 42.

[39]Neubeck and Cazenave, *Welfare Racism*, 78–92.

[40]Ellen Reese, *Backlash against Welfare Mothers: Past and Present* (Berkeley: University of California Press, 2005), 114–15; James T. Patterson, *America's Struggle against Poverty in the Twentieth Century* (Cambridge, Mass.: Harvard University Press, 1994), 179.

dren, to work if adequate child care was available.[41] Those failing to comply would lose their portion of the grant. Legislators also endeavored to manage the shifting sexual norms that so many found alarming by enacting another amendment that froze benefits for families with a child born out of wedlock. Practical and political complications prevented the full implementation of these punitive reforms. After facing criticism for punishing innocent children for their parents' moral lapses, Congress repealed the benefit freeze for families with children born out of wedlock two years after it was enacted. Lack of child-care funding and jobs prevented wide-scale enforcement of the work requirement and it was rarely strictly implemented.[42]

In addition to containing more coercive features, the 1967 amendments attempted to entice recipients into the workforce by implementing the $30 and one-third rule. The policy disregarded the first $30 of monthly earnings as well as one-third of the remaining income for calculating recipients' eligibility for ADC benefits. In practice, this allowed recipients to maintain some cash support from the state as they earned new income from wage work. The amendments represented a further departure from the original intent of ADC, which was to enable mothers to raise their children without relying on income from wage labor.[43] Lawmakers also addressed the erosion of grants' buying power by mandating that states adjust benefit levels to reflect a community's standard of need.

The 1967 amendments had barely gone into effect when President Nixon set out to more dramatically transform the welfare program. He announced his proposal in a nationally televised speech on August 8, 1969. He opened by explaining that the country grappled with two fundamental but intertwined crises: "We face an urban crisis, a social crisis—and at the same time, a crisis of confidence in the capacity of government to do its job."[44] Nixon proposed to address these crises by replacing AFDC and its intricate social work regulations and bureaucracy with a new, simplified cash benefit to all families with dependent children living in poverty. Nixon's Family Assistance Plan (FAP) was originally based on the concept of a negative income tax or guaranteed minimum income, which had been gaining support throughout the 1960s. A negative income tax triggered payments from the government to beneficiaries when

[41] Daniel P. Moynihan, *The Politics of a Guaranteed Income: The Nixon Administration and the Family Assistance Plan* (New York: Random House, 1973), 283.

[42] Nadasen, Mittelstadt, and Chappell, *Welfare in the United States*, 42–47.

[43] Brian Steensland, *The Failed Welfare Revolution: America's Struggle over Guaranteed Income Policy* (Princeton: Princeton University Press, 2008), 70–73; Kornbluh, *The Battle for Welfare Rights*, 97–100.

[44] Quoted in Moynihan, *The Politics of a Guaranteed Income*, 221. The entire speech is reproduced in Moynihan's book.

earnings fell below specific levels, effectively building an income floor below which no citizen would be allowed to fall.[45]

Throughout 1970 and 1971, lawmakers floated competing versions of the guaranteed income program, some with higher benefit levels, others at lower levels with more stringent work provisions. As originally introduced, the FAP guaranteed a minimum income for all families, granting $500 a year for each of the first two family members and $300 a year for each remaining member. Therefore, the state would pay a family of four with no additional wages $1,600 a year, approximately $9,000 in 2010 dollars. The FAP proposed to subsidize the income of low-wage earners, regardless of family composition. This feature was the most profound modification to AFDC, which only served families with an absent parent, usually assumed to be the father and primary wage earner. (To counter the alleged incentive for husbands to leave their families to make their wives eligible for ADC, legislators in the early 1960s enacted legislation allowing some unemployed fathers to claim welfare benefits.) Under the FAP, families could keep the first $720 of annual earnings in addition to their state benefits. As earnings increased above that amount, the welfare grant decreased by fifty cents for every additional dollar earned until the grant disappeared. A family of four could have earnings up to $3,810 before they lost state support. In this way, the planners hoped to address the two principal criticisms that plagued AFDC: that the policy discouraged wage work and that it encouraged the breakup of families. The FAP was designed to ensure that families with wages and two parents would always be better-off financially than those without.[46]

The FAP remained the centerpiece of the Nixon administration's domestic legislative agenda until it abandoned the proposal in 1972. In the interim years, the policy was widely debated in the political mainstream as a viable approach to income inequality and the "welfare mess" in the United States. While support for guaranteed income proposals existed most substantively among liberals and the Left, conservative economists, such as Milton Friedman, had endorsed similar visions, or the "nega-

[45] Steensland, *The Failed Welfare Revolution*, 30–34.

[46] On including unemployed fathers, see Nadasen, Mittelstadt, and Chappell, *Welfare in the United States*, 34–38. On the FAP, see Chappell, *The War on Welfare*; Jill S. Quadagno, *The Color of Welfare: How Racism Undermined the War on Poverty* (New York: Oxford University Press, 1994), 118; Moynihan, *The Politics of a Guaranteed Income*; and Steensland, *The Failed Welfare Revolution*. The FAP initially included a significant work incentive, which administrative officials characterized as a work requirement. The program mandated that employable recipients who refused to work or enter job training would forfeit their portion of the family's benefit. Mothers with preschool-age children and those unable to work would not face this penalty. However, the program did not actually force recipients into work, it merely withheld a percentage of support and relied upon recipients to act in their own economic interests and join the formal workforce.

tive income tax," as market-based strategies that incentivized workforce participation. The concept was supported at various points by groups of major corporations, who saw in the plan a vehicle to subsidize wages and secure social peace by appeasing restive urban spaces.[47]

Nixon officials hoped that the FAP would address both the "welfare crisis" and the "backlash" it supposedly generated. It was originally conceptualized as a program to address the unrest associated with African Americans and aimed to ameliorate the urban turmoil by restoring African American men as patriarchs and breadwinners in their families.[48] However, in the months leading up to Nixon's announcement, the FAP morphed into a policy aimed at white, male, low-wage workers. The president's political strategists intended the policy to build loyalty for Nixon among his coveted "silent majority" by offering new state support to disaffected white working-class voters, especially from the South.[49]

The FAP renounced the features of AFDC that were designed to accommodate the unique position of single mothers. With low grant levels for unemployed parents, it was designed to encourage women to rely upon a male breadwinner or wage work to make ends meet. For this and other reasons, the NWRO vehemently opposed the FAP, claiming that it trapped women in unwanted or potentially unsafe relationships and coerced them into low-wage, dead-end jobs without sufficient income to raise a family. They were particularly opposed to the standard grant levels, which were considerably higher than ADFC benefits in many southern states but lower than benefit levels in urban centers in the North and West, where welfare-rights organizers were most active.[50] Although the FAP prohibited states from decreasing benefits, NRWO organizers saw it as comparable to the fixed flat grants and other cost-saving measures

[47] Reese, *Backlash against Welfare Mothers*, 121–23; Chappell, *The War on Welfare*, 58–64.

[48] Administration officials believed that reestablishing traditional gender authority would help restore social peace. This was based on assumptions most notoriously espoused in the 1965 "Moynihan report" about the allegedly pathologizing effects of matriarchal families in black communities. Daniel P. Moynihan, *The Negro Family: The Case for National Action* (Washington, D.C.: U.S. Department of Labor, Office of Policy Planning and Research, 1965); Quadagno, *The Color of Welfare*, 123–24.

[49] Steensland, *The Failed Welfare Revolution*, 116. For detailed information about the debates within the Nixon administration over the policy and politics of their welfare proposal, see 78–119.

[50] States whose welfare benefits were already above $1,600 annually were required to supplement the federal contributions to maintain existing grant sizes. The states whose grants fell below these levels, mostly in the South, would be brought to the new minimum levels. All states stood to gain new federal assistance with their welfare budgets, a fact welcomed by many state and county officials. Nixon administration officials hoped this would slow the tide of migrants fleeing the low wages, joblessness, and paltry income supports of the South for the social turmoil of the North's urban centers.

they fought at the state level across the country. The organization instead endorsed the idea of a guaranteed *adequate* income and advanced legislative proposals with universal coverage (not just serving families with dependent children), a benefit floor of $5,500, and robust legal and procedural protections.[51] Welfare-rights activists insisted that benefit levels be high enough to allow single parents the opportunity to forgo wage work if they chose to do so.

The FAP promised to have as profound an effect on the cultural and political landscape as it would have on welfare administration. By expanding the program to serve the working poor, the FAP would have eliminated a program dedicated predominantly to serving unemployed, single mothers—increasingly from communities of color. The program designers intended the FAP to lessen the stigma of state support by folding AFDC caseloads into a program also serving the employed poor. President Nixon's policy advisor, Daniel Patrick Moynihan, emphasized this dimension of the plan in a memo to Nixon, explaining that under the FAP "receiving assistance is not conditioned upon being dependent; the working poor receive it as well as the non-working poor. Thus the great stigma of welfare is removed."[52] This feature of the FAP seemed to have appealed to Nixon and he encouraged his speechwriter in a memo to emphasize that the plan "takes away the degradation of social workers snooping around, of making some children seem to be a class apart."[53] Such comments suggest that policymakers understood that the stigma of welfare was produced in large part *through* degrading administrative procedures and eligibility qualifications, not—as many claimed—through the receipt of any state assistance. Since political discourse persistently defined normative, taxpaying citizens and productive workers in opposition to welfare recipients, removing the subordinated category risked eliminating a touchstone of growing importance in U.S. political culture. Proponents did not sell the FAP as an effort to erase the distinction between programs serving employed and non-employed poor people, but the implications were not lost on members of the Nixon administration, many of whom opposed the policy on exactly these grounds.[54]

Nixon officials also intended for the FAP to confront a crisis of state legitimacy.[55] Nixon integrated the theme into his August 1969 speech, claiming that the new system would "show that government can be made to work." At the conclusion of his address, he reiterated this mission, asserting that his proposal could help turn the corner "from an

[51] Kornbluh, *The Battle for Welfare Rights*, 137–60.
[52] Steensland, *The Failed Welfare Revolution*, 143.
[53] Joan Hoff, *Nixon Reconsidered* (New York: Basic Books, 1994), 119.
[54] Steensland, *The Failed Welfare Revolution*, 110.
[55] Moynihan, *The Politics of a Guaranteed Income*, 214.

ominously mounting impotence of government to a new effectiveness of government."[56] Nixon planned to build his political constituency by offering concrete material benefits to working poor families. This is not to overplay the radicalism of the FAP, which would have amounted to a public subsidy for low-wage employers and increasingly contained many restrictive features. In later iterations of the proposal Nixon also added more punitive features to the proposal that, for example, intensified beneficiaries' supervision and parents' work requirements. Members of the Nixon administration amplified conventional anti-welfare rhetoric in their advocacy for the FAP. Although the FAP united the working and nonworking poor programmatically, the rhetoric the administration used to sell the proposal constructed a sharp, hierarchical divide between the two groups. For example, at a speech in April 1971 before the Republican Governors Association, Nixon decried the state of the welfare bureaucracy:

> It is incredible that we have allowed a system of law under which one person can be penalized for doing an honest day's work and another can be rewarded for doing nothing at all. . . . The person on welfare can often have a higher income than his neighbor who holds a low paying job.[57]

By describing welfare recipients as "doing nothing at all," his language obscured the parenting responsibilities that enabled families to qualify for welfare in the first place. Instead of faulting economic transformations for the preponderance of low-paying jobs, Nixon directed public hostility about economic hardship toward people's neighbors and the social service bureaucracies' ill-conceived program regulations.

A central part of the demeaning cultural script of welfare was the idea that recipients were not "working" or paying taxes and squandered their grants on frivolous consumer goods.[58] There was even a hit country song, Guy Drake's "Welfare Cadillac," that topped the charts for more than a month in 1970. The song caricatured a family living in a dilapidated, neglected house while using their welfare checks toward the payments on a brand-new Cadillac.[59] In the midst of his struggle to overhaul AFDC, President Nixon asked Johnny Cash to sing "Welfare Cadillac" during a performance at the White House in 1970. (He also requested Cash sing Merle Haggard's "silent majority" anthem "Okie from Muskogee," which pilloried the counterculture.) When Cash caused waves by refusing

[56] Ibid., 226.

[57] Transcript of Nixon's speech on welfare reform at the Republican Governors Association, April 19, 1971, Box GO104, Folder: Welfare-Background/News Releases, 1/4, RRGP.

[58] Nadasen, *Welfare Warriors*, 196–99.

[59] Guy Drake, "Welfare Cadillac," *CowboyLyrics.com*, http://www.cowboylyrics.com /tabs/drake-guy/welfare-cadillac-6468.html.

the administration's request, the president's staff backed off and encouraged Cash to choose his own lineup. Nixon went on to pursue other ways to manage the welfare crisis while building bridges to the populations singing along approvingly to "Welfare Cadillac."[60]

No Responsibilities, No Representation: Reagan's Vision for Welfare Reform

As Nixon struggled with Congress over the FAP, California lawmakers, spurred on by Governor Ronald Reagan, took matters into their own hands and attempted to control welfare through reforms at the state level. The welfare reforms advanced by Nixon and Reagan responded to the same host of interlocking political problems and shared many objectives and cultural assumptions. They both aimed to reform AFDC and to position wage work and the "traditional family" as the remedy for family poverty. In key ways, however, Reagan's approach was at odds with Nixon's. Instead of enlarging the state's economic responsibility by subsidizing low wages, Reagan's reforms constricted families' ability to make ends meet by combining state benefits and wage work. Instead of blurring the boundaries between deserving and undeserving poor by joining working and nonworking beneficiaries into one program, Reagan further restricted the groups eligible for welfare benefits and positioned those sustained by AFDC in a degraded civic category without full standing. Instead of illustrating state competency through a streamlined federal benefit, Reagan's reforms emphasized the abuse, waste, and fraud within government programs. Where the FAP positioned the poor as rational actors that could be susceptible to financial incentives, Reagan's reforms rejected the work incentives and instead assumed that many recipients were shiftless—even criminal—and best managed through increased surveillance and coercive work mandates.

The efforts in California, driven largely by Governor Reagan, would become particularly high profile nationally and arguably more influential in the trajectory of AFDC than the FAP. By the time he became governor, Ronald Reagan had long been an ardent critic of the welfare state and big government. His involvement with domestic anti-communism politics while president of the Screen Actors Guild helped transform him from a New Deal Democrat into a conservative Republican.[61] After the overwhelming defeat of Barry Goldwater in the 1964 presidential election, he

---

[60]"Nixon's Numbers," *TIME*, April 13, 1970.

[61]Matthew Dallek, *The Right Moment: Ronald Reagan's First Victory and the Decisive Turning Point in American Politics* (New York: Oxford University Press, 2004), 32.

became the standard-bearer for the burgeoning grassroots conservative movement that flourished in Southern California.[62]

Criticism of AFDC would be a constant feature of Reagan's political career. Through his rhetoric and policymaking, he was instrumental in forging popular narratives about welfare and making AFDC a potent issue throughout subsequent decades. Reagan claimed he was reticent when his advisors recommended making welfare a central theme in his 1966 campaign for the governorship of California. In a letter to an assemblyman in 1966, Reagan confessed that "there was a time when I thought [welfare] might be a dangerous subject, something like Barry [Goldwater] and Social Security." However, after registering the intense popular support from his potential voters for his anti-welfare message, Reagan realized that the welfare program served to organize people's frustration about their responsibilities to the state. His letter explained that "I am becoming more aware that the man on the street has decided he's supporting too many families not his own, and he wants something done."[63]

Reagan took diverse steps to manage the state budget during his first administration. While he would eventually reduce taxes, he actually increased taxes upon assuming the governorship. As early as 1967, he focused on the problem of welfare fraud and convened a panel to determine the actual extent of fraud in the system.[64] It was not until he approached his second term that Reagan became determined to tackle a more wholesale reform of California's welfare programs. There was not widespread confidence that this was a wise political move. Robert Carleson, a key architect of Reagan's welfare reforms, explained that

in those days the worst thing a governor could possibly do, and it wasn't happening anywhere in the country, was to take on this insoluble mess, because to clean it up, you had to step on so many toes politically and emotionally that it was considered something every governor should stay away from. I have been told that he [Ronald Reagan] gritted his teeth and said, "It's got to be done so we're going to do it."[65]

[62] On the history of the conservative moment and its relationship to Reagan's political career, see ibid.; Lisa McGirr, *Suburban Warriors: The Origins of the New American Right* (Princeton: Princeton University Press, 2001); and Rick Perlstein, *The Invisible Bridge: The Fall of Nixon and the Rise of Reagan* (New York: Simon and Schuster, 2014).

[63] Quoted in Dallek, *The Right Moment*, 198.

[64] Ronald Reagan to Chairman Nelson Howard, July 11, 1967, Box GO19, Folder: Welfare Fraud: Report on Welfare Fraud, RRGP; speech opening conference on July 10, 1967, 2 pp., Box GO19, Folder: Fraud (includes Cases), RRGP.

[65] Oral history of Robert Carleson, "Stemming the Welfare Tide" (1983), OH R-44, p. 48, Ronald Reagan Gubernatorial Era Project, California State Archives, Sacramento, CA (hereafter CSA). Carleson overstates this point since other governors, particularly

When the governor considered making tackling the "welfare mess" a centerpiece of his agenda, all but one of his advisors argued against it.

Reagan did face alarming predictions about the implications of AFDC's growing caseloads for the state budgets. Popular opinion judged California's welfare program to be spiraling out of control, and administrators warned that the mounting costs could bankrupt the state. In 1967, the state fiscal director warned the new governor that, due in part to expanded eligibility, program costs could increase 268 percent for the period 1960–68.[66] The state's program had grown more rapidly than the average of all state programs. Forty percent of the national caseload increase during the 1960s was attributable to the increases in just California and New York.[67] Average monthly AFDC caseloads in California grew from under 150,000 in fiscal year 1966 to over 440,000 in fiscal year 1972.[68]

Although Reagan was concerned about the fiscal implications of California's welfare program, he also had political and ideological motives for tackling it. Reagan's reforms were connected from the beginning with the larger project of discrediting the policy approaches entailed in Nixon's FAP. Reagan and Nixon had competed for the 1968 Republican presidential nomination and many predicted they would be rivals again in 1972. As Reagan jockeyed for leadership of the Republican Party, his battles over the FAP specifically and welfare more generally helped build his profile and distinguish his approach to governance. According to Carleson, the governor's reforms were about federalism: "one last effort to prove that the state, even under all of the federal rules and regulations that existed at the time, could do the job."[69]

While Reagan remained circumspect and ostensibly loyal to his party's leader through portions of the FAP debate, his objections to the president's program were widely recognized. During the few years the FAP was before Congress, Reagan testified against the plan in the Senate, lobbied California's congressional delegation to withhold its support for it, and opposed the reforms in various other public settings.[70] A 1970 *Washington Post* article stated simply that "everyone knows it is Gov-

Nelson Rockefeller, attempted to control welfare costs during this period. See Kornbluh, *The Battle for Welfare Rights*, 106–13.

[66] William Crafton, "The Incremental Revolution: Ronald Reagan and Welfare Reform in the 1970s," *Journal of Policy History* 26, no. 1 (2014): 29.

[67] Patterson, *America's Struggle against Poverty in the Twentieth Century*, 178.

[68] State of California, Department of Social Welfare, *Public Welfare in California, Series AR 1-14*, FY 1971–72, appendix F.

[69] Oral history of Robert Carleson, "Stemming the Welfare Tide," 50.

[70] See, for example, press release from Reagan administration opposing the Family Assistance Plan-HR 16311, May 5, 1970, Box GO19, Folder: Welfare Reform Act [HR 16311], 1/4, RRGP and Ronald Reagan to Members of California Congressional Delegation

ernor Reagan leading a rearguard action against [the FAP]."[71] Reagan characterized the FAP as an unprecedented, foolhardy expansion of the welfare system. In an open telegram to the chairman of the Senate Finance Committee, Senator Russell Long, Reagan explained that his reservations about the program "stem from both financial anxiety and philosophical antipathy." He saw the FAP as an expansion of welfare and ascribed the same deleterious effects to both programs:

> [The FAP legislation] includes substantial incentives for desertion; in some cases, it could encourage the dissolution of families. . . . [I]t would further weaken the moral fiber and fiscal integrity of the nation; it would drain the productive wellspring of America. Many individuals who are now being encouraged to break loose from welfare would, under the new provisions of the Act, find it more comfortable to sink back into a state of federal dependency.[72]

As opposed to enhancing their capacity to support their families, government assistance diminished the social position of the working poor by placing them in a state of dependency. In Reagan's view, it was dependency on government, not the material condition of poverty or demeaning administration, that denigrated poor families. Reagan and his allies were emboldened when the FAP languished at the close of the 1970 congressional session. After passing the House, it stalled in the Senate Finance Committee following wavering support from the Nixon administration, criticism from the NWRO, and opposition from politicians within both parties.[73]

While attempting to scuttle Nixon's national reforms, Reagan also clashed with the White House over the administration of California's AFDC program. He defiantly refused federal orders to implement the cost-of-living increases mandated by the 1967 amendments to the Social Security Act. California grant levels were woefully inadequate and did not approach the amount official government figures—which were notoriously low—deemed necessary for families to survive financially. Benefits had not been increased for twelve years and had lost much of their buying power through their failure to keep pace with inflation.[74] State officials considered the minimum income for a family of four to be $328

Who Voted against HR 16311, May 4, 1970, Box GO19, Folder: Welfare Reform Act [HR 16311], 2/4, RRGP.

[71] "Mr. Agnew on the Road," *Washington Post*, September 24, 1970, A20.

[72] Draft of telegram from Ronald Reagan to Senator Russell Long, [May 1970?], Box GO19, Folder: Welfare Reform Act [HR 16311], 1/4, RRGP.

[73] Kornbluh, "Who Shot FAP?" 134–35, 139.

[74] Lou Cannon, *Governor Reagan: His Rise to Power* (New York: Public Affairs, 2003), 350.

a month, but the most AFDC provided was $221, only 67 percent of the recognized need. California risked losing millions of dollars in federal welfare funds in penalty for Reagan's noncompliance.[75]

Facing mounting fiscal pressures and the risk of federal intervention, the governor resolved to have a plan in place to reform welfare if reelected to a second term. In August 1970, he convened a task force to develop his own recommendations. Reagan's chief of staff, Edwin Meese, penned a memo—sent under the governor's name—that announced the group's formation and outlined its mission of formulating administrative and legislative solutions to the welfare crisis. Sent to all senior staff and cabinet members, the memo introduced the binary schema that saturated the entire subsequent political debate: "This study will place heavy emphasis on the tax-payer as opposed to the tax-taker; on the truly needy as opposed to the lazy unemployable."[76] Lest there be any doubt about the state's position vis-à-vis welfare recipients, the memo concluded:

> I am determined to reduce these programs to essential services at a cost the taxpayers can afford. This is our NUMBER ONE priority. Therefore, I am asking you to make available your best employees including directors for this all-out war on the tax-taker. If we fail, no one ever again will be able to try. We must succeed.[77]

This rhetoric suggested that the state's responsibility be limited to helping those citizens deemed productive and contributing. Declaring war on tax-takers positioned welfare recipients (or recipients imagined to be unworthy) not merely as a marginal group within society but as a wartime adversary without claims on the state.

Operating in secret and staffed by managers from agencies outside the welfare bureaucracy, the task force conducted hundreds of interviews and sifted through relevant state and federal regulations.[78] In December 1970, it reported to the governor that the welfare system was indeed careening out of control and dragging the state toward certain fiscal disaster. Attributing the problem to overly expansive interpretations of the enabling laws and regulations, the task force recommended a series of reforms, predominantly aimed at controlling costs, restricting eligibility,

[75] C. K. McClatchy, "Reagan Hits Needy Children, Aged," July 31, 1970, Box GO186, Folder: Research File Health and Welfare-Welfare, 1970, 3/5, RRGP. Articles from clippings files sometimes do not include the newspaper name or date.

[76] Cannon, *Governor Reagan*, 349.

[77] Ibid.

[78] Robert B. Carleson, *Government Is the Problem: Memoirs of Ronald Reagan's Welfare Reformer* (Alexandria, Va.: American Civil Rights Union, 2010), 1–13; California Department of Social Welfare, *Welfare Reform in California . . . Showing the Way* (Sacramento, Calif., 1972), 8–11.

prompting workforce participation, and increasing the contributions required from families, particularly absent fathers. These recommendations provided the framework for the detailed program of administrative and legislative reforms that Reagan championed at the outset of his second term.

California was not alone in facing staggering welfare costs; states across the country struggled to find ways to manage their budgets. Some attempted simple across-the-board cuts to grant levels.[79] New York State, for example, also faced conflicting pressures on its welfare program from activists, budgets, and increasingly galvanized anti-welfare public opinion. Although they also increasingly pursued welfare fraud, they emphasized cuts or capping grants and overall budget allotments in efforts to contain program costs. New York City, for example, implemented a flat grant in September 1968, and the legislature, at Governor Rockefeller's urging, cut welfare budgets by 8.5 percent in 1969.[80]

California attacked the problem differently, through more targeted reforms that restricted eligibility and thinned out the rolls. The Reagan administration released a publication in 1972 explaining California's approach and positioning it as a model that deserved national emulation. Aptly titled *Welfare Reform in California . . . Showing the Way*, the publication compared California's efforts to control welfare costs to the strategies of other states:

> Whereas some states were eliminating entire programs (such as AFDC-U) or rolling back grants across the board, California's reform planners chose to "purify" the system, the goal was to preclude or uproot those from the system who legally "didn't belong there," while making grants more equitable—even increasing them as warranted—among eligibles who really did.[81]

Reagan's team predicated the strategy of winnowing the welfare rolls on the premise that an influx of ineligible or undeserving people had caused the growth in program costs.

The reforms rested on the assumption that significant numbers of recipients were committing fraud and ultimately helped etch that assumption into public opinion. Although program administrators often claimed that purging the welfare rolls of ineligible or unworthy beneficiaries would redeem public faith in the welfare system, this strategy probably had the opposite effect. Incessant political and media attention to waste,

[79] Kornbluh, *The Battle for Welfare Rights*, 140.

[80] Ibid., 106–13, 139; Nadasen, *Welfare Warriors*, 93–97.

[81] California Department of Social Welfare, *Welfare Reform in California . . . Showing the Way*, 10.

fraud, and abuse solidified public suspicion of AFDC and welfare recipients. It framed the budget crisis as a product of deceitful, lazy recipients and an incompetent bureaucracy rather than as a function of demographic, administrative, and economic shifts. The Reagan administration reforms relied on shifting, historically structured assumptions that circulated through public policy debates, popular media, the workplace, and family conversations.

The Engines of Grassroots Anti-Welfare Politics

Elite anti-welfare rhetoric developed dialectically with anti-welfare discourse at the grassroots. They sculpted and amplified each other but were not always totally aligned. Both built upon very old transactional notions of citizenship and the distinctions between the deserving and undeserving poor to make sense of the profound economic and social transformations of the 1960s and 1970s. The letters Reagan received from constituents typically articulated opposition to unworthy people receiving benefits, not opposition to state services per se. Many letters were from people claiming to be upstanding, productive citizens who nonetheless were unable to get critical services, take vacations, or make ends meet. While these writers felt that the contemporary distribution of rights and obligations was unfair, they typically did not categorically object to the state offering benefits or government intervention in general. In this sense, elite and popular anti-welfare discourse in California often diverged in important ways. Where Reagan was ideologically opposed to expanding state power and welfare's interference with market operations, popular discussions rarely hinged on whether or not the state should ensure citizens' economic security or on disagreements over big government or small government. In constituent correspondence, the debates over AFDC circled primarily around the terms of the social contract—over who could legitimately claim rights and benefits. Many constituents saw welfare as directly responsible for disturbing broader economic and social trends; others focused on welfare as a symbol and symptom of the country's wrong turn.

Popular discourse often reflected the assumption that welfare policy should be structured by the concept of "less eligibility"—a notion that has long governed policy decisions about poor relief, unemployment insurance, and, as we will see in this book's final chapters, prison conditions. According to this rationale, people receiving aid (or being held in prison) must be kept worse off than the lowest wageworkers. There would be no incentive to perform menial or unattractive labor if welfare was more attractive or provided a higher standard of living. Constituents explained in their letters that this was precisely the danger of their current condition. One woman wrote that "the lines in the banks on the first of the month are full of people wearing the latest fashions, fresh from beauty salons, and driving new cars. . . . Many of [the welfare recipients] live better, and can afford more luxuries than the dumb working people." She warned of the consequences of this dynamic: "I can't afford to continue to support all of these free loaders. If something isn't done, I will be forced to quit working and go on welfare, so that I can afford to go on living in California."[82]

While welfare recipients were by definition poor, letter writers' frustration reflected some quantitative shifts in the relationship between low wages and state benefit levels. Welfare grants historically provided benefits significantly below what one could earn doing the typical lowest-paying wage work. For example, in 1961, the average welfare grant amounted to only 60 percent of what a full-time, low-paying job in retail would pay.[83] States with higher percentages of African Americans had even wider gulfs between welfare benefits and earnings from low-wage employment and therefore had a more dramatic "work incentive."[84] However, legal challenges and pressure from welfare-rights organizing in the 1960s disrupted the patterning of benefits that endeavored to ensure low-wage work remained more attractive than state aid. The value of benefit packages increased in the 1960s, particularly after the enactment of the food stamp program in 1964. By 1976, the combined benefits of AFDC and food stamps were on average 81 percent of state retail wages and 91 percent of low wages in retail, agriculture, and the service sectors. Although public discourse typically attributed this phenomenon to increasing benefits, the eroding value of low wages was also instrumental in closing the gap.[85]

Many letter writers displayed a particular concern about access to consumer goods. Citizenship and consumerism had become intertwined in American society in the prosperous decades after World War II, where access to material goods was increasingly understood as a marker of full political belonging.[86] While this new material abundance was omnipresent in political rhetoric and corporate advertising, popular rhetoric assumed that welfare recipients, especially poor people of color, were not entitled to the fruits of the postwar consumer boom.[87] Many who

[82] Gladys V. to Ronald Reagan, [January 1971?], Correspondence Unit Administrative, Box 1971/71, 1/2, RRGP.

[83] Soss, Fording, and Schram, *Disciplining the Poor*, 89.

[84] Ibid., 90.

[85] Ibid., 96–97.

[86] Cohen, *A Consumer's Republic*; Kornbluh, *The Battle for Welfare Rights*.

[87] Cohen, *A Consumer's Republic*, 368–88.

struggled to access consumer goods and services themselves directed their hostility toward the welfare program.

The popular resonance of anti-welfare politics was also connected to the burgeoning anti-tax movement rooted in California's sprawling and increasingly powerful suburban spaces. California's prosperity and rapid growth in the postwar decades caused a dramatic influx of people, which increased demand for all state services. It simultaneously drove up real estate prices, which increased state tax appraisals. The resulting substantial increases in tax rates and property value assessments between 1965 and 1970 helped animate a suburban anti-tax populism that would leave an indelible stamp on California's politics.[88] While welfare was only one element of the growing pressure on state budgets, constituents seized on the program to evidence claims that the state misappropriated taxpayers' resources on wasteful programs and illegitimate populations. The woman quoted earlier about recipients' expensive consumer goods explicitly linked the rising tax burden to welfare costs:

> I the undersigned; the oppressed, depressed, suppressed, over taxed, working taxpayer, demand immediate action on tax relief. The past year has seen staggering increases in income tax and property tax. In some cases, the property tax increase is 100%. We have been told that increased welfare payment is the major cause of the increase. If this is so, I feel it is time for California to take a hard look at welfare.[89]

The author did not just oppose the unwanted fiscal drain of the program's costs; she also saw welfare as a fundamental affront to the perceived social contract. It seemed to her that people who performed their responsibilities—working and taxpaying—did not have economic security and access to consumer goods, while those on welfare seemed to have economic security without any civic obligations. Another woman explained that the pressure of taxes galvanized her hostility toward the program and inspired her to write to Reagan. She explained, "I am 50 years old and I will lose my house that I have worked for many years, because I can not keep up the taxes. I am still self supporting and when I see these young people sitting home waiting for their welfare check I get angry."[90]

A Mexican immigrant whose family had worked long hours to open a small business connected his frustration with welfare to the era's political

---

[88] Self, *American Babylon*, particularly 282–88.
[89] Gladys V. to Ronald Reagan.
[90] E. A. M. to Ronald Reagan, January 13, 1971, Box 1971/71, 1/2, Correspondence Unit Administrative, Box 1970/79, 1/2, RRGP.

upheaval and a feeling that the wrong people were claiming rights. He told Reagan that "there are in this country two classes of people, those of us who work and who have a great feeling of responsibility, those who do not work and consequently are absolutely [irresponsible], and what irony! the latter who do nothing but vegetate, destroy, paint and burn public and private property have more guarantees and advantages in all aspects."[91] Many anti-welfare letters echoed the public frustration with the maldistribution of rights and responsibilities that saturated Rockefeller's constituent mail. A woman who worked with aid beneficiaries in her capacity as a nurse explained that "I have noticed that these [AFDC] families seem to have one trait in common. They are all totally devoid of any sense of responsibility for their own conduct, of their own welfare, or the production and care of offspring." She critiqued the emphasis on marginalized groups' rights. "We hear so much about 'rights' these days," she wrote. "What about the 'rights' of the tax paying citizen who is losing his home and going without things he needs, because the government takes his money from him as fast as he earns it."[92] This woman interpreted the increasing tax burden as a function of carrying the weight of immoral and unworthy AFDC recipients. Putting scare quotes around "rights" gestures to the extent to which rights appeared in much public discourse as fluid and under negotiation, instead of legally fixed or settled social fact.

While politicians typically interpreted public hostility to AFDC as a mandate for welfare-state retrenchment, many of the letters to public officials could also have been read as critiques of welfare programs as *too small* and *too limited*. One woman lamented that her daughter with serious physical disabilities was unable to qualify for state support or get private health insurance; she complained that "if my daughter had illegitimate children or was a drug addict she could get medical care." She paired her call for a new state medical insurance program with suggestions of cuts and limitations for the programs serving people she perceived as causing their own misfortune.[93] One man expressed his frustration in the language of discrimination and rights that circulated widely at the time: "Welfare laws and regulations infringe upon the rights of tax payers. In some cases it allows the recipients to have more rights than those who are paying for the programs . . . which, of course, is discrimination [ellipses in original letter]." He explained:

[91] Salvador A. to Ronald Reagan, October 1, 1970, Correspondence Unit Administrative, Box 1970/78, 1/2, RRGP.

[92] Dora E. N. to Ronald Reagan, August 3, 1970, Correspondence Unit Administrative, Box 1970/79, 1/2, RRGP.

[93] Mrs. Geraldine S. to Ronald Reagan, August 19, 1970, Correspondence Unit Administrative, Box 1970/80, RRGP.

Medical cards enable the welfare recipient to receive benefits the tax payer (and that's *me*) cannot afford. . . . The welfare program, which I support by my taxes, can give my own children services that I cannot afford to give them. What it amounts to is, I am paying for medical services for another man's child but withholding them from my own children because the cost is too high . . . or obtaining the services on credit and have to sweat out the payments? Should I quit working so that my family can have these benefits?[94]

He critiqued welfare on the grounds that coverage was not expansive enough to cover his family, yet his insistence that he and recipients were categorically different types of citizens (by virtue of "taxpaying") foreclosed the option of political solidarity with recipients, even as he threatened to join their ranks.

Another letter reflected the extent to which the stigma of receiving assistance inhibited people from claiming benefits: "It just makes our hair stand on end when we see these able bodied people live on us and suck out the blood of the working people who are too proud to hold out their hands and laugh in our face because as they feel we are the 'suckers.'" This woman's frustration with her limited sick leave intensified her frustration with recipients, who, she assumed, did not have to work: "I went to work two months after having part of my body removed because of cancer. I am still working very hard and have to see the money go to loafers."[95] These letters suggest broader popular support for AFDC was undermined as much by the welfare state's paltry benefits and limited protections as by its alleged generosity or leniency toward unworthy beneficiaries.

These letters also reveal that debates over AFDC became a site for forging common sense about women's roles and responsibilities. Many letter writers said that their hostility to welfare stemmed from the fact that it allowed women to stay home with their children, a division of familial labor long celebrated and defended, especially for middle- and upper-class women. However, as those arrangements eroded for more and more women, people insisted that poor women not be spared the pressure to work for wages. One letter explicitly addressed the changing cultural norms that attenuated and challenged the original maternalist vision that had structured AFDC. The author opened by establishing her unequivocal support for state support for groups she considered deserving and genuinely needy:

[94]Terrance B. to Ronald Reagan, September 3, 1970, Correspondence Unit Administrative, Box 1970/80, RRGP.

[95]Mrs. William S. R. to Ronald Reagan, September 23, 1970, Correspondence Unit Administrative, Box 1970/79, 1/2, RRGP.

I am not against welfare for the blind, physically handicapped or the aged. Nor am I against aid to the needy children left fatherless whose mother cannot provide for them because of illness. These people should be helped. My concern lies with the young and the healthy. The unwed mothers, divorcees, dope addicts, marginal cases and aliens.

She articulated her opposition to welfare by identifying a gulf between social norms and social practice. "According to our Cultural Society and welfare rules and regulations mothers are not asked to go to work," she explained. "These rules seem to apply only to mothers on welfare. I work with many mothers who much leave their children with babysitters. Why can't these young unwed and divorced mothers work?" Her letter suggested that her frustration flowed from the contrast between her circumstances and those of welfare recipients: "It also hurts to leave my child with a babysitter because I want a better future for her and yet knowing there are unwed and divorced mothers being paid to stay home with their children and instead are out partying and possibly adding a new illegitimate child to our welfare rolls."[96]

These articulations tended to efface the work of child-rearing that welfare recipients performed. When letter writers did acknowledge that alternative child-care arrangements were needed if parents were to take jobs, they tended to underestimate both its cost and availability. In the reply to constituents who recommended that all recipients be required to labor outside the home, the governor's office emphatically denied that poor women provided any meaningful labor, either to their families or society at large:

> You are one of many concerned citizens who have suggested that welfare recipients be required to participate in a public work project in return for the grant they receive—and I agree with you. The taxpayer can rightfully expect that the healthy and able recipient perform *some* function of benefit to that segment of society who foots the bill. The need to eliminate "welfare without work" as a way of life is particularly appropriate in light of the skyrocketing costs of our welfare program.[97]

This elision of domestic labor had consequences for all families struggling to manage time and resources as women entered the workforce in growing numbers. However, it should not be surprising that the most intense devaluation of women's parenting labor focused on AFDC, a pro-

[96] Mrs. Betty L. to Ronald Reagan, August 28, 1970, Correspondence Unit Administrative, Box 1970/79, 1/2, RRGP.

[97] Ronald Reagan to Mrs. James F., December 3, 1970, Correspondence Unit Administrative, Box 1970/78, 1/2, RRGP.

gram popularly understood to serve African Americans. Black women's domestic and familial roles had been denied, denigrated, or obscured in various ways for generations.

Welfare recipients vocally demanding rights and benefits in organized protests also fueled antagonism to AFDC. One woman wrote, "On the news this morning I heard about the Long Beach Mothers who are on welfare, making demands for more money for clothes for their children. How dare they make demands of any kind. I don't think being helped by others is anyone's right, [it's] a privilege and I am getting to the point (along with many others) that I do not feel this program should continue as it is."[98] While most recipients were legally entitled to the benefits they received (as well as other benefits that they were organizing to procure), this letter positioned beneficiaries as supplicants and rejected any notion of a right to welfare or assistance that attached to citizenship. She explained to Reagan that "at the age of 47, when it became necessary for me to work, I went to school, and I got a job. I think the majority of the above mentioned females could do the same."[99] Since she had entered the workforce, she felt other women should be expected to do the same.

Many of the people who wrote in opposition to AFDC expressed interests that diverged from those of politicians and administrators. Where the poor and working-class opponents often bemoaned the limited state support available, politicians, especially those ideologically opposed to the welfare state, were looking for ways to limit state spending and commitments. Yet while many of the anti-welfare letters to Reagan were critiquing the welfare state as too small, too difficult to access, and too paltry, few expressed solidarity with the program beneficiaries they deemed unworthy. Therefore, state support was not as controversial as its beneficiaries, and many of the letters could be read as expressing the desire for (or the threat to desire) the very services and freedom welfare was imagined to offer. Instead of demanding an expansive vision of state support or social citizenship, many constituents demanded a reduction in the benefits for and rights of people perceived as undeserving. One man who could not afford medical insurance offered a list of policy recommendations:

1. The welfare rolls should be published in the local newspapers as should the names of persons delinquent in payment of taxes and persons receiving traffic fines.
2. Some limit should be put on the number of children an unwed mother can receive benefits for.

[98] Mrs. Ardath H. to Ronald Reagan, [October/September 1970?], Correspondence Unit Administrative, Box 1970/79, 1/2, RRGP.
[99] Ibid.

3. Welfare recipients should receive goods and services only and more effective training as to the uses of these instituted . . . doing away with the "Welfare Cadillac." I believe the goods and services distributed be of a staple nature—no alcoholic beverages, cigarettes, color televisions, etc. The benefits should only include food, clothing, shelter and medical benefits.[100]

Such reforms assumed that accepting state support entailed the forfeiture of privacy and reproductive and consumer choice. They recommended establishing a fair distribution of benefits and rights through civic degradation and deliberately *leveling down* the living standards of aid recipients.

While many proposed reducing benefit levels, controlling recipients' consumption, or mandating labor for private or public organizations, others instead recommended limiting recipients' political and social rights. The San Lorenzo Valley Property Owners' Association also suggested that the state publish the names of all people receiving state aid: "Our burden is mounting by leaps and bounds. How long can a taxpayer stand by and endure this waste. We want the helpless cared for, but the grafters should be prosecuted. We, the Board of Directors of San Lorenzo Valley Property Owners' Ass'n Inc. firmly believe if all the recipients of welfare had their names published maybe it would force some of the leeches to stop their demand for free-loading."[101] While the letter acknowledged that some people needed care, the welfare program was broadly "waste," which warranted public shaming of the entire caseload, presumably both the "helpless" and the "leeches." The response to this letter from the Reagan administration dodged the policy proposal by lamenting (inaccurately) that this age-old custom would not be allowed by federal law. They encouraged the organization to lobby the principal target of Reagan's ire: federal officials and lawmakers imposing more uniform and robust welfare benefits: "Our major obstacle in solving the runaway welfare situation are federal rules and regulations, complicated by court decisions favoring the recipient, needy or not."[102]

Some of those who advocated removing political rights did not use fiscal justifications but rationales grounded in contractual conceptions of citizenship. California state senator Jack Schrade proposed in 1970

[100]Terrance B. to Ronald Reagan, September 3, 1970, Correspondence Unit Administrative, Box 1970/79, 1/2, RRGP.

[101]San Lorenzo Valley Property Owners' Ass'n, Inc., to Ronald Reagan, October 10, 1970, Correspondence Unit Administrative, Box 1970/79, 1/2, RRGP.

[102]Reagan to Miss Audry F., Corresponding Secretary for the Board of Directors of San Lorenzo Valley Property Owners' Ass'n, Inc., October 19, 1970, Correspondence Unit Administrative, Box 1970/79, 1/2, RRGP.

to deny habitual welfare recipients the right to vote. Paul Harvey, a popular conservative radio commentator, championed the proposal in his newspaper column. He explained that "now, his proposal merely sounds revolutionary. Actually, in Colonial America this was the policy. In the beginning of our nation only taxPAYERS were allowed to vote. Sen. Schrade is daring to say what a lot of taxpaying Americans have been thinking, that when you get behind in your dues you lose the right to run the club."[103] Buttressing his proposal with a reference to laws that stripped paupers of civil and political rights, Harvey inverted the traditional American axiom "no taxation without representation" to argue that there should be no representation without taxation.

The notion of a "culture of poverty" undergirded these debates and drew more attention during the 1960s. According to this theory, poor communities responded to economic deprivation with a series of cultural accommodations that in time actually perpetuated their subordinated economic position. Its proponents assumed that disorganized families, led by bad or unfit mothers and subsided by welfare, bequeathed social pathology to their children, who in turn proved incapable or unwilling to enter the economic and social mainstream. This notion of a culture of poverty was most famously associated with the 1965 report "The Black Family: A Case for National Action." The report became popularly known as the Moynihan Report, after its author, Daniel Patrick Moynihan. In it, he argued that the persistent poverty in African American communities was rooted in slavery and subsequent racial oppression. African American men withdrew from their families because they were historically prevented from assuming the role of breadwinner, leaving dysfunctional female-headed households that transmitted social pathology. Since Moynihan's report generated huge controversy and attention, it remains the most well-known articulation of the "culture of poverty" thesis. However, visions of a "culture of poverty" also developed through the production of popular and social scientific knowledge about differently racialized groups, particularly Puerto Ricans, both on the island and after migration to the mainland.[104] These logics circulated with the narratives about drugs and crime explored in previous chapters. They positioned welfare and black

[103] Paul Harvey, "Addictive Welfare," *Observer-Reporter*, Washington, Pa., October 20, 1970, A4.

[104] The anthropologist Oscar Lewis was one of the first to popularize the concept in the early 1960s in studies of Mexicans and Puerto Ricans. Laura Briggs, *Reproducing Empire: Race, Sex, Science, and U.S. Imperialism in Puerto Rico* (Berkeley: University of California Press, 2002), 162–83.

and Latina women's parenting at the root of crime, urban unrest, and racial and economic inequality.[105]

These narratives became more dominant as welfare reform debates intensified, but they were never uncontested. Welfare-rights organizers asserted a right to economic security as a function of legal citizenship, parenting, or other civic contributions. Welfare-rights organizers grounded their claims on the state in their role as "mother citizens" and championed women's roles in raising and cultivating the next generation of citizens. They insisted that parenting was demanding work, especially when poor. At a hearing in 1967, George Wiley, a leader of the NWRO, explained to Long's Senate Finance Committee that "welfare mothers already have more than a full time job—raising their children on inadequate welfare grants."[106] Activists directly challenged "culture of poverty" narratives positioning poor black women as weakening society by generating pathological children. Instead, they insisted that they were performing valuable social and civil labor by rearing productive and contributing future citizens.

It was not just organized welfare recipients who attempted to refute the stereotypes about AFDC beneficiaries. In 1971, the Department of Health, Education, and Welfare printed 100,000 pamphlets titled "Welfare Myths vs. Welfare Facts," which it distributed broadly. Using extensive charts and statistics, it explained that less than 1 percent of the rolls were able-bodied unemployed men, that families spent an average of twenty-three months receiving AFDC, that the majority of recipients were white, and that 68 percent of children were born to married parents. Taking aim at the notion recipients had surplus resources to spend on cars and alcohol, it published survey findings where recipients explained they would spend any extra money on food, clothing, and shoes for their children.[107] Individual social workers also attempted to intervene in the public representations of AFDC. One held Governor Reagan directly responsible for misrepresenting the program and wrongly blaming dishonest caseworkers and recipients for expanding welfare costs:

> The reason for higher costs certainly is not because we are giving excessive amounts of money to the clients as they live on a very low subsistence level. . . . Welfare costs are increasing because of the increase in caseloads caused by poor people moving into this rich state and by technological unemployment. Contrary to what you have been saying in your speeches,

[105] For the "culture of poverty" generally, see Katz, *The Undeserving Poor* and Briggs, *Reproducing Empire*, 162–83.

[106] Michelmore, *Tax and Spend*, 84.

[107] "HEW Paper Blasts 'Myths' Linked to Welfare Recipients: Idea That Extra Cash Is Used for Cars, Liquor Hit," *Los Angeles Times*, November 17, 1971, 2.

most welfare recipients, in my experience, want to be self-supporting and independent but cannot because of physical, educational, language, racial or other similar barriers beyond their control.[108]

These and similar efforts to counter the anti-welfare politics aimed to not only illuminate AFDC recipients' caregiving labor and other evidence of civic belonging but also assert that they were, in fact, very poor.

Becoming His Own Lobby: Reagan Mobilizes for Welfare Reform

It was in this political milieu that Reagan's administration moved to reform the state's welfare program. The governor first implemented a series of administrative reforms that did not require approval from the Democrat-controlled legislature. Reagan appointed Robert Carleson—an assistant director from the transportation department with no prior experience in welfare administration—to head the Department of Social Welfare during the transition. Carleson had been an enthusiastic member of Reagan's task force and had formulated most of the committee's recommendations. Carleson first moved to rectify the welfare department's allegedly incompetent, negligent management by replacing whole swathes of leadership and staff. The report that touted the state's reform program explained that the expertise and bureaucratic habits of social workers were antithetical to the administration's new orientation: "Out the window went the tradition of having the Department run by social workers or unwitting captives; in the door marched a management-legal-fiscal-oriented team intent upon reshaping welfare into a viable system under which both the genuinely needy and the troubled taxpayer would find equanimity and relief."[109] These comments reflected the administration's assumption that taxpayers and welfare recipients were fixed, distinct social categories with antagonistic interests. They explicitly submerged the purported state accountability to the program's beneficiaries that welfare-rights activists had seized upon to leverage larger grants and administrative accountability.

A series of seemingly banal reforms revealed the state's efforts to reorient the program from servicing welfare recipients to serving "the public." In an oral history interview years later, Carleson explained that he needed to purge the department's administrators, most of whom were social workers

---

[108] John B. to Ronald Reagan, June 1, 1970, Correspondence Unit Administrative, Box 1970/80, RRGP.

[109] California Department of Social Welfare, *Welfare Reform in California . . . Showing the Way*, 10.

who "really believed that they were representing the people who came in the door. They weren't representing the people who were paying the bill or who were running the department."[110] The department reform constrained social workers, who had a "tendency to regard themselves as advocates for their clients," to use their discretion in favor of recipients when regulations were vague.[111] Other reforms tightened eligibility, revised income limits, and instituted new efforts to prevent and correct abuse and fraud.[112]

Ostensibly because of the budget crisis, the department leadership submitted these new regulations as emergency measures to be implemented immediately, bypassing the usual review and comment period where officials anticipated resistance and challenges from welfare-rights groups.[113] Many of the reforms desired by the Reagan administration, however, needed to be enacted legislatively, and the governor requested permission to address a joint session of the legislature to introduce his proposed reforms. The Democratic leadership, who were aware that the governor hoped to gain political advantage from the speech, made the unusual decision of refusing Reagan the platform.[114] Reagan characterized the Democrats' move as protecting the embattled welfare program, and he vowed to take his plan for action directly to the people. He instead unveiled his plan on March 3, 1971, at a public speech in Los Angeles. The televised address and surrounding controversy attracted considerable media attention.[115]

Unlike the federal and state officials willing to tolerate the "uncontrolled upward spiraling of the welfare caseload," Reagan declared that he stood resolved to tackle the problem.[116] His speech acknowledged that the welfare system failed to provide sufficiently for the "truly destitute" but did not attribute this to inadequate benefit levels. Instead, the system failed because its incompetent administration allowed suspect and unneedy populations to infiltrate the rolls. He explained that "[welfare] is spread thin in attempting to provide for too many who are not needy but who through loopholes are legally eligible to claim welfare benefits, and too many who are receiving aid illegally because there is just no way to

[110] Oral history of Robert Carleson, "Stemming the Welfare Tide," 35.

[111] Reagan officials also made benefit calculations the purview of "eligibility workers" who were trained in technical regulations but were paid less since they did not have social work degrees. California Department of Social Welfare, *Welfare Reform in California . . . Showing the Way*, 25.

[112] Ibid., 11.

[113] Oral history of Robert Carleson, "Stemming the Welfare Tide," 60.

[114] Tom Goff, "Reagan Spurned on Legislature Talk," *Los Angeles Times*, February 26, 1971; oral history of Robert Moretti, "Reflections of an Assembly Speaker" (1983), OH R-24, pp. 170–71, Ronald Reagan Gubernatorial Era Project, CSA.

[115] Cannon, *Governor Reagan*, 351.

[116] Ibid.

prevent their cheating."[117] When the Reagan administration introduced its detailed welfare reform package in the legislature, the governor positioned his reforms as a model for the nation, clearly signaling that his proposals were intended to counter Nixon's Family Assistance Plan. "No other solution is in sight anywhere in the nation," he declared. "As usual, California is leading the way with courage and imagination down the always uncertain and sometimes slippery path of reform."[118]

At the outset, the Democratic-controlled legislature did not feel insurmountable pressure to acquiesce to the governor, and his package languished in various committees through June. In the interim, Reagan officials initiated a full-scale campaign to organize public understandings of the crisis and generate support for the administration's reforms. The governor consistently portrayed his punitive proposals as the only commonsense response to a corrupt system careening out of control. In one statement to the legislature, Reagan outlined the essential contours of his arguments for reforms: "Changes in our laws are imperative if we are to restore the balance between the legitimate interests of the taxpayer, and those of the honest, truly dependent welfare recipient."[119] He again portrayed welfare recipients—even the "honest" ones—and taxpayers as opposing and separate categories with inversely related interests. In claiming responsibility only for the "honest, truly dependent welfare recipient," Reagan absolved the state of accountability to the significant number of recipients he considered illegitimate and dishonest.

Reagan's vision of reform directly challenged welfare-rights activists' demands for freedom to choose whether to enter the workforce or to decline employment they deemed undesirable. In an interview with *U.S. News & World Report*, Reagan used the growing number of employed mothers to undermine AFDC's traditional mission of removing women from the workforce while raising children. Celebrating the story of a woman and her mother who carefully coordinated child-care responsibilities in order to manage their shifts as firewatchers, he asked, "When you look at that—well, by what right does a welfare worker say that just because a woman has children no one should expect her ever again to be self supporting? There are millions of women who are out working and supporting their kids."[120] Where in other settings conservatives bemoaned

[117] Quote from welfare speech, March 3, 1971, Box GO107, Folder: Welfare-Memoranda + Correspondence-March 1971, RRGP.

[118] Robert Fairbanks, "Nixon and Reagan Talk, Find Views on Welfare Are Similar," *Los Angeles Times*, April 3, 1971, A1.

[119] Ronald Reagan to the Members of the Legislature of California, March 19, 1970, Box GO186, Folder: Research File-Health and Welfare-Welfare, 1970, 2/5, RRGP.

[120] "Welfare: America's No. 1 Problem," *U.S. News & World Report*, March 1, 1971, Box GO186, Folder: Research File-Health and Welfare-Welfare, 1971, 2/6, RRGP.

how jobs took mothers away from the home and their children, here Reagan valorized poor women's wage earning and deemphasized and effaced their caregiving labor. In his interview, Reagan went on to explain that women agitating for welfare rights lacked a work ethic:

> I remember a statement in one hearing where one of these women from the Welfare Rights Organization got fired up and screamed out: "And don't talk to us about any of those menial jobs." Now, I don't think jobs are menial. You know, here's a woman who is demanding her right to be supported by the working people, and she's saying to millions of other people who are chambermaids in a hotel or maids in homes—she is insulting them and saying that somehow they're beneath her and that she will only work if you can guarantee that the job will be at the executive level.[121]

Such pronouncements positioned welfare recipients' activism as an affront to other struggling families and insisted that recipients, widely imagined to be black and Latina women, were antagonistic to other wage-earning women.

In early April, the *New York Times* ran an opinion editorial by Reagan titled "Welfare Is a Cancer." In it, he explained that welfare is "a cancer that is destroying those it should succor and threatening society itself." Not only had welfare failed those unfortunate destitute people who had no other way to support themselves, but "it has failed those who want to find their way into productive lives as people—individuals with a purpose and a goal—not a faceless mass whose destiny is the dole." With this language, the governor positioned productivity, individuality, and social value as antithetical to receiving welfare. At the editorial's conclusion, he again reiterated the dichotomous positioning of welfare receipt and full citizenship, declaring that the "only way to measure the success of the program is not by how many people have been added to the rolls, but how many have been removed and made productive citizens."[122] Within these discursive confines, there were few ways to be a welfare recipient *and* have legitimate voice in the polity. "Productive" citizenship was given specificity through the contrast to welfare recipients and the particular collection of negative attributes ascribed to them.

Although Reagan officials were outwardly confident of public support for their reforms, they left little to chance. In addition to scheduling extensive public appearances by the governor himself, the staff took the unusual step of organizing a citizens' committee to generate public pressure on the legislature for reform. The committee was a bipartisan

---

[121] Ibid.

[122] Ronald Reagan, "Welfare Is a Cancer," *New York Times*, April 1, 1971, Box GO186, Folder: Research File-Health and Welfare-Welfare, 1971, 3/6, RRGP.

group of reform supporters from around the state, which included administrators, a town mayor, a minister, a union leader, a law student, and a divorced working mother who chose not to receive welfare. Not a single welfare recipient served on the committee.[123] At the press conference announcing the committee's formation, a reporter questioned the governor about appointing his own advocacy group: "Aren't you in effect organizing your own pressure group and will it be part of their function to—to communicate with the legislature?" Reagan explained that he intended his committee to counterbalance the high-profile welfare-rights activism:

> Yes, I've been perfectly frank about it. I think there has to be a voice of the people that is heard, and I believe from my observation that the overwhelming majority of the people, regardless of party lines, are totally convinced that we are on a wrong path and that welfare is, as has been described here, a mess, and it must be reformed. Now, I am—if you look at the hearings that have been held so far, if you look at the demonstrations that have been held so far, a stranger in our midst would get a completely different idea. He would believe that public opinion was on the other side, and I think every one of you knows that public opinion is not on the other side.

Reagan explained that he intended his committee "to simply reveal where the people stand."[124] This rhetoric again underscored the distinction between full citizens—whom the state was charged to serve—and welfare recipients. Through such pronouncements, Reagan helped to produce the evidence of public support he claimed legitimated his efforts.

The statewide citizens' committee coordinated the work of 120 local committees, which were largely organized by local chamber of commerce branches across the state.[125] The chamber of commerce selected welfare as one of its main issues and dedicated significant resources to aid Reagan's campaign. The chamber loaned executives to staff the local committees, which ranged from ten to a few hundred members. They also ran ads in newspapers to pressure recalcitrant lawmakers. For example, one conservative Democratic senator would confront a full-page advertisement in his district's hometown paper that inquired, "Why is Senator Collier holding back welfare reform?"[126]

The citizens' committee also printed thousands of glossy brochures describing the welfare crisis and Reagan's proposed reforms. Next to

[123]Tom Goff, "Reagan Picks Panel to Help 'Sell' Welfare Plan," *Los Angeles Times*, March 31, 1971, 26; transcript of press conference of Governor Reagan, March 30, 1971, Box GO186, Folder: Research File-Health and Welfare-Welfare, 1971, pp. 1–15, 2/6, RRGP.
[124]Ibid., 12.
[125]Oral history of Robert Carleson, "Stemming the Welfare Tide," 73–75.
[126]Ibid., 75.

photos of Franklin Delano Roosevelt, Robert Kennedy, and Reagan, the brochure featured their quotes about welfare's destructive, degrading effects on recipients' spirits and the national fiber. "Remember!" the pamphlet proclaimed. "The burden you bear promises to grow larger every year . . . unless reforms are made NOW!" Supporters could tear off a section of the brochure to send to their state legislators after checking off which aspects of the plan they "particularly liked." For many voters, there was probably little to oppose in Reagan's reforms as the brochure described them: "Requiring work-for-welfare for the able"; "removing free loaders from the welfare rolls"; "limiting the amount of aid being paid those with high income"; and "tracking down absent, negligent fathers."[127] Californians sent thousands of these cards into legislative offices through the spring and early summer of 1971, increasing the pressure on lawmakers to deliver some measure of welfare reform.[128]

In the event that the committee's public relations and letter-writing campaign did not convince its opponents, the Reagan administration secretly prepared to field a ballot initiative on welfare reform. The staff planned to rely on the infrastructure established by the welfare reform committees to quickly gather the needed signatures and place the measure before voters in the 1972 primaries. The initiative threatened incumbents who had not supported reform by providing a readymade issue for their challengers. Reagan's staff designed the initiative to pressure both recalcitrant Democrats and Republican supporters of Nixon and the FAP. "Supporters of FAP knew that if Reagan succeeded in welfare reform in California, the largest state, their efforts to nationalize welfare were dead," Robert Carleson explained in his autobiography:

> Therefore, we were fighting not only the Democrats in Sacramento; we were fighting the Nixon Republicans in Sacramento and Washington. This situation made a Reagan-led welfare reform initiative in the 1972 primary a threat to all of his opponents—Democrat and Republican, state and federal. We code-named the secret initiative plan "Operation Crossfire."[129]

Someone in the governor's office probably leaked the plans for Operation Crossfire to key members of the legislature as resistance slowly softened among Democrats and Nixon loyalists in the Republican caucus.

---

[127] California Citizens' Committee for the Governor's Welfare Reform Program, Welfare Reform Pamphlet, Box GO186: Folder: Research File-Health and Welfare-Welfare, 1971, 1/6, RRGP.

[128] Carleson, *Government Is the Problem*, 25.

[129] Ibid., 24.

The popular support Reagan threatened to marshal against his opponents reflects the power of political rhetoric to frame poverty, and wrenching social and economic transformations, as a problem arising from a discrete group of pathological deviants. The constituency mobilized by these anti-welfare politics was less alarmed by the threat of big government than by the notion that welfare recipients had violated the social contract and forfeited claims on the state. As popular expectations regarding women's work continued to change, politicians used welfare recipients to advance definitions of valuable, dignified work by graphically representing its opposite. They drew a sharp distinction between welfare "dependence" and wage labor, demeaning the first to exalt the latter.[130] The discussions surrounding these transformations incessantly championed the virtue and American character of wage work, no matter how menial or unpleasant. Of course, the very real psychological and social benefits of being positioned above welfare recipients did little to improve low-income workers' economic conditions.

Through his high-profile campaign, Reagan articulated particular understandings of the causes of and remedies for the "welfare mess" that would eventually become political common sense: that welfare policy must privilege the rights of "taxpayer" over the "tax-taker" recipient through degrading administrative and political rituals. At the time, Reagan's approach to welfare was not seen as obvious or inevitable. In fact, it was President Nixon's FAP that seemed poised to become the nation's approach to family poverty. Reagan's welfare reforms, while sharing some of Nixon's assumptions and aims, were an attempt to derail the FAP and establish Reagan's conservative credentials on the national stage. His plan made access to benefits more conditional and degraded the civic status of recipients through surveillance and new work and reporting requirements. As Reagan's framing of the "welfare mess" gained more traction, alternative visions advanced by welfare recipients of even more robust social rights and guaranteed incomes receded from the public debate. As we shall see, the intensifying attention to welfare fraud and the recruitment of the penal system would be instrumental in narrowing the spectrum of debate and in positioning poor women receiving welfare as suspect citizens.

[130] For the historical development and political work of the concept of "dependency," see Nancy Fraser and Linda Gordon, "A Genealogy of 'Dependency': Tracing a Keyword of the US Welfare State," *Signs* 19, no. 2 (Winter 1994): 309–36.

CHAPTER FOUR

Welfare Is a Cancer

ECONOMIC CITIZENSHIP IN THE AGE OF REAGAN

On June 28, 1971, Robert Moretti, the Democratic speaker of the California Assembly, broke the political impasse with Governor Reagan by sending him a letter calling for productive and substantial bipartisan negotiations on welfare.[1] Reagan claimed in his frequent retellings of the story that Moretti was hounded to the bargaining table by the political pressure his campaign had generated. He would tell of how Moretti arrived at his office and declared, "Stop the cards and letters. I'm ready to negotiate a welfare reform act."[2] Starting in late July 1971, the parties entered into almost two weeks of intense deliberations, led primarily by Moretti and Reagan. Reagan was an accomplished negotiator seasoned by years as president of the Screen Actors Guild and emerged delighted with a final reform package. Accounts differ over which side prevailed on substantive policy matters, but few would dispute that Reagan benefited politically by forcing welfare reform onto the agenda. A Reagan aide subsequently claimed that through savvy negotiating, the governor disguised which provisions were most important to him and secured 80 percent of his desired reforms, surrendering to the Democrats on nothing they deemed vital.[3] Moretti, on the other hand, maintained that the legislation reflected the Democrats' principles and objectives. He later explained that his team happily supported the new eligibility restrictions and antifraud measures that Reagan's team presented as Democratic concessions: "We [Democrats in the welfare negotiations] had no desire to protect the goddamn welfare cheats. We were just as glad to get rid of them as he [Reagan] was, but we were interested in protecting the aged, the blind,

---

[1] Speaker Robert Moretti to Gov. Ronald Reagan, June 28, 1971, Box GO186, Folder: Research File-Health and Welfare-Welfare, 1971, 3/6, RRGP.

[2] Steven F. Hayward, *The Age of Reagan: The Fall of the Old Liberal Order: 1964–1980* (New York: Crown Forum, 2009), 244; Lee Edwards, *The Essential Ronald Reagan: A Profile in Courage, Justice, and Wisdom* (Lanham, Md.: Rowman and Littlefield, 2005). Others suggest that Moretti was motivated by a desire to deliver some significant legislative achievements after four years of gridlock with the Reagan administration. Cannon, *Governor Reagan*, 350–60.

[3] Carleson, *Government Is the Problem*, 15–33.

and the disabled mostly, and the children."[4] This enthusiastic bipartisan support for anti-fraud measures is a key to understanding the power and durability of anti-welfare politics.

While opposing fraud appeared to be a commonsense—even essential—political posture, the imperative to crack down on welfare cheats rested upon (and ultimately reified) contested narratives about citizenship, deservingness, and the mechanisms driving up welfare caseloads. This chapter examines the unique role that civic degradation—particularly intensifying criminalization and anti–welfare fraud campaigns—played in further stigmatizing welfare recipients and AFDC. Campaigns that positioned welfare recipients as criminally suspect helped cast the entire welfare program as *robbery*—an unjust and forcible transfer of resources from worthy, hardworking Americans to unworthy poor people. It was this logic that rationalized reorienting the mission of welfare from rehabilitating marginalized parents to protecting the "taxpayers" from the "tax-takers."

This chapter highlights the ways charges of criminality produced the racially freighted caricature of the "welfare queen," suppressed poor women's voices and claims on the state, and undermined support for the welfare state more broadly.[5] Much popular opposition to welfare did not arise from an aversion to assisting "deserving" poor parents but from the conviction that recipients as a group refused to work or otherwise contribute to the polity. Public opinion polls confirm that most Americans supported providing aid to those understood as genuinely needy or incapable of wage work. But political rhetoric and institutional reforms increasingly evacuated AFDC of "deserving" populations, leaving the program more and more vulnerable to political attacks. New reforms would institutionally and symbolically separate AFDC from the pro-

---

[4]Robert Moretti, "Reflections of an Assembly Speaker" (1983), OH R-24, p. 174, Ronald Reagan Gubernatorial Era Project, CSA.

[5]Although it is rarely a focus in historical work, the perception that welfare recipients were fraudulent and deceptive was a primary factor in undermining support for the program. For other scholarship that has also examined the role of welfare fraud, see Solinger, *Beggars and Choosers*, 139–82 and the research of legal scholar Kaaryn Gustafson, *Cheating Welfare: Public Assistance and the Criminalization of Poverty* (New York: New York University Press, 2012). I have also been particularly influenced by scholarship on the "welfare queen" generally, especially Dorothy E. Roberts, *Killing the Black Body: Race, Reproduction, and the Meaning of Liberty* (New York: Pantheon Books, 1997); Wahneema Lubiano, "Black Ladies, Welfare Queens, and State Minstrels: Ideological War by Narrative Means," in *Race-ing Justice, En-gendering Power*, ed. Toni Morrison (New York: Pantheon Books, 1992), 323–63; Ange-Marie Hancock, *Politics of Disgust: The Public Identity of the "Welfare Queen"* (New York: New York University Press, 2004); and Laura Briggs, "La Vida, Moynihan, and Other Libels: Migration, Social Science, and the Making of the Puerto Rican Welfare Queen," *Centro Journal* 14, no. 1 (Spring 2002): 74.

grams for "legitimately dependent adults," such as the blind, aged, and disabled. The belief that welfare recipients abused the system and shirked labor animated opposition to AFDC.[6] The relentless political and media attention to welfare fraud tangibly linked criminality with the already considerable stigma against AFDC and poor, single—usually black— motherhood.[7] The spectacle of the actual indictments framed welfare recipients as dishonest criminals, eclipsing their status as mothers and citizens. Ultimately these policies converged with other state initiatives, such as punitive criminal and drug policies explored in the other parts of this book, to help solidify the public perception of a racialized, unassimilable "underclass" in U.S. society.

Welfare fraud was often a language for resisting a more expansive vision of social citizenship. The anti-fraud campaigns presented the caseload increases that resulted from new rights and access to welfare as the handiwork of malevolent "welfare queens." Stories of recipients' laziness and opulent consumption masked the often brutal social reality of welfare receipt. The focus on racialized deviants obscured the fact that the structure of the economy and low welfare grants made fraud predictable, if not inevitable. Politicians' rhetoric depicted recipients as "nonworkers" and an isolated type of poor person, but this separation of welfare recipients from the working class or working poor often dissolved on the ground.[8] Contrary to the claims of many politicians, welfare was often only one in a collection of strategies families used for economic survival and not necessarily a significant part of recipients' core identity. Welfare recipients floated between wage work and welfare, often using both simultaneously since rarely was just one of these enough to support their families. The state responded to these conditions with criminalization and surveillance instead of social or economic intervention. Since anti-fraud efforts typically targeted welfare recipients with unreported income, these campaigns penalized people who *were working outside the home* and receiving welfare. Therefore, while the era's anti-welfare politics positioned recipients as lazy nonworkers, in practice fraud campaigns criminalized recipients who earned outside money. These politics obscured welfare recipients' wage

[6] Martin Gilens, *Why Americans Hate Welfare* (Chicago: University of Chicago Press, 1999), especially 64.

[7] Arrests and criminal indictments have historically served key roles in heightening stigmatization. See, for example, Ellen Schrecker's discussion of how criminal prosecutions of communists during the 1940s hardened public opinion against the party. Ellen Schrecker, *Many Are the Crimes: McCarthyism in America* (Princeton: Princeton University Press, 1998), 120.

[8] For some background on this debate, see Michael Katz, ed., *The "Underclass" Debate: Views from History* (Princeton: Princeton University Press, 1993).

and childrearing labor in public discourse while further restricting the financial resources of low-income parents.

This chapter first explores how Reagan's welfare reforms degraded the civic status of welfare beneficiaries through constricted eligibility standards, heightened bureaucratic scrutiny, work requirements, and increased reliance on criminal prosecution in handling fraud and child-support collections. It then traces the way Illinois politicians used anti-fraud campaigns to accommodate dynamics in their own state. And it was from the interaction between the Illinois campaign and Reagan's political rhetoric that the moniker "welfare queen" entered the political lexicon. I juxtapose legislators' fiscal and political motivations for these policies with the experiences of recipients struggling to make ends meet when neither welfare nor wage work provided sufficient income. The chapter also examines the role of the thousands of informants who reported recipients for earning wages, sexual impropriety, or owning "inappropriate" consumer goods. Public participation compounded with legislators' punitive policy responses to solidify welfare recipients' status as the antithesis of "workers" and the opposite of taxpaying, respectable, productive citizens. The spectacle of surveillance and prosecutions convinced many citizens that welfare recipients were deceitful and undeserving and produced a criminogenic "culture of poverty."

Coercing Recipients, Protecting Taxpayers: The California Welfare Reform Act of 1971

With most of the details hammered out in negotiations, the California Welfare Reform Act of 1971 moved through the legislature easily. It passed the Assembly 60–9. The *Los Angeles Times* explained that the only opposition came from "the very liberal and the very conservative." John J. Miller, an African American legislator representing Oakland, charged that the program would "take from the working poor to feed the nonworking poor." Assemblyman Peter Schabarum, a conservative Republican from Covina, also protested the redistribution that the bill entailed, but complained that it did not cut welfare costs far enough: "Middle-class suburbia deserves a better shake." The State Senate passed the bill 31–8 with only Democrats opposing.[9] Governor Reagan signed the bill at an exuberant bipartisan press conference on August 12, 1971. He relished his victory, telling reporters, "I expect to be happy for the

---

[9]Tom Goff, "Welfare Reforms Sent to Governor: Compromise Clears Legislature," *Los Angeles Times*, August 12, 1971, A1, 30.

next few weeks."[10] Because the bill reflected a political compromise, its provisions were not totally ideologically consistent. Contrary to Nixon's proposed FAP, these reforms marginally benefited the populations with no outside income while dramatically constricting state support to those working for low wages. California increased grant levels to come into compliance with federal mandates, and the legislation codified ongoing cost-of-living increases to grants. Once implemented, the state, which had only provided between 67 and 71 percent of recognized need, finally covered 100 percent of the amount deemed necessary to survive.[11]

The reform package was also loaded with new features that intensified the scrutiny and stigmatization of poor parents receiving aid. The Reagan administration declared that one of the four central objectives of the bill's reforms was to "strengthen family responsibility as the basic element in our society."[12] Instead of accomplishing this by offering wage supplements to install male earners as heads of households, the Reagan administration relied heavily on the criminal justice system and other sanctions and mandates. The Reagan administration construed parents' lack of economic contribution primarily as a moral and criminal failure and relied on punitive mechanisms to induce support payments. The Department of Social Welfare's report on the new law rationalized enlisting the penal system in collecting child support because they assumed the parents in question were already criminals: "Non-supporting absent fathers are often unstable individuals frequently known to the district attorney through his other work."[13] The administration assumed people in this population would only respond to coercion and punitive state intervention: "The district attorney has a far better chance at making these men 'believers' than any other local official, as he literally holds the key to the jail cell."[14] Recognizing that prosecutors were often loath to deal with child-support issues, the law included economic incentives and annual audits to entice district attorneys to devote more of their scarce resources to what were previously low priorities.[15] It allowed the state to

[10] Garin Burbank, "Governor Reagan and California Welfare Reform: The Grand Compromise of 1971," *California History* 70 (Fall 1991): 285.

[11] California Department of Social Welfare, *Welfare Reform in California . . . Showing the Way*, 20.

[12] Ibid., 13.

[13] Ibid., 41.

[14] Ibid.

[15] The law allowed counties to retain a significant percentage of the revenue district attorneys collected. In case financial incentives failed to motivate district attorneys, the law established annual audits of the collections programs designed to politically pressure the elected district attorneys to procure all child-support reimbursements. For details, see ibid. and Synopsis of the Welfare Reform Act of 1971, Box GO105, Folder: Welfare-HR 1(4), RRGP. There was also extensive and detailed coverage in the media. See, for example, Hall

garnish absent parents' wages and increased the responsibility of stepfathers for their children from previous relationships. In order to facilitate any future child-support collection efforts, the law also mandated that from this point forward every birth certificate identify the child's putative father with his Social Security number.[16] Coercing identification of the father created risks for women attempting to escape domestic violence and bound all women and children more tightly to fathers, husbands, and the state.

Where the FAP approached recipients as rational economic actors who would respond to economic incentives, architects of the Reagan plan assumed recipients were lazy and had to be coerced into the labor market. To do so, the reforms introduced a work requirement mandating that able-bodied recipients with school-age children and adequate daycare were to accept whatever job was offered or enter a training program. If these two options were unavailable, the state became the employer of last resort and provided a job in the community. These work assignments offered no wages and recipients were compelled to work eighty hours a month in exchange for their benefits. Since these work programs were technically not allowed under the federal legislation enabling AFDC, the Reagan administration lobbied the Nixon administration for a waiver allowing this experimental program in California.

In negotiations with the Nixon administration over the court order to increase benefit payments, Reagan had agreed to bring California into compliance and to curtail his assault on the FAP. In return, Nixon agreed not to withdraw millions in federal welfare funding and eventually granted California the waiver from federal law needed to implement the pilot workfare program. Nixon perceived Reagan as a political threat and potential challenger in the 1972 elections and recognized that welfare was a powerful tool to hammer him with from the right. A *Los Angeles Times* article explained the president's predicament: "On the strength of this one issue, if it is handled adroitly, Reagan could mount an impressive national political campaign. The White House is aware of this fact, which is probably why it backed down this month and agreed not to cut off $700 million in welfare funds for California."[17] By granting the waiver, Nixon may have bought himself some temporary respite from Reagan's attacks, but he cleared the way for the governor to implement punitive

---

Leiren, "Work-for-Welfare Plan Will Start in 3 Months," *Los Angeles Times*, March 27, 1971, SG10 and Jules Witcover, "Welfare Plan Given Support, Reagan Says," *Los Angeles Times*, February 25, 1971, A26.

[16] Synopsis of the Welfare Reform Act of 1971; Goff, "Welfare Reforms Sent to Governor," A1, 30.

[17] D. J. R. Bruckner, "Reagan Is Faring Well with Hot Political Issue Provided by Poor," *Los Angeles Times*, April 9, 1971, B10.

work provisions in California. Even at the time, the Nixon administration recognized the potential danger of allowing California to implement "successful" reforms.[18]

Cracking Down on Chiselers and Cheats

While the workfare provisions of Reagan's legislation forced recipients into jobs, the other prong targeted recipients already in the workforce. The alleged welfare-fraud pandemic was an overriding justification for welfare reform generally, and Reagan's package included a number of provisions designed to crack down on the problem. He intended his reforms to purge the rolls of non-needy recipients who collected grants illegally or through some "loophole." His language consistently blurred the distinction between people with jobs who received welfare through fraud and those who qualified legitimately for aid despite their workforce participation. The governor committed himself to purging the program of both categories and suggested that both were "cheats" and "chiselers," even though many were legally eligible for aid. In order to encourage labor force participation, the 1967 Social Security amendments had allowed people to retain a portion of their benefits as they added earned income. The governor charged that the way benefits were calculated under these regulations allowed people to collect welfare who lived comfortable—even lavish—lifestyles. A *Reader's Digest* article described the way Reagan framed the issue in his speeches:

> "How many of you know you are paying welfare to a man making $16,800 a year?" he asked. He told of an all-too-typical welfare mother receiving $339 a month who took a $582-a-month job. "Did she go off the rolls?" Reagan asked. "Not at all. Instead they reduced her grant by $29. Here is an individual making $892 a month, a good portion tax-free, and eligible for free medical care and food stuffs—and you're picking up the tab."[19]

In these comments, he indignantly equated the regulations allowing recipients to add some earned income with fraud, ignoring the multiple rationales for the policies.

While his political rhetoric maligned these recipients as "chiselers," his target was the policies allowing AFDC to be used as an income support. To curtail the practice, his reform package included a series of mechanisms intended to constrict the ability of people to supplement welfare with low

[18] Steensland, *The Failed Welfare Revolution*, 169.
[19] William Schultz, "California Cleans Up Its Welfare Mess," *Readers Digest*, August 1973, 67–70, Box GO105, Folder: Welfare-Clippings, 2/4, RRGP.

wages. In an era when both welfare and low-wage work often failed to provide sufficient income to support a family, these changes promised to have profound implications for people's daily lives. Through tightening and eliminating income disregards and work-expense deductions, the law reduced the amount and type of income people could receive and still be eligible for welfare. The Reagan administration proposed to change the application of the $30 and one-third formula established by the 1967 Social Security amendments. Prior to the welfare reforms, intake workers based their eligibility decisions on people's income level *after* subtracting the allowed earnings and work-expense deductions. They wanted to simply use gross income (with no deductions for child-care expenses and the like) to determine whether someone qualified for state support. While a seemingly technical detail, using gross income instead of net income in eligibility calculations would considerably reduce the number of people eligible for benefits, disqualifying many with relatively higher earnings but still struggling financially.

In addition to limiting people's ability to legally receive aid while employed, the reform package took new steps to crack down on fraud and purge the rolls of people who were technically ineligible for benefits. While consternation about unworthy or non-needy people receiving state benefits has been a part of state aid since its inception, welfare fraud took on a new urgency in the 1960s and 1970s. Fraud inquiries are inherently politicized, and recipients have always been subject to considerably more scrutiny in AFDC than in other programs. Yet efforts to ferret out fraud almost always stumble over the rudimentary problem of defining which behaviors technically constitute fraud. Actions interpreted as criminal theft in one instance could be construed as error or overpayment in another. Assumptions about the social position of program beneficiaries were embedded in policy, since administrators responded to the same behaviors differently depending on which population they served. California regulations directed that cases of suspected fraud in the AFDC program be referred to the district attorney to pursue criminal indictment. However, if the fraud was committed by a recipient of Old Age Assistance or Aid to the Blind, restitution was sought first by request and then civil action, and only after those failed were cases transferred to the criminal system. In practice, this meant that fraud within those programs virtually never resulted in criminal action.[20] This was one of the many mechanisms that reinforced and affirmed the civic standing of entitlement program beneficiaries while positioning AFDC recipients in a suspect, subordinated status.

[20] State Social Welfare Board, "Report on Welfare Fraud," July 1968, Box GO19, Folder: Welfare Fraud: Report on Welfare Fraud, pp. 16–17, RRGP.

Upon entering office in 1967, Reagan had authorized a panel to investigate the extent of welfare fraud and identify ways "to weed out welfare cheats now on California's welfare rolls."[21] In the following years, a series of publicized studies discovered alarmingly high levels of fraud. Instead of basing estimates on the number of prosecutions, the new reports uncovered vast reservoirs of undetected fraud by carefully auditing sample sections of the caseload, searching for unreported income and other deception. A study released in 1970 found that 15.75 percent of the sample had some evidence of fraud, mostly unreported income.[22] Subsequent reports estimated still higher levels.[23]

Politicians often used these reports of endemic fraud as evidence of the low moral character of many welfare recipients. More quietly, however, officials were aware that low grants and low wages made fraud unsurprising. In his oral history interview, Robert Carleson explained that the AFDC bureaucracy tolerated widespread misreporting of income because everyone realized that it was impossible to subsist on grants that had not increased since 1958. He explained that "the benefits were too low and people really couldn't make it on those benefits, so the whole system was looking the other way."[24] The brutal economic conditions made law enforcement officials reluctant to pursue criminal sanction since "the district attorneys weren't going to prosecute welfare fraud and go before a judge when this person was only getting $221 and they needed more money."[25] After the Reagan administration increased benefit levels (under pressure from the federal court order and the threat of losing federal funds), they took few other steps to address the economic factors that might logically give rise to welfare fraud.

Instead, they tackled the high-profile problem through a series of reforms that intensified surveillance of the caseload. The California Welfare Reform Act required that the income declarations of aid applicants be verified through cross-checking, as opposed to accepting their reporting on faith as had been the case earlier and was the norm for tax filing. The law made welfare recipients more transparent to state authorities by granting the Department of Social Welfare the ability to access files held by other agencies, such as income tax returns and other employment and

---

[21]Text of Reagan's speech opening conference on welfare fraud, July 10, 1967, Box GO19, Folder: Fraud, RRGP.

[22]"Recipient Fraud Incidence Study," January 1970, Box GO19, Folder: Welfare Fraud—The Recipient Fraud Incidence Study, RRGP.

[23]*Fraud Control, California and New York* (Washington, D.C.: U.S. Department of Health, Education and Welfare, Social and Rehabilitation Service, Assistance Payments Administration, 1975), 8.

[24]Oral history of Robert Carleson, "Stemming the Welfare Tide," 40.

[25]Ibid., 41.

unemployment records. The periodic eligibility reviews filled out by welfare recipients became formalized legal declarations and thereby turned any false reporting into perjury.[26] The Reagan administration leveraged the newest computer technology to integrate and synchronize records of the various bureaucracies, diminishing the chance of collecting aid in various localities or from multiple programs.

The most important new anti-fraud program was called the Earnings Clearance System. It allowed the state to cross-check recipients' declared earnings with wages reported by employers for unemployment insurance. The discovery of significant discrepancies between these amounts signaled fraudulent reporting and was one of the most common types of welfare fraud. The first run of the program in late 1971 found 41 percent of the targeted sample had significant discrepancies between the wages reported by employers and recipients. Following significant publicity about the program, the second run in early 1972 found unreported income in 26 percent of the sample.[27] The Department of Social Welfare claimed that the Earnings Clearance System increased fraud investigations by 50 percent.[28] To handle the new influx of cases demanding scrutiny and follow-up, officials formed new administrative units, both within the welfare bureaucracy and the district attorney's office, which were tasked specifically with ferreting out welfare fraud. Legislation increased the penalties for fraud, making the unlawful receipt of more than $200 a felony punishable by up to ten years' incarceration.[29]

Not surprisingly, the state's commitment to fraud detection resulted in dramatic increases in investigations and scrutiny of welfare recipients by the penal system. In the fiscal year 1970, welfare officials opened just under 11,000 investigations and referred over 3,600 cases to law enforcement who initiated prosecution in just over 1,600.[30] Between 1971 and 1972, fraud convictions doubled.[31] Ninety percent of the fraud in 1972 consisted of recipients concealing or underreporting income.[32] In fiscal

[26] Synopsis of the Welfare Reform Act of 1971; Goff, "Welfare Reforms Sent to Governor: Compromise Clears Legislature."

[27] Department of Social Welfare press release re: Earning Clearance System, February 26, 1973, Box GO187, Folder: Research File-Health and Welfare-Welfare, 1973, 1/3, RRGP.

[28] Ibid.

[29] California Department of Social Welfare, *Welfare Reform in California . . . Showing the Way*, 66.

[30] *Disposition of Public Assistance Cases Involving Questions of Fraud* (Washington, D.C.: U.S. Department of Health, Education, and Welfare, National Center for Social Statistics, 1972, 1973, 1974, 1975, 1976, and 1979). Until 1974, these numbers include suspected fraud in all public assistance programs, not just AFDC. See note to Figure 4.1.

[31] Schultz, "California Cleans Up Its Welfare Mess."

[32] *Fraud Control, California and New York*, 8.

year 1974, courts ordered AFDC recipients to repay almost $9 million to the state.[33] Between fiscal year 1970 and 1975, the number of cases investigated multiplied five times. State officials reported that in 1975 there were over 52,000 cases with questions of fraud, 14,392 referred to law enforcement, and 7,692 with initiated prosecution.[34]

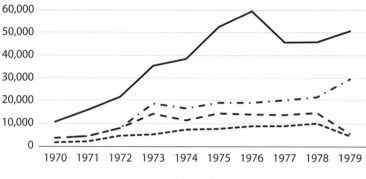

—— Cases Involving Questions of Fraud
— · — Cases with Facts Sufficient to Support Questions of Fraud
— — Referred to Law Enforcement
--- Prosecution Initiated

Figure 4.1. California public assistance fraud investigations, 1970–79. (*Source*: National Center for Social Statistics, *Disposition of Public Assistance Cases Involving Questions of Fraud, Fiscal Years 1970–79* [Washington, D.C.: U.S. Department of Health, Education, and Welfare, Social Security Administration, Office of Research and Statistics, 1973–1979])
Note: Number of convictions not reported. Until 1974, these numbers included suspected fraud in AFDC, Medical Assistance, and Adult Programs (defined as Aid to the Blind, Old-Age Assistance, and Aid to the Permanently and Totally Disabled). AFDC cases were the large majority, with the other programs never exceeding 20 percent of the cases suspected and prosecuted. After 1974, the Adult Programs were transferred into a federally administered program, Supplemental Security Income (SSI), and ceased to report fraud to this report. The numbers after 1974 still included suspected fraud in medical assistance, but AFDC was over 95 percent of the cases.

Welfare fraud became a frame through which a variety of problems were mediated, ranging from the budgetary pressures of growing AFDC caseloads to the most intimate family conflicts. Conditioned by the state's

[33] Ibid., appendix U.
[34] *Disposition of Public Assistance Cases Involving Questions of Fraud.*

emphasis on and responsiveness to the issue, citizens used fraud as an avenue to elicit government intervention in their lives. Some endeavored to use the campaign to publicize the behavior of unruly family members. In one example, an engineering professor wrote a long letter detailing his concern about his ex-daughter-in-law's parenting. While the narrative contained few actions that technically constituted welfare fraud, it recited a series of anecdotes juxtaposing the mother's frivolous consumption with her children's poor hygiene, dress, and nutrition. He recounted his alarm upon realizing his grandchildren were accustomed to eating their cereal with water instead of milk: "In this affluent age what would cause kids to expect water on cornflakes? The answer is found in the behavior and habits of their mother Mary Jane." Although the state had little control over how recipients spent their stipends, the grandfather assumed that stories of Mary Jane's disturbing consumer consumption evidenced the need for intervention in her case. The professor synopsized the situation:

> Briefly it is the story of Mary Jane, a young mother who, for no other reason than laziness and selfishness had become a welfare moocher. All of her cash income from welfare, plus everything she can gain by selling free food and gifts from any source is spent on her own clothes and travel. Within the past year she has spent 6 weeks in Guadalajara, a month in New York area and eastern seaboard towns, and two weeks in Hawaii. . . . Meanwhile, her 4 and 6 year old daughters, quite unnecessarily, suffer from malnutrition and a variety of illnesses, live in filth and are growing up in a psychological and moral atmosphere which is about as low as it can get.

After a full-page diagram graphically representing the various characters, their interrelationships, and class positions, the professor detailed how the mother locked her children in an unventilated basement and ignored the ongoing kidney infection of one of the children. Instead of framing such behaviors as child abuse or neglect, the professor sought remedy through the governor's anti-fraud campaign. He explained in his letter that stories such as these were the key to inciting public outrage and organizing political support for welfare reform. He recommended that the governor exploit these narratives in his political battles:

> This leads to the suggestion that you give wide publicity to a series of case histories. The amount and variety of material is almost infinite. A good writer could present them in a manner sufficiently interesting and exciting to upstage much of what we hear and see in the media. Presented as true stories in frequent newspaper columns, broadcasts and /or news confer-

ences these would surely result in reactions as violent and sincere as the reactions to Mary Jane's stories have been. I am confident that there would follow a wave of public protest strong enough to overwhelm your legislative opponents.[35]

While there is no reason to suggest Reagan took a lesson from this professor, the letter quite accurately prophesied the role individual anecdotal narratives played in rationalizing punitive reforms and benefit-level retrenchment.

The spectacle of purging ineligible recipients from the rolls did little to redeem the image of AFDC. On the contrary, continual reports of fraud convictions and investigations only further stigmatized the program and its beneficiaries. Public suspicion was only confirmed through the hundreds and hundreds of articles uncovering people living shamelessly in luxury at the public expense.[36] Strengthening the links between welfare and the criminal justice system, both symbolically and programmatically, hardened public antagonism and created greater symbolic distance between recipients and normative families. The news reports chronicling fraud ignited fierce public indignation and mobilized hostility to the program and its beneficiaries. A form-letter response to citizens' letters about fraud indicated there was heavy volume of mail on the topic, which probably convinced Reagan to continue emphasizing the issue. It also acknowledged the critical role the media played in amplifying Reagan's message. The stock response assured constituents that Reagan and most other taxpayers shared their outrage:

> We receive hundreds of letters daily from overburdened taxpayers citing news accounts of welfare fraud—accounts which have been investigated and verified, not merely rumored. We have a responsibility to restore a balance between the legitimate interests of our taxpaying citizens and those of the genuinely dependent welfare recipient.[37]

Amid the ongoing public spectacle of welfare fraud exposés and prosecutions, Reagan positioned himself as the agent who restored equilibrium to a social system many felt favored the poor and minorities over "taxpaying citizens."

[35]Dudley R. to Ronald Reagan, May 16, 1971, Box GO180, Folder: Research File-Health and Welfare-Background from RR Files, RRGP.

[36]There are files full of press clippings on welfare fraud in Reagan's Gubernatorial Papers. See press clippings in RS 196, Folder: Welfare Fraud (1970–71), 1/3, 2/3, and 3/3; RS 196, Folder: Welfare Fraud (1971), 1/2, 2/2, RRPL; and RS 196, Folder: Welfare Fraud (1972–73), 1/2, 2/2, all in RRGP.

[37]Form letter from Ronald Reagan to unnamed constituent, Box GO186, Folder: Research File-Health and Welfare-Welfare, 1970, 5/5, RRGP.

Public attention to fraud ebbed and flowed over the following years, usually connected to political initiatives or media coverage of an extreme individual case. The controversy generated by the case of Geraldine Chapman in 1975 provides a window into legislators' ongoing struggles over how to interpret recipient behavior. Chapman was arrested in Sacramento in December 1974 for unauthorized credit card use. In the course of their investigation, police inadvertently discovered she had been defrauding the state's welfare programs by collecting AFDC and food stamp benefits through five different claims. Chapman ultimately pled guilty to three counts of welfare fraud for illegally collecting approximately $18,000.[38] The case inspired legislators to revisit existing anti-fraud procedures. During a public hearing in the California Assembly, lawmakers and program administrators explicitly debated the implications, both practical and political, of recruiting the criminal justice system to manage welfare fraud.

Legislators now considered importing penal rituals into the welfare bureaucracy to augment the criminal penalties and increased emphasis on prosecutions they had enacted under Reagan. They considered plans to fingerprint all aid applicants and offer "bounties" or cash rewards for uncovering fraud. In his testimony during the public hearing, Phillip Manriquez, the acting deputy director of the State Department of Benefit Payments, argued against tactics of civic degradation. He claimed that Chapman was an atypical case involving a person possessing "extraordinary determination with unusual abilities and resources at her command."[39] (She had previously worked for the Department of Motor Vehicles and had a thorough knowledge of the complicated procedures to produce identity documents.)[40] Manriquez explained that the only technique available to prevent such schemes was a proposed new program called the CALSPAN system, which would fingerprint all new AFDC applicants and electronically cross-check them to verify identity and prevent people from drawing benefits from multiple jurisdictions or under different aliases. His department opposed the system on the grounds that it stigmatized beneficiaries and that the implementation costs would outstrip any savings. Such a program, Manriquez testified, "would be an expensive proposition in both dollars and human terms":

> More important than that is the impact that a finger printing process would have on innocent applicants. In our opinion subjecting all applicants to fin-

[38] Committee on Human Resources, "Welfare Fraud Controls," transcript of public hearing, California State Assembly, December 8, 1975, i.
[39] Ibid., 6.
[40] Ibid., 5.

gerprinting is demeaning and will cause unnecessary anguish to thousands of people for the purpose of being able to prosecute what would amount to an infinitesimal number of highly sophisticated individuals who will try to beat even the CALSPAN system.[41]

Fingerprinting welfare recipients, he argued, ran counter to evolving political norms:

The trend has been over the last several years to establish public policies which enhance individual rights—the rights to privacy, and it seems to me that the trend has been to restrict more and more the taking of fingerprints to the law enforcement process. So, the people I talk to, many of them, associate the fingerprint process with the booking process.[42]

Manriquez and other department staff also testified that fingerprinting would do little to counter the most typical types of fraud, such as the failure to report outside income or a man living in the home.[43]

Assemblyman John Briggs challenged Manriquez's assumption that the more sinister types of fraud, such as that committed by Chapman, were relatively infrequent. He explained that the seemingly innocent caseload could contain any number of criminals: "My point is there could be 300 Geraldine [Chapmans] out there. There is no way to know. . . . It is like this paint on the wall, there are elephants on the wall, but the color of the paint disguises them. They are really there, but you just can't see them."[44] Only fingerprinting could unmask the otherwise indeterminable number of dissembling and deceitful recipients.

Others lawmakers encouraged department staff to consider a possible relationship between fraud, grant levels, and the cost of living. Chairman Kenneth Maddy asked, "Do you think some of these people that are stealing would be stealing if there was a grant level that would be at . . . subsistence level, but not—$292 a month—I don't know what you live on, but $292 a month just isn't going to make it today."[45] Stealing, in this particular lawmaker's opinion, could be interpreted as a function of the benefit levels instead of recipients' criminality, greed, or laziness. The chairman also worried that prosecuting "the mother who is picking up some additional money because the money we are giving her is not enough" would ultimately have the inadvertent effect of increasing dependence on state welfare programs. He explained that the

[41] Ibid., 7.
[42] Ibid., 16.
[43] Ibid., 28–30.
[44] Ibid., 117.
[45] Ibid., 140.

criminal record "for all intents and purposes makes her totally unemployable for the future."[46] The debates at this hearing reveal politicians
and state officials grappling with the appropriateness of conscripting
the penal system in welfare administration and openly struggling over
whether to interpret fraud as a function of individual criminality or
economic constraints. In the short run, the reluctance of some state officials to subject welfare recipients to techniques of civic diminishment
and penal rituals won out. Lawmakers decided not to institute fingerprinting or bounties at this juncture, but they would not always make
the same choice.

Charting Welfare's Future: The Aftermath of Reagan's Reforms

The evaluation of the California's Welfare Reform Act's programmatic
effects quickly became contested political terrain. The Reagan administration claimed that its program caused dramatic reductions in caseloads, pruned the rolls of the high-income recipients, and increased
support to the most destitute. To evidence the law's accomplishments,
they highlighted the caseload declines that started before the law went
into effect and accelerated into 1972. Between 1972 and 1974, the average monthly AFDC caseload decreased from 442,187 to 406,405.[47] In
an era when most officials would have been delighted to simply slow
the rate of growth, caseload decreases were big news. Others, however,
disputed Reagan's claims of success and attributed the decreases to general economic improvement, lower unemployment, smaller family sizes,
and the leveling off that was inevitable once most eligible families were
enrolled in AFDC. In the long run, the reforms did little to control costs,
and welfare expenditures more than doubled in the decade following
the enactment of the act.[48] By fiscal year 1976, the number of caseloads
was higher than before the law passed, although the rapid growth of
previous decades slowed.[49] Economist Frank Levy attempted to quan-
tify the effects of the reforms while accounting for economic trends. He
concluded that California's welfare reform program probably had little
impact on cost and should be credited for only 6 percent of the much-

[46] Ibid., 56.
[47] Oral History of David Swoap, "The Continuing Story of Welfare Reform, 1965–
1983" (1983), OH R-43, p. 39, Ronald Reagan Gubernatorial Era Project, CSA.
[48] Burbank, "Governor Reagan and California Welfare Reform," 287–88. Some of the
cost increases are attributable to the high inflation during the 1970s.
[49] State of California, Department of Social Welfare, *Public Welfare in California, Series
AR 1-14*, FY 1974–75, appendix A.

vaunted caseload decline.[50] The early workfare experiment inaugurated by the California Welfare Reform Act never materialized in a robust or widespread form. At its height in 1974, only 4,760 of the 182,735 who were eligible participated and Governor Jerry Brown had abandoned the enterprise by 1975.[51]

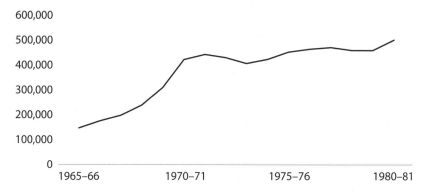

Figure 4.2. Average monthly AFDC caseload in California, FY 1965/66–1980/81. (*Source*: State of California, Department of Social Welfare, *Public Welfare in California, Series AR 1-14*, FY 1965/66–1980/81)

While increasing benefits to families with no additional income, Reagan's reforms diminished the support that had previously been available to poor families with outside earnings. One "poverty lawyer" characterized the reforms as a "very perverse, Marxian redistribution of income amongst the poor" that reduced the benefits of the top third of welfare recipients to increase payments to the bottom third.[52] The thousands of fraud investigations entailed unprecedented interventions and scrutiny into many recipients' lives and even more dramatic consequences for those indicted, convicted, or forced to pay restitution to the state.

Although debates continued about the programmatic effects of California's reforms, the political implications were indisputably profound. Reagan's welfare program steered national welfare policy away from guaranteed income proposals and toward an alternative, more restrictive path. The federal government and several states carefully moni-

[50] "'Work-or-Else' Welfare Program Called Failure," *Los Angeles Times*, April 13, 1976, B3; Burbank, "Governor Reagan and California Welfare Reform," 288.

[51] Jonathan Bell, *California Crucible: The Forging of Modern American Liberalism* (Philadelphia: University of Pennsylvania Press, 2012), 247.

[52] Quoted in Jack Thomas, "Reforming Welfare in the Reagan Style," March 16, 1975, *Boson Globe*, Box GO187, Folder: Research File-Health and Welfare-1974, 3/3, RRGP.

tored developments in California, and by 1974 twelve states had implemented one or more of California's reforms.[53] The law propelled him further into the national limelight and helped establish the terms of the national welfare debate for decades to come. It was instrumental in establishing what has become common sense about poverty, work, parenting, and the state's capacity to meaningfully intervene in society. In the short term, Reagan's programmatic accomplishments through the California Welfare Reform Act positioned him as the Republicans' innovator in welfare policy, displacing and discrediting the Nixon administration's approach to the problem. Through its claims to success, Reagan's program proved (to Republicans especially) that there was an alternative, efficient path out of the "welfare mess" that did not include a massive expansion of state entitlement programs. By the time the Nixon administration introduced the revised, more restrictive version of the FAP to Congress in 1971, commentators viewed California's welfare reforms as the principal competing vision. Reagan's "success" in California made the FAP seem like an unnecessary risk. Lou Cannon, a Reagan biographer who covered him for years in the capital press corps, explained, "The Family Assistance Plan had been on life support since Reagan first opposed it. The CWRA [California Welfare Reform Act] drove the final nails in the coffin."[54]

Daniel Moynihan explained that fears of Reagan attacking the FAP loomed over President Nixon's daily morning meetings: "The Right, in the person of Reagan, had come within breathing distance of the Republican nomination in 1968. The question had to be asked whether the president, who had barely held his conservative support in 1968, would not lose it in 1972."[55] These were not the unfounded fears of a paranoid president. There was evidence that Reagan's political efficacy, especially regarding welfare, had people wondering if he was not uniquely suited for the presidency. The American Conservative Union newsletter reported that conservatives were questioning their endorsement of Nixon: "For the first time political observers have noticed a private, though not yet public, willingness on the part of Southern GOP leaders to admit they may have been mistaken in backing Nixon over Gov. Ronald Reagan in 1968."[56] Senator Russell Long, who was a forceful opponent of the FAP, called Reagan to testify before the Senate Finance Committee to illustrate the ways California had allegedly tamed the welfare monster without instituting a new social safety net. In his welcome to the gover-

[53] State of Wisconsin Legislative Research Bureau, "Welfare Reform: A Look at Three States," Informational Bulletin 74-IB-5, March 1974, 6.

[54] Cannon, *Governor Reagan*, 361.

[55] Moynihan, *The Politics of a Guaranteed Income*, 375.

[56] Ibid.

nor, he explained that "we are particularly happy to have you here today because of the efforts you have made to develop a work program rather than to continue to build upon a program that encourages people to quit work in order to obtain more and more tax-paid hand-outs from the Government."[57]

In 1972, the U.S. Senate Finance Committee voted to sever the FAP from the welfare bill, H.R. 1, and not a single Republican voted to support Nixon's plan. The president, with diminishing enthusiasm for his signature domestic policy proposal, abandoned any effort to reintroduce or amend his program. In October, H.R. 1 passed Congress with no guaranteed income plan. The legislation did include, however, a series of provisions designed to press recipients into work. Senator Long designed the provisions with guidance from Robert Carleson, California's welfare director who now advised the powerful chair of the Senate Finance Committee.[58] In the same period that the proposal for a federally guaranteed income floor for poor families floundered, Congress with little controversy erected one beneath the blind, aged, and disabled. The new Supplemental Security Income (SSI) program united the various state aid programs serving these adult "deserving" populations into a more uniform, federally administered and funded aid program. They also approved automatic cost-of-living adjustments for Social Security benefits to prevent the erosion of grants through inflation.[59] These administrative readjustments further distanced the civic position of the recipients in other means-tested and social insurance programs from the stigmatized status of AFDC beneficiaries.

In 1973, Nixon affirmed California's position in the vanguard of welfare policy by appointing Robert Carleson as U.S. welfare commissioner and special assistant for welfare to the secretary of health, education, and welfare.[60] From this post, Carleson worked to encourage other states to adopt California's approach to welfare. Carleson and other conservatives in the Nixon administration became increasingly influential as the administration approached its notorious demise in the wake of the Watergate scandal. Nixon catered to conservatives in Congress because their support represented his best chance to avoid

[57] Senator Long, Hearings on H.R. 1, the Social Security Amendments of 1971, U.S. Senate Committee on Finance, 92nd Cong., 1st and 2nd Sess., Part 4, February 1, 1972, 1873, https://archive.org/details/socialsecurityam00unit_22.

[58] Steensland, *The Failed Welfare Revolution*, 169–76.

[59] Hoff, *Nixon Reconsidered*, 134–35; Patterson, *America's Struggle against Poverty in the Twentieth Century*, 196–98.

[60] Lou Cannon, "Reaganism on the Potomac," August 1974 and "National Welfare Reform: How Other States Copy Us," *Sacramento Union*, February 5, 1974, both in Box GO187, Folder: Research File-Health and Welfare-1974, 3/3, RRGP.

impeachment proceedings. Commentators recognized that these dynamics served to entrench Reagan loyalists in Washington. Journalist Lou Cannon prophetically reported at the time that "it now seems likely that Reagan appointees and Reagan programs will outlast President Nixon."[61]

Although fraud investigations were hardly Reagan's innovation, California's efforts and resulting expertise helped inspire and shape efforts in other states. As the news media amplified and reinforced the governor's claims of success, the Reagan reforms became models for other states. One critic of the governor explained that the media helped position California's reforms as a national model by failing to scrutinize Reagan's rhetoric of success. He explained that "there are a number of reporters who didn't believe what Reagan was claiming, but nobody took the time (to check it out)."[62] The upshot, he explained, was that other state officials accepted the effectiveness of Reagan's approach.

When the National Welfare Fraud Association formed to increase coordination among all the local efforts, there was a Reagan staffer at its head. Richard Peterson had been tapped to establish an "operations security" office within the welfare program when California resolved to formally enlist law enforcement in the fight against fraud in the early 1970s. He brought twenty years of professional experience but little of it with social welfare agencies. (He had worked first in Air Force Intelligence and subsequently with domestic police and prosecutors.) Peterson hoped the new association would produce a nationwide database of welfare recipients that would prevent individuals from opening duplicate cases in different jurisdictions. He also wanted to implement a nationwide identification card that would be required to cash benefit checks. Peterson claimed that these efforts to remove ineligible and "chiseling" recipients would redeem the image of truly needy and deserving beneficiaries. He explained to the *Los Angeles Times*, "We've got to eliminate these greedy people, these con artists, so the welfare recipient can become dignified again."[63] The motto of the organization was "Eliminate the Greedy; Help the Needy." The article, however, proceeded to explain that others saw this anti-fraud campaign as having an opposite effect: "Civil libertarians and welfare rights organizations wonder how what they consider the beginnings of a 'spy network' can restore any dignity to recipients." The head of California's welfare-

[61] Cannon, "Reaganism on the Potomac."

[62] Thomas, "Reforming Welfare in the Reagan Style."

[63] William Endicott, "Reagan Official Heads National Welfare Fraud Investigators," *Los Angeles Times*, June 17, 1973, B1.

rights organization, Helen Little, suggested that instead of exonerating recipients from suspicion, the hunt for fraud positioned the entire caseload as suspects. "This looks like another one of those Reagan philosophies that everyone on welfare is cheating until proven otherwise," she explained.[64]

The spectacle of purging ineligible recipients from the rolls certainly did not redeem the image of AFDC. The campaigns activated racialized and gendered stereotypes to explain complex social transformations as the fault of distinct, degraded social groups. Anti-fraud campaigns helped organize and amplify distinct, derogatory public scripts about families receiving AFDC and further concretized the association between cultural pathology and African American and Latina mothers. During the same period that anti-fraud and anti-welfare rhetoric escalated, the public increasingly associated AFDC with people of color and support for welfare declined dramatically. Sixty percent of poll respondents endorsed more public spending for welfare in 1960, while only 20 percent did in 1973.[65] Where a plurality in 1961 thought the state invested "too little" in welfare, the plurality in 1977 thought the state spent "too much." By 1976, 85 percent of poll respondents agreed that "too many people on welfare cheat by getting money they are not entitled to."[66]

California's reforms staked out a tough stance toward welfare that further marginalized recipients. They entrenched a logic that obscured the influence of market forces and interpreted poverty as the result of individual, cultural, and racial pathology. Other politicians, anxious to upstage Reagan or at least keep pace, rushed to match his rhetoric and replicate his policies. Nelson Rockefeller, who had preempted Reagan with his drug policy, hurriedly ratcheted up his attacks on the welfare program and welfare cheats. An article in the *Sacramento Bee* chronicled the competition between the two presidential hopefuls and speculated on who would appear tougher: "In New York this year they are saying Rockefeller, with his anti-narcotic program, has out-Reaganed Reagan on the law and order issue. Rockefeller also mimicked Reagan on the welfare fraud issue."[67]

Welfare reform became the cornerstone of Reagan's political legacy as governor of California.[68] Although innumerable factors propelled the

[64] Ibid.

[65] Reese, *Backlash against Welfare Mothers*, 117. See also Gilens, *Why Americans Hate Welfare*.

[66] John Gardiner and Theodore Lyman, *The Fraud Control Game* (Bloomington: Indiana University Press, 1984), 1.

[67] "Reagan, Rockefeller Stand Together as Conservatives," *Sacramento Bee*, December 12, 1973, Box GO153, Folder: Research File: Campaign 1976, RRGP.

[68] Cannon, *Governor Reagan*, 360.

man and his policies onto the national stage, Reagan consistently trumpeted his welfare reform success throughout the following decade to evidence his capacity for grappling with the nation's formidable social problems. Years later, Robert Moretti, Reagan's adversary in the initial 1971 negotiations, discussed the political consequences of the law: "That was the basis on which, I think, he became president or certainly one of the main factors, because he continually pointed to, and still points to, welfare reform in California."[69] Throughout his future campaigns, Reagan continually recounted his exploits disciplining the excessive, permissive welfare system of California. During his 1976 speaking tour, he juxtaposed his success with stories of the extravagant abuses of Linda Taylor, the Illinois "welfare queen" whose story we turn to next.

Although state officials never fully implemented California's workfare program, the reforms normalized the notion that welfare recipients could and should be required to perform labor in exchange for their grants—a notion that moved to the center of welfare reform debates in the following decades. When he did eventually win the presidency, Reagan brought his blueprint for welfare reform to the White House. He took many off guard by how quickly and effectively his administration attacked the welfare system. One historian observed that "the administration moved so quickly on welfare because it had over a decade of preparation. It hit the beach running, but running on a course set a decade before."[70] And California's welfare reforms cast a long shadow that extended even beyond Reagan's presidency. A chief architect of the reforms, Robert Carleson, remained a powerful force during subsequent welfare debates and was instrumental in drafting and passing the legislation that ultimately ended the federal entitlement program. The seminal 1996 welfare reform law that abolished AFDC is widely understood, especially in conservative circles, to be the culmination of the project begun in California in 1971.[71]

Creating the Welfare Queen: Illinois State Anti-Fraud Initiatives

Although Reagan commandeered the welfare queen story for his own campaigns, the scandal surrounding Linda Taylor originally emerged from the local politics of Illinois. In the mid-1970s, bad publicity, federal scrutiny,

[69] Oral history of Robert Moretti, "Reflections of an Assembly Speaker," 174.

[70] Quoted in Steensland, *The Failed Welfare Revolution*, 222.

[71] Carleson, *Government Is the Problem*. See especially the opening quotes from various conservative leaders testifying to the long-term impact of California's reforms and Carleson specifically.

and spiraling program costs combined to inspire state lawmakers to launch a high-profile anti-fraud campaign.[72] Where California's welfare reforms were driven by the governor's office, the main impetus for reform in Illinois was a powerful bipartisan committee of state legislators called the Legislative Advisory Committee (LAC) to Public Aid. This committee was charged with advising and assisting the agency that actually administered the welfare program, the Illinois Department of Public Aid (IDPA). Led for most of this period by Republican state senator Don Moore from Midlothian and emboldened by the high-profile fraud case of Linda Taylor, the LAC became singularly committed to reducing welfare rolls through stringent eligibility reviews. Although Republicans enjoyed significant support from Democratic lawmakers, they strategically championed the anti-fraud cause throughout much of the 1970s in their struggle to regain control of the General Assembly.

The Illinois anti-fraud campaign reveals how the themes that coalesced in California translated in the politics of other states and the ways that citizens—both the targets and fervent supporters of the anti-fraud initiative—understood and influenced politicians' anti-fraud efforts. Illinois was both a forerunner of and a model for the anti-fraud efforts that accelerated across the nation throughout the decade. Despite the fervency and high-profile nature of the state's anti-fraud initiatives, the exponential growth in fraud arrests and investigations during the 1970s in Illinois corresponded roughly with national trends.

Illinois's welfare rolls surged between 1967 and 1973.[73] Controversy regarding incompetent management had circled around the Department of Public Aid since the late 1960s and the state's high error rates put Illinois in danger of being sanctioned by the federal government. Often indistinguishable from bureaucratic bungling and the results of chronic understaffing, mistakes in cash grant amounts were handled administratively prior to 1973. Fraud by recipients was rarely prosecuted since it was extremely difficult to prove criminal intent. When an overpayment was detected, the state simply readjusted the grant amount or dropped the recipient from the rolls.[74]

In 1974, the *Chicago Tribune* began covering the bizarre case of Linda Taylor, who came to be known as the original "welfare queen." She was charged in 1974 with defrauding Illinois's welfare programs by collecting welfare cash grants, Social Security, and food stamps under multiple aliases. At a time when welfare fraud was already a national preoccupation, Taylor's story generated sensationalized media coverage in her hometown of

[72] Gardiner and Lyman, *Fraud Control Game*, 147.
[73] Ibid. See also *Annual Report: Illinois Department of Public Aid, 1974* (Springfield, Ill.: Office of Public Information, 1974), 19.
[74] "Welfare Cheats Find 'Easy Street' Has a Dead End," *Chicago Tribune*, March 26, 1978, sec. 1, 25.

Chicago and across the country. Although the specifics fluctuated dramatically between accounts, news media and politicians described her deceptive techniques in careful detail. One *Chicago Tribune* article reported she had at least 27 different names, 31 addresses, 25 phone numbers, and several husbands (most dead except for one 26 years her junior).[75] Another explained that Taylor had illegally received more than $200,000 by using more than 100 aliases in 12 different states.[76] Taylor's physical form was as elusive as her legal identity. Investigators alleged she had 30 different wigs and had claimed benefits as a white woman, an African American woman, and a Filipina.[77] Although prosecutors were ultimately only able to prove Taylor had defrauded the state of $8,000 using four separate aliases, the case was a huge embarrassment for the welfare administration. Instead of treating Taylor's actions as an anomaly, key conservative politicians and state bureaucrats claimed they were symptomatic of the permissiveness and incompetence of the entire welfare system. They used the controversy to spur an extensive campaign to crack down on welfare fraud; this served the politically expedient goals of pruning the caseloads and discrediting and disciplining the welfare bureaucracy.

Although Chicago journalists dubbed Taylor the "welfare queen," high-ticket welfare fraud was hardly Taylor's only legal transgression.[78] The *Chicago Tribune* recounted tales of Taylor's alleged robberies, bigamy, and kidnapping and told how she had collected fees as a "voodoo doctor" and tried to claim the inheritance of a policy runner who had died with $700,000 in his home from his illegal gambling operation.[79] An in-depth exposé published in 2013 also implicated Taylor in kidnapping and murder.[80] Instead of framing welfare as one of myriad avenues Taylor used for her nefarious enterprises, political rhetoric in the 1970s

[75] Ibid.

[76] Jane Fritsch, "Welfare Queen Becomes Case Study," *Chicago Tribune*, October 29, 1978, 42; Bliss, "Cops Find Deceit—But No One Cares."

[77] George Bliss, "Panel Probes Welfare Cheating Charges," *Chicago Tribune*, September 30, 1974, 1.

[78] David Zucchino, *Myth of the Welfare Queen* (New York: Scribner, 1997), 65.

[79] William Griffin, "Policy Chief's Estate an 11-Year Game," *Chicago Tribune*, February 20, 1975, 1; George Bliss and William Griffin, "Probe Aid Queen Tie to Kidnapping," *Chicago Tribune*, March 21, 1975, 3; William Griffin, "'Welfare Queen' Is under New Probe," *Chicago Tribune*, April 10, 1975, A8; William Griffin, "Welfare Queen's Role—Was It Voodoo Spell?" *Chicago Tribune*, July 29, 1975, 6; William Griffin, "Medical 'Practice' Just That for Welfare Queen," *Chicago Tribune*, July 14, 1975, 3; George Bliss, "'Welfare Queen' Charged with Stealing Furnishings," *Chicago Tribune*, February 26, 1976, A6.

[80] Josh Levin, "The Welfare Queen," *Slate*, December 19, 2013, http://www.slate.com/articles/news_and_politics/history/2013/12/linda_taylor_welfare_queen_ronald_reagan_made_her_a_notorious_american_villain.html.

positioned her as a representative AFDC recipient and a product of the welfare bureaucracy.

Connecting queens to popular images of welfare recipients symbolically transmitted multiple messages with derogatory racial, gender, and class subtexts.[81] Surrounded by extravagant luxuries and services, queens are assumed to perform neither caregiving work nor waged labor. Linking these images to welfare recipients discredited poor women's voices and insinuated that their claims of material hardship were disingenuous and malicious. By evoking socially unsettling images of politically powerful women, the phrase "welfare queen" also had racial connotations. It implicitly referenced popular beliefs, associated most frequently with the Moynihan Report, which attributed the "pathology of the Black family" to its alleged matriarchal structure. Since it could instantly convey multiple stereotypes, it should not be surprising that the moniker "welfare queen" quickly gained such currency.

State legislators used the Taylor case to call for a comprehensive crackdown on welfare abuse. IDPA responded to the political pressure by initiating a series of bureaucratic efforts to identify ineligible recipients. In February 1975, it instituted a "redetermination program," which called for caseworkers to visit the home of each welfare recipient three times a year. The program resulted in the cancellation of more than forty thousand cases in the first two rounds.[82] To find people who were illegally working, state officials used newly developed computer technology to cross-check the names of people receiving welfare with lists of state employees or recipients of unemployment insurance. Despite the worsening economic climate, bureaucrats strived for "caseload stabilization": stopping and even reversing the caseload increases. Through these programs, the IDPA dropped people from the program faster than new eligible cases were added, and caseloads stabilized in 1974 for the first time in more than three years. The caseload even decreased for a few months that year despite the recession.[83]

Still frustrated by the alleged lack of cooperation by the IDPA, the LAC initiated numerous efforts to coerce collaboration through threat, public humiliation, and enticement. Legislators worked closely with the media to publicize stories about the inefficient welfare bureaucracy and

---

[81] For writings about the implications of the welfare queen in later periods, see the important discussions in Roberts, *Killing the Black Body*; Lubiano, "Black Ladies, Welfare Queens, and State Minstrels," 323–63; and Hancock, *Politics of Disgust*.

[82] Report to the Legislative Advisory Committee by James Trainor, director of the Department of Public Aid, March 17, 1976, Legislative Advisory Committee, Administrative Files, 616.002, p. 8, Illinois State Archives, Springfield (hereafter ISA).

[83] *Annual Report: Illinois Department of Public Aid, 1974*, 32. See also graphs on pages 10 and 11.

the behavior it tolerated.[84] Although the IDPA employed fraud investigators, the LAC hired its own staff of off-duty police officers to track down ineligible welfare recipients.[85] In practice, this meant identifying the two behaviors that most frequently constituted fraud: failing to report additional earned income or an extra wage earner (usually a husband or a boyfriend) living with the family.

The LAC also established an anonymous, twenty-four-hour-a-day hotline that people could call to report suspected fraud. LAC investigators circulated memos to police stations that implored officers to include welfare fraud in the crimes they watched for during patrols.[86] After researching cases, LAC staff would hand over the files to welfare caseworkers for termination or readjustment of the cash grants. If there was sufficient evidence, they would send the cases to the state attorney's office for criminal prosecution. The members of the committee staff would then proceed to badger the reluctant and understaffed state attorney's offices and local law enforcement into prosecuting the cases.[87] The LAC also sponsored legislation designed to entice prosecutors to pursue welfare fraud more enthusiastically. Concerned that low penalties discouraged prosecution, legislators crafted a bill that allowed welfare fraud to be tried as a felony instead of a misdemeanor. Other legislation allowed the state attorney's office to keep 25 percent of the money recovered from welfare recipients after successful prosecutions. In 1977, the state attorney's office established a separate division dedicated to prosecuting welfare fraud.[88]

To eliminate theft and prevent recipients from falsely reporting missing and stolen welfare checks, Public Aid started mailing all grants directly to banks and currency exchanges instead of people's homes.[89] Recipients had to report in person to collect their checks and were required to present three forms of identification and sign a

[84]Neal Caauwe, Fred Pennix, Gerald Kush, and Jack Sherwin, progress report by investigative unit of the Legislative Advisory Committee, November 14 and 19, 1974, Legislative Advisory Committee, Administrative Files, 616.003, p. 6, ISA.

[85]Gardiner and Lyman, *Fraud Control Game*, 155.

[86]Caauwe et al., progress report by investigative unit of the Legislative Advisory Committee, 1.

[87]In numerous letters, investigators and other committee staff demanded progress reports on leads from LAC. The committee also called representatives from the state attorney's office before the committee to testify as to why they were not more effective at convicting welfare cheaters. See, for example, "Testimony of Mr. Gross before the Legislative Advisory Committee on Public Aid," March 22, 1977, Legislative Advisory Committee, Committee Meeting Minutes, 616.001, pp. 89–123, ISA.

[88]Gardiner and Lyman, *Fraud Control Game*, 163.

[89]Ibid., 161, 188.

receipt so that signatures could be verified.[90] Although this program was expanded to the entire state in 1977, it was tested in Chicago starting in 1975. Intensive scrutiny of all welfare recipients illustrated the extent to which these policies were directed at a stigmatized group of people, not specific criminals within a group of respected citizens. Both the language used and the location of the pilot programs revealed a particular concern about urban, usually African American and Latina, welfare recipients. Efforts to start fingerprinting the entire caseload were perhaps the most dramatic evidence that officials viewed all recipients as suspect. Although fingerprinting ostensibly served the administrative purpose of preventing recipients from collecting grants under multiple aliases, it also clearly reinforced an already stigmatized position by linking the recipients to explicit images of criminality.[91] Despite its obvious parallel to the way in which criminals were processed, the plan received considerable support.[92]

By the time Linda Taylor was finally sentenced to three to six years in prison, media attention and public outrage had shifted from her individual story to the hundreds of fraud cases that the state's campaign had unearthed.[93] In October 1978, the *Chicago Tribune* remarked on how the pervasiveness of welfare fraud made Taylor's case seem less extreme and instead simply representative of a larger pattern:

> Once the focus of national outrage, the flamboyant and mysterious Chicago woman has relinquished her throne to hundreds of others who have developed equally outrageous schemes to bilk the welfare system of millions of dollars each year.[94]

Although the idea of the welfare queen never lost its link to fraud and criminality, its original connection to Linda Taylor and high-ticket welfare fraud receded as welfare queens multiplied before the public gaze. Over the course of the decade, Illinois devoted increased resources to investigating fraud. In 1979, agencies initiated over 5,800 investigations and referred almost 2,000 cases to law enforcement for prosecution. Of-

[90] Report to the Legislative Advisory Committee by James Trainor, director of the Department of Public Aid, March 17, 1976, 7.

[91] Sociologist Harry Murphy called this practice "deniable degradation." Harry Murphy, "Deniable Degradation: The Finger Imaging of Welfare Recipients," *Sociological Forum* 15, no. 1 (2000): 39–63.

[92] "Way to Curb Aid Abuse; Judge Backs Welfare Fingerprinting," *Chicago Tribune*, April 24, 1979, 3; Robert Carleson, Commissioner of Welfare, Department of Health, Education and Welfare, to Don Moore, chairman of Legislative Advisory Committee, October 29, 1974, Legislative Advisory Committee, Meeting Minutes Summaries, 616.002, ISA.

[93] Jay Branegan, "State Calls Courts 'Soft' on Aid Fraud," *Chicago Tribune*, February 19, 1978, 44.

[94] Fritsch, "Welfare Queen Becomes Case Study," 42.

ficials initiated around five times more cases in 1979 than they had in 1971 and referred ten times as many cases to law enforcement. Although practices varied among states, this remarkable growth in fraud investigations was paralleled at the national level.[95]

Initiatives sponsored by the LAC enjoyed wide support within the Illinois General Assembly. For example, the bill to raise penalties for welfare fraud sailed through the Democratic-controlled House of Representatives by a vote of 124–26.[96] The main critics of these policies were African American legislators and community leaders from Chicago. For example, Senator Richard Newhouse of Chicago spoke out in the community and in the Senate. At a public meeting in 1977, he explained:

"Welfare cheaters" has become the new code word for the poor, for minorities in general and those temporarily down on their luck. Here in Illinois, we presently have three separate agencies seeking out "welfare cheaters" at goodness knows what cost to the taxpayer.[97]

In 1978, Senator Newhouse issued a press release condemning the state for "squandering more than $3 million peeking under the beds of welfare recipients."[98] He also challenged the much-publicized idea that the anti-fraud efforts resulted in savings for the state: "Then—with appropriate fanfare—the state proudly proclaimed that it had recovered the magnificent sum of $1 million as the result of its $3 million effort."[99] He insisted that anti-fraud efforts were racially charged initiatives designed to stigmatize the poor, especially from black urban neighborhoods. Jesse Jackson called the fraud investigators "welfare bloodhounds" and pointed out that the state made no similar effort to track down the $100 million of uncollected income taxes.[100]

Although Illinois was not monolithically behind efforts to crack down on welfare fraud, only a few legislators wasted political capital on impeding anti-fraud initiatives directed against socially stigmatized poor

[95]Gardiner and Lyman, *Fraud Control Game*, 93; *Disposition of Public Assistance Cases Involving Questions of Fraud*. These numbers reflect those cases suspected of deliberate and, therefore, possibly criminal fraud. They do not reflect the number of people whose grants were adjusted and canceled through other routine aspects of the anti-fraud initiatives, such as the redetermination and data-matching programs discussed earlier. It is extremely difficult to access the number of recipients directly materially affected by the campaigns. For example, many people probably removed themselves from the rolls to avoid scrutiny or sanction after hearing about the new policies. Those cases would obviously not be reflected in the official numbers.
[96]Transcripts of Illinois House Debates, November 11, 1977, 10.
[97]"Leaders Meet on Poor," *Chicago Defender*, November 26, 1977, 3.
[98]Press release by Senator Richard Newhouse, February 21, 1978, Legislative Advisory Committee, Administrative Files, 616.003, ISA.
[99]Ibid.
[100]"Jesse Rips State Welfare Plan," *Chicago Tribune*, May 31, 1974, 8.

parents. In fact, bureaucratic inertia was probably legislators' biggest adversary in their efforts to politicize the fraud issue and shrink the welfare program. To implement their policies, the LAC had to pressure two reluctant, overburdened agencies into expending their limited resources on criminalizing actions that had previously been handled administratively. This transformation could not happen overnight and required considerable political and bureaucratic mobilization. As the LAC's chief investigator acknowledged in a front-page *Wall Street Journal* article, "We're trying to convince people that welfare fraud is a crime just as bank robbery and homicide."[101] Despite these struggles, legislators had powerful allies in their campaign: a significant percentage of the public and the media. The more people heard about welfare fraud, the more infuriated they became; many even embraced the opportunity to join in the campaign themselves.

Cadillacs, Turtles, and Revenge: Community Participation in Identifying Fraud

Most of the public became informed about the state's anti-fraud efforts through the media. Although some media, such as the African American newspaper the *Chicago Defender*, published articles critical of the campaign, other papers tacitly assisted the investigations. Members of the LAC worked closely with journalist George Bliss from the *Chicago Tribune* in his multiple exposés about Linda Taylor and the resistance of IDPA to initiate further investigations. Investigators' reports acknowledged his help in generating public pressure on welfare administrators.[102] The LAC clearly saw the *Tribune* as a partner in their efforts, as illustrated by a letter to the *Tribune* editor that concluded: "We certainly appreciate the support of the *Chicago Tribune* in our ongoing investigations."[103]

In addition to echoing the indignant and alarmed tone of state legislators, newspapers publicized the state's hotline for reporting welfare cheaters. They frequently included the phone number in stories about the LAC's efforts and occasionally even designated separate space in their articles to promote the state's hotline.[104] Set apart from the article with lines

[101] David Garino, "Chasing the Cheats; Drive against Fraud in Obtaining Welfare Is Gaining Momentum," *Wall Street Journal*, November 18, 1976, 1.

[102] Caauwe et al., progress report by investigative unit of the Legislative Advisory Committee, 2.

[103] Joel Edelman, executive director of LAC, to Clayton Kirkpatrick, editor of the *Chicago Tribune*, February 17, 1976, Legislative Advisory Committee, Administrative Files, 616.003, ISA.

[104] See, for example, Branegan, "State Calls Courts 'Soft' on Fraud," 44.

or a box, the announcements were essentially advertisements for the ho-tline and a clear endorsement of the state's campaign. A 1976 article that ran in the *Markham Star Tribune* assured readers that there was no risk in reporting fraud and that all tips would be taken seriously: "All calls will be confidential and callers are not required to identify themselves. All reports will be checked."[105]

The *Chicago Tribune* also published lists of names of those charged with welfare fraud. When the state's attorney started returning indict-ments in groups of fifty or seventy-five, the paper would run all the names, along with addresses and places of illegal employment, at the end of the article in smaller print.[106] This public shaming of welfare re-cipients broadcasted the LAC's message more powerfully than simply re-peating legislators' allegations or speeches. Reading about actual indict-ments played a key role in convincing the public that the welfare program wasted their tax dollars on financially secure, manipulative criminals.

People responded to this news of rampant welfare fraud in various ways. Some angry citizens wrote letters to their paper's editorial page. One man demanded that judges who handed down light sentences for welfare fraud be removed from their jobs immediately and asked, "Aren't such judicial decisions tantamount to aiding and abetting criminal acts?"[107] Another woman, furious about the waste of "our money," wanted to be a part of the effort to hunt down welfare cheaters:

> I could think of a hundred people, including myself, who are tired of seeing our money wasted, and would love the opportunity to volunteer for a part in the investigations, without a penny for it. Just for the satisfaction of do-ing something! But that's the trouble with the system, they'll never let the people become involved.[108]

It seems that these sentiments were not aberrations. As the anti-fraud investigations produced more and more convictions, the public became increasingly invested in identifying and punishing "cheaters." Concern seemed to intensify throughout the decade as people became convinced that fraud was endemic to the entire program. One legislator wrote to encourage the LAC to expand their work after reviewing a poll from

[105] Ted Chan, "Welfare: What Can a Small Staff Accomplish?" *Markham Star Tribune*, April 1, 1976, 1.

[106] See, for example, Jay Branegan, "Jury Indicts 53 for $508,000 in Welfare Fraud," *Chicago Tribune*, July 20, 1978, 2; Jane Fritsch, "31 More Indicted in Welfare Fraud Probe; Total Now 342," *Chicago Tribune*, May 1, 1979, 3; and Jane Fritsch, "75 Indicted in Wel-fare Fraud, Netting More than $1 Million," *Chicago Tribune*, June 29, 1979, D1.

[107] Al Jaburck, letter to the editor, "Fraud Sentences," *Chicago Tribune*, March 5, 1978, sec. 2, 4.

[108] Letter to the editor, *Chicago Tribune*, May 18, 1978, sec. 3, 2.

his district that revealed 96 percent of his constituents thought "too many people on welfare are receiving benefits to which they are not entitled."[109] In 1978, a poll of 800 Illinois voters showed that 84 percent ranked controlling welfare and Medicaid fraud and abuses their *highest* legislative priority, polling above controlling crime and government costs generally.[110]

In the fiscal year of 1977, the state's fraud hotline received 10,047 calls, with the numbers mounting each month.[111] Between 1977 and 1980, it received more than 30,000 tips.[112] Since the tippers reported specific instances of welfare fraud, these numbers suggest extensive involvement by people who frequently interacted with or lived near welfare recipients. Although the intake records for the hotline are not available, it is possible to piece together anecdotal evidence about why people participated in this campaign. Tippers rarely had a clear understanding of what technically constituted fraud and instead turned in the more traditional targets of state sanction, such as morally stigmatized unmarried mothers. Many tips were inspired by a sense of frustration and injustice about a cheater who seemed to be getting ahead unfairly. The tippers expressed anger that others were getting financial support that they had not "earned." These complaints echoed the state's assumption that work did not include unpaid domestic labor or raising children. Tippers directed their complaints at objects of personal frustration and were remarkably unsuccessful at identifying criminal behavior. The almost 32,000 tips resulted in the adjustment or cancellation of 3,400 grants; thus the informers found actual fraud only about 10 percent of the time.[113]

Tippers were most frequently alerted to fraud by seeing material possessions denoting status. These complaints reflected the assumption that welfare recipients should not have access to consumer goods. Research on the NWRO has illustrated the importance of inclusion in the consumer economy for welfare-rights activism.[114] Recipients shared with wider society a definition of citizenship that entailed access to commodi-

[109] Rep. Thomas Miller to Don Moore, February 10, 1976, Legislative Advisory Committee, Correspondence Files, 616.004, ISA. The poll was taken in December 1975–January 1976 in Illinois's 10th legislative district (which included South Holland, Dolton, Harvey, Lansing, Riverdale, and Thornton).

[110] Remarks by Samuel Skinner, *Secretary's National Convention on Fraud, Abuse, and Error: Conference Proceedings* (Washington, D.C.: U.S. Department of Health, Education and Welfare, 1978), 21.

[111] "Welfare Fraud 'Hotline' Pays Off for Taxpayers," *Chicago Tribune*, January 1, 1978, sec. 3, 6.

[112] Gardiner and Lyman, *Fraud Control Game*, 155.

[113] Ibid.

[114] Kornbluh, "To Fulfill Their 'Rightly Needs': Consumerism and the National Welfare Rights Movement," *Radical History Review* 69 (Fall 1997): 76–113.

ties signifying a dignified standard of living.[115] Like other women in the United States, female welfare recipients insisted that they were entitled to consumer goods, such as perfume or a decent dining room table. These activists articulated a different claim to rights and dignity, one based on their position as mothers and citizens, which did not depend on participation in wage work. By claiming entitlement to material comforts by virtue of their citizenship, recipients directly challenged dominant ideas about the social and material value of domestic and caregiving labor.

While activists defended poor families' right to be included in the consumer society, many other people were offended when they saw welfare recipients possessing certain material goods. Tippers who notified the state about fraud assumed that nice or new possessions were sufficient evidence to establish the guilt of the welfare recipient. In one typed, anonymous letter sent to a state senator, the author reported that the family next door to him had a house full of children and that the parents floated between welfare and wage work. Offended by the family's unimpeded access to various commodities, the author explained, "They made the comment that whatever they want they will go buy. . . . They go to town every week and spend between $40 and $50 for new clothes and foolishness. They buy turtles, guinea pigs, white mice and a lot of toys that are broken up in one day."[116] The crime, in this writer's mind, was illustrated by the existence of frivolous toys and pets. Although there was no explicit fraud stated in the letter, the investigators followed up on this tip and found that the family had not received aid for more than a year.[117]

Although not stated explicitly, it seemed that the tipper could not afford such luxuries for his or her own family and found the comparison with his or her neighbors disturbing. The author wrote, "These people are living high on the hog and sitting home doing nothing and we have to get out and work to support them."[118] Tippers assumed that their neighbors were not contributors to the state organs that funded welfare programs. This rhetoric created a dichotomy between "taxpayers," which served as a proxy for full citizens, and welfare recipients, who were presented as not contributing to the polity and therefore having no claim to the benefits of citizenship.

Other examples suggest that tippers may have felt that welfare gave their neighbors unfair advantages, especially when used to subsidize low-wage work. Chief Investigator Tom Coughlin explained to reporters that the best informants were "the outraged, average community taxpayer." He explained,

[115]Ibid., 79. On consumerism and citizenship, see Cohen, *A Consumers' Republic*.

[116]Anonymous letter to Senator John Carroll, [1970?], Legislative Advisory Committee on Public Aid, Administrative Files, 616.003, ISA.

[117]Memo regarding Geraldine H., October 13, 1971, Legislative Advisory Committee, Administrative Files, 616.003, ISA.

[118]Anonymous letter to Senator John Carroll, [1970?].

"One man called here and started chastising me. . . . He accused me of not doing my job because the man across the street was on aid, working, and driving a new car." In this case, the new car, a symbol of status and consumerism, angered the neighbor and inspired him to inform the authorities. The investigator explained that there was nothing he could do unless the tipper could name the place of employment. An hour later, the tipper called the investigator back to report that he had looked through his neighbor's window with binoculars and, upon seeing his work shirt, found out he was employed at Sears.[119] While press and law enforcement might have condemned spying on people as a violation of privacy in another context, welfare recipients had entered a suspect category and thus surveillance was encouraged.

One man wrote a letter to LAC chairman Moore to remind him that food stamp fraud was also a problem. Although he had no specific person to report, he simply wanted to alert the authorities that there were a lot of people using food stamps and some of their actions made him suspicious: "What makes this so noticeable is that some of these people using food stamps are often dressed in fine clothing and purchasing items considered for expensive taste. Need I say more?"[120] The concluding question revealed that the author assumed a common understanding about the limits of recipients' rights to nonessential or frivolous commodities. According to this logic, people surrendered their cherished American rights of consumer choice once they started receiving food stamps. Simultaneously, it became any citizen's right to monitor, judge, and report recipients' decisions. By excluding welfare and food stamp recipients from this consumer society, tippers were also reinforcing the image of recipients as a separate and degraded category of citizen.

The campaign against fraud also caused people who were bothered by deviant social behavior to feel that the state might intervene to discipline their neighbors. Another anonymous letter, written in 1974, testified to the power of the media's representations of welfare queens: "In [the] wake of recent newspaper stories concerning welfare cheaters, I would like for you to investigate another 'unfortunate' person who is collecting food stamps and welfare checks while riding around in a white late model Cadillac."[121] Again, this tipper named no act that technically constituted welfare fraud. Instead the welfare recipient's guilt was established by her access to status symbols and her sexual impropriety. The letter detailed the woman's use of her parents' Cadillac, her lack of attention to her child, and her "marathon sexual activities." It concluded, "As a concerned

---

[119]"1,000 Cheats a Month," *Chicago Defender*, December 17, 1977, 1.

[120]John K. to Don Moore, June 24, 1974, Legislative Advisory Committee, Administrative Files, 616.003, ISA.

[121]Anonymous letter addressed to "Gentlemen," July 1974, Legislative Advisory Committee, Administrative Files, 616.003, ISA.

citizen of this area, I think you should investigate this woman's daily activities (and nightly ones as well)."[122] This tipper seemed more interested in convincing the state to regulate the recipient's sexual behavior than addressing her use of the welfare program. By highlighting her inappropriate connection to a key symbol of postwar prosperity, the Cadillac, the complaint interlaced traditional assumptions with more contemporary concerns.[123] It connected the older rhetoric that considered normative sexual behavior a condition for receiving aid with the more modern anxiety regarding poor women's inclusion in the consumerist society.

Like citizens on probation and parole, welfare recipients were located by these campaigns in a subordinated civic status that could be exploited by family members, friends, and neighbors. Revenge and animosity motivated people to report their acquaintances for welfare fraud. Although it is difficult to establish what percentage of the tips were thus inspired, it is not surprising that this would occur. The state promised to investigate all leads and did not require any proof or documentation from the anonymous tippers. Even welfare officials occasionally acknowledged that the calls were not always civically motivated. As one Public Aid employee explained, "We get a lot of grudge calls from people upset with their neighbors, and we have a couple of callers who just give us doses of music, but we're obligated to check all calls if they give us the necessary information."[124]

A few specific examples illustrate this phenomenon. In one case, it was clearly a woman's estranged husband who informed authorities she was working while receiving welfare. He even went on a stakeout with LAC investigators to help identify her.[125] In another example, a couple testified against their downstairs neighbor who had not reported to Public Aid that her husband resided with the family. The defendant attempted to have her neighbors' testimony thrown out on the grounds that they had frequently fought and were biased against her. It also turned out that the witnesses were themselves under investigation for welfare fraud and may have been hoping for leniency by cooperating with their neighbor's prosecution.[126] Although the files do not clearly establish what happened,

[122] Ibid.

[123] For a discussion of how African American ownership of luxury goods, especially the Cadillac, challenged white cultural norms, see George Lipsitz, "'Swing Low, Sweet Cadillac': Antiblack Racism and White Identity," in *The Possessive Investment in Whiteness* (Philadelphia: Temple University Press, 1998), 158–83.

[124] Egler, "Welfare Fraud 'Hotline' Pays Off for Taxpayers."

[125] Welfare fraud report on Beverly B., [February–March 1975?], Legislative Advisory Committee, Administrative Files, 616.003, ISA.

[126] *People of the State of Illinois vs. Bobbie Baugh*, 80-1456 (Appellate Court of Illinois 1st District, 4th Division, May 28, 1981). Although most of the events regarding this case occurred around 1977, it did not reach the appellate level until 1981.

it seems that the parties involved reported each other and were certainly using the state to settle personal scores.

These examples suggest that people became involved in the fraud campaign for reasons that deviated from the state's motivations. Not aware of the specifics of welfare policy, neighbors watched recipients for signs of social and cultural transgressions. They duly noted evidence of sexual impropriety, even though the state could no longer legally deny benefits using this criterion. Since neighbors were notoriously ineffective at identifying actual welfare fraud, the hotline's main success seems to have been allowing citizens to harness the state's power to address concerns in their personal lives. Their participation, however, further legitimized the state's campaign and added another technique for monitoring poor families. This street-level surveillance enabled citizens to intervene in the *performance* of recipients' stigmatized position; it impeded recipients' ability to subvert that position by acquiring consumer goods connoting status.

The Crime of Survival: Welfare Recipients and Fraud Prosecutions

The LAC legislators were likely correct when they charged that welfare fraud was prevalent in Illinois in the 1970s. Many recipients probably committed fraud as the state defined it, as it was difficult to survive on the checks from Public Aid.[127] The final section of this chapter investigates some strategies recipients used to subsist on paltry cash grants and how they reacted to the state's anti-fraud initiatives. Welfare recipients were personally, racially, and socially diverse. However, they supposedly all shared two conditions: poverty and parenthood. They probably also shared an awareness that it was incredibly difficult to support a family on a welfare grant.[128] In 1974, the welfare grant for a family of four in Illinois was approximately $288 per month, plus $65 in food stamps. Based on 1972 prices, this was 35 percent below the lowest floor set by the federal government for a four-person family.[129] Even after adding wage work, many families still lived below the federal poverty line.[130] The difficulty of subsisting on AFDC was exacerbated by the failure of the already low grants to keep pace with the era's rampant inflation. The national reces-

[127] See Kathryn Edin, "There's a Lot of Month Left at the End of the Money: How Welfare Recipients in Chicago Make Ends Meet" (Ph.D. diss., Northwestern University, 1989).
[128] Neubeck and Cazenave, *Welfare Racism*, 100.
[129] Lee Strobel, "Coalition of 40 Groups Backs 10 Percent Aid Payment Hikes," *Chicago Tribune*, June 11, 1974, 3.
[130] For one example, see Mae Gentry, "Man Indicted for Fraud Blames Welfare System," *Chicago Defender*, October 14, 1978.

sion, which started in 1973, further intensified the economic insecurity of poor families. Unemployment rose to 8.3 percent by 1975 and real weekly earnings declined at a -0.4 percent annual rate during the 1970s.[131]

The state's indictments illustrate that many of the cases that became defined as fraud involved people who were trying to supplement welfare grants with additional income from low-wage work or living with another wage earner. Herbert Saul was a typical case. He was sentenced to two years' probation and $13,024 in restitution for working at a furniture store while also receiving welfare. He explained his crime to a journalist concisely: "I have a wife and three kids and I'm loaded with medical bills. That is all I can say."[132] Although recipients were depicted as lazy, the main crime constituting welfare fraud was *working*, holding a job on top of raising children. Similarly, although welfare recipients were often represented as promiscuous single mothers, Public Aid often sanctioned women for living with a husband or partner after claiming to be single, deserted, or separated.

Investigators' files also illuminated the techniques parents used to make ends meet while on welfare. Many recipients chose not to notify welfare administrators when they got a new job in order to avoid having their cases reassessed and grants reduced. Although many people held low-wage jobs with formal employers, one woman's grant was reduced because she failed to report babysitting income.[133] Some worked under different names, usually maiden names, or used fake Social Security numbers to avoid detection by Public Aid. Other recipients reported checks missing and cashed both the original and the duplicate. One woman paid her nephew's friend $40 to rob her on the way home from cashing her welfare checks. After she reported the money stolen, the fake robber returned the original money.[134] In one bizarre case, investigators struggled to ascertain who had been cashing the checks of a man murdered months earlier.[135]

It is impossible to determine the true extent of fraud without access to extensive interviews or surveys where recipients felt safe enough to tell the truth about their behavior. Surveys conducted during the 1970s in Seattle and Denver showed that 50 percent of recipients admitted to

[131]Cohen, *A Consumer's Republic*, 389.

[132]William Juneau, "Aid Cheat Ordered to Pay Back $13,024," *Chicago Tribune*, June 28, 1974, 1.

[133]Welfare fraud report on Anna B., March 10, 1977, Legislative Advisory Committee, Administrative Files, 616.003, ISA.

[134]Welfare fraud report on Luretha M., April 17, 1975, Legislative Advisory Committee, Administrative Files, 616.003, ISA.

[135]Welfare fraud report on Lancie W., March 10, 1977, Legislative Advisory Committee, Administrative Files, 616.003, ISA.

"cheating" in order to get by financially.[136] In an interview with the *Chicago Tribune*, an ex–fraud investigator for IDPA estimated that 25 to 50 percent of welfare recipients committed some degree of fraud. She explained that "the extent of the fraud varies. Some of it is rather minor, some of it is huge. But people are forced into committing fraud because of the silly rules of the system."[137]

Many of the less extreme techniques mentioned thus far must have been relatively well known, and recipients shared information about how to supplement grants without being detected. One woman told a reporter how she was terrified to find out that people were suddenly being jailed for working while on welfare:

> "I had a good job," she said, "but then I got laid off. I had a baby and so I got on welfare. But then I got my job back and everyone told me to just stay on welfare and not tell them that I was working again. So I did. Everyone was doing it. . . . But now what am I going to do? Go to jail?"[138]

She and other welfare recipients had come to believe that this behavior was not risky or could not be detected. The woman went on to explain how the extra income from fraud impacted her family: "I moved from my apartment with roaches to a decent apartment. I could go to the store and load up the basket instead of buying hamburger and chicken necks. I could send my baby to Catholic school."[139] In this case, she felt fraud enabled her to raise her family's standard of living to what would be considered comparable to that of an average American family. Other recipients also felt that the state's anti-fraud campaign blocked one of their few available avenues for economic advancement. When one woman was arrested for working while receiving welfare, the investigator reported that "she felt she was getting arrested for trying to upgrade herself, and she thought this was just terrible." She then informed investigators that when she got out of jail, she intended to kill herself and her two children.[140]

Some committed fraud out of what they considered dire financial need. The *Chicago Defender* carried a story about Shelley Miller, a father of three, who was indicted for illegally collecting aid while he was employed as a community service worker for the Chicago Department of Human

---

[136] Edin, "There's a Lot of Month Left at the End of the Money," 253. Edin suggests that the percentage might have been even higher since many respondents were probably not convinced of the survey's confidentiality.

[137] Derrick Blakley, "Red Tape of Public Aid Job Pushes Her off Payroll, onto Welfare Rolls," *Chicago Tribune*, June 25, 1974, 4A, 1.

[138] "Welfare Cheats Find 'Easy Street' Had Dead End," 25.

[139] Ibid.

[140] Welfare fraud report on Beverly B.

Services. In the article, he admitted to lying about this income but refused to plead guilty because he held the system responsible for his situation:

> Prior to applying for this assistance two years ago, my family was nearly starving. I couldn't buy clothes for my wife or shoes for my kids. . . . The money we were receiving from Public Aid we weren't stealing from the poor, because we are the poor. And if you add that $261 a month to my income of $5,000 a year, I still was below the poverty line.[141]

The article explained that Miller was an upstanding and active member of the community who was recognized by both Mayor Richard J. Daley and Alderman Vito Marzullo for his work with West Side youth. Because of his pride in his commitment and connection to his community, Miller explained to the reporter that he almost cried when he was asked to resign from his job:

> I grew up on the West Side. I've worked in the community with the youth and I've never been involved in crime. But if I'm convicted and put on probation, then it will be three strikes against me. I'm black, I don't have a college education and I'll have a criminal conviction on my record.[142]

He claimed the indictment would cripple his ability to support his family, who were already struggling to get by.

The state's crackdown probably had equally severe implications for many others in similar situations. The lives that were most disrupted were those of family members where a parent was incarcerated or received a criminal record. These campaigns drastically expanded the population subject to formal criminal scrutiny. Between fiscal year 1971 and 1979, the number of referrals for prosecution increased five times and actual prosecutions increased over three times. When controlling for the growth in AFDC, the number of both referrals and prosecutions multiplied approximately three times during this period.[143] Since a significant portion of investigations never ended up referred to criminal prosecutors or resulting in formal charges, the statistics probably understate the breadth and impact of the campaign for the entire AFDC caseload. In 1971, welfare agencies referred 0.04 percent of the caseload to law enforcement; in 1979, they referred 1.5 percent. Although only 0.51 percent of the entire caseload nationally was actually prosecuted in 1979, the welfare department opened cases investigating 6.7 percent of the families receiving benefits. This represented a dramatic increase in just a matter of years since

---

[141] Gentry, "Man Indicted for Fraud Blames Welfare System."

[142] Ibid.

[143] Gardiner and Lyman, *Fraud Control Game*, 93–94. Figure 4.3 represents fraud investigations in all public assistance; these numbers just reflect investigations in the AFDC program.

officials investigated only 1.6 percent of AFDC families in 1971.[144] It is reasonable to assume that even more families were scrutinized but never officially had a case opened. Therefore, the intensification of anti-fraud efforts during this period subjected significant segments of the caseload to actual or threatened scrutiny by the penal system.

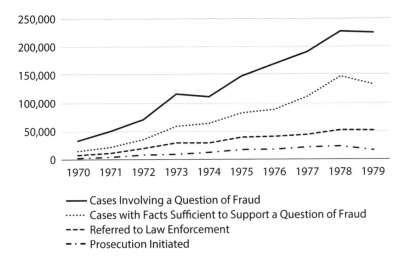

Figure 4.3. National public assistance fraud investigations, 1970–79. (*Source*: National Center for Social Statistics, *Disposition of Public Assistance Cases Involving Questions of Fraud, Fiscal Years 1970–79* [Washington, D.C.: U.S. Department of Health, Education, and Welfare, Social Security Administration, Office of Research and Statistics, 1973–1979.])
Note: Number of convictions not reported; not all states reporting all years. Until 1974, these numbers included suspected fraud in AFDC, Medical Assistance, and the Adult Programs (defined as Aid to the Blind, Old-Age Assistance, and Aid to the Permanently and Totally Disabled). AFDC cases were the large majority, with the other programs never exceeding 20 percent of the cases suspected and prosecuted. After 1974, the Adult Programs were transferred into a federally administered program, Supplemental Security Income (SSI), and ceased to report fraud to this report. The numbers after 1974 still included suspected fraud in medical assistance, but AFDC was over 95 percent of the cases.

Welfare recipients endeavored to mitigate the consequences of such scrutiny through various strategies, such as legal challenges and fair hear-

---

[144] Ibid., 89–95. See also *Disposition of Public Assistance Cases Involving Questions of Fraud*. Until 1974, these numbers include suspected fraud in all public assistance programs, not just AFDC. See note to Figure 4.3.

ings. Miller, for example, collected more than 120 signatures in a petition to support his not-guilty plea. In addition to the families convicted criminally, thousands more had their grants reduced or eliminated through new stringent administration. The deployment of new technologies that cross-checked the welfare rolls with employee lists forced many to choose between welfare or wage work, neither of which provided sufficient income. Anti-fraud efforts contributed to the increased surveillance of poor urban neighborhoods. Recipients were forced to comply with continual bureaucratic examinations of their personal and financial decisions. This heightened presence of state officials intertwined with the increased policing that followed the massive social and political upheavals of the late 1960s and 1970s and contributed to the growing criminalization of inner-city space.

Many of the strategies implemented to prevent fraud had consequences for poor communities generally. For example, Mary Cowherd, a resident of Chicago's Robert Taylor Homes, testified before a legislative committee about the consequences of the decision to send all welfare checks to currency exchanges instead of people's homes. She explained that on the day that the checks arrive "it looks just like a bread line . . . it's like a concentration [camp] line. . . . Then you go to the currency exchange and they charge you 5 or 6 dollars to cash a check. And then . . . you get ripped off outside of the place."[145] Since the whole community could see who had just cashed their check, the state's anti-theft initiative turned recipients into "sitting ducks" and put them at risk of being robbed. The punitive policy was therefore both demoralizing and counterproductive. It also forced all recipients to perform in a degrading theater that constructed them as a distinct, suspect segment of society.

This formal monitoring by various state agencies was intensified by the fact that neighbors, acquaintances, and ex-lovers had the power to report recipients to Public Aid. Welfare-rights activist and recipient Kathi Gunlogson explained:

> I really feel like when someone applies for Public Aid, they are giving up a great majority of their constitutional rights. And one of those things is privacy. If somebody down the block from you sees somebody moving in a new table, which they may have given you, and you never had one before, they can go and call Public Aid and tell them that you are going against

[145]Testimony of Mary Cowherd before Sub-Committee on Emergency Assistance on LAC, November 29, 1976, Legislative Advisory Committee, Administrative Files, 616.003, p. 66, ISA.

the laws. And Public Aid [does] not have to tell me who that person is that informed on me. But they can decide to cut my grant.[146]

Gunlogson's anecdote illustrates that recipients understood that consumer goods triggered fraud complaints. In becoming a welfare recipient, Gunlogson felt that she had forfeited her right to privacy and the right to face a hostile accuser. She argued that these conditions amounted to stripping welfare recipients of the intertwined rights of citizenship and participation in the consumer economy.

Although opinions about the welfare program undoubtedly varied among recipients, some claimed it criminalized the poor, especially people of color. In testimony before members of the state legislature, recipient Frank Smith articulated a similar sense that welfare policy deliberately degraded recipients. He explained:

> I think that the Department [IDPA] is geared to cause people to commit crimes. . . . [T]hey treat us as if we are less than human beings. . . . You know, but I have personally went out and committed a crime, a crime I call survival. And a lot of guys that's sitting down there in Menard [Prison] right now committed that crime of survival because they were unable to take care of their families. And it's mainly because of the Department of Public Aid not taking them at heart once they come to you and have no other place to go.[147]

Smith felt that the financial options were so constrained that poor people could not survive without breaking the state's rules. His language united welfare policy and criminal law into a single, undifferentiated oppressive structure. Indeed, he saw his survival within these structures as essentially and inevitably a criminal act. Shelley Miller, the recipient profiled in the *Chicago Defender*, echoed these sentiments when he explained that welfare forced people to "live worse than animals." He claimed that the structure of the welfare program made crime inevitable by "forc[ing] people who are unemployed and on welfare to go out there and commit crimes because they don't provide enough on their welfare budget to coincide with the cost of living today."[148]

---

[146] Verbatim testimony of Kathi Gunlogson, February 2, 1979, Commission to Rewrite the Public Aid Code, Meeting Minutes and Transcripts, 557.003, p. 122, ISA.

[147] Testimony of Frank Smith before Sub-Committee on Emergency Assistance, November 29, 1976, Legislative Advisory Committee, Administrative Files, 616.003, pp. 26–28, ISA.

[148] Gentry, "Man Indicted for Fraud Blames Welfare System."

Examining recipients' perspectives on fraud highlights the immense gap between legislators' rhetoric and the material conditions of poor families. The architects of anti-fraud initiatives were not in conversation with welfare recipients or with statistics about falling wages and rising prices. Their policies were designed to discipline the welfare queen: a deviant woman burdened by neither work nor family. They almost never acknowledged that the welfare grant kept families living in poverty.[149] Claims of culturally transmitted criminality elided the effects of economic transformations, particularly the economic abandonment and high levels of unemployment in racially segregated urban areas. Their language and policies reflected the assumption that only wage labor constituted "work." In this rhetoric, work and welfare were diametrically opposed and the caregiving labor that welfare was originally designed to remunerate was rendered invisible or irrelevant.

Efforts to crack down on fraud not only undermined public support for poor parents and AFDC but became evidence for the more general incompetence of the state. Politicians recognized that more was at stake than just ballooning budgets: the public faith in government's capacity, already shaken by years of protest and scandal, was also in jeopardy. President Carter acknowledged this dynamic in a 1978 speech responding to the escalating preoccupation with fraud throughout government. He explained that "this administration has declared war on waste and fraud in government programs. We are concerned with more than saving dollars, crucial as that is today. . . . We must restore and rebuild the trust that exists in a democracy between a free people and their government."[150]

In the postwar era, policymakers had shifted AFDC's emphasis on supporting mothering through cash grants to reforming mothers into independent wageworkers. In the face of mounting welfare rolls and wrenching economic and social transformations that escalated in the 1970s, reform campaigns in Illinois and California asserted a new priority: protecting the "taxpaying public" from the "tax-eating" welfare mothers. Instead of new financial supports or guaranteed family incomes, they restricted welfare recipients' ability to use low-wage and informal work to subsidize stagnating welfare stipends. Just as Rockefeller used the alleged incorrigibility of drug pushers to explain social turmoil and

---

[149]For example, in 1974, even after a 10 percent cost-of-living increase, the cash grant in Illinois totaled $3,804 a year for a family of four. The poverty threshold, according to the federal government, was $5,038. It should also be noted that the federal poverty thresholds are frequently critiqued for underestimating the actual costs of living, especially in metropolitan areas. *Annual Report: Illinois Department of Public Aid, 1974*, 27; "Historical Poverty Tables—Poverty by Definition of Income," U.S. Census Bureau, http://www.census .gov/hhes/poverty/histpov/rdp01a.html.

[150]Quoted in Gardiner and Lyman, *Fraud Control Game*, 2.

rationalize scaling back commitments to treatment and reintegration, the opponents of AFDC presented "welfare queens" as the source of social upheaval and economic hardship within state and family budgets. They used her purported laziness and criminality as the grounds to deny calls for broader social rights and undermine newly established welfare rights and income supports. Unlike earlier policies that positioned poor women as rational economic actors who would respond to market incentives, the new policies positioned recipients as in need of tough discipline: work mandates and increased coercion and surveillance. They responded to recipients' wage earning with costly punishment: increased scrutiny, stigmatization, and criminalization. These campaigns constricted the amount of financial support available to poor parents at a time of narrowing economic opportunities, especially in increasingly economically abandoned urban centers.

Anti-welfare legislators and their grassroots supporters cast these reforms in terms of a social contract. They claimed that recipients had forfeited their claims on the state because they had failed to uphold the obligations of citizenship: performing wage work, paying taxes, and following the law. Since "independence" and paid employment were the principal avenue to poor women's full citizenship, anti-welfare policymakers fiercely contested welfare recipients' participation in the political community with full standing. And the surveillance, criminalization, and new work mandates further entrenched these claims by actively subordinating the civic status of aid beneficiaries. The political spectacle of "getting tough" solidified a salient, maligned social category against which productive workers and taxpayers were defined. Elites used the degraded civic status of welfare recipients to buoy the social and cultural (but emphatically not the economic) position of low-wage work. In a period of growing female participation in the workforce, anti-welfare politics portrayed recipients as the antithesis of workers and in the process contributed to the broader cultural trend of erasing or demeaning caregiving labor. The focus on crime, laziness, sexual impropriety, and fraud suppressed poor parents' voices and claims on the state. It obscured—if not completely disguised—the economic and social challenges facing the nation.

PART III

Criminals

But there is a movement underway now which has already had a profound impact in some parts of the nation and which promises to turn the entire criminal justice system upside down, for good or bad, before it has run its course. This movement goes by the generic title of "determinate sentencing." It has its origins in the civil rights and prisoners' rights struggles of the late sixties but has since been enthusiastically embraced by both liberals and conservatives, by prison reformers and police chiefs. Determinate sentencing is clearly an idea whose time has come, even though its definition heavily depends on the person who is defining it.

—Michael Serrill, *Corrections Magazine*, September 1977[1]

In 1976, California state lawmakers from across the ideological spectrum joined together to abolish the central pillar of half a century of penal practice: the indeterminate sentence. With their enactment of a new fixed sentencing scheme, the state became the first in the nation to declare the official mission of incarceration to be the punishment—not rehabilitation—of people convicted of crimes. These sentencing reforms became one of the first and most significant manifestations of a trend that would sweep the nation over the following decade. By the mid-1980s, every state in the nation had either enacted or considered reforms moving away from indeterminate sentencing.[2]

---

[1] Michael Serrill, "Determinate Sentencing," *Corrections Magazine*, September 1977, 3. Quoted in John Irwin, *Prisons in Turmoil* (Boston: Little, Brown, 1980), 223.

[2] Griset, *Determinate Sentencing*, 39–60, especially 55. California was technically the second state to abolish indeterminate sentencing. In 1975, Maine enacted determinate sentencing reforms but gave the judiciary vast discretion over the length of punishments within wide sentencing ranges.

Ever since the Progressive Era, prisons' purported primary function was to rehabilitate criminals, not to avenge their crimes, and sentencing policy had reflected this mission. Instead of a fixed prison term set upon conviction, the judge handed down an indeterminate sentence—a range of, for example, three years to life. Parole boards actually controlled the duration of incarceration, periodically evaluating prisoners and setting a release date once they deemed a prisoner sufficiently reformed. When longstanding critiques of the state's efforts to rehabilitate criminals escalated in the 1970s, support for indeterminate sentencing quickly eroded, leading lawmakers to replace it with determinate sentencing. Under determinate—or fixed—sentencing, the prison terms for particular offenses were set by law, adjusted by the judge to reflect a person's prior criminal record and other mitigating factors, and announced at the time of sentencing.

Criminologists and sociologists have long argued that abandoning the "rehabilitative ideal" and embracing increasingly long determinate sentences were foundational steps on the road to mass incarceration.[3] This final study of the book examines how the reorientation in the prison's stated mission transpired in California. Chapter 5 argues that prisoners themselves catalyzed these changes through their resistance to what many felt were the discriminatory, degrading, and coercive features of the rehabilitative regime in California's prisons. It then maps the diverse and unlikely collection of law enforcement professionals, leftist radicals, and law-and-order activists who all joined prisoners in their rejection the "rehabilitative ideal."

In the chapters that follow, I am more concerned with the political and cultural logics animating sentencing decisions than with the determinate sentence as a legal instrument. When legislators abolished indeterminate sentencing, they transferred to the legislature the authority to set the prison terms for different crimes. However, moving sentencing policy into the political arena need not inevitably lead to harsher sentencing.[4]

---

[3]For analyses of the significance and causes of the fall of the "rehabilitative idea," see Griset, *Determinate Sentencing*; Garland, *Culture of Control*; Malcolm M. Feeley and Jonathan Simon, "The New Penology: Notes on the Emerging Strategy of Corrections and Its Implications," *Criminology* 30, no. 4 (1992): 449–74; and Gottschalk, *The Prison and the Gallows*, 37–40.

[4]No penal system is isolated from these political forces, but comparative research tends to assume that institutional arrangements that insulate criminal justice decision makers from direct populist pressure tend to punish less. The following three books have different emphases and arguments but all scrutinize how different political and institutional configurations explain variations across states and nations in levels of punishment: David Downes, *Contrasts in Tolerance* (Oxford: Oxford University Press, 1988); Barker, *The Politics of Imprisonment*; and Nicola Lacey, *The Prisoners' Dilemma: Political Economy and Punishment in Contemporary Democracies* (Cambridge: Cambridge University Press, 2008).

Not every crime evokes a populist demand for retribution, and crime increases do not mechanically trigger harsher punishment. Comparative research reveals that escalating punishment can be a less attractive political choice in communities with more social cohesion, fewer socially vulnerable targets, or other more effective strategies for mitigating crime and its social milieu.[5] Furthermore, determinate sentencing schemes were not inherently more punitive than indeterminate ones. Texas, for example, largely retained indeterminate sentencing and saw huge increases in incarceration rates during the late twentieth century.[6] And even once draconian minimum sentences—indeterminate or determinate—were on the books, they did not automatically translate into a massive expansion in prison populations unless other actors within the penal system enthusiastically implemented them.[7] Prosecutors can decline (and often have declined) to pursue long sentences by either not indicting or charging defendants with crimes carrying lesser punishment.

In short, historical actors at all levels of the criminal justice system could have chosen to keep punishment and prison populations stable. They could have, as some predicted at the time, decreased reliance on the prison even further. But in the final decades of the twentieth century, they chose otherwise. Chapter 6 tracks how California politicians, as one lawmaker explained, went "berserk in terms of punishment" and helped balloon the prison system to a scale few could have imagined possible in the early 1970s.[8] While determinate sentencing in itself does not ratchet up punishment, the ensuing battles in California over setting prison terms became a vehicle for the ascendance of what I call the "toughness imperative." "Law-and-order" politicians in both parties used the displacement of the rehabilitative ideal to assert a new vision for the prison. They interpreted the upheaval in California's prisons as evidence that corporal

[5] See, for example, Lisa Lynn Miller, *The Myth of Mob Rule: Violent Crime and Democratic Politics* (New York: Oxford University Press, 2016) and Whitman, *Harsh Justice*.

[6] New York's Rockefeller Drug Laws were very severe indeterminate sentences with high mandatory minimums and a maximum sentence of life in prison. Many states developed mixed systems where some crime categories carried indeterminate sentences and others determinate, and both saw increases in time served in the late twentieth century. Gottschalk, *The Prison and the Gallows*, 38–40.

[7] For a critique of focusing too narrowly on legislation without attention to state-level criminal justice actors (especially prosecutors), see John F. Pfaff, "The Micro and Macro Causes of Prison Growth," *Georgia State University Law Review* 28, no. 4 (2012): 1239–73 and John Pfaff, *Locked In: The True Causes of Mass Incarceration and How to Achieve Real Reform* (New York: Basic Books, 2017).

[8] Oral history of Howard Way, "Issues in Corrections: The Adult Authority, Determinate Sentencing, and Prison Crowding, 1962–1982," conducted in 1984 by Julie Shearer, Ronald Reagan Gubernatorial Era Project, p. 31, Regional Oral History Office, Bancroft Library, University of California–Berkeley, 1986, CSA.

containment and harsh, degrading punishment were the only viable response to street crime. Similar to the logic undergirding tough welfare and drug policy, the need for tough sentencing rested upon and reified intertwined claims of state and individual failure. It was predicated upon the idea that most criminals were governable only through punishment and incapacitation and state efforts to rehabilitate them were futile and counterproductive. This vision of incorrigible deviants rested upon, mobilized, and reinstantiated older caricatures of violent, uncontrollable African American men. According to this logic, the state must contain and pacify these populations to ensure "public safety," but it had neither the capacity nor the responsibility to answer to them as citizens.

As was the case in the welfare and drug-policy debates explored in previous chapters, "getting tough" was one of many responses considered in the face of reports of rising crime rates, political upheaval, and unruly prisons. The function and even the future of the prison were in question for a moment in the 1970s. The following chapters trace how—in the span of a decade—toughness and a newly fortified carceral archipelago became the only viable response to the threats that haunted the political imaginary.

CHAPTER FIVE

Unmaking the Rehabilitative Ideal

Prisoners and their representatives played a central role in undermining the therapeutic rationale for incarceration in California. Many felt the indeterminate sentence was at the heart of the hypocrisy and oppression of penal practice. Although their voices were not always audible to those outside of prison walls, prisoners were actively engaged in political deliberations about the institutions that governed them. By the early 1970s, prisoners appeared to be on the verge of gaining more voice, responsibilities, and authority within prisons and in negotiating criminal policy in California. They testified on the conditions they endured, issued reports on their grievances, and almost secured the right to organize unions within the prison. They helped sculpt the arguments that discredited the indeterminate sentence and convinced legislators, activists, and other commentators of the hollow promise of rehabilitation.

This chapter explores how the indeterminate sentence operated in California during the 1960s and early 1970s to illustrate why many opposed it so fervently. Not only did prisoners agitate against the indeterminate sentence, but their resistance and upheaval revealed that the promise of parole (or the threat of its denial) no longer pacified the institutions. Prisoners' uprisings, union organizing, and legislative advocacy signaled the indeterminate sentence's growing ineffectiveness in maintaining control within prisons and were a critical and underappreciated force in discrediting the "corrections" ethos. Law enforcement professionals, prisoners' family members, activists, and legislators from the Left and the Right all came to oppose the status quo for distinct reasons, thereby hastening the fall of the rehabilitative ideal.

Scholars often attribute this fall to criminologists' and other penal specialists' loss of faith in corrections after influential research allegedly demonstrated that "nothing works" to reform prisoners.[1] In this chapter, I move prisoners and struggles for power within carceral institutions more to the center of the story. Reports and studies about the limits of rehabilitative programming were very important in their own right, especially

[1] On the importance of abandoning the rehabilitative ideal and the limitations of attributing it primarily to critical reports and penal professionals, see Garland, *Culture of Control*, particularly 53–73.

212 • Chapter Five

in the context of rising crime rates, but they were also indicators of a broader and increasingly audible critique of "corrections" that prisoners shaped through their activism, writing, and resistance within institutions.

Bringing attention to the role prisoners played in destabilizing the rehabilitative ideal does not imply that activists bungled into inadvertently enabling the subsequent punitive ascendancy. Many actors at the time did not predict the fierce countermobilization that lay ahead and, in fact, had some reason to believe things were heading in the opposite direction. When "law-and-order" proponents won out in these struggles, it was mostly because they marshaled vast social, economic, and cultural resources that were largely unavailable to prisoners and their allies. When they mobilized against these stigmatized and suspect populations, those advocating for more punitive policy had behind them the force of history. Just as in welfare and drug policy, proponents of "getting tough" positioned their policy as protecting taxpaying citizens from threatening populations without legitimate claims on the state. But in the period before the onset of California's punishment binge, prisoners and their allies offered distinct critiques of the rehabilitative regime and alternative visions for replacing it.

The Long History of Reforming Prisons and Reforming Prisoners

The determinate sentencing laws of the 1970s were part of a long history of reforms attempting to make state punishment more legitimate and effective. The indeterminate sentence was a key Progressive reform born out of distaste for penal practices that were established during the Jacksonian era, which were the result of "civilizing reform" to the habits of punishment of the colonial period. In the early days of the republic, Americans, influenced by European Enlightenment philosophers such as Cesare Beccaria, began to question the effectiveness and morality of corporal punishments, such as public pillory, flogging, and execution. Reformers insisted that these practices were not only inhumane but also ineffective in controlling crime or inspiring respect for government authority. States began instead to confine offenders in prisons, which were previously reserved for debtors and those awaiting trial or corporal punishment.[2]

---

[2] Michel Foucault's famous work exploring this transformation is *Discipline and Punish*. For work on the United States, see Louis Masur, *Rites of Execution: Capital Punishment and the Transformation of American Culture, 1776–1865* (New York: Oxford University Press, 1991).

Beginning in the 1820s, new generations of reformers, often Quakers, advanced the notion that punishment should discipline and reform the deviant's mind, not merely hurt, scar, or kill the body. Believing that new social mobility and instability caused criminality, these reformers designed prisons to offer the solitude, silence, discipline, work routine, and moral guidance thought to be lacking in society. Reformers hoped that isolating offenders from corrupting influences would enable their eventual reintegration, while prisons, in turn, could provide a positive model to society. In practice, these new institutions became violent, coercive, and corrupt, often marked more by torture and idleness than penance and rehabilitation.

It is therefore not surprising that Progressive Era reformers scrutinized the prison and its unfulfilled promise. These activists, overwhelmingly white middle-class reformers concerned about the social consequences of rapid industrialization, urbanization, and mass immigration, fundamentally revamped penal practices while maintaining earlier reformers' faith in prisons' capacity to rehabilitate offenders. Abandoning the earlier hope that an ideal prison routine would cure all deviance, they insisted that each prisoner's treatment must reflect the individual's unique background and circumstances. In alliance with prison officials, Progressives rebuilt the institution, largely abandoning the lockstep shuffle, enforced silence, and infamous striped uniform. They allowed new freedoms, such as visitation and correspondence.

They instituted sentencing reforms that reflected their emphasis on individual casework. Progressives argued that the fixed sentence length, set by judges at an offender's trial, was merely retributive and did not account for a person's unique past and progress within the institution. In its place, they implemented the indeterminate sentence, where judges—under the legislature's general guidance—issued a sentence range determined by the crime committed and the person's circumstances. The power to actually release prisoners, however, was transferred to parole boards. These boards monitored the prisoner's progress and decided when the convict was reformed and ready to reenter society. For those people best treated in their communities, states instituted a system of probation, which released offenders directly after conviction and supervised them in their communities to ensure good behavior and compliance with the court's specific terms.

These reforms entrusted the state with immense power and discretion, which rested on the faith it had the capacity to transform deviant characters into productive citizens.[3] Progressives did not call for the

---

[3] David H. Rothman, *Conscience and Convenience: The Asylum and Its Alternatives in Progressive America* (Boston: Little, Brown, 1980), 71.

revolutionary remaking of society, especially the economic and racial order, to reduce crime. Although many believed criminality often grew out of poverty, they saw no need for radical economic restructuring, merely the profound and concerted intervention by a well-meaning state. The criminal offender was characterized as ill, demanding the expert care of trained specialists. Just as a doctor could not predict when a patient would fully recover, reformers argued that experts needed to monitor criminals individually to determine when they were sufficiently reha-bilitated. The massive transfer of discretionary power to unaccountable parole boards and probation workers did not disturb Progressive reform-ers, who trusted in the benevolence of the state and specialist expertise. In fact, many argued that only the state had the capacity and responsibility to reconcile the antagonistic interests in society, cure the various forms of social deviance, and integrate the maximum number of people into mainstream, middle-class norms.

From the onset of these reforms, therefore, there was a fundamental legal tension in the commitments to normalization and incorporation. As progressive reforms spread throughout the country, legislators and courts did not fundamentally challenge the assumptions of "civil death" that states embraced in the mid-1800s. Based on the premise that people who violated the law forfeited their rights as citizens, states continued to with-draw a series of rights from those convicted of crime. The exact clusters of rights abridged and denied varied by time and place, but many states, for example, barred convicts from juries, elected office, and the franchise. While some sanctions ended upon release from prison, many persisted and continued to formally degrade convicts' citizenship even after the completion of their formal punishment.[4]

The indeterminate sentence first appeared in the 1870s, and by 1922, thirty-seven states had adopted some form of indeterminate sentencing and forty-four states had instituted parole boards.[5] By 1923, half of all people held in state prisons were serving indeter-minate sentences.[6] This swift transition cannot be explained by the moral suasion of idealistic reformers alone. A majority of criminal justice officials found something convenient or profitable in the transi-tion to greater indeterminacy. District attorneys found that probation and sentence ranges strengthened their hand during plea bargaining. Through indeterminate sentences, prison wardens gained invaluable leverage over prisoners, since they held the power to extend an in-dividual's sentence almost indefinitely. Less reliant on physical disci-

[4] McLennan, "The Convict's Two Lives," 191–219.
[5] Griset, *Determinate Sentencing*, 10.
[6] Rothman, *Conscience and Convenience*, 44.

pline, prisons also gained new social legitimacy by replacing corporal punishment and their custodial mission with a curative, rehabilitative institutional purpose. Politicians appeared humane in their approach to crime while simultaneously deflecting public outrage about crimes committed by released offenders onto parole boards that did not have to answer to the public in elections.

Despite the advantages it provided to the various institutional actors, indeterminate sentencing failed to deliver on its promise. From the outset, rehabilitation remained a largely elusive goal. Recidivism rates stayed high and therapeutic programs were usually lacking in quality and availability. Likewise, probation was poorly implemented, with inconsistent supervision and little treatment. Although it is difficult to isolate the exact effects of the indeterminate sentence over time and across various state administrations, it probably increased the average time people served in prison. Prisoners also deeply resented being subjected to the arbitrary power of parole boards and guards.[7]

The rehabilitative ideal was not embraced evenly across that nation. Race profoundly structured its implementation. The legacy of slavery, a demand for cheap labor, and a violent commitment to maintaining white supremacy combined to produce convict-leasing systems across the South that barely paid lip service to the new rehabilitative trends until decades after the concepts ascended in other areas.[8] Northern systems embraced rehabilitative rationales and programming but typically assumed that African Americans were not viable candidates. As various immigrant ethnic groups were slowly absorbed into the category of "white" and cast off the stigma of criminality, blackness and criminality fused more tightly. The assumption that African Americans had innate criminal proclivities foreclosed the possibility of rehabilitation and in practice helped limit their access to, for example, the mutual benefit leagues and vocational training.[9] Therefore, although the commitment to rehabilitation was a central ideological column that supported the criminal justice system, these programs were sustained more by their usefulness to politicians and prison authorities than by their ability to fulfill their promise.

[7]Ibid., 72–116, 194.

[8]See Angela Davis, "Race, Gender and Prison History: From the Convict Lease System to the Supermax Prison," in *Prison Masculinities*, ed. Don Sabo, Terry A. Kupers, and Willie London (Philadelphia: Temple University Press, 2001), 35–45; David Oshinsky, *Worse than Slavery Parchman Farm and the Ordeal of Jim Crow Justice* (New York: Free Press, 1996); Alex Lichtenstein, *Twice the Work of Free Labor: The Political Economy of Convict Labor in the New South* (London: Verso, 1996); and Perkinson, *Texas Tough*.

[9]Muhammad, *The Condemnation of Blackness*; Muhammad, "Where Did All the White Criminals Go?"

California Prisoners under Indeterminate Sentencing

California became the exemplar state correctional system by the 1960s, and its rehabilitative programs and indeterminate sentence were considered national models.[10] Although parole had operated earlier as a mechanism to mitigate excessive sentences and relieve overcrowding, the state's indeterminate sentencing system was established in 1917.[11] The rehabilitative promise gained momentum in the World War II era, when labor scarcity and patriotic zeal made the barriers between prisoner and respected citizen more permeable.[12] It was the leadership of Governor Earl Warren that fully committed California to the rehabilitative ideal. In 1944, he signed the Prison Reorganization Act that created the California Department of Corrections and the state's parole agency, the Adult Authority.[13] The central features of the rehabilitative prison were classification, treatment, and the indeterminate sentence. Through classification, administrators attempted to sort prisoners, for example, by their proclivity for disorder or violence and assumed capacity for reintegration into mainstream society. Officials also proscribed an individualized program of education, training, and therapy to facilitate rehabilitation. By the 1950s, institutions offered a wide assortment of programming aiming to catalyze individual transformations. They ranged from individual and group therapy to vocational training to formal educational opportunities, such as high school and higher education.

Indeterminate sentencing was a cornerstone of the therapeutic prison. California's system granted almost complete discretion over male prisoners' sentences to the Adult Authority. The separate, but parallel, Women's Board of Terms and Parole monitored female prisoners. Judges sentenced convicted offenders to "the term proscribed by law," which was usually a broad sentence—for example, one year to life. After serving a percentage of their minimum term, prisoners appeared before the parole board, usually every year, to be considered for release. The Adult Authority consisted

[10] Eric Cummins, *The Rise and Fall of California's Radical Prison Movement* (Stanford: Stanford University Press, 1994), 274.

[11] On the history and origins of parole in California, see Jonathan Simon, *Poor Discipline: Parole and the Social Control of the Underclass, 1890–1990* (Chicago: University of Chicago Press, 1993) and Sheldon Messinger, John Berecochea, David Rauma, and Richard Berk, "The Foundations of Parole in California," *Law and Society Review* 19, no. 1 (1985): 69–106.

[12] Volker Janssen, "When the 'Jungle' Met the Forest: Public Work, Civil Defense, and Prison Camps in Postwar California," *Journal of American History* 96, no. 3 (2009): 702–26.

[13] Joshua Page, *The Toughest Beat: Politics, Punishment, and the Prison Officers Union in California* (New York: Oxford University Press, 2011), 17–18.

of nine members appointed by the governor for four-year terms. They broke into teams of three (or two) to conduct approximately twenty-five hearings a day, each customarily lasting between seven and twenty minutes. One member would interview the prisoner about his activities in prison, his attitude toward his crime and imprisonment, and anything else that might appear of interest in the file. The other board members were often silent because they took turns leading interviews and were busy reading the files of the cases to follow.[14] Adult Authority members based their decisions on their interview and the prisoner's central file. The file could hold comments and reports from judges, district attorneys, psychiatrists, and prison guards. Prisoners had no representation or access to the information in their files that weighed so heavily in the hearings' outcomes. Guards and other correctional staff did not write formal recommendations for parole boards, but they recorded any disciplinary infractions, complaints, and hearsay they deemed relevant in the files.

There were no transcripts and few formal records of the hearings, and parole boards were not compelled to explain their verdicts. There was no way to appeal the Adult Authority decision. Not surprisingly, therefore, the principal complaint against the parole boards was that they exercised their considerable authority arbitrarily and inconsistently. For example, two people imprisoned at the same time in the same place for the same crime could be released years apart. Sordid anecdotes of murderers getting paroled before burglars spread quickly in prison yards and caused significant hostility and unrest. Although the Adult Authority's parole decisions could be unpredictable, they exhibited trends that reflected general societal prejudice and panics. Many felt that boards were unfairly responsive to shifting political winds. People suspected, for example, that the Adult Authority would hesitate to parole a person convicted of drug trafficking during periods of heightened public concern about narcotics.[15] There were racial and gender disparities in time served as well. Women, whose hearings were conducted by the separate women's parole board, often served less time than men for similar crimes. Critics alleged, with some statistical support, that people of color, both men and women, fared worse before parole boards.[16] As originally conceived, the indeterminate

---

[14] "Transcript of the Hearing on the Indeterminate Sentencing Law by Senate Select Committee on Penal Institutions," December 5 and 6, 1974, Senate Select Committee on Penal Institute Working Papers: 1972–1976, LP161: 201, p. 37, CSA.

[15] Irwin, *Prisons in Turmoil*, 81.

[16] The effects of race are more difficult to isolate than those of gender. There was also variation in these patterns between different crime categories. For example, see Michael H. Tonry, *Sentencing Matters* (New York: Oxford University Press, 1996), 7 and Erik Olin Wright, *The Politics of Punishment: A Critical Analysis of Prisons in America* (New York: Harper and Row, 1973), 113–20.

218 • Chapter Five

sentence's ability to adjust to an individual's unique circumstances was its most innovative, promising feature. In practice, it produced what appeared to many prisoners as uneven and arbitrary administration and the antithesis of justice.

If the board was not inclined to divulge its logic, prisoners could never be sure of the actual grounds for their decisions. They articulated this frustration to sociologist Erik Olin Wright, who conducted a series of interviews about prisons for his 1973 book, *The Politics of Punishment*. One prisoner explained that "the people on the [Adult Authority] board are God and they know it. They have you in their hands. They control your salvation, your heaven and your hell. Once a year you stand before that God and they decide whether or not you stay in hell for another. And that God is unpredictable. . . . You never know what they want."[17] This led to an atmosphere of paranoia and tension within institutions, and prisoners would spend hours analyzing board members' questions and rulings, trying to find patterns in their decisions or clues to how the board would rule in their own cases. In some instances, examiners might suggest that an individual would be well served by further vocational education, addiction treatment, or religious instruction. However, since prisoners appeared before different examiners each year, there was no guarantee that the suggestions offered would further prospects for parole from the next year's panel.

Many attended therapy and programs to demonstrate their "positive adjustment" for the board. These dynamics helped undermine the therapy groups since prisoners were convinced counselors' assessments of their temperament and outlook were factors in parole decisions. While many prisoners endeavored to figure out what activities or behaviors would maximize their chance of being released, a clean record with participation in programming was no guarantee. For example, one African American prisoner with a perfect disciplinary and work record felt confident before his hearing that the parole board would give him a release date. He had attended Alcoholics Anonymous and group therapy, received his high school diploma, and begun taking college courses. Nonetheless, he explained, "the Adult Authority shot me down a year. They said they didn't feel I was sincere. They said I was just con-wise and was playing a game with them." Worried that prisoners were trying to manipulate the system, boards could interpret good records as evidence of a prisoner's duplicity. The man explained that the decision left him disoriented about how to conduct himself within the institution: "Now I don't know what to do. If I get any write-ups or stop going to therapy, they will take this as proving

[17] Quoted in Wright, *Politics of Punishment*, 127–28.

that I was faking it before. But if I don't do anything new, they will just say the same thing next year."[18]

One man, knowing that his conviction and previous record guaranteed at least five years behind bars, implemented a long-range plan designed to produce the appearance of a prison-induced transformation. He explained:

> [I] deliberately [got] a lot of write ups during my first two years. I probably spent half my time in the hole, always for petty things. I'd swipe extra food from the lunch line or report late for work. So I built up a terrible disciplinary record. Then in my third year here I got only a couple of beefs. And since then I have a clean record. I figure the Adult Authority will look at this and think that I am "improving," that I have learned my lesson.[19]

These dynamics left some prisoners with the impression that parole boards were less concerned with facilitating prisoners' economic or social inclusion than in producing docile political subjects. Another of Wright's interviewees explained that "the AA [Adult Authority] doesn't care how many positive things you have done in prison. They don't care if you graduate from high school or learn a trade. What they want is for you to feel guilty for your crime. They want prisoners who are conformists, whose spirits have been broken. What they can't take is a man with pride."[20]

Prisoners frequently complained about the power of "silent beefs," the negative reports in their files from unknown sources. Since there were no strict codes designating what evidence was admissible, prisoners claimed that parole boards used information against them that had never been proven in court. Take, for example, the story of an eighteen-year-old sentenced to five years to life for an armed robbery in which no one was injured. His file contained a letter from the district attorney accusing the young man of a vicious double homicide. Even though the district attorney was unable to prove the case after three jury trials, the prisoner believed the Adult Authority held the charges against him in parole hearings, causing them to keep him in prison for fifteen years—eight years longer than the average time served for first-degree murder and fourteen years longer than the average for a first-offense robbery.[21] Prisoners also claimed that they were penalized for conducting legally protected acts, especially pursuing legal appeals regarding their individual case or prison

---

[18] Ibid., 129–30.

[19] Ibid., 129.

[20] Ibid., 130.

[21] Jessica Mitford, *Kind and Usual Punishment: The Prison Business* (New York: Vintage, 1974), 101. Clearly told from the perspective of the prisoner, there is no way to corroborate Mitford's interpretation of the board's motivation.

conditions. While it was infrequently acknowledged officially, organizing and prisoner leadership was a formula for the denial of parole. As one prisoner explained, "If they know you are with the militants, they will just let you sit here."[22] Even associating with known "writ writers" could compromise one's chances of parole. The indeterminate sentence, therefore, was both a powerful tool for maintaining control and a source of unrest and frustration.

California's therapeutic commitment not only produced tension between prisoners and their keepers; it also contributed to divisions between guards and staff members working within treatment programs. Treatment staff and counselors often felt that guards and administrators did not take their roles seriously. "It is pure tokenism," one counselor explained. "They only have counselors in order to say publicly that they have 'rehabilitation.'"[23] On the other hand, guards resented the ascendance of the treatment professionals within institutions and were skeptical of the entire emphasis on corrections. These antagonisms intensified as treatment staff became less inclined to see the prisoners as sick or otherwise defective during the 1960s and guards suspected them of alliances or affinity with prisoners. Custodial staff often felt they shouldered the responsibility for maintaining physical order and safety and were unfairly blamed for any fallout from confrontations with prisoners.[24] Laced through these resentments was the assertion that rehabilitative programming did not simply fail but actually exacerbated the problems they aimed to ameliorate. The later drive to replace the indeterminate sentence grew out of these longstanding struggles over authority within prisons.

The rehabilitative emphasis coexisted uneasily with the penal system's habits of civic subordination. Perhaps most inconsistent with the rhetorical emphasis on reincorporating prisoners into society was the practice of considering people convicted of crimes in a legal status of "civil death." This extended beyond denial of civil rights during imprisonment to the critical period of parole supervision. The document issued to parolees explicitly announced their limited civil rights. "Your Civil Rights have been suspended by law," it explained. "You may not marry, engage in business, nor sign certain contracts unless your Parole Agent recommends, and the Adult Authority approves, restoring such Civil Rights to you."[25] Parolees had many employment rights restored and gained access to disability compensation, unemployment insurance,

[22] Quoted in Wright, *Politics of Punishment*, 39.

[23] Quoted in ibid., 80.

[24] Irwin, *Prisons in Turmoil*, 130–37.

[25] "Appendix II: Conditions of Parole," *Convict Report on the Major Grievances of the Prison Population, San Quentin*, February 26, 1969, Box 37, Folder 2, p. 46, Jessica

and Social Security upon leaving prison. Nonetheless, the requirement to disclose their criminal record to potential employers hindered their access to decent jobs. People released from prison claimed this barrier to licit work impeded their ability to attain economic independence—the hallmark of successful rehabilitative and civic standing. Until 1974, California law denied people who had served time in state prisons the ultimate symbol of civic belonging—the vote—for life, even after they had served their time and were removed from parole. After 1974, prisoners were still prohibited from voting while incarcerated and on parole.[26] Therefore, the emphasis on individual rehabilitation coexisted in practice with customs of civic degradation that delimited the social, political, and economic standing of people convicted of crimes. Interestingly, many of these civil disabilities attached to the status of convict, not prisoner. The prisoners' rights activism would help secure new protections for people while they were incarcerated, but the rights revolution did less to prevent the state from retracting rights and benefits on the basis of a criminal conviction.[27]

Rebellion against and within the Prison

In addition to being home to the most robust prison treatment programs in the nation, California was also the site of the most active prisoners' organizing during the 1960s and 1970s.[28] Prisoners never spoke with one voice and embraced a wide range of critiques and politics. Despite their differences, many shared a skepticism of the state's program of correction and its commitment to reintegrating those marked as convicts. Experiencing the indeterminate sentence and the institution of civic death as part of a single, oppressive system, prisoners attacked them both. In the process, they also challenged prisoners' symbolic role in society, the limitations on their rights, and social assumptions about the responsibility for crime and deviance. Others pointed to the conditions of U.S. prisons

---

Mitford Papers, Harry Ransom Humanities Research Center, University of Texas at Austin (hereafter HRC).

[26] Jeff Manza and Christopher Uggen, *Locked Out: Felon Disenfranchisement and American Democracy* (New York: Oxford University Press, 2008), 78.

[27] McLennan, "The Convict's Two Lives," 191–219. See also Mary Katzenstein, "Rights without Citizenship: Activist Politics and Prison Reform in the United States," in *Routing the Opposition: Social Movements, Public Policy and Democracy*, ed. Valerie Jenness, Helen Ingram, and David Meyer (Minneapolis: University of Minnesota Press, 2005), 236–58.

[28] For detailed histories of the movements in California, see Dan Berger, *Captive Nation: Black Prison Organizing in the Civil Rights Era* (Chapel Hill: University of North Carolina Press, 2014) and Cummins, *Rise and Fall of California's Radical Prison Movement*.

and fundamentally questioned the virtue of a society that would produce and tolerate such institutions.

Prisoner organizing and organizing around prison issues was intimately intertwined with social movements outside of the prison. It was enabled by the legal challenges from imprisoned World War II resisters and the Nation of Islam during the 1950s and early 1960s, whose efforts opened up prisons to increased public scrutiny and reformed penal operation, especially regarding racial segregation and religious observation.[29] Outside movements became more attentive to prison issues as arrests during protests and civil disobedience brought new groups into contact with the penal system and highlighted the role of the law in defending what many came to consider a brutal and unjust status quo. In the 1960s, prison crowding, political changes, and the growing percentage of black and Latino prisoners ushered in an era of increased revolt and instability within institutions. Large numbers of prisoners joined independent study groups, educating themselves about their ethnic and racial heritage and reading critical political writings. Tension mounted as African American prisoners, influenced by the Nation of Islam and the growing civil rights movement, resisted the racism in prison administration and among white prisoners. Many became more politicized and organized, and turned toward more radical critiques, particularly black nationalism and Marxism. Uprisings became more commonplace over the following decade, with at least five nationally in 1967, twenty-seven in 1970, thirty-seven in 1971, and forty-eight in 1972.[30] Some of these uprisings were more explicitly political and others were responses to tensions among prisoners and staff that were often exacerbated by prison conditions or officials' incitement of racial divisions within incarcerated populations.

Following a violent confrontation between ethnic and racial groups at San Quentin prison in 1967, organizers called for prisoners to deemphasize their divisions and identify as an oppressed collective that had a common enemy in the administration. The fact that treatment staff—such as librarians, counselors, and teachers—took up weapons to help guards regain control of the prison further strained prisoners' faith in rehabilitative programs.[31] In late 1967, a San Quentin underground newspaper, *The Outlaw*, publicized a list of grievances, paramount among them the Adult Authority. It called for prisoners to put aside racial divisions and participate in a general strike beginning on February 15, 1968. The nonviolent "Convict Unity Holiday" lasted a week and, at times, shut down

[29]Toussaint Losier, "'. . . For Strictly Religious Reason[s],'" *Souls* 15, no. 1–2 (January 2013): 19–38; Gottschalk, *The Prison and the Gallows*, 171–75.

[30]Gottschalk, *The Prison and the Gallows*, 178–79.

[31]Cummins, *Rise and Fall of California's Radical Prison Movement*, 90–91.

75 percent of the prison. Outside of San Quentin's gates, between 400 and 500 people rallied in support of the striking prisoners, entertained by bands such as the Grateful Dead.[32]

During the strike, a group secured permission from the warden to collect grievances about the institution.[33] The activists gathered 4,500 comments from the four major cell blocks and compiled the complaints into a report to the state legislature.[34] However, the San Quentin warden refused to release the more than seventy-page "Convict Report on the Major Grievances of the Prison Population" to the legislature when the authors submitted it for duplication and approval. Not deterred, the activists made copies clandestinely and delivered the contraband document to legislators in front of three reporters and a surprised warden.[35] The first sentences of their report read:

> Prison "time" does not rehabilitate. On the contrary, it corrodes whatever creative individuality a person possesses, and operates against realistic readjustment on release. . . . The California Adult Authority and the Department of Corrections, while mouthing policies of "rehabilitation" to sell their staggering budget to the Legislature, in reality follow the philosophy of "punishment," and terms are fixed and release dates are determined accordingly.[36]

According to the report, punishment and control were the true objectives of the penal system and rehabilitation merely hypocritical legitimization. In fact, the authors insisted that prisons accomplished the opposite of their purported goals, as prisoners became less prepared for life outside the longer they were imprisoned:

> The California penal system has little or no corrective or rehabilitative value. We feel to the contrary, that it is more likely to be destructive to the individual character, and that, overall, the prison environment as presently constituted has a design such that it serves as the primary obstacle to the necessary and desired reformation of character of those so imprisoned.[37]

The authors saw "civil death" as an absurd and backward way of preparing people for full citizenship, writing that "the theory that an offender

---

[32] Irwin, *Prisons in Turmoil*, 84–89; Cummins, *Rise and Fall of California's Radical Prison Movement*, 116–18.

[33] Buck Walker, "History of a Convict Report on My Anniversary," *Convict Report on the Major Grievances of the Prison Population*, San Quentin, February 26, 1969, Box 37, Folder 2, p. 79, Jessica Mitford Papers, HRC.

[34] Cummins, *Rise and Fall of California's Radical Prison Movement*, 129.

[35] Walker, "History of a Convict Report on My Anniversary," 79.

[36] Ibid., 4.

[37] Ibid., 12.

may come to appreciate more highly the values of citizenship by having that citizenship, and its inherent values, taken from him is an obvious exercise in illogic."[38] They continued, "While fairness and equity and the rights of man are being preached at him, the prisoner finds that he cannot find fairness in his treatment, nor equity in his term of imprisonment, and his rights are non-existent. He is treated like an animal, and told to act like a man."[39] Through the report, the authors positioned themselves as a legitimate authority on managing criminality and the conditions of their captivity. Prisoners, frustrated by prison officials' response to their agitation, staged a second convict strike at San Quentin in August 1968, demanding fair wages and an end to the indeterminate sentence.[40]

While many radical prison activists called for open insurrection against the state, more moderate elements pushed for limited legal reforms through courts and the legislature. Together, this agitation helped inspire renewed attention in the capital to prisoner rights issues. Among the most critical changes was the California legislature's 1968 revision of Section 2600 of the penal code that retreated from considering prisoners "civilly dead." The bill, which became known as the Prisoners Bill of Rights, guaranteed inmates' access to most printed materials and the right to correspond privately with legislators and legal counsel (although letters could still be monitored for contraband). Prisoners also secured the right to inherit personal property and own their written material. These changes unleashed a flood of confidential correspondence to lawmakers and provided a new window into the vast range of prisoner grievances. Prisoners' letters also helped spark a series of lawsuits throughout the early 1970s in which the courts steadily expanded prisoners' rights.[41]

The developing affinity between prisoners, Black Power groups, and New Left activists in the Los Angeles and San Francisco Bay areas brought unprecedented attention to the conditions and social significance of incarceration. Activists both in and outside the prison called into question the fundamental legitimacy of the prison, positioning prisoners not as individual deviants but as members of an oppressed class—often considered political prisoners—whom the state targeted because they resisted subjugation. Activists challenged dominant notions of criminality, arguing that survival within a racist, capitalist system forced many to commit acts defined as crime. In his influential 1968 book, *Soul on Ice*, Eldridge Cleaver rejected the notion that crimes were caused by a person's individual pathology that demanded therapeutic treatment. Cleaver, a former

[38] Ibid., 9.
[39] Ibid., 11.
[40] Irwin, *Prisons in Turmoil*, 87.
[41] Cummins, *Rise and Fall of California's Radical Prison Movement*, 130–33.

San Quentin prisoner and Nation of Islam minister who eventually became a charismatic leader of the Black Panther Party, argued that crimes could be considered insurrectionary acts, or at least desperate attempts by subjugated people to lash out at their oppressors.[42] Many in California's New Left looked to Cleaver and other radical prisoners as potential movement leaders and prisons as a central battleground in their struggle against the American state.[43]

The most famous person who served an indeterminate sentence in California was George Jackson. Convicted for the armed robbery of a gas station at eighteen years old, Jackson received a sentence of one year to life in prison. At the time of his death in 1971, Jackson had served eleven years. It was his behavior within prison, not his crime, that stretched out his sentence indefinitely. While incarcerated, he became an outspoken and high-profile revolutionary writer and a flashpoint for both the Left and Right in debates surrounding prisons. While incarcerated, Jackson read and studied voraciously. Like Malcolm X, Jackson credited his politicization to the education he gave himself while in prison. "I met Marx, Lenin, Trotsky, Engels, and Mao when I entered prison and they redeemed me," he wrote. "For the first four years I studied nothing but economics and military ideas."[44] He became an active Marxist organizer and educator and eventually joined the Black Panther Party.

In January 1970, prison officials at Soledad prison charged Jackson and two other prisoners with murdering a white guard (supposedly in retaliation for a guard's shooting of three black prisoners days before). The case became an international cause célèbre for many who believed the three men, widely known as the "Soledad Brothers," were innocent and targeted for their political work. Jackson became even more notorious when, in August 1970, his brother, Jonathan Jackson, stormed a Marin County courtroom. He freed and distributed weapons to several San Quentin prisoners present in the court, and together they took five hostages (including the judge) and demanded the immediate release of the Soledad Brothers. The judge and all the abductors, save one, were killed in the shootout with police as Jackson tried to make an escape.

A collection of George Jackson's letters titled *Soledad Brother* was released in the fall of 1970, bringing him more supporters among the New

---

[42]Eldridge Cleaver, *Soul on Ice* (New York: McGraw-Hill, 1968). On the origins and history of the Black Panther Party, see Donna Murch, *Living for the City: Migration, Education, and the Rise of the Black Panther Party in Oakland, California* (Chapel Hill: University of North Carolina Press, 2010).

[43]See Cummins, *Rise and Fall of California's Radical Prison Movement* and Berger, *Captive Nation*.

[44]George Jackson, Jean Genet, and Jonathan Jackson Jr., *Soledad Brother: The Prison Letters of George Jackson* (Chicago: Chicago Review Press, 1994), 16.

Left and antagonism from the Department of Corrections. In it, Jackson rejected the notion that criminals were socially maladjusted or ill, and instead saw crime as a function of racially concentrated class oppression and imprisonment as a transmutation of racial slavery.[45] He challenged the notion that prisons cured criminals:

> The textbooks on criminology like to advance the idea that prisoners are mentally defective. There is only the merest suggestion that the system itself is at fault. Penologists regard prisons as asylums. Most policy is formulated in a bureau that operates under the heading Department of Corrections. But what can we say about these asylums since *none* of the inmates are ever cured. Since in every instance they are sent out of the prison more damaged physically and mentally than when they entered.[46]

To understand crime and punishment, Jackson explained, the gaze must shift from the prisoner to the keeper:

> For a real understanding of the failure of prison policies, it is senseless to continue to study the criminal. All of those who can afford to be honest know that the real victim, that poor, uneducated, disorganized man who finds himself a convicted criminal, is simply the end result of a long chain of corruption and mismanagement that starts with people like Reagan and his political appointees in Sacramento. . . . To determine how men will behave once they enter the prison it is of first importance to know that prison. Men are brutalized by their environment—not the reverse.[47]

He argued that prisoners were increasingly seeing themselves not as defective individuals but as essentially enslaved by the state. And just as slavery could not be reformed and only abolished, Jackson rejected the possibility of reforming the prison system and called for revolution.[48] "Most of today's black convicts have come to understand that they are the most abused victims of an unrighteous order."[49]

Jackson claimed that the indeterminate sentence had previously forestalled political resistance, but its efficacy was crumbling: "Up until now, the prospect of parole has kept us from confronting our captors with any real determination. But now with the living conditions of these places deteriorating, and with the sure knowledge

[45] For a more detailed discussion of Jackson and other radical imprisoned intellectuals, see Berger, *Captive Nation* and Dylan Rodriguez, *Forced Passages: Imprisoned Radical Intellectuals and the U.S. Prison Regime* (Minneapolis: University of Minnesota Press, 2006).

[46] Jackson, Genet, and Jackson, *Soledad Brother*, 25.

[47] Ibid., 18.

[48] For a thorough discussion of the particular importance of the metaphor of slavery, see Berger, *Captive Nation*.

[49] Jackson, Genet, and Jackson, *Soledad Brother*, 26.

that we are slated for destruction, we have been transformed into an implacable army of liberation."[50] Jackson explained that the system was intent on crushing the insurrectionary movement and the parole boards demanded total surrender in exchange for freedom: "No black will leave this place if he has any violence in his past, until they see that thing in his eyes. And you can't fake it—resignation, defeat—it must be stamped clearly across the face."[51] Jackson was determined that "they'll never count me among the broken men," but he believed that prison officials would "not be satisfied until they've pushed me out of this existence altogether."[52]

Despite tensions between the radical and more moderate prisoners, they came together to organize a strike at Folsom Prison in November 1970. Prisoners refused to work or participate in programming for nineteen days. Among the list of demands, prisoners included the right to unionize, an end to the indeterminate sentence and the Adult Authority, and prison compliance with state minimum-wage and working conditions regulations.[53] Officials broke the strike, but afterward prisoners, ex-prisoners, and outside allies banded together to form the United Prisoners Union, an organization dedicated to building a rank-and-file collective to influence penal policy and practice.[54]

In California, the Prisoners Union was generally more white and moderate than the radical prison groups connected to George Jackson. They repudiated violent resistance and eschewed Marxist revolutionary rhetoric and were more directly engaged in policy discussions. In their publications, they also distanced themselves from reformers, particularly those who had helped build the contemporary institution. Willie Holder, one of the group's leaders, explained the union's mission in this way:

> The Prisoners Union is an organization of convicts, ex-convicts and interested citizens dedicated to bringing about change in a decadent, barbaric prison system, a system designed to de-humanize men and women in the most agonizing ways that only men can devise, one that has over the years of penology become ultrasophisticated; a sophistication that would shame a sophist but only elicits the word REFORM from the penologists. . . . We

[50] Ibid.
[51] Ibid., 218.
[52] Ibid., 27–28.
[53] Cummins, *Rise and Fall of California's Radical Prison Movement*, 202.
[54] Oral history interview of Jan Marinissen, "'To Let the Legislature Know': Prison Advocacy and the American Friends Service Committee in California, 1960–1983" (1983), conducted 1981 and 1983 by Gabrielle Morris and Sarah Sharp, OH R-23, p. 11, Ronald Reagan Gubernatorial Era Project, Regional Oral History Office, Bancroft Library, University of California–Berkeley, CSA.

in the Prisoners Union do not want reform, we want a permanent change. This means a good hard look at structure.[55]

However, unlike the more revolutionary prisoners, the Prisoners Union accepted prisons as a legitimate state entity and endeavored to influence the terms and condition of confinement.[56] Like Jackson, they advocated for convict unity. Unlike him, they warned against riots, which they felt played into prison officials' hands.[57]

The Prisoners Union built membership within the prisons and with support outside. The group disseminated its views through its newspaper, *The Outlaw*. The Prisoners Union began using the name after authorities suppressed the original underground publication in late 1968.[58] Inside organizers, most notably the Nation of Islam member Harlan Washington, united previously warring factions within San Quentin prison. The union organized mass interracial meetings until the warden realized what was happening and transferred leaders to other institutions. By 1973, more than 3,000 prisoners belonged to the Prisoners Union, and *The Outlaw* boasted a circulation of 5,000 within the prisons, with 25,000 total subscribers by mid-decade.[59]

Through the work of its outside activists, which included a number of formerly incarcerated men, the organization often represented prisoners in debates in the legislature and the media. Because of its engagement with public policy, the group figures more prominently in the history of California's determinate sentencing law. However, the black nationalist and more explicitly revolutionary prisoners, while less directly engaged with policy discussions, still loomed large in the broader political context. The California Department of Corrections and other political elites were pressed to address prison conditions in part because of controversies arising from interactions with the revolutionary prisoners. State authorities probably engaged with the Prisoners Union because they were relatively more politically palatable than the revolutionary prisoners.

George Jackson's prediction of his own demise became to pass in August 1971 when prison guards shot and killed him during what authori-

[55] Untitled article, *Outlaw* 1, no. 2 (December 1971), Reel 274, p. 1, Underground Press Collection.

[56] On the political and racial divisions between the Prisoners Union and the more revolutionary black nationalists, see Berger, *Captive Nation*, 185–92.

[57] Untitled article, *Outlaw* 1, no. 1 (November 1971), Reel 274, p. 1, Underground Press Collection.

[58] Untitled article, *Outlaw* 1, no. 3 (January–February 1972), Reel 274, p. 11, Underground Press Collection.

[59] Mitford, *Kind and Usual Punishment*, 324; Cummins, *Rise and Fall of California's Radical Prison Movement*, 218–19.

ties claimed was an escape attempt. Three guards and two prisoners were also killed during the confrontation, their throats slit before authorities retook the area. The details of the confrontation remain sharply contested to this day, and inconsistencies within the shifting official narrative made movement participants immediately suspicious that Jackson had been the victim of a targeted political assassination by the state. For many on the Left, he became a martyr and his death further evidence of the true brute nature of the American system when faced with radical challenge. For the Right, George Jackson epitomized many of the perils threatening the nation: the danger of organized, militant people of color, the failure of the liberal state to maintain order, and the lack of respect for traditional authority, especially law enforcement. For many "law-and-order" constituents, the fact that leftist activists lionized Jackson, an imprisoned revolutionary Marxist, proved how far things had deteriorated and how desperate was the need to reestablish order and sanity.[60]

These sentiments only intensified in early September when the prisoners of New York State's Attica Correctional Facility, catalyzed by the news of George Jackson's death and mounting frustration at official intransigence at their pleas for change, seized control of a block of the prison after a spontaneous melee. They held forty-two guards hostage and demanded improvements in prison conditions and treatment. After days of negotiations and accompanying national media frenzy, Governor Rockefeller ordered state police to attack the prison. In their brutal retaking, state agents killed ten hostages and twenty-nine prisoners. The siege underscored the ongoing polarization in the public, which was divided between horror at the state's action, which many considered a brutal massacre, and disgust that social order had deteriorated to the point where mutinous prisoners were voicing demands through mediators of their choosing.[61]

Throughout this period, there was a fascination with prisoners that permeated popular culture. The rebel protagonist of the popular 1967 film *Cool Hand Luke* was a convict. Paul Newman played the prideful prisoner the state was intent on breaking. The film highlighted Luke's virtue by juxtaposing an oppressive, venal penal system to his perseverance, loyalty, anti-authoritarianism, and independence. The next year, Johnny Cash recorded a concert before the incarcerated men at Folsom Prison. Singing most of the songs from the perspective of criminals and prisoners, Cash bluntly described crimes, voiced antipathy toward prison administration, and expressed a longing for repentance and social connection unmediated

[60]See Cummins, *Rise and Fall of California's Radical Prison Movement*, 151–87.
[61]Wicker, *A Time to Die*; Persico, *The Imperial Rockefeller*, 140; Thompson, *Blood in the Water*.

by the state. He even debuted a song, "Grey Stone Chapel," which was written by a prisoner in the audience—directly giving voice to the supposedly civilly dead. Initially skeptical of such a risky project, Columbia Records released *Johnny Cash at Folsom Prison* with little fanfare and promotion. Nevertheless, the album slowly gained popularity among underground deejays and eventually climbed up the pop and country charts.[62]

In 1969 Cash recorded another concert, this time at California's San Quentin State Prison. It was also released as an album and had more commercial successful than *Folsom Prison*. Throughout the album, Cash again explicitly allied himself with the prisoners and often in stark opposition to the state, mainstream society, and prison administrators. When introducing his brand-new song "San Quentin," Cash explained that "I try to put myself in your place, / And I believe this is the way that I would feel about San Quentin." Cash's song focused on San Quentin's effect on prisoners, not society or crime rates. Narrated from the perspective of a prisoner, Cash's song denied that San Quentin served any positive social purpose for those kept there. Instead of rehabilitating, Cash claimed the prison warped and scarred. The song expressed a deep bitterness toward the institution and a dream of a time when the physical structure would crumble and die. His audience evidently appreciated the sentiments and demanded Cash sing it a second time.[63]

With prisoners and outlaws remaining powerful symbols in a society deeply divided over the legitimacy of traditional authority structures, the people confined in them continued to challenge administrators and agitate to improve their conditions. Between revolutionary prisoners, riots, and union organizing, California's prisons seemed to authorities to be increasingly unmanageable. The entire system seemed unstable and poised for profound change by the early 1970s. Prisoners, more impatient and politicized than at any time in recent history, faced brutal repression but also unprecedented opportunities for alliances with sympathetic groups and movements on the outside. And most prison activists shared prisoners' withering opposition to the Adult Authority and indeterminate sentencing. In efforts to establish control over the institutions, California officials cracked down on activism and engaged in counterinsurgency operations within the prisons. Officials banned groups connected to political organizing, especially targeting those dedicated to revolutionary education. They began to more aggressively ask about political sympathies and affiliations at parole board hearings.

[62]Michael Streissguth, *Johnny Cash at Folsom Prison: The Making of a Masterpiece* (Cambridge, Mass.: Da Capo Press, 2004), 157.

[63]For lyrics, see Johnny Cash, "San Quentin," *SongMeanings.com*, http://songmeanings.com/songs/view/3530822107858574054/.

However, the wave of strikes and uprisings revealed limits to these strategies of control. One prisoner explained how he reached the decision to join prisoners striking at Susanville in these terms: "I've always been poor. That is all there is in prison—poor people. I am beginning to realize that there isn't a war on poverty in this country; there is a war on poor people. . . . Poor people have to start fighting back." After the strike, he lost his parole date and was transferred to San Quentin. "After the strike I was asked why I got involved, since I had a parole date already set. I told them I got involved because it was necessary. I wasn't threatened or anything. I chose to get involved. It was absolutely necessary. I doubt if it will change anything up there, but I still had to be part of the strike."[64] The Adult Authority, which had been an integral tool for maintaining order and control in California's prisons, seemed now to be a source of disorder. It certainly had shown itself incapable of containing the upheaval and insurrection. With this backdrop of solidarity, militancy, and chaos in California's carceral institutions, various groups, motivated by divergent interests, turned their attention to the policy that seemed to symbolize all that was wrong with the system: the indeterminate sentence.

Discrediting Indeterminate Sentencing in California

The indeterminate sentence had few fervent supporters by the mid-1970s. Opponents condemned parole boards for being overly lenient, excessively punitive, or wholly arbitrary. Despite rhetoric that positioned prisoners as civilly dead and nonviable actors in the public sphere, prisoners sculpted the shape and texture of the criticism of indeterminate sentencing. They produced the disorder within the prison that made existing management strategies untenable, and the content of their criticism influenced the critiques of the indeterminate sentence, particularly the reports and books written on the Left. The writings of radical prisoners heavily influenced attitudes about incarceration in the movements of the New Left. An active cohort of radical criminologists, many of whom were concentrated in the School of Criminology at the University of California, Berkeley (until state officials disbanded it in 1976), connected with movements and prisoners and articulated sharp critiques of the rehabilitative project.[65] Prolific correspondence by less prominent prisoners informed legislators and social critics, such as Jessica Mitford, about the realities of penal practice.

---

[64] Quoted in Wright, *Politics of Punishment*, 137.
[65] Johann Koehler, "Development and Fracture of a Discipline: Legacies of the School of Criminology at Berkeley," *Criminology* 53, no. 4 (November 2015): 513–44.

One of the first and most prominent critical reports about the indeterminate sentence was *Struggle for Justice*, published in 1971 by the Quaker-led American Friends Service Committee (AFSC). The organizing within prisons and among formerly incarcerated people directly informed *Struggle for Justice*. For example, John Irwin participated in the committee that crafted the AFSC report. Irwin served five years in California prisons for armed robbery and went on to become an influential sociologist and leader in the Prisoners Union. Published around the same time as the revolt in Attica, *Struggle for Justice* received considerable attention from the press and served as a mobilizing tool for activist organizations. The AFSC organized community meetings and public discussions about the penal system around the release of the report. Where previous reports attributed the failures of correctional programs to insufficient funding or flawed implementation, *Struggle for Justice* questioned the legitimacy of the entire rehabilitative project. Challenging the fundamental tenets of the therapeutic model, the AFSC argued that indeterminate sentencing put a benevolent disguise on punitive practice and was deeply implicated in the oppression of the poor, minorities, and other marginalized groups. Seeing crime as an outgrowth of systemic inequality, the authors ultimately saw the best hope for remedies in government policy that reallocated power and resources within the nation. They proposed that incarceration be used minimally and sentences become standard and proportionate, dictated by the crime committed and not the quirks of the individual criminal.[66]

A few years later, the journalist Jessica Mitford published *Kind and Usual Punishment*, an influential and scathing attack on the legitimacy of the entire penal system. A work of muckraking based largely on evidence from California, Mitford's book aimed at a wide, popular audience.[67] Mitford's meetings and correspondence with prisoners directly informed her presentation of penal practice. She identified hypocrisy, paternalism, and brutality in the system and called for systematic restructuring of penal practice. She saw hope in the nascent prison union movement, which she believed fundamentally challenged the legal and discursive separation of the prisoner from society:

> The union movement is no modest reform proposal, no effort to gild the cage. By striving to establish the rights of the prisoner as citizen and worker, it seeks to diminish the distinction between him and those on the other side of the walls. In a profound sense the ultimate logic of such a movement

[66]American Friends Service Committee, *Struggle for Justice: A Report on Crime and Punishment in America* (New York: Hill and Wang, 1971). See the discussion of the literature critical of rehabilitation in Garland, *Culture of Control*, 53–73.

[67]Mitford, *Kind and Usual Punishment*.

is abolition, for to the degree that those distinctions are obliterated, to the same degree the prison is stripped of its vital functions.[68]

These critics often presented the commitment to therapeutic custody as a thin veneer painted over a brutal, violent, repressive system. They charged that cloaking these oppressive functions with benevolent, therapeutic rationales shielded their true operation but also legitimized them. The belief that these policies crushed individual authenticity and produced conformity led some critics to actually favor explicitly retributive and punishing rationales. In their estimation, abandoning the normalizing, reformative aspirations of prisons and embracing a punitive rationale was a more honest reflection of the prison's social function.

Michel Foucault's now canonical analysis of the prison was itself informed by writings by prisoners and black radicals in the United States. The philosopher was active in prison organizing in France and read the writings of imprisoned intellectuals such as George Jackson.[69] *Discipline and Punish* portrayed efforts to reform a prisoner's behavior or "soul"—as opposed to inflicting pain on the body—as a permanent feature of modern Western society and critical to larger projects of discipline and normalization. Foucault saw the power the state exerted through rehabilitation programs as a more refined, but not significantly less coercive, method of maintaining power relations in society.[70] During a 1972 interview conducted after a visit to Attica, Foucault argued that the prison's therapeutic mission and programming obscured the ways that crime was symptomatic of political struggle over social inequality. He asked: "Doesn't everything that concerns reintegration, everything that is a psychological or individual solution for the problem, mask the profoundly political character both of society's elimination of these people and those people's attack on society?"[71] Foucault's critique of the coercion implicit in therapeutically orientated incarceration not only would have resonated with many prisoners but likely drew on their activism and writings.

These high-profile critics on the Left were joined by more mainstream and conservative commentators. Conservative critics such as Ernest van den Haag and James Q. Wilson argued that retribution and fixed

---

[68]Ibid., 324.

[69]See Eugene Wolters, "Michel Foucault, Prisons and the Future of Abolition: An Interview," *Critical-Theory*, June 25, 2016, http://www.critical-theory.com/michel-foucault-prisons-and-the-future-of-abolition-an-interview/; Brady Thomas Heiner, "Foucault and the Black Panthers," *City* 11, no. 3 (2007): 313–56; and Berger, *Captive Nation*, 153–55.

[70]Foucault, *Discipline and Punish*.

[71]Interview of Foucault conducted in 1972 after a visit to Attica prison, originally published in *Telos* in 1974. Reprinted as John Simon, "Michel Foucault on Attica: An Interview," *Social Justice* 18, no. 3 (Fall 1991): 26–34, quote on page 34.

sentencing had a legitimate role in penal practice.[72] Legal professionals also took aim at the indeterminate sentence. In a widely debated work, Federal District Court judge Marvin Frankel called for the state to link the degree of punishment directly to the crime committed and not the individual offender. He advocated for sentencing commissions—removed from political pressure but subject to judicial and legislative approval—to set guidelines for the fixed sentences associated with each crime.[73] In 1974, the criminologist Robert Martinson synthesized decades of empirical studies on therapeutic programs into an oft-quoted and highly influential article titled "What Works?—Questions and Answers about Prison Reform." The article was often cited to evidence the increasingly resonant mantra (but not necessarily accurate representation of the research) within criminology that "nothing works": that rehabilitative efforts were fundamentally ineffective and did not significantly reduce recidivism.[74] This emphasis on the state's impotence in the face of rising criminality helped undermine what remained of the Progressive Era faith in government's ability to regulate marginality and conquer deviance.

Declining support for the rehabilitative mission coincided with the attacks from intellectuals and professionals on the Left and the Right. While these writings alone did not drive the rapid disavowal of the indeterminate sentence, such critiques certainly facilitated the process.[75] In the case of California, legislators turned their attention to prisons and sentencing policy because the prisoners themselves made it difficult to do otherwise. Contemporary observers identified the catalyzing role played by those inside the prisons. In John Irwin's 1980 book *Prisons in Turmoil*, which chronicled transformations in the state's prisons during the 1960s and 1970s, he explained that "the developments inside the prison, among prisoners who initially were helped and influenced only slightly by outsiders, set off processes that then dominated prison events for several years."[76] One journalist explained that "out of the violence and turmoil inside American prisons that boiled over in the late '60s and early '70s, a

[72] Ernest van den Haag, *Punishing Criminals* (New York: Basic Books, 1975); James Q. Wilson, *Thinking about Crime* (New York: Bantam Books, 1975).

[73] Marvin Frankel, *Criminal Sentences: Law without Order* (New York: Hill and Wang, 1973). Other key monographs were David Fogel, *We Are the Living Proof: The Justice Model for Corrections* (Cincinnati: W. H. Anderson, 1975); Norval Morris, *The Future of Imprisonment* (Chicago: University of Chicago Press, 1973); and Andrew Von Hirsch, *Doing Justice: The Choice of Punishments: Report of the Committee for the Study of Incarceration* (New York: Hill and Wang, 1976).

[74] Robert Martinson, "What Works?—Questions and Answers about Prison Reform," *The Public Interest* (Spring 1974): 22–54.

[75] For a challenge to the notion that these works alone could have dislodged the rehabilitative ideal, see Garland, *Culture of Control*.

[76] Irwin, *Prisons in Turmoil*, 88.

new consensus is emerging. Mainly, that the basic assumptions on which prisons have been operating for the last 50 years have been disastrously wrong."[77] And in prisoners' efforts to explain the escalating revolts and desperation within the institutions, they again and again blamed sentencing practices. The McCay Commission, appointed to investigate the uprising at Attica, found that the indeterminate sentence and parole release "were by far the greatest cause of prisoner anxiety and frustration."[78]

Prisoner hostility toward sentencing practice in California must have been exacerbated by Ronald Reagan's direction of the Adult Authority in the late 1960s. As governor, Reagan faced prison crowding and fiscal constraints, but he rejected calls to build new prisons. He instead used the indeterminate sentence as a mechanism to manage corrections budgets by calling on the Adult Authority to reduce prison populations.[79] In practice, this meant granting parole to larger percentages of the prisoners at their annual hearings, thus relieving population pressure by releasing more prisoners. This policy decreased California's prisoner population from 29,000 to 19,000 by the end of 1971.[80] Even though this policy shift did not statistically increase crime rates, prison unrest and newspaper reports of crimes committed by parolees—especially the high-profile murder of an Orange County schoolteacher—pushed parole board decisions into the public spotlight.[81] Probably because of these pressures, Reagan reversed course in January 1972 and had aides meet with Adult Authority members to request that they "get tough" in their parole reviews. As one newspaper article explained, the fallout from this "secret meeting" was "that sentences of virtually all male felons in California prisoners were arbitrarily stretched out." It continued, "This decision came at a time when the Adult Authority had been progressing toward more early releases and the recidivism rate was near the lowest point in California's history."[82] The results of Reagan's order were dramatic: between 1971 and 1973, the percentage of prisoners actually paroled fell from 44.7 percent to 29.5 percent.[83] And parole revocations increased, climbing

[77] "New Penology Concepts Emerge, Display Prison 'Wrongs,'" August 22, 1975, Modesta California Bee, Corrections Administration News Digests: 1975, F3717:377, CSA.

[78] Griset, Determinate Sentencing, 36.

[79] Charles Maher, "Building of Prisons to Be Debate Issue," Los Angeles Times, June 18, 1979, B3.

[80] Oral history of Jan Marinissen, "'To Let the Legislature Know,'" 13.

[81] Oral history of Howard Way, "Issues in Corrections," 45; Ronald Dewolk, "How Wide Did Procunier Open the State's Prison Gates?" California Journal, January 1976, Corrections Administration News Digests: 1976, F3717:1638, CSA; Robert Fairbanks, "More Parolees Being Sent Back to Prisons," Los Angeles Times, July 4, 1976, C1.

[82] George Williams, "Reagan Order Jams Up Prisons," Sacramento Bee, January 28, 1975.

[83] Ibid.

from 1,654 in 1971 to 2,255 in 1973.[84] In 1971, more than 70 percent of prisoners who came before the parole board received release dates. After the order, that number plummeted, and by 1975 less than 20 percent of prisoners were given the certainty of fixed release dates at their hearings.[85] This could only have intensified prisoners' belief that sentencing in California was arbitrary, political, and unfair.

An article published in *The Outlaw* captured the hostility many of them felt toward the indeterminate sentence:

> The Indeterminate Sentence and Adult Authority or parole boards are perpetrators of a terminal disease; a cancer devised by man to dehumanize men, women and children. They are the most sophisticated, nonjudicial, arbitrary, paternalistic, arrogant, abusive, inhumane, insensitive, manipulative, bureaucratic, redtape, double-talking, bullying administrative body that sits in judgment over other human beings.[86]

In fact, it is virtually impossible to overstate prisoners' hatred of the indeterminate sentence. Jessica Mitford reported that it was prisoners' number-one complaint:

> At a meeting of ex-convicts, I asked what they conceived of as the major grievance of the California prison population. There was near unanimity: surprisingly, the wretched physical conditions of prison life are by no means the major concern. The food, they say, is generally lousy. Medical treatment amounts to criminal neglect in many instances. The highly touted vocational training is a fraud. . . . But these features of prison existence, disheartening, degrading, and dangerous though they are, pale in importance, say the convicts, beside the total arbitrariness of the bureaucracy that rules every aspect of their existence. One former inmate summed it up: "Don't give us steak and eggs; get rid of the Adult Authority! Don't put in a shiny modern hospital; free us from the tyranny of the indeterminate sentence."[87]

An *Outlaw* article echoed this appraisal, bluntly asserting that the Adult Authority was the primary political issue for California's incarcerated population: "The abrogation of the indeterminate sentence is the first and foremost proposal that must be submitted to the legislature. This is more paramount than any facet of reform in relation to the penal system in California."[88]

[84]"Terminal Cancer: Part 2," *Outlaw* 3, no. 3 (May 1974), Reel 274, p. 2, Underground Press Collection.

[85]Williams, "Reagan Order Jams Up Prisons."

[86]"Terminal Cancer," *Outlaw* 3, no. 2 (March 1974), Reel 274, p. 2, Underground Press Collection.

[87]Mitford, *Kind and Usual Punishment*, 95.

[88]Larry West and Kenneth Divans, "Prisons or Slavery," *Outlaw* 1, no. 2 (November 1972), Reel 274, pp. 6, 9, Underground Press Collection.

Most disdained the Adult Authority's arbitrary power over their lives and the uncertainty and tension produced by living year to year without a certain release date. Ideologically, prisoners varied in their assessment of indeterminate sentencing; some faulted the entire premise, while others condemned the administration of principles they generally accepted. Fewer opposed the availability of services, education, or therapy within prisons; instead, they opposed the way they were coerced into programs in order to gain their freedom. Many critiqued the hypocrisy of a system that claimed to cure but actually punished. They experienced this allegedly benevolent institution as torturous—made all the worse by its professed claims to rehabilitate. One prisoner wrote to Jessica Mitford, "That the indeterminate sentence is predicated on one's supposed adjustment in the institution and chance of making it on the outside is just so much rubbish. Punishment is the hallmark of this penal system, just as it is in most of the others."[89] Advocates echoed prisoners' claims that punishment was already the reality of the system: "Although punishment is no longer a fashionable rationale for criminal justice, the punitive spirit has survived unscathed behind the mask of treatment."[90]

The cynicism about the operation of penal institutions does not mean that all prisoners and their allies thought it impossible for the state to facilitate rehabilitation. In their writing, organizing, and study groups, they forwarded their own visions of redemption and reintegration. Many people argued that the key to true rehabilitation lay in removing the legal and symbolic barriers to full citizenship. Two authors writing for *The Outlaw* linked calls for conjugal visits and jobs to a need to preserve their manhood:

> This [minimum-wage jobs in prison] would enable prisoners to make allotments to their families, thus maintaining their status as the bread winner. . . . Prisoners should be allowed to maintain their responsibilities as providers and continue their sex life. These are the two components essential for his manhood. Should a prisoner be denied his manhood because he is a prisoner?[91]

Among male prisoners, visions of rehabilitation were often connected to wider concerns about restoring or securing masculinity, which many felt was deliberately undermined by prison administration.

Some prisoners expressed frustration with bureaucratic administration and social science expertise. One man wrote to Jessica Mitford

[89] Frank Hatfield to Mitford, November 12, 1972, Box 59, Folder 3, Jessica Mitford Papers, HRC.

[90] American Friends Service Committee, *Struggle for Justice*, 26.

[91] West and Divans, "Prisons or Slavery."

that he preferred dealing with brute punishment than "compassionate professionals":

> God help us from the "gung ho" professionals who want to help us. Too of-
> ten they're just as dangerous as the retired, military orientated, correctional
> officer, who sees every "number" as a threat, psychopath, and lunatic, who
> should be treated as such. At least he'd find his satisfaction in harassing
> you, or clubbing you to death. While the compassionate professionals will
> keep you incarcerated, for however long, in the interests of helping you.[92]

The same author explained that true reform entailed allowing prisoners a degree of self-determination and listening to what they needed: "Perhaps if they began putting rehabilitation into the hands of the experts (US). Rather than the 'professionals,' there could be such a thing as rehabilitation. But of course even this poses problems in itself. FACT: the professionals have failed."[93] Such sentiments were undoubtedly bolstered by the cynicism throughout U.S. society for bureaucratic expertise and, more specifically, by the mounting attacks within the criminal justice field on the effectiveness of rehabilitative programs.

The stigma people experienced after leaving prison only intensified their scorn for authorities' claims of reintegration and rehabilitation. The prejudice and hardship people faced upon release belied officials' declared intention of reintegrating people into society as full citizens. The families of prisoners also felt that, in practice, prison administration served to segregate and subordinate former prisoners within the polity. A flyer produced by a San Francisco organization of families and friends of incarcerated people articulated this critique:

> We find we are stigmatized by the public just for loving a convict. We risk
> losing jobs if our associations with convicts are known and may run the
> same risk in friendships. Often we are unable to rent housing, obtain credit,
> and we have difficulty being licensed for various professions. We are penal-
> ized for telling the truth. When our men are released, the stigma they carry
> makes it extremely difficult to find employment, and they even lose some
> of their rights as citizens. Society refuses to take any of the responsibility,
> responding only with never-ending blame; the myth of rehabilitation serves
> only to salve the social conscience.[94]

From this perspective, the "myth of rehabilitation" cloaked the true operation of the penal system and meant little for those actually subject to the system.

[92] Adrian S. A. to Mitford, July 22, 1971, Box 15, Folder 2, Jessica Mitford Papers, HRC.
[93] Ibid.
[94] Flyer: "Connections," n.d., Box 37, Folder 3, Jessica Mitford Papers, HRC.

Other prisoners rejected the entire premise of rehabilitation and challenged the state and dominant society's definition of deviance and criminality. These critics challenged not just the coercive and ineffective nature of therapeutic programs but also the normative assumptions about the ideal citizens the programs aspired to build. An article in *The Outlaw* explained how the training programs that parole boards advocated did more to enforce the performance of dominant gender roles than prepare people for a trade. She wrote:

> None of [their] courses or trades can be related to the real job statistics on the outside. Sisters in prison are encouraged to participate in group therapy; where a sister tends to role play when the pressure is on, or to superficially pretty herself, when all the time she'd being geared toward rehabilitation; breaking the sisters into society's role: passive, brainless and obedient. For our brothers, they are encouraged in the same ways, only to be programmed to fit his predefined role as a "man in society." By doing this to our brothers and sisters the prison officials are attempting to mold them into submissive subjects of society.[95]

These assessments were embedded in a sweeping structural critique of how power operated in society and have echoes of the themes that would appear so prominently in Foucault's *Discipline and Punish*.

Prisoners resisted the efforts of corrections programs to create docile citizens, as well as the penal system's role in producing deviance and constructing them as "others." Many prisoners denied having an individual pathology and instead saw their criminal actions as stemming from economic, racial, and social injustice. One prisoner wrote to Jessica Mitford:

> We no longer personally assume the identity, or assimilate the labels of "the sick," "the evil," or "the criminal," and we are thusly further liberated. Crimes are often committed with brazen faces—but they are always committed with underlying desperation of one form or another. We are tugged, towed, twisted, shoved, held back, shaped and formed through physiological, sociological, and environmental factors which are, or were evidently beyond our control. In retrospect, we see that we are no less than the overt reflection, or the symptom of the illness of society from which we are derived.[96]

This rejection of being labeled as "criminal" was buttressed by the wider trend, most pronounced among intellectuals and activists on the Left, of

---

[95] Debbie Castro X, "Programmed People," *Outlaw* 1, no. 3 (January–February 1972), Reel 274, p. 7, Underground Press Collection.

[96] Raymond B. to Mitford, June 7, 1971, Box 59, Folder 3, pp. 19–20, Jessica Mitford Papers, HRC.

interrogating how mainstream culture maintained an unjust status quo through constructing marginalized people as deviant.

"The System Began to Crumble"

By the mid-1970s, the indeterminate sentence would become an unviable policy. Prisoners opposed the rehabilitative ideal on both ideological and practical grounds in the growing number of forums open to their input. Simultaneously law-and-order advocates, who perceived the rehabilitative mission as ineffective and indulgent of prisoners, joined the attacks against the indeterminate sentence. Therapeutic programs became easy targets for critics long hostile to welfarist strategies who claimed parole boards released violent and dangerous criminals too soon, endangering the public in an era of skyrocketing crime rates. Critics on the Left argued the opposite: the policy kept people in prison too long, reflecting an overreliance on ineffectual and punitive custody. Prison administrators, who yearned to cool down their turbulent institutions and alleviate the pressure of intense public scrutiny, were increasingly open to alternative techniques for maintaining order. With many critics and few ardent defenders, the indeterminate sentence would not withstand the ensuing assault. While these groups had little in common beyond their opposition to the indeterminate sentence, together they overcame the institutional inertia and the remaining supporters of the policy.

Administrators' reaction to prison overcrowding and disorder further exacerbated the governance crises within prisons. Officials responded to violence, gang tension, and political disturbances with lockdowns, segregation units, and transfers between institutions. These strategies of population control limited prisoners' access to therapeutic, vocational, and educational programming and further undermined claims that rehabilitation was the principal object of incarceration. Limitations on mobility and activities, in turn, caused more frustration and unrest.[97]

As early as 1971, the Adult Authority and Governor Reagan's head of corrections, Raymond Procunier, initiated reforms to start informing prisoners of their release dates within the first months of their incarceration. Officials believed this would contain the unrest and frustrations caused by the uncertainty of open-ended sentences.[98] The plan lost momentum, however, in the midst of Governor Reagan's "get-tough" crime

[97]Heather McCarty, "From Con-Boss to Gang Lord: The Transformation of Social Relations in California Prisons, 1943–1983" (PhD diss., University of California–Berkeley, 2004), 293–94.

[98]William Endicott, "Adult Authority Approves Plan to Set Release Dates for Inmates," *Los Angeles Times*, October 19, 1971, A1.

policies and was ultimately abandoned.[99] Not long after, courts introduced new urgency by issuing a collection of opinions that challenged the existing sentencing practices.[100] Throughout the 1960s, prisoners, with the assistance of activist lawyers, successfully challenged their status and treatment. The resulting legal decisions enhanced due process protections for prisoners and criminal defendants. Richard McGee, who headed the California Department of Corrections from 1944 to 1961, saw the courts' new assertion of prisoner rights as the catalyst for the shifts in sentencing. In a law journal, he offered his explanation for the sudden traction of reform efforts:

> The California [indeterminate sentencing] law and the manner in which it was administered has been subjected to criticism from many sources and for numerous reasons for many years. As long ago as the late 1940s, I remember standing before a legislative committee to defend the law against an abortive attempt to repeal the act. . . . It was not, however, until the Federal courts began taking note of the constitutional rights of prisoners and parolees that the system began to crumble.[101]

The subsequent efforts to adjust penal practices with the court's new orders created openings for people intent on abandoning indeterminate sentencing all together.

In *Re: Lynch* (1972) and *Re: Foss* (1974), the California Supreme Court intervened in California's practices, declaring there must be symmetry between the crime committed and the punishment given. They found the upper limit of some sentences to be unconstitutionally long and thus cruel and unusual punishment. The implications for the 1975 case *Re: Rodriguez* extended beyond the individual petitioner and the state felt forced to revise its practices. Rudolpho A. Rodriguez, a Santa Monica man imprisoned for twenty-two years for lewd conduct with a child, challenged the Adult Authority's right to incarcerate him indefinitely.[102] Corrections officials classified Rodriguez—despite his near-perfect record in prison—as a "warehouse case" and repeatedly refused to release him or set a parole date. He was diagnosed with schizophrenia (although "in

[99] William Endicott, "State Parole: Gates Open to New Ideas," *Los Angeles Times*, May 8, 1975, 24.

[100] Earlier decisions had weakened the indeterminate sentence by establishing proportionality tests for sentence lengths, undermining parole boards' authority to hold "unrehabilitated" offenders indefinitely. See discussion of *In Re: Foss* and *In Re: Lynch* in Griset, *Determinate Sentencing*, 50–52.

[101] Richard McGee, "California's New Determinate Sentencing Act," *Federal Probation* 42 (1978): 3.

[102] Daryl Lembke, "Man Confined 22 Years for Sex Crime Challenging Indeterminate Sentence Law," *Los Angeles Times*, February 23, 1975, 22.

remission") and declared unfit to reenter society. Rodriguez's lawyers claimed that his feelings of persecution were actually caused by interminable incarceration and multiple rejections by the parole board.[103] While the court upheld the legality of indeterminate sentencing, it concurred with Rodriguez's lawyers that the Adult Authority had violated the cruel and unusual clause of the state constitution by not setting a release date proportionate to the crime (or by never setting a date at all and potentially holding him for his entire life). Together, these rulings diminished the weight of therapeutic considerations in sentencing by ordering that parole boards must also strive for consonance between the crime committed and time served.

Meanwhile, in the legislature, John Nejedly, the Republican state senator from Walnut Creek and chairman of the Senate Select Committee on Penal Institutions, started exploring proposals to replace California's indeterminate sentence. Nejedly would shepherd the plan to replace the old sentencing scheme through the legislature. Compared to other ex–district attorneys, he was moderate on criminal justice issues and held the arbitrary and unjust application of indeterminate sentencing responsible for prison unrest. In December 1974 he first introduced Senate Bill 42 (SB42), the determinate sentencing bill that would slowly wend its way through multiple revisions to eventually sweep away almost sixty years of penal practice.

The looming threat posed by SB42 and the recent court rulings intensified pressure on the Adult Authority. Raymond Procunier, the controversial, blunt-talking prison administrator who previously headed the Department of Corrections, was tapped by Democratic governor Jerry Brown to lead the Adult Authority and its effort to align its practices with the shifting legal and political landscape. Hoping administrative reforms could stave off a more drastic overhaul, in April 1975 Procunier issued Directive 75/20, which ordered parole boards to immediately set offenders' release dates commensurate with their crime and prior criminal records. The move, backed by Governor Brown, was widely interpreted as a bid to contain damage from attacks on the Adult Authority from prisoners, the courts, and the legislature. It would not be successful. In reevaluating all prisoners to set release dates, the new policy inspired the release of approximately 5,000 prisoners, many of whose sentences had been arbitrarily stretched out by Reagan's "get-tough" order in 1972.[104] This, in turn, set off an avalanche of attacks from law enforcement and

[103]Daryl Lembke, "State High Court Upholds Indeterminate Sentences," *Los Angeles Times*, May 10, 1975, A20.

[104]Dewolk, "How Wide Did Procunier Open the State's Prison Gates?"; Fairbanks, "More Parolees Being Sent Back to Prisons," C1.

other law-and-order proponents, who charged that the surge of released felons endangered society.[105] Such claims were undoubtedly bolstered by news reports that Rudolpho A. Rodriguez, the man whose lawsuit helped spur these releases, was rearrested only four months after his parole for fondling a young girl.[106]

It was the courts, however, that derailed the Adult Authority's efforts to save the indeterminate sentence. In early 1976, they struck down Procunier's directive on the grounds that it failed to conform to the indeterminate sentencing law's mandate that parole boards consider an individual's rehabilitation in prison when setting prison terms. Since Directive 75/20 ordered sentences fixed before a prisoner's progress could be evaluated, the Adult Authority could not account for personal development in prison.[107] Thus the last administrative effort to salvage indeterminate sentencing was thwarted by the policy's insistence that sentence length reflect a prisoner's attitude behind bars. By the time the court struck down Procunier's administrative directive, SB42 had already passed the Senate by wide margin. The proposed legislation abolished the indeterminate sentence and replaced it with a sentencing grid that detailed set prison terms for various offense levels. Under the new scheme, a judge would choose among three possible sentences for each crime category: an average or median sentence, which would be used in most cases; a mitigated sentence, which reduced the term to account for extenuating circumstances; and an aggravated sentence, which lengthened the sentence when some factor made the crime exceptionally objectionable. In addition, all prisoners would qualify for "good time," which allowed for a one-third sentence reduction for good behavior in prison. The new system retained parole supervision upon release for an established period of time, usually just one year.

As the law moved through various committees, the diverse coalition of prisoners, prisoners' advocates, and law enforcement fundamentally agreed on the failure of the state's rehabilitative mission and the need for certainty in sentencing. They differed sharply, however, on policy specifics, most significantly the appropriate length of sentences. SB42 resolved these disputes in the short term by not succumbing to calls to either lengthen or shorten prison terms and holding them relatively steady. The

[105] See, for example, Robert Fairbanks, "California Prisons Freeing Massive Surge of Felons," *Los Angeles Times*, October 23, 1975, B1.

[106] See William Farr, "Molester Who Served 22 Years Faces New Sentence," *Los Angeles Times*, March 11, 1976, C1 and William Farr, "Man Whose Case Upset Parole Policy Back in Jail," *Los Angeles Times*, October 28, 1975, 3.

[107] William Endicott, "Court Strikes Down New California Parole Policy," *Los Angeles Times*, January 10, 1976, 1; Robert Fairbanks, "State High Court Lets Fixed-Term Prison Plan Die," *Los Angeles Times*, April 3, 1976, A1.

sentence lengths in the proposed bill roughly corresponded to the average time prisoners had served under the indeterminate sentence. With the possibility of an additional one-third reduction for good time, people had reason to believe that sentences would actually be reduced under the new system.[108]

Many prisoners and prisoner advocacy organizations fervently supported abolishing the indeterminate sentence and played an active role in shaping SB42. The sponsoring legislative committee received testimony and input from prisoners throughout the process. Willie Holder, a leader of the Prisoners Union, testified regularly before the committee and developed a familiar rapport with legislators. Throughout 1975 and 1976, as SB42 moved toward final passage, the Prisoners Union remained at the table in negotiations over what would replace the indeterminate sentence, pressuring politicians to reduce sentence lengths, abolish parole supervision, and limit the amount of arbitrary discretion in the system.

This involvement reflected the highly controversial assumption among some groups that prisoners and ex-prisoners might be a source of expertise on their own punishment. Outside groups, such as the AFSC and the Prisoners Union, kept California's incarcerated men and women informed about legislative negotiations and identified the key officials to pressure throughout the process.[109] Soliciting prisoners' participation in designing policies that governed them moved against the tradition of a prisoner's "civil death." It countered the long practice of rhetorically and physically severing prisoners from the "public" while they were incarcerated, on parole, and even long after they were released.

Many incarcerated and formerly incarcerated people felt their separation from the "public" acutely, which contributed to their cynicism toward the Department of Corrections' claims to rehabilitate. This issue surfaced at a Senate hearing in an offhand exchange between Raymond Parnas, a law professor who had helped craft SB42, and Willie Holder, who had served twenty years on and off for burglary and forgery:

HOLDER: The prime goal of all criminal justice legislation should be to increase prisoner confidence as well as public confidence in the administration of justice.

PARNAS: Excuse me for interrupting you, but I simply wanted to indicate that in drafting this statement we considered prisoners part of the public, and by saying improve or increase public confidence we meant to include prisoners, ex-convicts, convicts, what have you.

HOLDER: Having been an ex-convict, you know, a good majority of my life, and a citizen just about the same amount of time, you know, I felt

[108] Griset, *Determinate Sentencing*, 48–49.
[109] Oral history of Jan Marinissen, "'To Let the Legislature Know,'" 20.

that I was excluded. I really did, and I'm sure that the prisoners that read this will feel that they were being excluded, too, because of all the monkeys that you've got on your back.[110]

Holder's testimony reiterated a common sentiment among prisoners that penal practices conspired to sharply distinguish them from full citizens, despite the insistence to the contrary.

Ironically, legislative advocacy around SB42—a law designed to repudiate the state's commitment to reintegrate convicts into the public—inspired some prisoners to feel recognized in the polity. One man held at California's Men's Colony wrote to Nejedly that "for the first time in ten years of being under the Department of Corrections' thumb, myself and every other state prisoner feels that we have a chance to be heard through your bill, SB42."[111] More remarkable, many politicians viewed prisoner support for SB42 not as a liability for their legislation but as evidence of its soundness. When the bill was before the Senate Judiciary Committee, Senator Nejedly presented six boxes, which held nine thousand letters from prisoners and their families, to demonstrate prisoners' overwhelming engagement and support for the proposed reform.[112]

Correspondence sent to legislators revealed prisoners' intense investment in the fate of SB42. In the letter just quoted, the prisoner described the anxious, hopeful mood in California's carceral institutions:

> At this very moment, on every prison yard, in every prison in California, the attention of the prisoners are drawn to one thing, the passing of your bill SB42. The anticipation is near the point of a person waiting on a last minute stay of execution, only to a lesser degree. What it is, is that we are waiting for the lights to be turned on. We have been kept in darkness so long that it doesn't even seem realistic. If we could see the light at the end of the tunnel there would be less time spent in despair, and less "living for the moment" and one could plan for the future, no matter how far away.[113]

[110]"Transcript of the Hearing on the Indeterminate Sentencing Law by Senate Select Committee on Penal Institutions," December 5–6, 1974, Senate Select Committee on Penal Institute Working Papers, 1972–1976, LP161:201, p. 103, CSA Notes.

[111]Letter from inmate ("name withheld to protect identity") to Nejedly, February 24, 1975, Senate Select Committee on Penal Institute Working Papers, 1972–1976, LP161:210, CSA.

[112]Nejedly explained that 95 percent of the letters supported abolishing the indeterminate sentence. "Fixed Prison Terms? Indeterminate Sentence Ban Gains in Senate," *Sacramento Bee*, April 16, 1975, Senate Select Committee on Penal Institute Working Papers, 1972–1976, LP161:211, CSA.

[113]Letter from inmate ("name withheld to protect identity") to Nejedly, February 24, 1975.

Another letter explained how closely prisoners monitored the legislation's progress:

> I was very happy to learn that your Senate Bill 42 got out of committee. You never realized how much all of the inmates here were hoping it would. All day they asked—has it passed the committee? Do you think it will go through? So much concern and so much thanks and happiness after learning that it did clear. You are to be congratulated and commended for such a humanitarian book of revised statutes that treat an inmate as a human being.[114]

Writers equated indeterminate sentencing with denial of citizenship rights and an assault on their very humanity, and connected passage of the bill with expanding prisoners' faith in the political system and society in general:

> I placed the copy of the Senate Bill no. 42 in the prison law library where it was read by hundreds of prisoners. . . . From my conversations with them, I gather that if this bill becomes law, there will be a rebirth of respect for the law and the State of California in the way which its justice is administered. To send a man to prison to destroy him is one thing; to send him to prison as a societal experience whereby he acquires a respect for the society is quite different and produces a better citizen.[115]

While these correspondents may have exaggerated the degree of prisoners' enthusiasm for Nejedly's benefit, prisoners appear to have followed SB42 extremely closely, believing it intimately intertwined with their fates.[116]

The Senate passed SB42, 36–1, on May 15, 1975. This wide margin reflected the diverse coalition arrayed against the indeterminate sentence from across the ideological spectrum. The bill stalled, however, a few months later in the State Assembly when the Criminal Justice Committee declined to vote on it. Liberal advocates thwarted SB42's progress, although the District Attorney's Association also opposed the bill on the grounds that sentences were too lenient. The Criminal Justice Committee was known to be among the most liberal in the legislature and was traditionally the source of progressive criminal justice legislation. The liberal members saw themselves as the brakes on "get-tough" legislation that came from other committees and the Senate. In part as a response to this committee's practice of scuttling the law enforcement lobby's agen-

[114] Charles L. to Nejedly, April 21, 1975, Senate Select Committee on Penal Institute Working Papers, 1972–1976, LP161:210, CSA.

[115] Ibid.

[116] The various official prisoner newspapers from California carceral institutions also reflected the high level of engagement reported in these letters. These papers, while censored, were typically written and edited by prisoners.

das, the organizations representing district attorneys and guards had embraced a long-term strategy to take crime control decisions directly "to the people." They hoped to circumvent or forestall judicial or legislative mechanisms that could insulate legislators from direct accountability for sentence ranges.[117]

When SB42 came before the committee, it heard testimony from the American Civil Liberties Union (ACLU) of Northern California, which opposed the legislation because the sentences were too long. Furthermore, since the bill allowed the legislature to set sentence lengths, the ACLU saw no mechanism to stop lawmakers from lengthening them in the future. They also called for increased administrative discretion in setting early release dates for deserving prisoners. Allegedly convinced by this testimony, the committee, led by longtime advocate of prisoners' rights legislation Alan Sieroty, chose not to vote on the bill. This effectively ended the legislation's chances of passage during the session, although it did not kill the bill outright.

The Prisoners Union was furious with the ACLU. They publicly attacked it for elitism and failing to consult with prisoners, and organized a picket in front of the ACLU office. Willie Holder charged that

> the ACLU lives in a world of abstract civil liberties and ivory towers, more appropriate to an academic setting than the reality of prison life. Their lobbyists rode in on a high horse right before the hearing and made pronouncements that the bill wasn't pure enough. They never asked convicts or us or any other prison group what their ideas and feelings were. I'd like to know who in the hell these people think they represent.[118]

These criticisms caused a rift between the ACLU's board of directors and its staff. After the public clash, the board sided with the Prisoners Union and prohibited its staff from working against determinate sentencing legislation in the future.[119] Prisoner activists complained that ACLU staff, despite their benevolent motives, failed to comprehend the profound differences between serving a fixed sentence and serving an indeterminate one. An article published in *The Outlaw* explained:

> What they [ACLU] cannot grasp is that quantitative time and qualitative time are not necessarily the same. If a man or woman has a flat three years

[117]Michael Campbell, "The Emergence of Penal Extremism in California: A Dynamic View of Institutional Structures and Political Processes," *Law and Society* 48, no. 2 (2014): 377–409, quote on 389.

[118]Averie Cohen, "Twenty-two Miles of Protest," *Outlaw* 4, no. 4 (September/October 1975), Reel 216, p. 11, Underground Press Collection.

[119]For the confrontation between the Prisoners Union and the ACLU, see Mike Snedeker, "The Indeterminate Sentence Lives and Breathes," *Outlaw* 4, no. 4 (September/October 1975), Reel 216, pp. 16–18, Underground Press Collection and Griset, *Determinate Sentencing*, 49.

to do, and knows that most other people who committed the same act are looking at the same three years, it is possible to kick back, think it over, get what you can from what's there, and make plans for getting out. The body is caged but the mind is free.

If a man or woman only spends two years inside, but all the while has hopes that a petition of some kind would cut them loose sooner (because others have made it), and fears that they would be trapped inside for far longer (because others have lost it) and wasted mental energy trying to fall into the right category for the Graders and Sorters—then that two years can be a draining, embittering eternity. It is Death Time; time that generates a "fuck 'em in their ass" attitude.[120]

As the author explained, many prisoners found that the discretion exercised by liberal, therapeutic treatment specialists seemed far more difficult to tolerate than the certainty of a fixed sentence, even if applied in the name of brute punishment. The Prisoners Union claimed that female prisoners also supported the repeal of indeterminate sentencing, even though they averaged shorter sentences than men for comparable crimes. Activists explained that being governed by the arbitrary whims of parole boards was so heinous that female prisoners would accept longer prison terms in exchange for the certainty of fixed release dates. Prisoners Union activist Patricia Holder explained to a reporter, "I'm not advocating longer sentences by any means but I've talked to the women in prison and they would rather do double time than do time under the Adult Authority. They'd rather know how much time they'll spend."[121]

———

Although SB42 stalled in the 1975 legislative session, the old rationale for penal custody was widely discredited and legally unviable. Indeterminate sentencing in California was destined to fall. Now lawmakers faced the more contentious task of constructing a new justification for incarceration. This process inspired fervent disagreements over prisons' core function, who should control them, and, ultimately, whose interests they should serve. People of all political persuasions used this critical juncture to advance their unique visions for the penal system. Proposals from the Left reflected aspirations to expand the rights, opportunities, and participation of marginalized groups while finding alternatives to coercive institutional practices. More radical voices called for fundamentally reor-

---

[120] Snedeker, "The Indeterminate Sentence Lives and Breathes," 4–5.

[121] "Fixed-Term Law Stretches Time for Woman Cons," *San Francisco Examiner*, June 16, 1977, Corrections Administration News Digests: 1977, F3717:1639, CSA.

ganizing society to alleviate the structural inequalities that caused crime and led certain groups, especially within communities of color, to be constructed as criminal. "Law-and-order" politicians forwarded policies that moved in the opposite direction, narrowing the populations that the state was committed to represent and protect by entrenching the boundaries between full rights-bearing citizens and criminals. They pressed for tough, punitive approaches that positioned law enforcement and militaristic (as opposed to welfarist) strategies as the best antidote to crime and disorder. Few at the time would have anticipated that a historically unprecedented era of carceral expansion was around the corner.

CHAPTER SIX

Going Berserk for Punishment

A PRELUDE TO MASS INCARCERATION

The indeterminate sentence arose as a political issue from struggles *within* prisons, but soon debates over sentencing policy became connected to wider and longstanding struggles over how to manage street crime and about the rights and standing of felons. Once the old rationale for penal custody was widely discredited, different groups advanced their own visions for the prison. Prisoners hoped that abolishing the indeterminate sentence would help reduce their stigmatization and mitigate their degraded status in the polity. Many hoped to open avenues out of prison and toward greater economic and social security. However, just as many felt they were making headway, the original coalition that displaced indeterminate sentencing dissolved and "law-and-order" advocates came to dominate the debate. The calls for tough crime-control strategies by elites developed dialogically with discourse among the general populace frustrated with expanding the rights of prisoners and criminal suspects. Instead of pursuing convicts' integration, lawmakers forwarded legislation that degraded their civil status by making punishment more severe and intensifying prisoners' rhetorical, physical, and legal segregation from "good" citizens.

The escalation of punishments was not simply a Republican or conservative project. Although Democrats ultimately reaped fewer political rewards than Republicans, they were instrumental in "stiffening" criminal penalties and entrenching a punitive logic. Democratic politicians endorsed get-tough political proposals, sometimes proactively and sometimes defensively. While lawmakers often debated the appropriate degree of punishment, elites in both parties usually proved willing to sacrifice the interests of criminalized groups for their own political gain or protection. At the heart of this dynamic was the development of a near-compulsive political imperative to appear tough on crime that relegated programmatic efficacy and cost to secondary concerns. By the 1980s, the notion that sentencing policy might address "root causes" of crime or help reintegrate prisoners into society was branded as permissive and "soft" and therefore politically untenable. Toughness in criminal sentencing policy became politically essential.

The "Modest Proposal" of Prisoner Unionization

In the mid-1970s, the California Department of Corrections (CDC) was still entertaining other tactics to manage unruly prisons. In 1975, high-level officials entered into negotiations with the Prisoners Union over plans to organize union-like structures to enhance prisoners' power and voice within institutions. Although the plan ultimately galvanized opponents and rationalized new efforts to curtail prisoners' influence, the negotiations were a high-water mark for the Prisoners Union. The union put forward what corrections administrators saw as a "reasonable and moderate" proposal to build trust between the parties. They planned to initially build union support and infrastructure inside a single institution and then slowly expand into others. The Prisoners Union proposed forming committees—comprised of one Prisoners Union member, one Department of Corrections representative, and one member chosen by both—that would rule on conflicts over appeals, transfers, and disciplinary matters, as well as examine prison policies generally. Although the committee's decisions would not be binding at first, the parties agreed they would carry moral and social weight.[1] Despite their limited initial proposal, the union openly declared that its ultimate aim was to abolish the Adult Authority, restore prisoners' human and civil rights, and act as representatives in collective bargaining over wages, conditions, and disciplinary hearings. For this brief moment, both corrections administrators and the Prisoners Union saw the possibility and appeal of sharing power and responsibility for administering prisons.

In January 1976 the administrators were about to introduce this plan to a wider group of corrections personnel when the California Correctional Officers Association (CCOA) got wind of it. Enraged, the union that represented corrections officers released the proposal to the press, accompanied by a scathing attack. They threatened to strike if such a plan were implemented and demanded the resignation of the director of corrections and the secretary of health and welfare for even considering such an "insane" and "idiotic" idea. Almost every major news outlet in California—and some national programs—carried the story, paired with the indignant comments of wardens and superintendents furious about the proposal. "Law-and-order" politicians soon joined the fray. H. L. "Bill" Richardson, state senator and Republican whip, who had

---

[1] Kempsky, Department Director of Policy and Planning, to J. J. Enomoto, Director of Corrections, "Notes on Meeting with Prisoners Union on June 27, 1975," Corrections Administration, Prison Issues: 1975–77, F3717:1475, CSA; Prisoners Union, "Proposal for Union in One Institution," Corrections Administration, Prison Issues: 1975–77, F3717:1475, CSA. See also Cumming, *Rise and Fall of California's Radical Prison Movement*, 255–57.

made crime his signature issue, told the press, "Any appointee who has actively helped in this insane effort should be fired. . . . We're talking about Bolsheviks, inside and outside who want to foment as much internal strife in this country as they possibly can."[2] While CDC administrators probably negotiated with the Prisoners Union because they saw the organization as a moderate alternative to the activism of more revolutionary prisoners, conservative legislators labeled all prisoner activism dangerous and viewed dialoguing with them as treasonous.

The political fallout of the leaked plan immediately shut down the negotiations to allow the Prisoners Union to organize in one institution. The union interpreted the resistance as politically motivated "calculated hysteria" but also saw a deeper significance in the refusal to grant prisoners authority within prisons. An article in *The Outlaw* explained:

> A more formidable obstacle, however, is an insidious, mistaken notion which we strongly believe is at the root of the prison administrations' unwillingness to accept the proposed plan. This is the belief that prisoners are fundamentally inferior. They are either dangerous animals or mostly weak people subject to domination by the few dangerous animals. They are, according to this view, incapable of participating in sustained, responsible action and becoming dignified, honorable human beings.[3]

According to this analysis, corrections employees rejected the notion that prisoners were capable of reasoned civic participation, especially the responsibilities of self-government. Their status as prisoners marked them as inherently incapable of self-determination or self-regulation and unable to responsibly choose who represented them. For prisoners, the adamant refusal to acknowledge their capacity for "responsible action" or as "capable human beings" underlined the hypocrisy of the Department of Corrections' claims of facilitating rehabilitation.

The Prisoners Union, however, retained more faith in the political system than the officials had in them. In a section of an *Outlaw* article titled "Prisoner Organizations Are Inevitable," the author advanced a familiar Whiggish understanding of American history whereby prisoners and other marginalized groups would inevitably gain greater rights and respect:

> One of the few consistent trends over the past few decades has been a slow, very painful, but steady increase in the rights of people formerly excluded from any decision making arena. The struggle is no less intense now; the

[2]Robert Fairbanks, "Wardens Rap Plan to Allow Prison Unions," *Los Angeles Times*, January 21, 1976, C1.

[3]"Right to Participate: A Modest Proposal," *Outlaw* 5, no. 1 (January/February 1976), Reel 216, pp. 1–2, Underground Press Collection.

outcome in any single situation is problematic, but overall the extension of power to more and more people cannot be stopped. . . .

Two hundred years ago, the only people who could vote were white male landowners who were not in prison. The requirements that a person own property, be of a particular race or a favored sex have been dropped; only those classed as felons remain disenfranchised. The process of extending basic recognition to prisoners has begun—100 years ago a Judge in Virginia could correctly say that prisoners forfeit all rights save the right to breathe.

Things are different now. Whether we will be the particular agents who enable a union of prisoners is an open question, dependent on forces larger than our energies or hopes. What is not open is the increased recognition of the humanity of people locked inside, and of what is necessary if they are to remain fully human; this includes the right to organize around the problems common to all.[4]

This level of faith in progress through struggle was probably diminishing for many activists in the mid-1970s. Many may have originally seen the long-term struggle as between a liberal rehabilitative regime and the expansion of marginalized people's autonomy; now there was clearly a strident "law-and-order" contingency ascending. It would pose a new threat to prisoners hoping to improve their conditions or enhance their civic standing.

Whom Should the State Protect?

Proclamations about the need for tougher responses to social disorder were remarkable in their redundancy and consistency. The arguments were repeated incessantly, eventually solidifying into mantras that echoed throughout discussions about crime and the role of the prison. Key tropes appeared and reappeared in citizen letters, politicians' speeches, newspapers, and conversations at family dinner tables and employee lunchrooms. Many of the same themes that animated discussions of welfare and drugs featured in these debates. People reported feeling endangered and enraged at the government's failure to protect them, which they equated with being robbed of their citizenship rights. They accused the state of protecting the rights of criminals and other outsiders at the expense of "taxpaying" and "law-abiding citizens." Letter writers were indignant about a topsy-turvy world where the wrong people had protection. In one representative letter, a woman explained:

[4]Ibid.

I think we have cried long and hard for the criminal, it is about time for the victims whose families weep in silence while the American Civil Liberties Union and ambulance chasing lawyers get front page coverage for the poor deprived, lonely, persecuted criminal who may finally serve some time in a correctional facility after having been picked up perhaps two dozen times for various offenses. . . . I certainly don't believe housing them in country clubs and spoon feeding them will ever make worthwhile citizens out of a criminal, particularly those involved in violent crime.[5]

The writer explicitly rejected the notion that decent prison conditions or therapeutic programs could "make worthwhile citizens." The letter did not propose that a tougher approach would be more effective at reforming criminals but instead rejected the possibility of ever making criminals into citizens.

Embedded in this type of critique was profound hostility to reliance upon therapy, rehabilitation, or structural reform to address crime. Many commentators insisted that attending to "root causes" emboldened and coddled criminals and actually made the problems worse. An editorial that articulated this logic ran in the *Herald Examiner*:

It has seemed that while more and more dollars have been allocated to crime prevention programs, and a greater emphasis at all levels of government on social services which address themselves to alleviating the conditions on which the criminal element thrives, we have witnessed not only more violations of the law, but a tendency toward more violence in the acts committed.[6]

Therefore, therapeutic approaches to criminality were not merely ineffective; they actually exacerbated violence and crime. Such letters portrayed social services as harmful, even jeopardizing the safety and security of law-abiding communities. Instead of expanding the groups within society that possessed full rights and autonomy, people felt that authorities' attention to marginalized, racialized populations negated the rights of average citizens. This zero-sum understanding of rights suggested an inverse relationship where those with full citizenship had their rights constricted when they were accorded to new groups. These interpretations clashed, not surprisingly, with those of prisoner activists who claimed that the constraints on the rights, standing, and opportunities of subordinated groups created disorder.

[5] Mary S. to Senator Nejedly, February 10, 1975, Senate Select Committee on Penal Institute Working Papers, General Correspondence: 1975–1976, LP161:225, CSA.

[6] William Banowsky, "American People Don't Want Nagging Fear," *Herald Examiner*, November 2, 1975, Corrections Administration News Digests: 1975, F3717:377, CSA.

The sentiment that the state no longer served the right people was particularly resonant in an era marked by government interventions on behalf of women, people of color, and other traditionally marginalized groups. A couple wrote to Senator Nejedly: "It is time we become less concerned with the rights of the criminal, and more concerned with the rights of the innocent victims. . . . We all know it is an erosion of the rights of the people to be protected. . . . Today wrong is right in the eyes of too many of our government who make the laws."[7] A letter to the editor echoed this same theme: "It is high time to reexamine our criminal laws and legal procedures and put the emphasis where it belongs—on the rights of all law-abiding citizens of California who are the direct or indirect victims of crime."[8] In this language, people asserted rights to state resources and protections by virtue of their position as taxpaying, law-abiding, productive workers. Positioning claims to full citizenship protection in this way negated the entitlement of other groups. It rested on the familiar assumption that those who commit crimes forfeited their ability to make claims on the state.

In another letter to Senator Nejedly, a man wrote that after eight armed robberies and eight burglaries, he was the "record holder in the City of Pittsburgh as a victim of crime." He explained:

I'm writing to you in a cry for help, not only for myself but for thousands of other citizens. . . . I'm going to work armed, even at home. . . . My question is What happened to our laws which is supposed to protect all citizens? Are our today's leaders getting soft? Some of them seem more concerned about the welfare of our prisoners, (bums, radicals, etc, etc,) then us who are trying to make a honest living. We need men with guts in today's society, to stand up and show us that we also have rights, also the right to work in peace without looking over our shoulders or keeping our fingers on the trigger. . . . All I and others want is to live in peace without fear.[9]

While it is not surprising that this person became enraged after being victimized sixteen times, it is interesting to note that his analysis positioned politicians' cowardice, "soft"-ness, and lack of guts as the cause of crime. The particular logic and gendered imagination embedded in this reasoning have often been obscured by their constant repetition and omnipresence. It assumed that any new rights or protections accorded to

[7] Mr. and Mrs. Wm. W. to Nejedly, March 10, 1977, Senate Select Committee on Penal Institutions Bill Files: SB42, LP218:231, CSA.

[8] In the department's news digest there is a large group of letters to the editor opposing the release of a surge of felons. Corrections Administration News Digests: 1975, F3717:377, CSA.

[9] Harry F. to Nejedly, February 26, 1976, Senate Select Committee on Penal Institute Working Papers, LP161:243, CSA.

marginalized groups represented the emasculation of state authority. The writer deplored how everyday citizens were forced to step into this leadership void and protect their families and property by arming themselves.

These issues were made all the more salient by the wider political and cultural context. In the mid-1970s, the nation was coming to terms with losing the war in Vietnam. The loss reverberated throughout society, leaving many with a desire—even a determination—to affirm American power, particularly of its military personnel and might. This was all the more acute for the many men who had direct personal or community ties with the military and worked in police department and guard forces (both of which prioritized the hiring of ex-military). Just as many argued that the fighting forces had been sabotaged by politicians who never allowed the military to "take their gloves off" in Vietnam, domestic law enforcement and prison officials felt hamstrung and sabotaged by new procedures protecting people charged with and convicted of crime.

Some of the era's more popular films reflected these themes as well. In fact, the frustrations with an incompetent yet obstructionist state probably contributed to the appeal of the vigilante movie during the 1970s, which became one of the defining film genres of the era. Clint Eastwood played the title role in the popular 1971 law-and-order film *Dirty Harry*. Eastwood played a maverick San Francisco cop, Harry Callahan, chasing a serial killer called Scorpio. Callahan's embrace of violent, extralegal tactics clashed with the ineffectual state hierarchy committed to following legal procedures. In a key confrontation, Callahan tortures a killer until he reveals the location of his latest victim. As if to emphasize Callahan's deviation from sanctioned police policy, Scorpio repeatedly asserts his right to a lawyer during the scene. Callahan soon finds the body and the murder weapon, yet the killer is released because police failed to follow proper procedure and therefore made the key evidence inadmissible in court. Infuriated by these legal hindrances, Callahan takes matters into his own hands, confronts the killer again, and executes him. For a populace obsessed with crime and the supposed ineptitude of liberal crime-control strategies, the film dramatically illustrated the appeal of vigilante justice. Although leading reviewers critiqued the film as "a right wing fantasy" and a "disturbing manifestation of police paranoia," the film was popular and followed by four other commercially successful *Dirty Harry* movies.[10] Vigilante justice became a staple of pop culture, depict-

[10]For the centrality in the 1970s of vigilante movies, see Peter Lev, *American Films of the 70s: Conflicting Visions* (Austin: University of Texas Press, 2000), 22–40; for the plot details, see Tim Dirks, "Dirty Harry (1971)," The Greatest Films, http://www.filmsite.org /dirt.html ; and for reviewers' quotes, see Lev, *American Films of the 70s*, 35. Following the model popularized by *Dirty Harry*, a popular 1974 vigilante film, *Death Wish*, also spawned four sequels exemplifying the public frustration with perceived rising crime and

ing ruthless force as the anecdote to disorder. Implicit in these treatments was the assumption that liberalism's strategies of social control had failed and that granting criminals rights and protections was foolhardy and dangerous.

"Law-and-order" advocates—particularly corrections employees—used this rhetoric to attack prisoners' new rights and recalibrate the balance of power within institutions. Prison guards and wardens, enraged by perceived attacks on their authority from both their bureaucratic managers and the prisoners they guarded, became an increasingly organized, influential force. In the mid-1970s, prison guards—or correctional officers, as they were called in California—were some of the lowest-paid law enforcement employees in the state. Their organization, the California Correctional Officers Association, had only limited sway with lawmakers and was not capable of reshaping procedures within prisons or crime policy more broadly. These workers had long resented the respect accorded to the more professionalized treatment staff, whom they often felt did not face the same suspicion, hostility, and physical dangers.

These frustrations only multiplied as prisoners gained new rights, which afforded them new protections that guards typically experienced as dangerous checks on their authority and discretion. The loosening of visiting and correspondence regulations gave lawyers and legislators new access to prisoners' grievances, which tended to feature complaints about guard behavior. The upheavals within prisons in the early 1970s, particularly the revolts and growing incidence of attacks on guards, led many officers to claim that new prisoner rights and protections exacerbated disorder. They also charged that state administrators were prioritizing prisoners' rights over staff safety. Custody staff's principal functions of order maintenance and security had long been (at least rhetorically) subordinated to therapy and corrections.[11] Therefore, guards and wardens often shared prisoners' hostility to the rehabilitative orientation in California's prisons, although for completely different reasons. The disorder and upheaval in prisons and the critiques of rehabilitation opened new space for a public debate over the appropriate function of prisons. By the mid-1970s, it was not settled whose visions or authority would prevail, and the officers and guards resolved to have a voice. Prison officers began to organize more assertively, forming a more formal, independent union unaffiliated with

police inefficiency. The vigilante violence depicted in the film is celebrated as the effective, appropriate reaction to a society rife with chaos and crime; the film helped make Charles Bronson one of the most popular movie stars of the 1970s. *The Exterminator* (I [1980] and II [1984]) and *Rolling Thunder* (1977) featured Vietnam veterans who translate their military experience into controlling rampant crime.

[11] Page, *Toughest Beat*, particularly 19–54. On guards' frustrations, see Irwin, *Prisons in Turmoil*, 123–52.

the AFL-CIO. H. L. Bill Richardson, a conservative state senator who had worked at the John Birch Society, would help teach them the way around the capitol, explaining the ins and outs of political donations and effective lobbying. In the coming decades, this organization would become one of the most powerful organized forces in California politics.[12]

While many prisoner activists proceeded on the assumption that society would continue to expand their rights and access to social and economic resources, law enforcement interests were determined not merely to return to the status quo by rolling back prisoners' recent gains but to remake the penal landscape altogether. Newly mobilized guard organizations connected with legislators intent on restoring "law and order" through longer sentences and further empowering law enforcement agencies. As opposed to making the boundaries between prison and society more porous, "law-and-order" reformers operated on the premise that law-abiding citizens were diametrically separate from criminal elements. Emboldened by their success at derailing the Prisoners Union's plan, wardens and the CCOA became more effective at rhetorically positioning their interests as synonymous with the public's, depicting themselves as the tough remedy for the violent chaos on the streets and within prisons.

Prisons Are Punishment: California's Legislature Enacts Determinate Sentencing

Despite the gathering strength of their political adversaries, the prisoners' rights movement and the Prisoners Union remained adamant in their support of SB42 during the following legislative session. This support persisted even as the political process exacted new compromises with law enforcement. During the 1976 session, SB42 encountered little opposition. After California courts struck down Directive 75/20, Governor Jerry Brown abandoned his efforts at administrative reform and supported the bill. He and his staff played a critical role in mediating conflicts and building compromise legislation palatable to all the parties involved. Despite some dissatisfaction about the sentence lengths, every major law enforcement organization, except for the California Probation, Parole and Corrections Association, joined Brown to support SB42.

While many prisoners and their advocates were pleased with Governor Brown's intervention and SB42's resurgence, close observers saw his involvement with the bill as more complex. Brown articulated little sympathy or affinity with those behind bars. Although the Right reviled Brown as a typical liberal, his views on criminal justice frequently diverged from

[12] Page, *Toughest Beat*, particularly 19–54.

those of the more liberal members of his party. In an oral history, Anthony Kline, Brown's legal affairs secretary from 1975 to 1980, explained
that the governor was not inclined to support prisoners' interests: "Jerry
Brown was not a bleeding heart liberal. I know there were a lot of people
who think that he must have been or were sure that he was, but let me
assure you—and I was there—when it came to sentencing issues, Jerry
Brown was not a liberal."[13] Although he did not drive punitive escalation
to the extent Rockefeller did in New York, Brown aligned staunchly with
"law-and-order" positions on criminal policy.[14]

Many anticipated a dark side to determinate sentencing for prisoners
and the Left. Michael Dufficy, the attorney who defended one of the San
Quentin Six who were charged in the confrontation in which George
Jackson was killed, told a reporter, "I think there is no question that this
bill is going to backfire for the liberals and the radicals."[15] The legislative
staff of the Criminal Justice Committee continued to register reservations
about granting lawmakers power over sentencing:[16] "The Legislature has
been a reactive body in the area of criminal sentences. Other than in the
case of marijuana, there has been no significant legislation that attempts
to reduce sentences."[17] The legislative staff recognized that these proposed reforms did not remove discretion and arbitrariness from the sentencing process, as the bill's proponents claimed. Instead, the sentencing
reforms enhanced prosecutors' power, since they determined the charge
and whether to pursue the enhancements. The committee staff explained
that "the ultimate sentencer becomes the Prosecutor who decides the
length of sentence by the enhancements he alleges."[18] The reforms shifted
the locus of decision making from judges and parole boards to prosecutors and lawmakers.

In negotiations over the final version of SB42, there was little resistance to abolishing the indeterminate sentence, which was politically and
legally unviable by 1976. The debate centered instead on the appropriate

[13] Oral histories of Anthony Kline, "Oral History interview of Hon. J. Anthony Kline,
Legal Affairs Secretary 1975–1980," conducted in 1990 and 1991 by Germaine LaBerge,
OH 92-7, p. 25, Regional Oral History Office, University of California–Berkeley, CSA. For
Brown's reluctance to spend political capital, see p. 22.

[14] Despite signing legislation that made punishment the principal function of incarceration, Brown did not completely abandon the notion that prisons could facilitate rehabilitation. Gilmore, *Golden Gulag*, 92.

[15] Mary Leydecker, "Many Not Cheering New Sentencing Bill," *San Rafael Independent*, September 2, 1976, Corrections Administration News Digests: 1976, F3717:1638,
CSA.

[16] Campbell, "The Emergence of Penal Extremism in California," 391.

[17] "Staff Concerns and Proposals over SB42," April 7, 1976, Assembly Criminal Justice
Committee, SB42, LP319:68, CSA.

[18] Ibid.

length of the fixed sentences, an ironic stumbling block considering that once lawmakers gained control over term lengths, there was no obstacle to constantly revising them. Kline explained this dynamic in his oral history interview:

> But once you took the power to set sentences away from the Adult Authority and placed it in the legislature, you were giving the legislature the ability to lengthen sentences. You also gave it the ability to shorten sentences, but it's politically unrealistic to think they would ever do that, and to my knowledge they have not.[19]

By keeping prison terms roughly consistent with California's earlier averages, the final bill maintained the compromise between competing interests and resisted pressure to either lengthen or shorten prison terms.

On August 4, 1976, SB42 easily passed the committee that had stalled its passage the previous year. Pressure from the Prisoners Union and the governor's involvement helped temper the incentive for the Democratic members to scuttle the legislation. The Assembly's Criminal Justice Committee voted 4–1 in favor of SB42. Alan Sieroty cast the only opposing vote, claiming that the law opened the door to a dangerous cycle in which lawmakers would perpetually extend sentences in response to public pressure or political motivations.[20] After further compromises, the bill finally passed both houses. On September 20, 1976, Governor Brown signed the groundbreaking determinate sentencing law and three other anti-crime bills at a press event surrounded by law enforcement officials.[21]

The new bill abolished the Adult Authority and the Women's Board of Terms and Parole and replaced the indeterminate sentence with a fixed, or determinate, sentencing system. The law aimed to standardize sentences and equalize the amount of time served for those convicted of similar crimes. Implicit in this endeavor was the discursive abandonment of the decades-long rehabilitative mission of prisons. The law spelled out this conversion with its famous declaration: "The purpose of imprisonment for crime is punishment." Corrections was no longer the official motive for incarceration in California.[22] The final version of the law replaced the discretion of the parole board with a middle, lower, and

[19] Oral histories of Anthony Kline, "Oral History interview of Hon. J. Anthony Kline, Legal Affairs Secretary 1975–1980," 24.

[20] Robert Fairbanks, "Repeal of Indeterminate Sentencing Appears Sure," *Los Angeles Times*, August 6, 1976, B3.

[21] Robert Fairbanks, "Brown Signs Bills on Crime and Tax Relief," *Los Angeles Times*, September 21, 1976, B3.

[22] Griset, *Determinate Sentencing*, 54–55; Albert J. Lipson and Mark Peterson, *California Justice under Determinate Sentencing: A Review and Agenda for Research* (Santa Monica: Rand Corp., 1980), 1–7.

upper term for each felony. Unless mitigating or aggravating factors existed, the judge was expected to sentence offenders to the middle term. Prison terms could be extended if prosecutors chose to charge any of the enhancements available for a variety of factors, and the law instituted "good time," a standard one-third reduction in sentence length for good behavior in prison. Most offenders faced a single year of parole upon release from prison. Community Release Boards replaced parole boards. The new board's authority was limited to decisions about parole suspension, "good time" reductions in prison terms, and release dates for prisoners serving life sentences (which remained indeterminate).[23]

Many prisoners and their advocates celebrated the passage of SB42. Abolishing indeterminate sentencing was considered a great victory, unthinkable only a decade earlier. Yet, early on, some prisoners warned that the particulars of the bill were not as favorable as many imagined. An incarcerated journalist cautioned his readers against unrealistic expectations in the California Medical Facility's newspaper:

> From talk on the yard there seems to be as many interpretations of SB42 as there are convicts. Unfortunately, many cons are extracting from the bill that part which is most favorable, blinding themselves to the various negative provisions. For instance, SB42 does not provide for a mandated mass exodus of overdue convicts on July 1, 1977. . . . Beware your local jailhouse lawyer, as he may subject you to a bitter disappointment later on. . . . Anyone who truly believes that SB42 is light stuff should re-read the bill. It may be great for first-timers, but don't come back for seconds . . . certainly not thirds.[24]

In this and other articles, prisoners ruminated over the new statutes, searching hopefully for clues about how the new law would affect their fate. Although many prisoners welcomed the end of indeterminate sentencing, some also anticipated that the full import of the new legislation was not yet evident.

Before the bill was even signed by the governor, "law-and-order" interests began attacking SB42 for being overly lenient. Motivated in part by the looming 1978 elections, politicians portrayed the bill's prison terms as dangerously short and warned of disastrous consequences should officials issue fixed release dates for the thousands of prisoners sentenced under the old indeterminate system. They rushed to call for repeal, revisions, and amendments to better protect the public. In the summer of 1976, H. L. Bill Richardson, started the Law and Order Campaign Committee.

---

[23] Lipson and Peterson, *California Justice under Determinate Sentencing*, 7.

[24] Carl Jordan, "Senate Bill 42—A Synopsis," *Vacavalley Star* 22, no. 1 (January 1977), California Medical Facility, F3717:1841, CSA.

Richardson, who had previously run an advertising agency, organized a direct mail fund-raising operation devoted to unseating "soft-on-crime" legislators and channeling public concern about rising crime to the political and financial advantage of conservative legislators.[25] This massive direct mail apparatus positioned conservative lawmakers as the protectors of public security, generated an influx of new funds, and discouraged lawmakers' opposition to "law-and-order" bills at the state capitol. It would become an increasingly powerful and feared force in California politics in the coming years. Richardson explained his new organization's mission in terms of correcting the maldistribution of rights in society: "There are already too many advocates for the rights of the criminal, and I do everything I can to speak up for the rights of the law abiding. Our side is outnumbered in the legislature, and I am trying to provide some balance."[26] The organization monitored elected officials' votes and comments concerning crime policy and kept their constituents informed. In its first two months, the committee raised over $1 million from around 220,000 individuals.[27] As sentencing decisions were pushed into the legislature and lawmakers took more and more public votes on crime bills, the Law and Order Campaign Committee garnered new ammunition to deploy in their campaigns.

SB42 soon became a pawn in the upcoming gubernatorial election battles. Edward Davis, the tough-talking, controversial chief of the Los Angeles Police Department, retired from the force and made a bid to become the Republican nominee for governor. His likely rival, Evelle J. Younger, also had a law enforcement background, having served as Los Angeles County district attorney before becoming state attorney general in 1971. Younger was certainly not aligned with prisoners' rights groups; he supported mandatory life sentences and declared in 1975 that "I'd rather run the risk of keeping the wrong man a little longer than let the wrong man out too soon."[28] But Younger had supported SB42, which became a political liability.

In a series of public pronouncements and opinion editorials, Davis relentlessly attacked the provisions in SB42 that required corrections employees to assign release dates for people incarcerated before the new law passed and therefore still serving indeterminate sentences. Referring to those prisoners held far beyond the average term for their respective crimes, he claimed that this policy would release a torrent of particularly violent felons who should instead be warehoused indefinitely by the state. In a provocative *Los Angeles Times* opinion editorial, Davis wrote: "A

[25] Robert Fairbanks, "Group Formed to Unseat 'Soft-on-Crime' Officials," *Los Angeles Times*, August 11, 1976, B3.
[26] Quoted in McCarty, "From Con-Boss to Gang Lord," 292.
[27] Ibid., 293–94.
[28] Fairbanks, "Group Formed to Unseat 'Soft-on-Crime' Officials," B3.

new escape tunnel has been dug for San Quentin prisoners, but this one had the help of the Governor and the Legislature. Because of this tunnel, you can expect a sharp increase in violent crime. More than 56% of the most violent and vicious criminals presently warehoused in state institutions will be released." In case there was any doubt about whether Davis was trying to generate panic, he continued: "Does that scare the hell out of you? Well, it should!" He portrayed this "prison break" as worse than mere bungling, charging the governor and courts with deliberately endangering law-abiding citizens:

> On one side of that door are the predators of society: while on the other side, in the relative quiet of our communities, lie the potential victims— fearful of possible intrusion. Who is going to provide these potential victims with compassion? . . . At the center of this turnstile sit the executive and legislative branches of government. Will these representatives of the people continue to add grease to the doors of justice?[29]

With this rhetoric, Davis played upon (and, in turn, escalated) fear of crime, while insinuating that he had the experience and resolve to protect the public from criminal predators and their unwitting accomplices: the executive and legislative branches of government.

Although Davis's claims were hyperbolic, his attacks on SB42 effectively painted Attorney General Younger and Governor Brown as "soft on crime."[30] Both now called for changes to the law. Senator Nejedly accused the candidates of knuckling under to Chief Davis's "vituperative" attacks. "These hysterics are all posturing to get some preeminence as the architect of law and order," he told the *San Francisco Chronicle*. "The governor's caught in the political maelstrom. Like the AG [Attorney General Younger], suddenly he's got problems with the bill."[31] These political realities did not escape the many prisoners who continued to watch policy developments very closely. An analysis written for the prisoners' newspaper at California Medical Facility explained the risks: "Considering that 1978 is an election year, and the political ambitions of the pervert from Los Angeles [Ed Davis], SB42 could become a political football with Chief Davis playing quarterback."[32]

[29] Edward Davis, "A New Escape Tunnel," *Los Angeles Times*, December 5, 1976, A1, A3.
[30] Michael Snedeker, "Prison Terms: Going Along with Hysteria," *Los Angeles Times*, January 27, 1977, C5.
[31] Larry Liebert, "New Sentencing Law Under Fire," *San Francisco Chronicle*, March 21, 1977, Corrections Administration News Digests: 1977, F3717:1639, CSA.
[32] Carl E. Jordan, "The Continuing Saga of SB42," *Vacavalley Star* 22, no. 2 (February 1977), California Medical Facility, F3717:1841, CSA.

Political Football: The Futile Scramble to Fix Prison Terms

With SB42 already passed, lawmakers clamored to modify the law before it became effective on July 1, 1977. Much of the controversy zeroed in on the provisions concerning issuing release dates to prisoners who still had open-ended sentences. Critics charged that the law triggered the release of criminals parole boards had deemed too dangerous to release after serving the average prison terms for their crimes. Governor Brown attempted to head off these attacks by forwarding his own revision, or "clean-up" legislation, which was introduced by Representative Daniel Boatwright as Assembly Bill 476 (AB476). Boatwright was a Democratic member of the Assembly and former deputy district attorney for Contra Costa County who championed "tough positions" on crime. Although the bill's sponsors resisted pressure to increase SB42's base prison terms, the law amended the cap on enhancements and limits on consecutive terms, thus enlarging the discretion of prosecutors to further lengthen sentences.[33] It extended routine parole supervision from one year to eighteen months. It also altered the retroactive sentencing of those who were being held under indeterminate sentences. The Boatwright Bill (AB476) empowered authorities to review, revise, and postpone the "tentative" release dates that Community Release Boards had begun issuing upon the passage of SB42.[34]

Politicians' rush to amend SB42 was clearly motivated by the new attacks characterizing the bill as overly lenient. One newspaper article read: "The proposed changes follow accusations by some law enforcement officials that sentences in the new law, scheduled to take effect this July, are too soft."[35] As opposed to discussing the punishments merely in terms of length (i.e., too long or too short), reporters and officials more frequently cast the bill as "soft" and overly indulgent. Depicting state programs, officials, and policy in such gendered terms instantly linked with larger themes in public discourse that disparaged welfare-state programs by portraying them as weak, effeminate, and therefore generally ineffective. On a more concrete level, politicians, Governor Brown in particular, wanted to avoid the political debacle that would undoubtedly ensue if any prisoners released under the new law were to commit any

---

[33] SB42 restricted judges' ability to impose consecutive sentences. Under the final Boatwright Bill, they were allowed to do so for those convicted of violent crimes. Robert Fairbanks, "Bill Seeking Longer Prison Terms Diluted," *Los Angeles Times*, March 31, 1977, C6.

[34] "Brown to Change New Sentencing Law," *San Francisco Chronicle*, February 10, 1977, Boatwright Papers, AB476, 1977, LP357:14, CSA; Griset, *Determinate Sentencing*, 56.

[35] "Brown to Change New Sentencing Law."

newsworthy crimes. Some critics suspected that lawmakers were planning to simply postpone release dates until after the 1978 elections.[36]

While the Right attacked AB476 as insufficiently severe, the architects of SB42 were alarmed to see the policy they had championed and carefully crafted career off course so suddenly. Raymond Parnas, one of the two principal drafters and negotiators of SB42, wrote a detailed analysis of these developments in the *Sacramento Bee*. He explained that SB42 was careful, rationally deliberated legislation resulting from two years of debate, public hearings, negotiations, and study, and eight different drafts. Boatwright's legislation, on the other hand, was hurriedly assembled and informed by little more than political pressure. At the article's conclusion, Parnas acknowledged that he and his allies had failed to anticipate the full consequences of transferring sentencing authority to politicians. He confessed that the liberal senator Alan Sieroty, one of SB42's few opponents, had anticipated this dynamic: "I would, however, hate to admit that Senator Alan Sieroty was right in distrusting the collective ability of his legislative brethren to withstand the pressures of the multitude for perpetually higher penalties."[37] Senator Nejedly also recognized that the shifting political landscape spelled serious problems for the delicate compromises in his determinate sentencing law. He wrote to one constituent that "the whole subject of crime and lengths of incarceration has become a political football which threatens the very existence of SB42. I think it is clear that some measure 'toughening SB42' will pass, or we will most certainly face a repeal or initiative measure drastically increasing sentences."[38] In another letter responding to a woman concerned about the cost and effectiveness of the longer sentences in AB476, Nejedly again warned of the gathering strength of "law-and-order" proponents:

> While harboring serious reservations about the contents of AB476, I have even greater reservations about attempts by law enforcement groups and individual legislators to "toughen" the bill still further. . . . Given the political clout of judges, district attorneys, sheriffs, police and other law enforcement groups, and the existing political climate, perhaps a bill such as AB476 was inevitable.

Emphasizing his conviction that longer sentences, while appearing "tough," did nothing to reduce crime, Nejedly continued, "I can only

[36] Bob Egelko, "Bid to Prevent Many Paroles Expected," *Los Angeles Times*, December 28, 1976, B3.

[37] Raymond Parnas, "A Case for Fixed Prison Terms," *Sacramento Bee*, March 27, 1977, Criminal Justice Committee, AB476:1977–1978, LP319:84, CSA.

[38] Nejedly to Ms. Jennifer B. R., June 15, 1977, Senate Select Committee on Penal Institutions, Bill Files: 476, LP218:232, CSA.

hope that as our prisons become overcrowded and crime remains unabated we will discard the fallacious belief that longer prison terms will somehow make our streets and homes safer."[39]

The changes heralded by AB476 were most alarming for prisoners themselves. They reacted immediately to the proposed legislation, recognizing the implications for the material conditions of their captivity and for the larger cultural milieu. In a letter to Senator Howard Way opposing AB476, the Prisoners Union's Willie Holder expressed a sense of betrayal by the legislative process:

> SB42 evolved over a two-year period of intense discussions with the author, liberal and conservative politicians, law enforcement, judicial associations, community groups, and the Governor. During these two years there were many compromises—all in good faith. Good faith like good will must withstand enormous pressure and requires strong convictions of a basic principle of equity. It is a highly unethical practice for the Governor to duck the leadership necessary to give what we and many others see as a compromise legislation, at best, a chance to work.[40]

Holder's comments suggest that the new bill violated the rules of fair play. The Prisoners Union activists felt double-crossed as the concessions they had secured through hard compromises and organizing were quickly swept away.

One letter to Assemblyman Maddy, the chair of Assembly Criminal Justice Committee, expressed a similar sense of betrayal over prisoners' exclusion from the political dialogue concerning their fate. The author asked, "First, why were over 9,000 letters from prisoners, their families, and other concerned groups used to help SB42 through the legislative process, and now that the Boatwright Bill [AB476] proposes to completely rewrite SB42 . . . no one is asking for our input or feelings."[41] The letter pointed to a wider trend where prisoner voices had become less legitimate and less audible as policy recommendations became more punitive.

The same writer spoke to the personal torment and disillusionment that resulted from extending the tentative release dates issued after SB42's passage. The prisoner requested that the governor and Representative Boatwright "tell my wife and children that I have to serve these added years of imprisonment because of the coming gubernatorial race and that it's nothing personal toward me. I can't explain it, all they know is that

[39] Nejedly to Virginia R., June 20, 1977, Senate Select Committee on Penal Institutions, Bill Files: 476, LP218:232, CSA.

[40] Willie Holder to Senator Howard Way, March 3, 1977, Senate Select Committee on Penal Institutions, Bill Files: 476, LP218:232, CSA.

[41] Samuel M. to Assemblyman Charles [sic] Maddy, April 5, 1977, Assembly Criminal Justice Committee, Bill Files: AB476, LP319:83, CSA.

I received a 'tentative date' and that Daddy is coming home."[42] Prisoners' letters attempted to impress upon legislators the impact of suddenly revising release dates, especially for their families and friends on the outside. Another man wrote to Representative Maddy:

> Do you have any idea how much SB42 meant to people like myself? Or how we have counted the days since last August 31st, waiting for the time to creep by until the first of July this year and a chance to be free again? . . . Can you imagine the resentment this kind of disappointment will cause among the men in prison expecting to go home this summer? . . . We are people too, with the same feelings as everyone else, and we can differentiate between justice and injustice. I've never gotten mad about any of the years I've spent in prison yet, because I knew what I was doing when I broke the law, so I could not rightly complain about paying for my actions.[43]

In this letter, the prisoner claimed that he believed himself to be in a reciprocal relationship with the state, where both sides had rights and responsibilities. He accepted the state's logic that a prison term was punishment for breaching this covenant but was dismayed when lawmakers violated this social contract by readily exchanging years of prisoners' lives for political gain. A public letter sent by more than five hundred prisoners at the California Medical Facility denounced AB476 as cynical maneuvering. It was all the more objectionable because it betrayed prisoners' nascent faith in the system:

> California prisoners have waited many years for an alternate system that would remove the inhumane and debilitating cloud of indeterminacy from our lives. Time and time again we of the convicted classes and our families have been used and manipulated in this political and economic game of chess in which human beings are considered expendable by those forces in control of this society. After years of struggle, bloody riots, demonstrations, and the death of many of us, we finally ceded to those who asked us to stop using violence and to learn to work within the system. From that point many compromises were made in order that SB42 could become a reality. . . . There are many reasons why the prisons of this state and this country remain full, but you know and we know that prisons are not full because of any soft or "PERMISSIVE" laws. We also know that the public will not be any better protected by longer prison sentences nor will punishment ever act as a deterrent to crime or unwanted social behavior.[44]

[42] Ibid.

[43] Howard Jay B. to Ken Maddy, chair of Assembly Criminal Justice Committee, April 1, 1977, Assembly Criminal Justice Committee, Bill Files: AB476, LP319:83, CSA.

[44] Form letter from prisoners at California Medical Facility to State Public Defenders Office, April 6, 1977, Assembly Criminal Justice Committee, Bill Files: AB476, LP319:83, CSA.

The letter charged that disingenuous politicking dashed prisoners' incipient trust in the political process and expelled them from dialogue just as they had become audible in the public sphere on matters that concerned their own custody.

They objected to the wanton disregard of their time, interests, and loved ones. To counter the persistent rhetorical erasure of their ties to society, many letter writers highlighted their connections to their communities, especially to family. They repeatedly asserted their own humanity and notions of justice, both of which they felt were compromised by law-and-order politics. One man explained:

> People tend to talk about years out of a person's life as if it were nothing, every day in prison is hard . . . and when you talk about 8, 10, and 12 years it's an eternity of misery. I've neither killed nor hurt anyone yet to be told that 13 years isn't a full pound of flesh, and that I have to give 3 or 4 more years to support a politician's platform and further his political career, is neither fair nor just and only breeds [negativity] and resentment.[45]

Frustration extended beyond disappointment with the policy changes proposed in AB476. Writers resented that their opinions and fates were so flagrantly, and deliberately, disregarded. They were alarmed by political elites' rhetoric that renounced state accountability to prisoners and implied further subordination within the polity.

Many letters warned of the consequences of betraying prisoners' trust and already strained faith in the justice of the legal system. Forty men imprisoned in Chino sent an open letter to Senator Nejedly, which opposed the proposed postponement of implementing SB42. They explained: "At Governor Brown's words, we were told SB42 would come into effect on July 1, 1977. We told our families. Plans were made. Now we might have to tell them, all the hopes were for nothing. . . . Some people ask why there is no faith in the system. Need we say more to understand?"[46] One prisoner warned that "the added years of punishment after we have received 'tentative' release dates under the provisions of a bill that was legally passed and signed into law—will, no doubt, cause an uproar and an injustice that will be remembered for years to come."[47] If politicians would not be motivated by compassion to reconsider the punitive policy, this writer suggested that they might do so in the interest of maintaining peace within institutions.

[45] Kenneth C., prisoner, to Assemblyman Maddy, [March 22, 1977], Assembly Criminal Justice Committee, AB476, LP319:83, CSA.

[46] Letter signed by forty Chino inmates to Nejedly, January 28, 1977, Senate Select Committee on Penal Institutions, Bill Files: AB476, LP218:237, CSA.

[47] Edward A. to Members of the Criminal Justice Committee, [March 21, 1977], Assembly Criminal Justice Committee, Bill Files: AB476, LP319:84, CSA.

In an effort to reason with policymakers, some prisoners painstakingly explained the realities of how policies operated in their daily lives. In response to the provisions in AB476 that extended the period of parole supervision, one man wrote at length about how parole actually functioned to prevent independence and reintegration into society as a law-abiding citizen:

> A lot of people will advise you that a longer parole term is necessary to control and guide the men released from prison. This is the opposite of the truth. The parole system does not exist to help the parolee remain out of prison. Its actual function, regardless of what anyone may say to the contrary is to perpetuate a high rate of recidivism and keep the prisons filled. . . . I could go straight and work, and get along fine, even on escape or when I was a bailbond fugitive. But a parole is such a handicap that I could not make it. They always insisted that I had to tell my employer about my past. The only jobs I could get was when I lied, or did not reveal my past, and I was fired when my parole officer told my employer the truth. On each parole, I was unemployed for months, until I gave up and took off. Then I started robbing again.[48]

Prisoners were therefore acutely aware of the political pressures motivating revisions to SB42. If lawmakers were going to ignore prisoners' perspectives, prisoners argued that politicians should at least consult the research on deterrence and recidivism. Their letters expressed indignation at the chasm between specialists' knowledge and the policy recommendations that grew out of the legislators' inflammatory rhetoric. One wrote, "We all know that AB476 is politically motivated, it is not based on any recommendations from learned bodies or national commissions, nor have the proposed amendments resulted from study, analysis, of public hearings."[49] Opponents of AB476 repeatedly decried the pretense of claiming that harsher punishment improved public safety. A prisoners' rights activist echoed prisoners' accusations: "The real reason why you legislators want to change SB42 is because of the scare tactics who have hit more newspapers. You do not hear organizations and people like myself who know—as you do—that long-term punishment is not and never has been a deterrent."[50]

Despite this fervent opposition, AB476 easily passed both chambers of the legislature. With little debate, the Senate approved the law by a vote

[48] Howard Jay B. to Ken Maddy.

[49] Edward A. to Members of the Criminal Justice Committee.

[50] Statement by Florence Kelly, n.d., Assembly Criminal Justice Committee, Bill Files: AB476, LP319:83. Kelly included with her statement a sample letter from prisoners opposing AB476. She said that five hundred men held at California Medical Facility at Vacaville signed a letter opposing AB476 and submitted it to Public Defenders Office.

of 27–6. In the Assembly, 59 approved passage and only one opposed the measure.[51] Governor Brown signed AB476 into law as emergency legislation on June 29, 1977, just two days before SB42 went into effect. This bill, however, did little to alleviate the political pressures on the Brown administration, which was now attacked from the right for failing to increase penalties sufficiently and from the left for succumbing to pressure from law enforcement. Again framing the debate in gendered terms of strength and weakness, Chief Davis attacked AB476 as a "sell-out," rejecting the claim that Boatwright's law "toughened" SB42 as "absolute malarkey."[52]

Prisoners resisted the new policy in every forum they could. In addition to writing lawmakers and coordinating advocacy with groups such as the Prisoners Union, they organized fund-raising drives within various California prisons in order to hire lawyers to challenge AB476 in the courts. For example, one committee organized more than sixty men to solicit donations on their respective floors at California Men's Colony, raising more than $3,000 to challenge the constitutionality of AB476.[53] Prisoners found the courts no more sympathetic to their pleas than the legislative branch, and AB476 went into effect without significant hindrances. The policy effectively prevented the feared exodus of criminals and kept release rates low.[54]

Confronted with these changes and the increasing calls for "law and order" in mainstream politics, some prisoners began to reevaluate or nuance the fervent rejection of the rehabilitative ideal. One in-depth commentary ran in the institutional paper of California Men's Colony and warrants being quoted at length. The article began by revisiting why rehabilitation had fallen from favor so suddenly:

> Across the country, the death knell is being sounded for rehabilitation programs in our prisons. Conservatives, who have always opposed the concept of rehabilitation, are watching in silent satisfaction as liberals and academ-

[51] "Both Houses Okay Longer Prison Terms," *Communicator* 23, no. 25 (July 1, 1977), California Men's Colony, F3717:1844, CSA.

[52] Richard Bergholz, "Brown Goes Unchallenged, Davis Charges," *Los Angeles Times*, May 3, 1977, E1.

[53] Prisoners raised over $3,000 in two separate fund-raising drives. Although organizers expressed disappointment that they did not raise more money, they claimed it was the most collected at any prison. "Fund Drive Nets $1,645 for Legal Defense 'Kitty,'" *Communicator* 24, no. 17 (May 12, 1978); "Legal Fund Committee Thanks Everyone for Their Help," *Communicator* 24, no. 19 (May 26, 1978); "News from Attorneys Is Bad But Not Hopeless," *Communicator* 24, no. 21 (June 9, 1978), all in California Men's Colony, F3717:1845, CSA.

[54] Otto Kreisher, "No Mass Exit of Felons Due from State Prisons," *San Diego Union*, July 1, 1977, Corrections Administration News Digests: 1977, F3717:1639, CSA.

ics rush to recant their faith in the ability of psychiatrists and psychologists to alleviate prisoners' antisocial tendencies. Once derided as barbaric and ineffectual, punishment is making a strong comeback as the radical-chic answer to the problem of crime in America. . . . Meanwhile, prisoner-rights groups complain that existing rehabilitation programs are, more often than not, forced on them. Such programs, they also charge, have turned prisons into an Orwellian nightmare where inmates, denied a firm date for getting out, are reduced to playing endless games to prove that they have achieved "insight" into the psychic causes of their crimes.

After acknowledging why rehabilitation lost support, the author warned of the dangers of discrediting therapeutic rationales for incarceration:

True, the time is long overdue to limit this power of psychiatrists and psychologists in deciding, almost single handedly, who goes to prison and how long they stay there. These "experts" should also be deterred from forcing their wares on a—quite literally—captive audience. . . . However, it should be clearly understood that treatment has always been the exception rather than the rule. Most of the time "rehabilitation" has just been a convenient excuse for placing enormous discretion in the hands of prison officials. . . . Yet the hasty retreat from the excesses and overpromises of the "rehabilitative ideal" poses a serious danger not only for prisoners after their release but also for the larger society. The danger is that legislators at both federal and state levels will seek to cut expenditures and balance budgets by seizing on the current climate of pessimism about rehabilitation to justify eliminating even the woefully inadequate amount of treatment now being provided.[55]

These warnings proved prophetic. While prisoners no doubt appreciated liberation from the arbitrary power of parole boards, they faced a climate that was increasingly hostile to providing them basic educational, recreational, and social services. By 1978, the Prisoners Union also registered their disappointment with the effects of SB42 in an *Outlaw* article:

We thought that when we exposed rehabilitation as a punitive, arbitrary system legislatures would adopt a rational, uniform sentencing system. . . . They have been drumming up fear of crime in the streets for several years and the result is an almost insane rage against a narrow slice of the whole, very large mass of criminal acts that go on in our society. This was accompanied by a demand for extreme punishment for the felons convicted of crimes which are presently receiving all the attention. What we ended up with here in California, and this seems to be the case in many other

[55] "Prisons: A Retreat from Rehabilitation," *Communicator* 23, no. 22 (June 10, 1977), California Men's Colony F3717:1844, CSA.

states, is the worst of both systems, the old rehabilitative system and the new "justice" (or better, punishment) system. We still have all the discretion needed to discriminate between the weak and the powerful and now more punishment is heaped on those selected. Now they call it punishment and feel righteous about it.[56]

According to this article, critics' success in revealing the arbitrariness and hypocrisy of corrections did not translate into the ability to control what replaced it. Proponents of tough policy seized the initiative and used penal policy to aggrandize the authority of law enforcement and denigrate marginalized citizens constructed as inherently and irredeemably criminal.

AB476 did little to mollify "law-and-order" advocates. It was an abortive attempt to stave off even more punitive policy and a harbinger of things to come. And these trends were not confined to the legislature. As law enforcement interests gathered strength in Sacramento, corrections employees struggled to assert more total control of prisons by wresting away authority from prisoners and upper-level bureaucratic management. Events at the rural prison in Susanville in 1977 sent a powerful message throughout California's prison system. The confrontations there illustrated the ongoing struggles to recalibrate the balance of power within prisons in the wake of fervent prisoner organizing. Previously a lower-security conservation camp, Susanville became a medium-security prison after local citizens fiercely opposed CDC plans to close the institution in 1973. The atmosphere at the prison was particularly tense, especially as the overwhelmingly black and Latino prisoners clashed with the predominantly white workforce. On February 9, 1977, prisoners organized a peaceful work stoppage to protest prison conditions and policy. Guards reacted violently, breaking the strike with riot sticks and almost 120 rounds of rifle ammunition. The attack injured ten prisoners, three from gunfire. Scandal erupted when the Department of Corrections' investigation into the incident blamed the confrontation on prison staff racism, terrible conditions, and failure to implement affirmative action programs.

"Law-and-order" advocates and corrections employees were horrified by this public rebuke, especially the CDC's move to discipline twelve guards involved in the clash.[57] Enraged officers retaliated by organizing their own work action, and more than 160 guards staged a

---

[56] *Outlaw* (Winter 1978), quoted in Irwin, *Prisons in Turmoil*, 227.
[57] Sigrid Bathen, "Susanville: Crisis Blamed on Racism, Poor Detention Facilities," *Sacramento Bee*, April 17, 1977, Corrections Administration News Digests: 1977, F3717:1639, CSA; Janssen, "When the 'Jungle' Met the Forest," 724–25.

sickout to protest the investigation specifically and affirmative action programs and expanded prisoner rights more generally.[58] In public comments, the CCOA charged that CDC administrators were in "cahoots" with the Prisoners Union and had "shifted the staff's authority to the inmates."[59] By presenting the guards' union as a check on the excesses of prisoners and CDC management, the CCOA enhanced its authority within institutions and its influence on public debates over the new direction in penal practice. The fact that guards were struggling to assert control over prisons was no secret. Assistant Director of Corrections Phil Guthrie explained to the *Sacramento Bee*, "There's a feeling, although sometimes it's vague, that changes in society and how prisons are run have caused a loss of control and reduced their [guards'] authority."[60] As the new determinate sentencing policy diminished therapists' and parole boards' authority, guards struggled for dominance in the new balance of power emerging within prisons. Through aggressive organizing and rhetorically positioning themselves as protecting "the public's" interest in safety and order, law enforcement (and the CCOA in particular) became increasingly influential in criminal justice debates.[61]

Prisoners' efforts to remain viable civic participants suffered other blows as the decade wound to a close. For years courts had heard arguments about prisoners' right to unionize, and in 1977 the U.S. Supreme Court overturned two lower-level decisions issued in North Carolina, ruling that prisoners had no guaranteed right to form a union. In their dissent, Justices Marshall and Brennan called the court's move "a giant step backwards" to "a time not so very long ago when prisoners were regarded as slaves of the state."[62] In choosing this language, the justices, perhaps unwittingly, echoed prisoners' and activists' analyses that asserted a continuum between racial slavery and a legal system that targeted people of color for imprisonment.[63] This court decision dashed the already waning hopes for prisoners' collective representation and an organized, independent voice within prisons. On a symbolic level, it was another public declaration of prisoners' subordinated status without the rights and protections of other citizens.

[58] "Prison Inmates say 'Guards Freaked Out,'" *Sacramento Bee*, March 27, 1977, Corrections Administration News Digests: 1977, F3717:1639, CSA.

[59] Bathen, "Susanville."

[60] Ibid.

[61] Janssen, "When the 'Jungle' Met the Forest," 725.

[62] "Convicts Denied Right to Unionize," *Sacramento Union*, June 24, 1977, Corrections Administration News Digests: 1977, F3717:1639, CSA.

[63] For a detailed discussion of the theoretical and political importance of African American prisoners understanding themselves as slaves, see Berger, *Captive Nation*.

As law enforcement made new gains in courts and within prisons, they also continued to push for criminal sentencing reforms at the California legislature. Only months after SB42 and AB476 went into effect, lawmakers moved again to increase prison terms. State Senator Robert Presley, another Democratic politician with a law enforcement background, led the charge. He had campaigned as the "Undersheriff of Riverside County" and credited his electoral victories—particularly the ability to attract Republican support within his swing district—to his stance on crime issues and his professional background.[64] Disturbed by the allegedly short sentences proscribed by the new fixed sentencing scheme, Senator Presley introduced legislation to extend the terms. His bill, Senate Bill 709 (SB709), added two to four years to middle and upper terms for violent crimes and some property crimes. For example, the indeterminate sentence for a convicted rapist had been three years to life in prison. Under SB42, rape was punished by a lower (or mitigated) term of three years, a middle term of four years, and an aggravated sentence of five years. SB709 increased the terms for rape to three years, six years, and eight years, respectively. The sentence for assault with the intent to kill, which had been two, three, or four years, depending on severity, was increased to three, five, or seven years by SB709.[65] A companion bill, Senate Bill 1057, extended the average length of parole supervision from eighteen months to three years. For those serving indeterminate life sentences who were to be released at the discretion of the new Community Release Board, SB1057 increased parole from three to five years.

Law enforcement interests and their political allies used the proposed fixed sentencing laws as a vehicle to assert a muscular vision of state power. Prosecutors and police groups, principally the District Attorney's Association, justified SB709 by presenting the punishments in SB42 as weak. In public pronouncements and media coverage, SB709 was characterized as an attempt to "strengthen," "toughen," or "stiffen" criminal penalties. Editorialists spoke of SB709 as "putting teeth" in determinate sentencing and described it as a "Bill with Backbone."[66] Officers also couched their calls for expanded parole supervision in gendered terms. A letter to Senator Presley from a unit supervisor of the Parole and Com-

[64] "Oral History Interview with Robert Presley" (2001, 2002, 2003), conducted by Patrick Ettinger and Julie Recher, OH 2003–4, p. 23, State Government Oral History Program, CSA.

[65] Lipson and Peterson, *California Justice under Determinate Sentencing*, 5. See also "Vote Nears on Extension of Prison Terms," *Los Angeles Times*, April 24, 1978, B3.

[66] "Stiffer Sentences—A Crucial Test Today," *Sacramento Union*, March 13, 1978; Cam Benty, "Move to Stiffen Criminal Penalties," *Orange City News*, February 10, 1978; "SB709 Attacks Violent Offenders," *Victorville Daily Press*, February 7, 1978. For all articles, see Senator Robert Presley Papers, Bill Files: SB709-B, LP220:59, CSA.

munity Services Division explained that "it appears to us that some legislators and outside groups wish to emasculate and eventually eliminate paroles, for whatever their reason." SB1057 was needed to "toughen" or "strengthen" parole workers and—the logic followed—in turn enhance public safety. The key to protecting the public was fortifying the power of law enforcement agencies.

While this reasoning became increasingly naturalized, some challenged the notion that extending parole or prison time enhanced public safety. In the debate surrounding SB709 and SB1057, opponents disputed whether the bills would provide enough social benefit to justify an additional $370 million in corrections spending between 1981 and 1986 alone. Governor Brown "raised questions about cost" but chose not to oppose the law in an election year.[67] Most politicians joined him in endorsing the revisions, and SB709 passed the Senate 27–2. The only opposing votes were Senator Nejedly, who originally shepherded SB42 to passage, and Alan Sieroty, who had opposed determinate sentencing from the beginning, fearing lawmakers' inclination to perpetually increase sentences.[68]

Legislators were right to worry about the political costs of opposing these "tough-on-crime" bills. When SB709 moved to the Assembly, H. L. Bill Richardson's advocacy organization, the Law and Order Campaign Committee, coordinated a media and grassroots campaign with the District Attorney's Association and other law enforcement groups. It unleashed intense pressure, especially on the members of the Criminal Justice Committee, who had historically thwarted efforts to increase punishments. In one mailing, the Law and Order Campaign Committee alerted 10,520 constituents of Criminal Justice Committee members that their representatives had not yet committed to supporting SB709.[69] After clearing the Criminal Justice Committee, the Assembly easily passed SB709 and SB1057. On September 5, 1978, Governor Brown signed these bills and three other anti-crime measures into law. He held a press conference at the Los Angeles Sheriff's office, again surrounded by law enforcement personnel.[70]

[67]Bob Egelko, "Vote Near on Extension of Prison Terms," *Los Angeles Times*, April 24, 1978, B3. Brown may have supported an alternate, more moderate bill proposed by Senator Nejedly, but it had little traction in the legislature.

[68]Robert Kroll, "Bill to Double Crime Penalties Draws Support in Sacramento," *Berkeley Gazette*, February 24, 1978, Senator Robert Presley Papers, Bill Files: SB709-B, LP220:59, CSA.

[69]Thomas Condit, Legal Affairs Director, CA District Attorney's Association, to Joseph Spangler, Law and Order Campaign Committee, March 21, 1978, Senator Robert Presley Papers, Bill Files: SB709-B, LP220:59, CSA. See also "SB709 Attacks Violent Offenders."

[70]"Brown, Younger Focus on Crime," *Los Angeles Times*, September 6, 1978, 3.

The Walls Are Getting Higher

Senator Presley believed his law "fixed" the major problems in California's new sentencing system and that legislators would resist "emotionalism" and not pursue further, more punitive changes.[71] However, as had happened after the passage of AB476, the clamor for harsher laws did not end. In the following decades, statutes that increased punishment, enhanced "victims' rights," or otherwise "toughened" policy became staples of California's politics. And the reward for championing such legislation was increasingly apparent. In 1978, H. L. Richardson introduced Senate Bill 1840, a law that in effect doubled the penalty for rape, making it greater than punishment for first-degree murder in some cases. When the Assembly Criminal Justice Committee blocked the legislation because it believed it created a warped, disproportionate penalty structure, senators used a rarely successful parliamentary maneuver that forced the entire Assembly to vote on whether to bypass the committee and bring the bill directly to the floor. Although the effort to bypass the Criminal Justice Committee failed by five votes, Richardson's Law and Order Campaign Committee used legislators' opposition on the procedural question to attack them as "soft on crime" and "soft on rape" in the upcoming election campaigns. Voters sent almost a dozen new Republican legislators to the Assembly who had made "tough" stands on crime central to their campaigns. Many of them were supported by funds from Richardson's campaign.[72] Legislators attributed some of their colleagues' subsequent defeat in the 1978 elections to these attacks and, not surprisingly, were even more reluctant to oppose the next round of anti-crime legislation.

Seizing the momentum, Senator Richardson repeated the same play in 1979 and introduced essentially the same rape bill, Senate Bill 13. When the Criminal Justice Committee again obstructed the legislation, opponents seemed on the verge of assembling a bipartisan coalition with enough votes to pry the law from committee and move it before the full body. Democrats, fearful of handing "law-and-order" proponents another vote to hammer them with in the 1980 elections, relented and the Criminal Justice Committee negotiated another hearing for Senate Bill 13. Soon afterward, the law passed the legislature. It mandated severe enhancements for repeat violent sex offenders and eliminated caps on consecutive sentences. In practical terms, it roughly doubled the sentences for serial rape, making California's penalties the most severe

[71]Lipson and Peterson, *California Justice under Determinate Sentencing*, 11.

[72]Ibid., 13; Martin Smith, "The Democratic Frankenstein," *Sacramento Bee*, October 23, 1979, Corrections Administration News Digests: 1979, F3717:16411, CSA.

in the country.[73] And with few mechanisms for arresting this trend, these were only the opening gamut. In the 1981 legislative session, crime was the principal issue. Lawmakers on both sides of the aisle introduced bills that in various ways enhanced the punishment for different crimes. Nearly one-third of the legislation introduced at one time during the session concerned crime.[74] Crime was also a defining issue in the gubernatorial contest in 1982, where conservative "law-and-order" candidate George Deukmejian narrowly defeated Los Angeles mayor Tom Bradley.

During this period, such political tactics were not just directed against recalcitrant legislators. Richardson also aimed his organization's political energy toward disciplining members of the judiciary. When California Supreme Court Justice Rose Bird authored a decision that undermined the 1975 "Use a Gun, Go to Prison" law, the Law and Order Campaign Committee invested almost a quarter of a million dollars into an effort to defeat her. Confronting an unprecedented public attack in what were usually routine reconfirmations, Bird barely retained her seat in the 1978 election.[75] Despite her victory, Richardson considered the campaign a success, explaining that it would serve as a warning to judges and the politicians who nominate them for the future. "It will make a sizable difference on the next selection for the court made by Gov. Brown when he knows full well that the potential is there for the public to not confirm an appointee," he explained to reporters.[76] Although Richardson's attempt to initiate a campaign to recall Bird in 1982 failed, the pressure on her (and, by implication, other judges who seemed "soft on crime") persisted and she was finally defeated in 1986 following a campaign that highlighted her consistent rulings against the death penalty. She was the first state-level chief justice in the country to lose her seat since the institution of popular reconfirmation votes for judges earlier in the century.[77]

The ascendancy of these punitive politics joined with mandatory sentencing, the state's growing population, the War on Drugs, and longer parole sentences and growing parole violations to balloon

[73] Lipson and Peterson, *California Justice under Determinate Sentencing*, 13; Griset, *Determinate Sentencing*, 56–57; "GOP Seeks to Revive Tough Antirape Bill," *Los Angeles Times*, August 22, 1979, B22; Jerry Gillam, "Bill on Repeat Sex Offenders Is Signed," *Los Angeles Times*, September 25, 1979, B3.

[74] Campbell, "The Emergence of Penal Extremism in California," 395.

[75] William Endicott, "Rose Bird Sees Positive Results: Says Voters Don't Want Decisions Based on Threats," *Los Angeles Times*, November 9, 1978, B3.

[76] Ibid., B3, 22. Richardson quoted on 22.

[77] Claudia Luther, "Effort to Recall Bird Dropped by Richardson: BIRD: Recall Effort Abandoned," *Los Angeles Times*, July 9, 1982, B1; "Voters Oust Rose Bird from California Court: Chief Justice Concedes after Polls Close," *Washington Post*, November 5, 1986, A35.

California's prison population.[78] Though the growth started before the passage of SB42, with prison commitment rates climbing steadily from 1972 onward, the rate of increase accelerated considerably after sentencing reform.[79] And although there is some scholarly debate over what caused the explosion in incarceration, contemporary observers drew a direct correlation between punitive new laws and increasingly crowded prisons. With mandated sentences, authorities lost the ability—employed successfully by Ronald Reagan when he was governor—to use parole releases to alleviate population pressure within institutions.

As the imperative to be tough solidified, criminal justice professionals generally became more punitive.[80] Those convicted were sentenced to prison and jail more frequently.[81] Some judges felt more willing to hand down prison time, knowing that the offender faced a set punishment and would not be held indefinitely.[82] Other judges and prosecutors were no doubt swayed by the increased scrutiny of their decisions and reports of an increasingly punitive mood. Between 1976 and 1983, the number of felons held in California prisons doubled from 18,113 to 38,025.[83] California's twelve prisons quickly filled to capacity, raising the politically dicey issue of whether to fund new prison construction or institute reforms to reduce the population that left lawmakers open to "soft-on-crime" attacks. In January 1979, institutions housed 20,000 prisoners in facilities designed to accommodate 19,000.[84] When the population reached 24,000 by 1981, 10 percent of the prisoners shared cells built to house one person.[85] By 1983, the system was at 140 percent of its designed capacity.[86] Crowding made conditions for everyone more tense and bitter, and exacerbated violence. Officials considered plans to house prisoners in tent cities.

[78] Page, *Toughest Beat*, 47.

[79] Lipson and Peterson, *California Justice under Determinate Sentencing*, 20–24.

[80] Ibid., 25.

[81] Ibid., 20.

[82] Dorothy Townsend, "Judges Give More Prison Sentences," *Los Angeles Times*, January 12, 1979, C2.

[83] California Department of Corrections, "Historical Trends: Institutions and Parole Populations, 1976–1996" (Sacramento: CDC Data Analysis Unit, 1996), 1a.

[84] Martin Smith, "Facing Up to Prison Costs," *Sacramento Bee*, February 9, 1979, Corrections Administration News Digests: 1979, F3717:1641, CSA.

[85] Claudia Luther, "State's Criminals Serving Tougher Sentences," *Los Angeles Times*, April 6, 1981, 23.

[86] Barry Krisberg, "California's Overflowing Prisons: Must We Wait for an Explosion?" *Los Angeles Times*, June 19, 1983, D3.

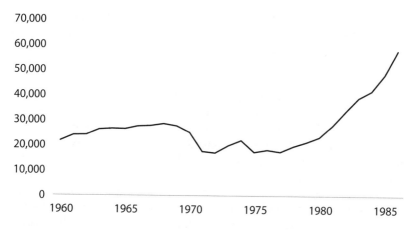

Figure 6.1. California prison population, 1960–85. (*Source*: U.S. Department of Justice, Bureau of Justice Statistics, *Historical Statistics on Prisoners in State and Federal Institutions, Yearend 1926–86* [Washington, D.C.: U.S. Department of Justice, 1988])

Because diverting precious state resources to prison construction was less popular than demanding "stiff" sentences, it was here where some state politicians made another stand against punitive trends. For a period in the late 1970s, the issue of prison costs reopened debates about punitive mandatory sentencing. When overcrowding prompted demands for construction funds, Assembly members blocked the proposals, arguing that other approaches would be a more productive use of resources. In article after article, journalists deliberated whether the public's taste for longer prison terms would translate into a willingness to fund building new structures and sustain a massive carceral apparatus. One editorial predicted that the price tag of punitive policy would inspire new reforms: "Despite the current tough mood of citizens toward criminals, it may be tempered somewhat when the high cost of this attitude really sets in. These incarceration costs may help renew interest in devising effective rehabilitative programs."[87] The issue was often presented as a duel between the public's two most pressing concerns: crime and taxes. As one *Los Angeles Times* article began: "As much as Californians want government spending held down, they also want criminals locked up."[88]

[87]"Heavy Burden of New Prisons," *The Enterprise*, April 11, 1979, Corrections Administration News Digests: 1979, F3717:1641, CSA.
[88]Charles Maher, "Building of Prisons to Be Debate Issue," *Los Angeles Times*, January 19, 1979, B3.

When members of the Assembly concerned about costs blocked major prison construction funding, the law enforcement community took the issue directly to the voters through ballot initiatives. Senator Presley, the conservative Democrat who had carried SB709 and many of the stymied prison construction bills, joined with Republican governor Deukmejian to spearhead two propositions authorizing $495 million in bonds for prison construction and $280 million for jails.[89] Presley remembered that the bond initiatives passed easily when put directly to the people, especially in Southern California: "It seemed to be a self-starter. We didn't put much of a campaign to get them passed. I think in the public, a lot more than in the Legislature, there seemed to be a law-and-order sentiment out there."[90] Californians approved bonds for prison construction every few years throughout the 1980s, authorizing over $2.5 billion to build a vast new carceral landscape.[91] The state, which had operated twelve prisons between 1965 and 1984, would open twenty-one new ones over the following quarter century.[92] Between 1983 and 1989, the felon population more than doubled again to 84,388.[93] By 2010, California's thirty-three prisons housed 165,000 people, more than double the 84,000 prisoners the institutions were designed to hold.[94]

Punitive shifts in criminal policy were frequently characterized as the inevitable response to the populace's growing concern about crime and the state's inability to manage it. Newspaper reports often took for granted that the public demand for security resulted in longer prison terms. A typical story from the *San Diego Evening Tribune* read: "The mood of the California public is reflected in recent actions by the legislature mandating stiffer penalties for crimes involving a gun and getting specific sentences for certain violent crimes."[95] Other articles reiterated the assumption that bottom-up pressure drove legislators' actions: "Over the last few years, in response to the public outcry over rising

[89] Campbell, "The Emergence of Penal Extremism in California," 398.

[90] "Oral History Interview with Robert Presley," 54. The interviewer's questions suggest that there were some educational campaigns to encourage passage of the prison bonds.

[91] Ibid., 53–55, 116–18; Campbell, "The Emergence of Penal Extremism in California," 398; Gilmore, *Golden Gulag*.

[92] Page, *Toughest Beat*, 48.

[93] California Department of Corrections, "Historical Trends: Institutions and Parole Populations, 1976–1996," 1a. I list only "felons" in CDC custody and am excluding other categories within the adult correctional institution population, such as "civil narcotics addicts" and "Youth Authority wards."

[94] Randal Archibald, "California, in Financial Crisis, Opens Prison Doors," *New York Times*, March 23, 2010; editorial, "California's Crowded Prisons," *New York Times*, February 13, 2009.

[95] "Stiff Laws Demand Prison Expansion," *San Diego Evening Tribune*, August 23, 1979, Corrections Administration News Digests: 1979, F3717:1641, CSA.

crime, the Legislature has enacted measures which set fixed prison terms, increased the length of sentences and limited judges' discretion in granting probation."[96]

Legislators also pointed to public pressure to explain their support for increasingly draconian punishments. Many felt trapped by insurmountable pressure from the public not only to address rising crime rates but to do so in a "tough" and punitive manner. Howard Way, a Republican who had cosponsored SB42 with Senator Nejedly, explained his dismay when colleagues voted for extreme anti-crime bills that he knew they found objectionable:

> No one wants anybody to be soft on crime. That's the kiss of death. That's why so many of my liberal colleagues, when I approach them on why they were casting some of those votes for harsh penalties, they would reply, "Just not to be labeled soft on crime." And they can just take one vote, you know, on one obscure bill, and say, "Look, he's soft on crime."[97]

In the same oral history interview, Way reiterated how this fear, coupled with legislators' newly acquired sentencing authority, affected the fate of SB42:

> Almost immediately the legislature began tampering with it [SB42]. Assembly Bill 476 increased terms and mandated sentences for certain crimes. And they continued to do that every year, which was very distressing to those of us who had pushed for determinate sentencing. And I think it would be fair to say that neither Senator Nejedly nor I anticipated that this would happen. As long as sentences and the punishment of crime is left in the hands of publicly elected officials, I think you're going to see this. I would go over and talk to my liberal former colleagues—Senator Petris, for example, would be one—"Why did you vote for this bill?" Well, there was just one simple answer: "I want to stay in office, and this is what my constituents want." And this is a very, very dangerous precedent. . . . What's happened here in California is that—and I have said this many times—we've just gone berserk in terms of punishment.[98]

With the state positioned as the guarantor of "public safety" and largely unaccountable for the welfare of those convicted of crime, there appeared to be no political posture liable of being branded *too tough*.

This punitive drive did not go uncontested. During the same period, there was ongoing and fervent organizing for a moratorium on prison construction. There were even efforts by erstwhile architects of the

---

[96]"Making Space for Prisoners," *Fresno Bee*, August 26, 1979, Corrections Administration News Digests: 1979, F3717:1641, CSA.

[97]Oral history of Howard Way, "Issues in Corrections," 49.

[98]Ibid., 31.

escalation in criminal sentencing to arrest the process. In 1983, Senator Presley introduced two bills to contain prison population growth; one was a short-term fix and the second attempted to wrest sentencing authority from the legislature. The first, Senate Bill 50 (SB50), aimed to relieve overcrowding by allowing the governor to identify nonviolent offenders for release 180 days before their original date. The second, Senate Bill 56 (SB56), would have created a commission to issue sentencing guidelines. The commission, modeled on one in Minnesota, would have been charged with rationalizing the structure of criminal penalties, which had become distorted through the myriad bills enacted since the passage of SB42. It would also, in theory, insulate criminal punishment decisions from direct intervention by the legislature. Of course, these laws were themselves subject to the same pressures. In an interview with the *Los Angeles Times*, Presley gave his legislation a 50 percent chance of passing. "The difficulty with it is political," he explained. "It is pure and simple. Legislators are afraid to vote for it."[99] Governor Deukmejian refused to sign either bill despite support from diverse groups such as the California Correctional Peace Officers Association (the revised name of the guards' union) and the ACLU. Claiming that the new determinate sentencing law was successfully reducing crime, the governor fiercely defended keeping legislators directly responsible for criminal sentencing policy.[100]

Commentators occasionally noted how attention to one explanation for disorder distracted from alternate theories. For example, when discussing the attacks on the judiciary in the late 1970s, an ACLU lobbyist explained, "It sounds great—you blame it [crime] on judges so people don't think law enforcement is responsible for not doing a good job."[101] The public could logically hold police and prosecutors responsible for rising crime rates instead of blaming liberal politicians, rehabilitative programs, and judges. Law enforcement was, after all, directly tasked with maintaining order and failed to apprehend or convict anyone for the majority of crimes reported. Yet political rhetoric, such as that aggressively deployed by the Law and Order Campaign Committee, was used in savvy, resonant ways that both accommodated and shaped the common sense of what was responsible for crime and what secured safety.

---

[99] John Hurst, "Change in Sentencing Laws Could Ease Prison Problem, PRISONS: Overcrowding Could Be Solved by Changing Laws," *Los Angeles Times*, December 27, 1983, B1, 3, 18. Presley quoted on page 18. Also quoted in Campbell, "The Emergence of Penal Extremism in California," 401.

[100] Campbell, "The Emergence of Penal Extremism in California," 401.

[101] Bob Egelko, "Group Opens Drive on Armed Criminals," *Los Angeles Times*, October 11, 1977, B3.

Two factors were integral to successfully positioning law enforcement and punitive policy as the commonsense solution to the era's perceived crisis in law and order. First was the ability of groups—usually associated with law enforcement—and legislators to connect themselves with muscular assertions of state power. These people projected a vision for government that was fresh, resolute, and unsullied by the increasingly fortified links between social disorder and liberalism. These visions were uniquely attractive at a moment when critics scrutinized traditional authority and expertise from every angle. Punitive policy's second key contribution was the symbolic and often technical denigration of the citizenship of highly marginalized, racialized groups. Debates about escalating criminal penalties were platforms from which people could resist the broader redistribution of rights, the demands to dismantle racist institutions, and the increased state accountability to marginalized groups. As opposed to balancing the diverse, conflicted interests in society, these laws portrayed the state's primary responsibility as serving and protecting taxpaying, law-abiding, "productive" citizens. The rhetoric and policy reaffirmed traditional notions of "the public" that rejected the recent fraught, incremental movement toward a more democratic multiracial society. The need for tough politics was dependent upon the perceived threat of black and Latino criminals, while the hyperincarceration of these populations continually fused race and criminality.

Staking out a "tough" position was a political and rhetorical maneuver that was most often associated with the Republican Party. Although in the final analysis these politics were most beneficial for the GOP, Republicans did not monopolize the issue, nor were they singularly responsible for moving it into the core of political culture. Although Republican George Deukmejian won the governorship in 1983, it was a Democratic governor and a Democratic-controlled legislature that oversaw California's stark punitive escalation until that point. In his analysis of what went wrong with determinate sentencing, Jan Marinissen of the AFSC argued that it was Democrats who undermined the promise of SB42: "The two people who did the greatest damage to the determinate sentence were Mr. Boatwright and Jerry Brown, of course. They were the two greatest perpetrators of screwing over what was initially a very good bill."[102] Efforts to head off conservatives by co-opting "law-and-order" politics—usually undertaken by more conservative Democrats associated with law enforcement—frequently divided the party. And while Democrats could rarely wrest the mantle of "toughness" away from Republicans, bipartisan participation in "law-and-order" politics

[102] Oral history of Jan Marinissen, "'To Let the Legislature Know,'" 32.

legitimized the core messages and assumptions about the appropriate responses to crime.

In fact, as opposed to seeing punitive politics as the fruit of Republican enterprise, many contemporary observers faulted Democrats for their own political vulnerability on "law-and-order" issues generally and determinate sentencing in particular. A columnist for the *Sacramento Bee* suggested Democrats had created the beast that now threatened them: "It has taken them a while to catch on, but Democratic lawmakers have awakened to the fact that, in helping to end the system of indeterminate prison sentences in California, they have created a Frankenstein monster which is threatening their political careers." The article continued by reminding readers that some had predicted this outcome, quoting Democratic Assembly member Alister McAlister's earlier warning that "I fear SB42 will return to haunt us."[103]

While many present Democrats as unwitting accomplices in penal expansion, these dynamics might better be interpreted as evidence of a broad consensus about the political and social disposability of racialized, criminalized groups for many in both parties. Lawmakers across the political spectrum were willing to sacrifice prisoners' interests for political gain or protection. Just as the worst excesses of McCarthyism depended on the broad social consensus about the dangers of communism, the most extreme "tough-on-crime" politics were predicated upon acceptance of the appropriateness of criminal targets and their subordinated status in the polity. In the end, the disagreements were usually not over the appropriateness of criminalization or punishment but over the appropriate degree of criminalization and punishment. While Democrats attempted to neutralize the political viability of these issues by adopting punitive postures, they rarely outflanked Republicans. It turned out there was virtually no upper limit on how far to escalate punishments. An Assembly staffer explained that "no matter how much we [Democrats] adapt, the Republicans can always take one more step to the right than we can. I expect them to try and to continue to make that an issue."[104]

The developing consensus favoring punitive penal strategies helped discredit any program or person that could be characterized as its opposite: "weak," "soft," or otherwise effete. Raymond Procunier, known for his blunt talk, explained that Republicans' monopoly of this tough politics allowed them political latitude unavailable to Democrats:

You've got a lot more freedom to be decent under the conservatives than you ever have under a liberal administration. Look what [Jerry] Brown did, appropriated all kinds of money, got tough on law and order, hollered "Kill

[103] Smith, "The Democratic Frankenstein."
[104] Ibid.

'em" and Old [Pat] Brown put some board members that should have never been on there, just to make it look like he was tough. Reagan did not have to look like he's tough, just like I don't, the way I talk and raise hell and bark and stuff. I don't ever have to do anything tough to make sure I'm tough.[105]

By painting liberal solutions as "soft," their opponents ensured that politicians advocating for therapeutic, systemic reforms to handle crime operated in uncomfortably cramped rhetorical space.

Prisoners were quite aware that lawmakers were using their lives to perform their tough resolve. After the disappointments following Boatwright's AB476, they were cynical about future political developments and the repeated escalation of punishments. One man sarcastically described this dynamic in a prison newspaper article about Senator Richardson's efforts to enhance rape penalties:

> With the legislative sessions coming to a close last week, our lawmakers held to their usual pattern of passing penal legislation that increases the terms of imprisonment for some crimes. This year they concentrated on rape penalties. Last year it was something about "use a gun, go to prison." Next year it will be: "Commit a crime, get the gas chamber."[106]

With the rise of increasingly punitive policy, space for prisoners in civil society and in public debates narrowed. Prisoners' civic participation, which was never widely celebrated, became increasingly unwelcome and controversial. And they clearly grasped the implications of these trends. One man depicted the situation in an article for the California Medical Facility's newspaper:

> You don't have to be a weatherman to know that things are getting hot for convicts. If you're semi-conscious, mildly literate and occasionally capable of adding two and two, then you know that, in a manner of speaking, the walls are getting higher, and the steel bars are getting closer together. Is seems like every time we turn around some new bill is being introduced, to give convicts more time for a given offense, or to expand the number of offenses for which a prison term is mandatory. Moves are being put on our visiting rights and our rights under the 1st, 6th, and 14th Amendments to the US Constitution. Lifers sentenced under the indeterminate Sentence Law are having their terms fixed under the Determinate Sentence

[105]Oral history of Raymond Procunier, "Administering Your Prisons: The Art of Corrections Management, California, 1967–1974," conducted in 1982 and 1983 by Gabrielle Morris, OH-R 2, p. 37, Ronald Reagan Gubernatorial Era Project, Regional Oral History Office, Bancroft Library at University of California–Berkeley, CSA.
[106]Ed Apodaca, "Senate Bill 13," *Communicator* 25, no. 39 (October 5, 1979), California Men's Colony, F3717:1846, CSA.

law, without fair compensation in the areas of good time and work cred-
its. . . . In terms of attitude towards prisoners, the people in the free world
are definitely regressing. Believe it.[107]

The only hope to counter these trends and be heard, the author argued,
was for prisoners to unite:

> We need a union to stand up for the continuously diminishing rights of
> convicts, so that there will be no return to the Dark Ages of penology.
> We need a union to act as a liaison between convicts, the public, and the
> powers that be. We need a union to promote a greater awareness of the
> problems of prisoners and how those problems relate to the free world. We
> need a union to identify the true causes of criminality, and when possible,
> to alleviate those causes. We need a union for access to the media, so that
> our position on matters that affect prisoners can be voiced.

The author went on to explain that these new dynamics foreclosed the
possibility that outside allies would make a prisoner's case:

> Who should we depend on for our survival? The police? Politicians? Profes-
> sors? No there is only ourselves. Ourselves and those precious few people
> in the free world who realize that there is a lot more to criminality than the
> commission of crimes; and who believe that no matter how badly some of
> us may stumble, the human spirit is always capable of redeeming itself.[108]

With fewer champions on the outside, prisoners saw their civic status further subordinated and their constricted avenues for intervening
in public dialogue further narrowed. The platforms for prisoners to be
heard, even by each other, shrank as criminal policy became more punitive. For example, the California Department of Corrections shut down
all prison-based newspapers in 1982, responding to prisoners' legal challenges to press censorship. Following pressure from the ACLU and allied
lawmakers, the papers were reopened under even stricter control, serving
essentially as administrators' organs.[109]

As these trends converged to further degrade convicts' status, law enforcement and "law-and-order" politicians expanded their power and prestige.
Their enhanced authority was predicated upon the perceived need to con-

---

[107] Joshua Nicholas Hill III, "Penguins, Prisoners, and Pinball Machines," *Vacavalley Star*
(July/August 1980), California Medical Facility, F3717:1841, CSA.
[108] Ibid.
[109] Cummins, *Rise and Fall of California's Radical Prison Movement*, 269.

trol and punish groups that were ungovernable through suasion and only responded to punishment and direct physical control. Instead of facilitating convicts' reintegration into society, the new policies charged state agents with guarding the boundary between criminals and law-abiding citizens. The rejection of prisoners' rights and belonging worked to secure the rights and security of normative, law-abiding citizens. In fact, the authority of law enforcement, their "law-and-order" political allies, and the reformulated legitimacy of the state itself were all predicated upon the repeated efforts to symbolically and physically exile prisoners from the political community. These rituals of punishment and degradation were incapable of actually expelling these people, extinguishing their civic agency, or severing the many ties to their communities. Nonetheless, the frantic, seemingly insatiable compulsion to purge, punish, and strip rights exerted unparalleled pressure on those marked as criminal.

The California legislature passed over one thousand crime-related bills between 1984 and 1991. Most enhanced punishments through extending sentences or changing the classification of certain offenses from misdemeanors to felonies.[110] While debates rage over the effect of increasingly punitive prosecution and sentencing on violent crime rates, experts agree that a majority of the dramatic decline in crime since the 1990s cannot be attributed to the prison boom. In fact, mass incarceration probably at a certain point exacerbated both state and nonstate violence, both inside and outside of prisons.[111] Nonetheless, the spectacle of "getting tough" was not senseless or futile. It enhanced its proponents' standing both within carceral institutions and in the political sphere. It propelled to dominance a tough strategy of governance that, while hardly stable and uncontested, helped resolve many political questions of the time—questions that prisoners had helped thrust into the public arena but were prevented from helping to answer.

---

[110]Page, *Toughest Beat*, 47.

[111]On causes of the crime decline, see Bruce Western, *Punishment and Inequality in America* (New York: Russell Sage, 2006); Franklin E. Zimring, *The Great American Crime Decline* (Oxford: Oxford University Press, 2007); Richard Rosenfeld, "The Case of the Unsolved Crime Decline," *Scientific American* 290, no. 2 (2004): 82–89; Steven D. Levitt, "Understanding Why Crime Fell in the 1990s: Four Factors That Explain the Decline and Six That Do Not," *Journal of Economic Perspectives* 18, no. 1 (January 1, 2004): 163–90; and Vanessa Barker, "Explaining the Great American Crime Decline: A Review of Blumstein and Wallman, Goldberger and Rosenfeld, and Zimring," *Law & Social Inquiry* 35, no. 2 (March 1, 2010): 489–516; National Research Council, *The Growth of Incarceration in the United States: Exploring Causes and Consequences*, ed. Jeremy Travis and Bruce Western (Washington, D.C.: National Academies Press, 2014).

Forging an "Underclass"

For communities whose sons and daughters fill U.S. carceral institutions as prisoners and staff, the penal system casts a long and constant shadow.[1] But for many others, the cumbersome project of cycling millions of Americans through prisons and jails is largely submerged from view. Perhaps this is why it is almost compulsory to begin discussions of mass incarceration with the shocking statistics. Academic and nonacademic authors routinely open by tracing the colossal dimensions of the American carceral apparatus—its staggering size, its unprecedented expansion since the 1970s, and its disproportionate impact on low-income communities of color. Writers will contrast the U.S. system to other nations' dramatically less punitive practices. Or they will use comparisons to other infamous mass incarcerations in history, such as the Soviet gulag. Through these strategies, we endeavor to force the shrouded carceral behemoth onto the political landscape. Yet the need to use these devices—the need to drag such gargantuan institutions into popular consciousness or to point out that millions of people are missing from their communities—is perhaps as revealing as the statistics themselves.

For a long time, the expansion of the U.S. penal system was similarly submerged in our historical narratives. Only recently have historians begun shedding light on the process of carceral expansion that accelerated in the 1970s.[2] Still, at this point, the advent of mass incarceration has not been fully integrated into larger accounts of U.S. history.[3] And while

[1] For a review of the research that explores how many citizens' primary contact with the state is via the criminal justice system, see Vesla Weaver and Amy E. Lerman, "Political Consequences of the Carceral State," *American Political Science Review* 104, no. 4 (2010): 817–33, particularly 818.

[2] There is much exciting new historical work and much more on the horizon. See, for example, two journal special issues showcasing just a section of the historical work underway on the "carceral state": Kelly Lytle Hernández, Khalil Gibran Muhammad, and Heather Ann Thompson, eds., "Historians and the Carceral State," *Journal of American History* 102, no. 1 (June 2015) and Donna Murch and Heather Thompson, eds., "Urban America and the Carceral State," *Journal of Urban History* 41, no. 5 (September 2015).

[3] Until very recently, many of the excellent syntheses and textbooks covering recent decades fail to mention the ballooning penal system at all or merely relegate it to a sidebar or brief mention. The longest discussion of mass incarceration I have found in a textbook is in Eric Foner, *Give Me Liberty: An American History* (New York: Norton, 2011), 1152–53.

the implications of crime and punishment have never been limited to the penal system, their recent history has been especially significant and dramatic. The political project of constructing the massive state apparatus profoundly influenced other central transformations of the postwar era.[4] Fully incorporating the burgeoning penal system into our historical narratives will not just add new passages in textbooks and new books to our shelves, it will force a new synthesis.

Chronicling the recent history of the U.S. welfare state presents different challenges. Instead of making visible the towering institutions in plain sight, scholars have the challenge of keeping the light on something that much political rhetoric insists has already retreated or will soon retreat into irrelevance. We endeavor to illuminate those sections of the safety net that have attenuated to mere gossamer threads and bring into view the robust state supports obscured by claims of their recipients' deservingness and independence. This is critical because social welfare programs continue to figure prominently in low-income communities. Welfare programs have become more privatized, shifted strategies, and redirected resources but have not abdicated responsibility for social regulation.

The tough policies enacted in the final decades of the twentieth century were both creative and destructive. They helped impoverish key social welfare programs and rework the reigning assumptions about the appropriate response to drug abuse, poverty, and crime. Simultaneously, they advanced a muscular vision of state power that expanded and further legitimized the state's penal apparatus. They entrenched stratifications within the polity. These degraded civic statuses were built through deeply rooted notions of civic death, contractual citizenship, and patterns of racial, class, and gender domination. They did not, however, simply reproduce the social and racial relations of earlier periods under a thin disguise. Enacting and implementing tough policy was part of renegotiating the terms of citizenship during the 1960s and 1970s as much as was the legislation and court rulings that expanded civil rights. The policies further subordinated the civic status of socially and economically marginalized citizens. They devalidated their

---

Alex Lichtenstein makes a similar point in "Flocatex and the Fiscal Limits of Mass Incarceration: Toward a New Political Economy of the Postwar Carceral State," *Journal of American History* 102, no. 1 (June 1, 2015): 113–15.

[4] For scholarship that positions mass incarceration as a central development in recent U.S. history, see, for example, Thompson, "Why Mass Incarceration Matters" and Marie Gottschalk, "Hiding in Plain Sight: American Politics and the Carceral State," *Annual Review of Political Science* 11, no. 1 (2008): 235–60. In *Governing through Crime*, sociologist Jonathan Simon argues that the practice and logic of new crime control strategies have seeped into American daily life and structured efforts to regulate the workplace, family life, and schools.

voices and claims and absolved the state of responsibility for their safety and welfare.

These politics responded to an especially volatile time in U.S. history, marked by momentous economic and social transformations. During the 1970s, traditional authority experienced a profound crisis of legitimacy.[5] Freedom movements, particularly African Americans' bitter confrontations with racist institutions across the country, contested the reigning citizenship practices. The state was undermined from within by its own practices and from without by an onslaught of criticism from social movements on the Left and Right. At roughly the same time, capital reorganizations and economic slowdowns caused dislocations and hardship for many working-class and poor families. The value of real wages eroded and job opportunities migrated from many urban centers. Women entered the workforce in unprecedented numbers, unsettling family dynamics and established gender roles.

These interlocking factors destabilized old social assumptions and economic arrangements and opened space for new ones. Welfare and criminal policy debates, like the ones examined in this book, became principal sites for this contestation. On this unstable stage and with varying degrees of social authority, groups met and struggled over whom the state should serve and protect. In concert with other social movements, welfare recipients and convicted people made new claims on the state. Their political engagement reshaped policy debates and undermined liberalism by laying bare the quiet brutality behind many rehabilitative claims and therapeutic regimes.

Those who advanced tough politics renarrated what were the limits of political will to address inequality and social movements' demands as problems of incorrigible drug pushers, welfare queens, and criminals. They argued that these populations were unable or unwilling to conform to social norms and ultimately incapable of self-governance. Tough policy transformed programs ostensibly designed to reintegrate marginalized populations into programs responsible for protecting taxpaying citizens from these groups. Lengthy quarantining of drug sellers in prisons and jails displaced an earlier, short-lived emphasis on treatment. Welfare reforms reoriented AFDC's mission from serving its beneficiaries to protecting taxpayers from recipients' abuses. Rejecting the earlier mandate

[5] It is a persistent trope about the 1970s that the nation witnessed a crisis of leadership and faith in government. President Carter declared in a renowned 1979 speech that "a crisis of confidence" was plaguing the United States. See, for example, Peter Carroll, *It Seemed Like Nothing Happened* (New Brunswick, N.J.: Rutgers University Press, 1990), 139–235; and Marc J. Hetherington, *Why Trust Matters: Declining Political Trust and the Demise of American Liberalism* (Princeton, NJ: Princeton University Presss, 2006).

to rehabilitate offenders, new sentencing policies claimed to serve and protect the public by removing the criminals from society.

Civic degradation helped remake knowledge about racial difference at a time when movements challenged and destabilized white supremacy.[6] By pairing punishment with stark limitations on rights and access to benefits and economic opportunities, tough politics degraded the citizenship of many poor African Americans and Latinos at the precise moment they were making forceful demands on the state and challenging their subordination through the welfare and penal systems. Positioning pathological individuals and racialized "cultures of poverty" as the source of social problems refuted activists' criticisms of broader social and economic relations. Supporters and architects of tough policy alleged that subordinated groups forfeited their rights and claims on the state by breaking the law or drawing state aid. The spectacles of civic degradation helped absolve the state of responsibility to subordinated groups' needs and demands.

The stock character that tough politics helped create—drug pushers, welfare queens, and criminals—were all propelled into the limelight by distinct economies and exigencies. However, these politics merged and intersected, and ultimately resonated together to create something larger than the sum of its parts. In 1977, the front page of *TIME* magazine announced the discovery of the "underclass," an entirely new social system divorced from the cultural norms and prosperity of the rest of the nation. The cover article described this population in menacing terms: "Behind its crumbling walls lives a large group of people who are more intractable, more socially alien and more hostile than almost anyone had imagined. They are the unreachables: the American underclass." Depicted as a minority within racial minorities, the underclass was the source of social turmoil: "Thus the underclass minority produces a highly disproportionate number of the nation's juvenile delinquents, school dropouts, drug addicts and welfare mothers, and much of the adult crime, family disruption, urban decay and demand for social expenditures."[7]

Building upon the centuries-old binary between the deserving and undeserving poor, the emergence in the 1970s of the "underclass" was nonetheless new and significant.[8] It explicitly united the cast of racial-

---

[6]On the perpetual reproduction of notions of racial difference, see Michael Omi and Howard Winant, *Racial Formation in the United States*, 3rd ed. (New York: Routledge, 2014).

[7]"American Underclass," *TIME*, August 29, 1977, http://www.time.com/time/magazine /article/0,9171,915331-1,00.html#ixzz0vSUjPldP.

[8]Herbert J. Gans, *The War against the Poor: The Underclass and Antipoverty Policy* (New York: Basic Books, 1995); Katz, *The Undeserving Poor*; Katz, *The Underclass*

ized characters into a distinct, self-perpetuating ecosystem. In this formulation, drug pushers, welfare queens, and drug pushers were not only gendered representations of poor, hyperstigmatized blacks and Latino/as but also the stages in a cycle by which the "underclass" reproduced itself. The sexually deviant, single mother transmitted her pathology to her children, destining them for delinquency, criminality, and welfare. Isolated and alien from society, the underclass was nonetheless a constant moral and physical threat to the nation. This threat, in turn, rationalized other punitive policies in the coming years.

Tough policy played an underappreciated role in solidifying this vision of a racialized underclass entrapped by a culture of poverty. These policies helped produce the political reality they purported to reflect, erecting barriers to the civic and economic participation of poor people, particularly within urban African American and Latino communities. In the final decades of the twentieth century, a dynamic interaction between the penal and social welfare systems consistently fortified the symbolic and legal barricade between the "underclass" and "public." The penal system used welfare-state programs to constrain felons' economic and social standing, just as the welfare system often enlisted the penal system and its rituals to signal the suspect position of recipients.

Throughout the 1980s and 1990s, the welfare queen took her place at the center of political debates over race, poverty, parenting, and inequality. The political attacks on welfare crescendoed in 1996 when Congress abolished welfare as an entitlement program and replaced it with TANF (Temporary Assistance to Needy Families). TANF relied heavily on "sanctions"—the reduction or eliminations of benefits—to punish recipients for noncompliance with regulations and work and reporting requirements. Along with work requirements and lifetime limits on aid, the legislation required that every state implement an anti-fraud program. In order to facilitate anti-fraud monitoring, administrators subjected recipients to administrative scrutiny and reporting requirements that courts have deemed violations of privacy rights in other settings. For a period in California, people applying for assistance underwent a similar ritual to that of being booked for a crime: they were photographed and fingerprinted. Many states followed California's lead and began collecting biometric data on all recipients to monitor the caseload, prevent fraud, and signal recipients' marginalized social position.[9]

Other welfare programs subject the caseload to the same surveillance procedures as those experienced by parolees. In July 2011, Florida began

Debates.
[9] Magnet, "Bio-Benefits," 169–84; Murphy, "Deniable Degradation."

requiring all recipients and applicants to undergo drug tests as a condition of receiving aid. Although only 2 percent of Florida recipients tested positive for drugs, mandated screening casts the entire caseload as criminally suspect.[10] Despite the policy's dubious constitutionality (a Florida judge halted the practice in October 2011), lawmakers in a majority of states have introduced similar legislation.[11] As of 2016, fifteen states had passed laws implementing drug testing or screening for TANF recipients.[12] These policies have revealed the level of drug use among TANF beneficiaries to be below that of the general population.[13] For example, the state of Utah spent over $30,000 in the first year of its program to find that twelve of the almost 5,000 aid applicants tested positive for drugs.[14] Instead of abandoning the practice in light of these findings, Congress in 2016 considered proposals, continually pushed by Republican governors, that would allow states to expand drug testing to food stamp recipients.[15]

States also have continued to circumscribe beneficiaries' freedom to make their own spending choices. In 2015, more than twenty states had laws forbidding welfare recipients from spending their benefits on items such as alcohol, tobacco, tattoos, body piercing, and bail bonds. The Kansas legislature passed a law in April 2015 that explicitly prohibited TANF recipients from using their benefit cards at movie theaters, nail salons, fortune tellers, strip clubs, swimming pools, professional sporting events, or cruise ships. It also prevented them from withdrawing more

[10] See DeWayne Wickham, "Drug Testing of Welfare Applicants a GOP Fishing Expedition," *USA Today*, August 28, 2011, http://www.usatoday.com/news/opinion/forum/story/2011-08-29/Drug-testing-of-welfare-applicants-a-GOP-fishing-expedition/50179484/1 and Sherman, "Judge Temporarily Halts Drug-Testing for Welfare Applicants."

[11] "Drug Testing for Welfare Recipients and Public Assistance," National Conference of State Legislators, March 28, 2016, http://www.ncsl.org/research/human-services/drug-testing-and-public-assistance.aspx.

[12] Most of these laws have found ways to circumvent the legal challenges Florida confronted by, for example, testing only those the department had "reasonable suspicion" of using drugs or were flagged through intake surveys. "Drug Testing for Welfare Recipients and Public Assistance."

[13] Tracy Moore, "The Terrible Push to Drug Test Food Stamp Recipients: By the Numbers," *Vocativ*, April 14, 2016, http://www.vocativ.com/308871/drug-tests-for-food-stamps-terrible-policy-by-the-numbers/.

[14] Ibid.; Michelle Price, "Only 12 Test Positive in Utah Welfare Drug Screening," *KSL.com*, http://www.ksl.com/?sid=26559995&nid=148&title=only-12-test-positive-in-utah-welfare-drug-screening&fm=home_page&s_cid=queue-11.

[15] Mary Clare Jalonick, "A Key Republican Is Renewing a GOP Push to Allow Drug Tests for Food Stamp Recipients and Find Savings in the Program," *US News & World Report*, February 11, 2016, http://www.usnews.com/news/politics/articles/2016-02-11/house-bill-would-allow-drug-testing-for-food-stamps.

than $25 a day from cash machines.[16] Such explicitly degrading restrictions, coupled with other forms of surveillance, sanctions, and biometric monitoring, further stigmatized welfare receipt, discouraged new claimants, and pushed families off the welfare rolls into increased economic insecurity.

Occasionally lawmakers acknowledge that welfare policies have been designed to regulate caricatures that have little basis in fact. In 2016, the California legislature abolished the "maximum family grant cap" they had implemented twenty-two years earlier to discipline welfare queens alleged to have had extra children to get an increase in public assistance. The senator who led the repeal effort explained that "I don't know a woman—and I don't think she exists—who would have a baby for the sole purpose of having another $130 a month." Ending the policy increased the grants for low-income families and terminated the degrading state inquires that forced women hoping to be exempt from the ban to prove a child was conceived through incest, rape, or faulty birth control.[17]

The penal and welfare systems have also interlocked in ways that blurred the administrative boundaries. The welfare system continued to use the penal system to prosecute fraud and collect child support. Welfare recipients' personal information became transparently available to law enforcement in new ways. For example, benefit administrators were often required to turn over recipients' contact information to police when they were crime suspects or potential sources of information. In a program called Operation Talon, authorities summoned food stamp beneficiaries wanted on warrants to the welfare office on the pretense of clearing up an administrative problem and then arrest them.[18]

Just as the welfare system relied on the penal system to signal the suspect position of recipients, the penal system enlisted welfare-state programs to denigrate the status of people convicted of crimes. In the final decades of the twentieth century, the emphasis on "getting tough" resulted not only in longer periods of physical exile in prisons and jails but the perpetuation of post-release strictures on key markers of citizenship: the franchise, access to the welfare state, and the ability to earn. Felons were often prohibited from serving in elected office or on juries.

[16]"New Kansas Law Limits Spending of Welfare Benefits on Concerts, Pools, Lingerie"; Ben Rooney, "Kansas Signs Sweeping Welfare Crackdown," *CNN Money*, http://money.cnn.com/2015/04/16/news/kansas-welfare-limits/.

[17]The Editorial Board, "California Deposes Its 'Welfare Queen,'" *New York Times*, July 23, 2016, http://www.nytimes.com/2016/07/24/opinion/sunday/california-deposes-its-welfare-queen.html.

[18]Kaaryn Gustafson, "The Criminalization of Poverty," *Journal of Criminal Law & Criminology* 99 (2009): 667–74.

In 2013, approximately 5.85 million people in the United States were disenfranchised as a result of a felony conviction, 75 percent of whom were not incarcerated but on probation or parole or had completed their sentence.[19] In many states, convicted felons could not be licensed in certain occupations, including careers—such as hairdressing—with few criminal temptations.[20]

Lawmakers have withdrawn access to social services and civil rights in ways that extend and expand punishment far beyond what is evident if focusing only on the penal system. In 1994, prisoners lost the right to receive Pell Grants, drastically curtailing their ability to receive higher education while incarcerated.[21] People charged with drug offenses were typically barred from access to federal student loans even after serving their sentence. The 1996 welfare reform law enacted a little-debated provision that gave states the power to permanently bar drug offenders from eligibility for food stamps and cash assistance.[22] In many cases, felons were prohibited from living in or visiting public housing for at least five years.[23]

Even more than brutally long sentences, it was the synergy and coordination between the welfare, penal, and other state institutions that so powerfully and indelibly mark people with criminal records. In popular imagination and administrative practice, the tangled webs of the penal and welfare systems lay most heavily in poor, urban communities of color. Together, these interlocking regulations effectively severed many paths to economic security, while simultaneously reinforcing the image of a criminalized, racialized "underclass" with markedly circumscribed rights, benefits, and popularly recognized claims on the state.

For Americans who do not encounter the penal system and stigmatizing welfare programs on a regular basis, the symbolic work of "getting tough" saturates their political culture. Tough politics helped entrench particular explanations of the social world. They constrained the boundaries of the political imaginary—of what was deemed feasible. These politics helped build a political landscape where drug sellers, welfare recipients, and criminals were held responsible not only for their own con-

---

[19]"Democracy Imprisoned: A Review of the Prevalence and Impact of Felony Disenfranchisement Laws in the United States," September 2013, Sentencing Project, http://sentencingproject.org/doc/publications/fd_ICCPR%20Felony%20Disenfranchisement%20Shadow%20Report.pdf, 4. On felon disfranchisement, see also Manza and Uggen, *Locked Out*. Felon disfranchisement laws vary markedly from state to state.

[20]Gottschalk, *The Prison and the Gallows*, 22.

[21]Marc Mauer, *Race to Incarcerate* (New York: New Press, 2006), 200.

[22]Patricia Allard, "Life Sentences: Denying Welfare Benefits to Women Convicted of Drug Offenses," February 2002, Sentencing Project, http://www.sentencingproject.org/doc/publications/women_lifesentences.pdf, 1–2. Recently many states have exercised their option to opt out of this ban.

[23]Alexander, *The New Jim Crow*, 141–45.

ditions but for many of the nation's most pressing social problems. They were instrumental in forging a virtuous national identity and perpetuating interlocking gender, racial, and class hierarchies. They helped forge common sense about the limits of government's capacity to foster social and economic security for the nation's residents. Even during periods of intense criticism of economic inequality and racially concentrated hyperincarceration, few challenged the contractual understandings of citizenship and the customs of civic degradation in the United States. Yet the history in this book suggests that as long as many economic, political, and social rights remain "earned" and social problems are interpreted as solely the product of pathological individuals, the United States will display an appetite for tough politics.

urban areas, "crises" in, 9–11, 19–23, 38, 137; drug control policies and, 54–61
Utah, surveillance in, 294

van den Haag, Ernest, 233
Vietnam War, 20, 30, 64–66, 256
vigilante movies (film genre), 256
violence and unrest. *See* prison unrest and strikes; protest movements
Von Luther, Sidney, 1n1, 97
voting rights, 125, 154, 221, 295

wardens. *See* prison administrators
War on Poverty programs, 20–22, 132
Warren, Earl, 216
Washington, Harlan, 228
Way, Howard, 209n8, 235n81, 281
"Welfare Cadillac" (song), 139–40
welfare policies: expenditures on, 1, 142, 178; fraud and, 122–23, 130–31, 145, 157, 164–65, 170–76, 182–83, 188, 197–203, 293; mothers' pensions and, 128; purging of non-needy recipients and, 169–70, 175, 183; rehabilitation and, 19, 130; work requirements and, 122, 134–35, 140, 168, 179, 293. *See also specific programs (e. g.,* AFDC*)*
welfare recipients, 6, 16, 24, 26; advocates for, 122, 127, 132–33, 152, 155; civic degradation and, 123–24, 126–27, 138–40, 144, 146–50, 152–54, 159–60, 164, 166, 170, 181, 183, 194–97; "criminalization" of, 7–12, 122, 162, 164–67, 170, 175–76, 189, 192, 200–201, 203; economic strategies of, 165, 177–78, 197–203; labeled as "welfare queens," 14, 24, 164, 166, 187, 205; voting rights and, 125, 154
welfare statistics, 130, 134, 155, 172–73, 178–79, 190, 200–201
white supremacy, 21, 126, 215, 292
Whitman, James Q., 17n39
Whitman, Michael, 89
Wiley, George, 155
Wilson, James Q., 233
Wilson, Malcolm, 106
WIN (Work Incentive Program), 134
women: citizenship of, 125–26; roles/responsibilities of, 24, 150–52, 158–59; separate spheres ideology for, 126, 128; as stigmatized unmarried mothers, 193
Women's Board of Terms and Parole (Calif.), 216–17, 260
Work Incentive Program (WIN), 134
work requirements, 122, 134–35, 140, 168, 179, 293
Wright, Erik Olin, 218

Younger, Evelle J., 262–63
Young Lords, 58
Yurick, Sol, 29